C000195273

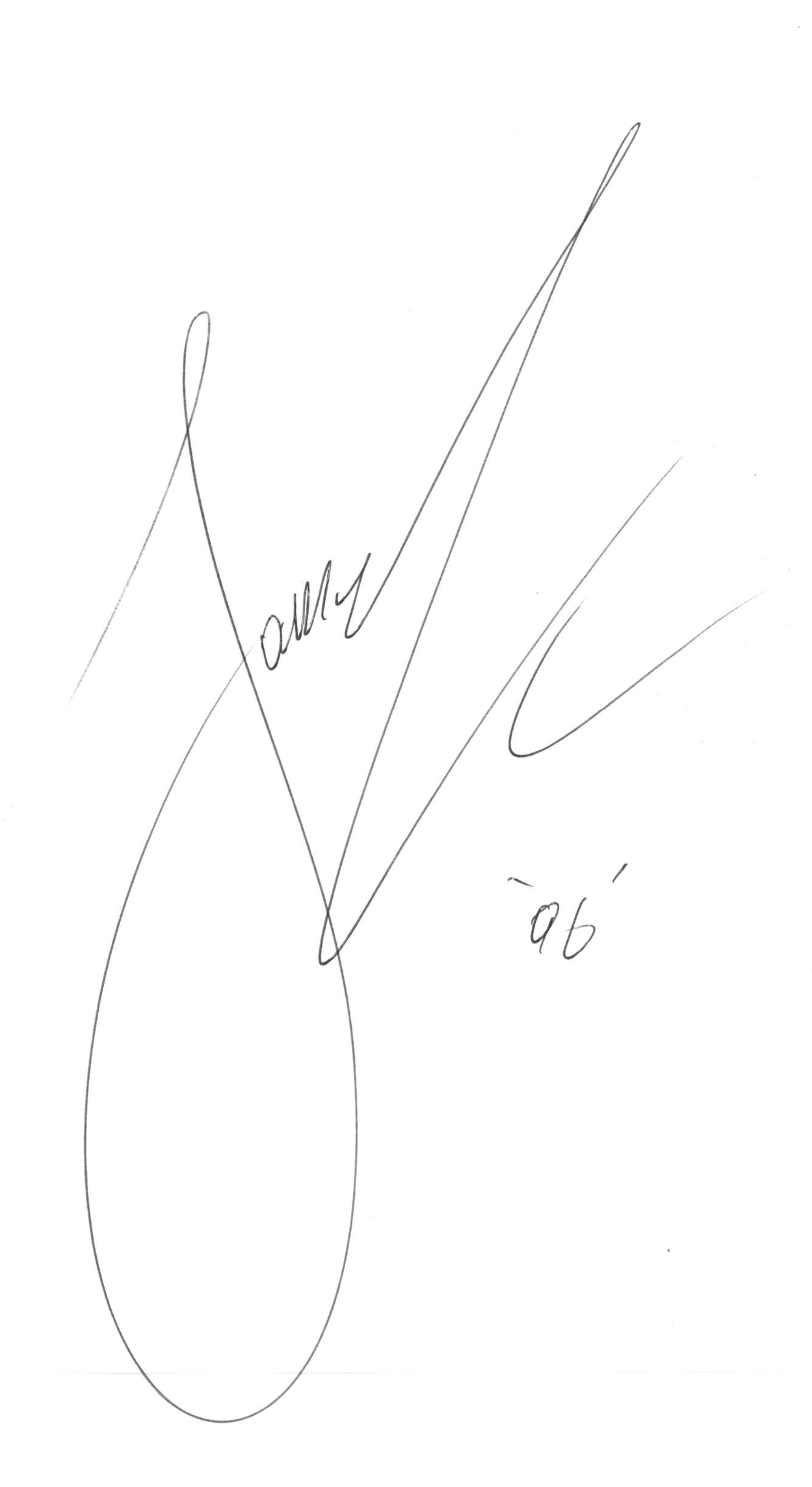

AUTOCOURSE

BRITISH MOTORSPORT YEAR 1995-96

CONTENTS

British Motorsport Year 1995-96
is published by
Hazleton Publishing Ltd,
3 Richmond Hill,
Richmond, Surrey
TW10 6RE.

Colour reproduction by
Barrett Berkeley Ltd, London.

Printed in England by
Jarrold Book Printing,
Thetford, Norfolk.

ISBN: 1-874557-61-6

PUBLISHER
Richard Poulter

EDITOR
Paul Fearnley

ART EDITOR
Steve Small

PRODUCTION MANAGER
Steven Palmer

MANAGING EDITOR
Peter Lovering

BUSINESS DEVELOPMENT MANAGER
Simon Maurice

SALES PROMOTION
Clare Kristensen

RESULTS AND STATISTICS
Paul Haines

TOURING CAR ILLUSTRATIONS
Ian Hutchinson
Nicola Fox

CHIEF PHOTOGRAPHERS
LAT Photographic

ACKNOWLEDGEMENTS

The Editor of *British Motorsport Year 1995-96* wishes to thank the following for their assistance: Simon Arron *(for recommending me)*, Charles Bradley, Gwyn Dolphin *(for standing in the rain at Brands Hatch in June)*, Kay Edge, Nicola Fox, Paul Haines, Ian Hutchinson, LAT Photographic (Kathy Ager, Charles Coates, Malcolm Griffiths, Bob McCaffrey and Steve Tee), Paul Lawrence, Peter Lovering, Nick Phillips, Marcus Pye, Marcus Simmons, Steve Small and Stewart Williams. And Jan.

Photographs published in *British Motorsport Year 1995-96* have been contributed by:

Chief Photographers, LAT Photographic; Action Images/John Marsh; Barry Ambrose/Photomart Photography; Allsport UK/Mike Cooper/John Gigichi/Anton Want; Bothwell Photographic/Bill and Mark Bothwell; Diana Burnett; Clive Challinor; John Colley Photography; Bruce Grant-Braham; Gary Haggity; Mary Harvey; Gary Hawkins; Darren Heath; Steve Jones; John Overton; Marcus Potts/CMC; Professional Sport/Tony O'Brien; Marcus Pye; Shutterspeed Photografik/Trevor Davies; Sutton Photographic/Gavin Lawrence; Colin Taylor Productions; Mick Walker; Words and Pictures/Colin McMaster/Bryn Williams.

DISTRIBUTORS

UNITED KINGDOM
Bookpoint Ltd
39 Milton Park, Abingdon
Oxfordshire OX14 4TD
Telephone: 01235 400400
Fax: 01235 861038

NORTH AMERICA
Motorbooks International
PO Box 1, 729 Prospect Ave.
Osceola, Wisconsin 54020, USA
Telephone: (1) 715 294 3345
Fax: (1) 715 294 4448

AUSTRALIA
Technical Book and Magazine Co. Pty
295 Swanston Street, Melbourne
Victoria 3000
Telephone: (03) 9663 3951
Fax: (03) 9663 2094

NEW ZEALAND
David Bateman Ltd
PO Box 100-242,
North Shore Mail Centre
Auckland 1330
Telephone: (9) 415 7664
Fax: (9) 415 8892

SOUTH AFRICA
Motorbooks
341 Jan Smuts Avenue
Craighall Park, Johannesburg
Telephone: (011) 325 4458/60
Fax: (011) 325 4146

FOREWORD

by John Cleland

To win the British Touring Car Championship when it is more competitive than ever before is a feeling that is only just starting to sink in. The enormous effort the team and I put into this season left little time for reflection, and there is a lot to remember when 25 races are packed into so little time.

With its rapid growth, the increase in its professionalism and manufacturer support, added to the spectacular nature of the racing, the BTCC has been crying out for a glossy, in-depth book such as this. *British Motorsport Year* will serve as an ideal reminder of what it was all about.

John Cleland

LAT Photographic

Such introductions are designed to accentuate the positive: the glorious colour photography, the pithy verbiage and inventive lay-out. And there can be little doubt that the recent massive growth of the *Auto Trader* British Touring Car Championship, and upon its back a host of professional single-seater and one-make series, has been crying out for a book such as this . . .

Yet I am confident that literally thousands of people will be disappointed by our offering. This warning is issued on the premise that no other country possesses such a diverse motorsport culture: I know that there are around 30,000 competition licence-holders out there – all potential purchasers of this inaugural *British Motorsport Year*, I hope – who will all be hopeful of seeing their name in print. Yet this is a sheer impossibility. In Britain and Ireland there are over 100 racing championships and, as such, we can only scratch the – admittedly very shiny – surface without producing something akin to the *Encyclopedia Britannica.*

Naturally, I also feel that there are a host of good reasons for pressing on with your purchase, and would ask those who have been initially disappointed in this manner to hazard a second look.

The strength of the BTCC and its supporting package has warranted such a volume for possibly the past three seasons now, and it is perhaps surprising, therefore, that the void is only now being filled. We have our rivals on the touring car front, but none in terms of coverage of the UK's other major racing series, nor in our strenuous efforts to equal *and* mirror the – oft unheralded – professionalism that abounds in all strata of the national motorsport scene.

This industry is one of the nation's best-kept secrets – one which the Government is happy to occasionally bask in the kudos of without offering a whiff of an incentive or a smidgin of aid. Yet the sport continues to thrive in most quarters, thanks in the main to an all-time high of manufacturer support.

Of course, the contents of this annual can but reflect this latter fact. But we are enthusiasts at heart, and have been dispassionate where necessary if we think that a manufacturer or team has transgressed. This is very definitely not an advert for them. However, the fact that most of what is currently happening is good, may make it appear that way.

As for my word-processor colleagues, I can only marvel at their knowledge, wrapped up as I am in my own touring car world. All the writers featured in this book either work for, or contribute to, a national motorsport weekly, and I am confident that nowhere will you find more insight into your chosen interest.

Or better photographs.

Any journalist who regularly has to crash out copy in the middle of the night will often cast a green eye over his camera-carrying colleagues, with their autofocus and variable shutter speed, but even I have to admit that one good photo can speak a thousand words - at least. *British Motorsport Year* will prove that. The bulk of the UK's top motorsport 'snappers' offered up work for its pages and you will reap the benefit.

And that's about it.

Personally, I will be glad to see the back of it - these few hundred words represent a very welcome last lap for me - yet I know from almost 20 unbroken years of experience with this publishing house's world famous *Autocourse* annual that I will dig out this book in ten years' time for a sentimental delve. TV and video catch the immediacy - its noise and movement - of this dramatic sport, but I hope we can prove to you that it possesses a greater permanence than that - even outside the heady world of Formula One.

Paul Fearnley
Ealing, London
November 1995

DRAWING PIN GOES HERE
DRAWING PIN GOES HERE

DRAWING PIN GOES HERE

THE BMW M3 CONVERTIBLE
BMW
DRAWING PIN GOES HERE

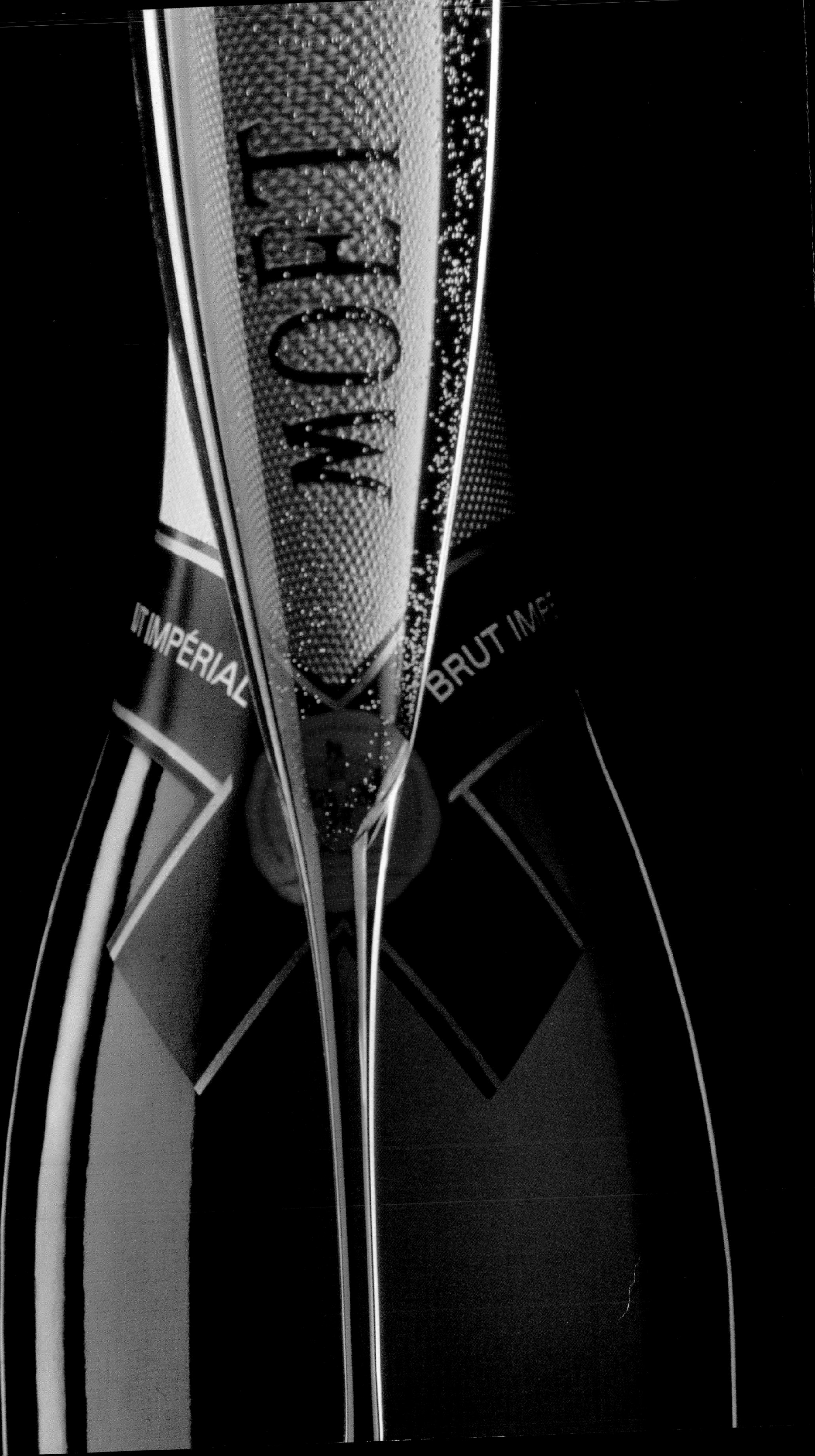
MOET
IMPÉRIAL
BRUT IMP

Tony O'Brien/Professional Sport

AUTO TRADER RAC

BRITISH TOURING CAR CHAMPIONSHIP

by Paul Fearnley

BIGGER, BUT

The five-year history of the two-litre touring car formula has witnessed a remarkable transformation: from its tentative first step in the 1990 British Touring Car Championship, it has been transplanted to all corners of the globe, while the unappetising racing recipe of front-wheel drive and around 300 bhp has produced a device that now laps quicker than the awesome Ford Sierra Cosworths it supported that same year.

The careful couching and targeting of the regulations is both the cause and effect: the category boasts an unheralded weight of support due to its accessibility for manufacturers with or without a strong sporting heritage; the British series in particular has benefited greatly from this over the past three seasons, and to gather nine or ten manufacturers within the tight confines of a single series is to fuel the furnace of technological development. In this respect, the 1995 *Auto Trader* RAC British Touring Car Championship ushered in a new era.

The most obvious manifestation of this was the spectacular failure of Alfa Romeo and BMW. Between them, in 1994, these two blue chip motorsporting marques scored 14 wins. This year they were rarely more than also-rans, and their further participation has been called into doubt. As the formula evolves, so it becomes more specialised, and in this atmosphere of the survival of the fittest, any stragglers were easily picked off: Alfa Romeo was distracted by its efforts in Class 1 touring car racing, while BMW learned the harsh lesson that it is no longer possible for it to flood the Super Touring market and remain competitive in the toughest championship of its type.

Further, a Super Touring programme can no longer be tacked onto an existing motorsport budget: Vauxhall Sport has scrapped its well-established UK rally team in order to ensure that Vectra continues where Cavalier left off; Alfa Corse was told to decide between Class 1 or Super Touring and its one-car Italian Superturismo campaign was abandoned in a trice. The stakes are that much higher than previously. In Formula One or Class 1 terms, its budgets are still under control. But for how much longer? If the stakes continue to rise, will enough importers still be able to fund a national programme? And on how many fronts will a manufacturer be able to – or wish to – bale these out?

Some manufacturers have already decided to channel their Super Touring commitments: Volvo allied itself to a three-year BTCC programme with the highly-successful Tom Walkinshaw Racing. Nothing was to detract from this but, even so, with a year still remaining, this partnership has yet to bear fruit in terms of titles for its marketing department to utilise. In order to win the said titles, Renault UK wheeled in Williams, a move which served to emphasise the toughening-up process the category is passing through. So is it now necessary to concentrate solely on the BTCC in order to win it?

Volvo and Renault clearly thought so, and their single-minded approaches reaped victories. But there is still more than one way to skin a cat – just – and BMW and GM are to be congratulated on their widespread successes this season. But had not Ray Mallock, a man central to the Vauxhall/Opel Super Touring programme, been based in the UK, would his aged Cavalier have been able to keep pace with Renault and Volvo? I somehow doubt it.

And this is the tip of the iceberg. Williams has a clean sheet of paper for 1996, and so a radical departure is expected in the design of the next Laguna. Volvo and Honda have already pointed the way to the next generation of Super Touring cars, and doubtless Vectra will follow.

Success in this formula now requires a much greater attention to detail, a short line-of-command for rapid development reaction, plus a full-time testing team, careful packaging of the engine and drivetrain, hours spent in the wind tunnel . . . it's got a familiar ring to it, hasn't it? Formula One is still the pinnacle of the sport, Class 1 has the greater technology and faster cars, but ask Derek Warwick which is the most competitive category he has ever contested . . .

And the BTCC beats out the rhythm worldwide. Where it has been, others will follow. So has it set a good precedent this season? It was unavoidable, but I think not. Only Japan and Germany can follow its lead, the rest will suffer . . . if they are not already. The basis of any national championship is its market leaders: if Ford and Vauxhall were to pull out of the BTCC the effect would be dramatic. In this respect, Alfa Romeo's withdrawal from Italy has been a huge blow to that championship. Germany and Japan have the power bases – Audi, BMW, Ford, Opel, and Toyota, Nissan, Honda – necessary to survive, but if the category continues on the path it has trodden this year, a siege mentality may develop, with manufacturers concentrating solely on their home markets.

From a purely selfish point of view, the British series is likely to avoid any such developments, centred as it is at the hub of the motorsport world. The kudos of winning the most competitive series is likely to attract new, eager manufacturers each year, but a weeding out of those not 100 per cent committed to the cause is in the offing. This may be a good thing: Alan Gow, the Managing Director of TOCA, has long stated that nine manufacturers is too high a number for all competitors to receive the same amount of benefit from the series. What the category must not lose totally, however, is its variety – one of the reasons it was created in the first place.

As it stands, however, there are still 16 manufacturers committed to Super Touring, with perhaps two or three more hovering on the sidelines, and they wouldn't be involved unless they thought they were benefiting from it. Certainly, the future of the British Touring Car Championship, which has just enjoyed its most competitive two-litre season to date, looks assured.

After the initial adverse reaction to the new wings, which brought with them the concern that the dicing element so crucial to the success of touring cars had been nullified, the season settled into a battle between Renault, Vauxhall and Volvo, with an occasional foray from Ford, and later Honda.

But there is no doubt that downforce played a bigger role than the FIA had envisaged when it released the new wing regulations in late '94. Or that it shortened braking distances, improved tyre wear and made it more difficult to overtake. But was the racing any less spectacular than previously? No one dry race struck me as a classic of its type, and the thrill factor of the wet races was obvious. So perhaps a little less grip would be beneficial. The problem with downforce is that it's addictive, and those in the business of making cars go faster bleat maddeningly when there is any suggestion of the removal of their new toy. But the spectacle often provided by Formula Three is a salutary lesson to be learned – more grip than grunt can grate.

There was also a general feeling that wings made the cars easier to drive; yet those who possessed an edge without them tended to maintain it with them. The better drivers still shone through. And those who were prepared to consider their moves, on tyres that gave them a bigger window in which to do so, benefited. There were still plenty of bent motor cars strewn about the place, but the frequency of the last-minute lunge diminished as the pilots got to grips with their new parameters.

One knock-on effect of the wings was increased speeds in the quicker corners, and the resultant safety concern. The fatal accidents that befell Gregg Hansford and Kieth O'dor during the season will hopefully shake this sector of the sport out of its 'safe in a tinbox' philosophy. The key to success in a two-litre touring car is to maintain its momentum. A metric tonne of motor vehicle has plenty of the latter and, perhaps lacking the ultimate drivability of the rear-wheel drive layout, the bulk of these machines tread a very fine line, especially in qualifying. Add to this the closeness of the racing, and the formula is not as safe as it first appears.

Of course, racing can never be totally safe. The danger element is undoubtedly part of the attraction. But the lack of urgency on the part of the FIA after Hansford's shunt in March was unforgivable. Lots of well-meaning words emanated from the governing body *and* the manufacturers, but little action was taken. For the cynical among us, it was if there were a strong belief that lightning wouldn't strike twice . . .

With the increasing prevalence of centralised build programmes, it should now be easier to impose new safety regulations. But it needs to be done sooner rather than later. The lessons learned from these accidents must be acted upon. If an increasing number of road cars are sold on their safety features, why should their racing cousins be any different?

Finally, the success of John Cleland must be applauded. The upfront Scot is not everybody's cup of tea, but when the burgeoning BTCC needed a character on which to build its public image, he was there. He's never likely to reach the Frank Bruno/'Gazza' level of public awareness, but he's as close as any touring car driver has got since Gerry Marshall in the mid-Seventies. Barring a minor brainstorm at Brands Hatch, a couple of bad starts, perhaps a wrong tyre choice at Knockhill and a tiny tap that sent Rickard Rydell wide – again at Brands Hatch – his year has been exemplary. After the near-miss in 1992, and the frustrations of the next two years, his never-say-die attitude has stood him in good stead. As the BTCC's TV profile continues to increase, his is a lead many touring car drivers would do well to follow – as long as they have the talent to back it up, that is. The man from Galashiels may talk a lot, but it's his driving that speaks volumes.

by Paul Fearnley

BETTER?

Gavin Lawrence/Sutton Photographic

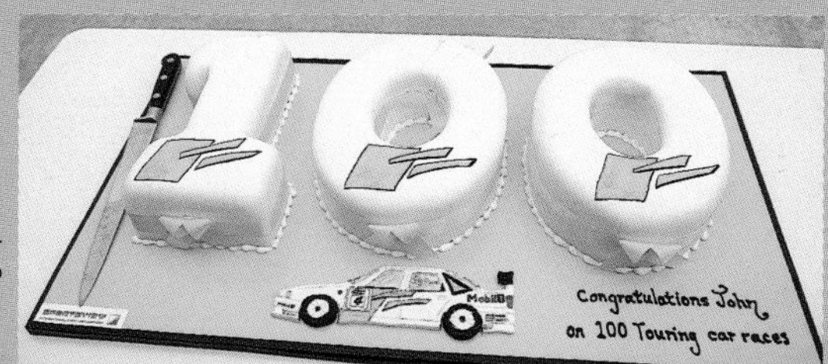

LAT Photographic

John Gigichi/Allsport

Bill Bothwell/Bothwell Photographic

Clockwise from above: **Tyre choice is everything. For once, the 'voice of the sport' is speechless – Johnny Cecotto shuts up Murray Walker. John Cleland had his cake. And fair share of champagne. Many hands make for innumerable autographs – Paul Radisich is swamped. A happy occasion for Volvo. The pit lane 'walkabout' is a veritable scrum.**

John Marsh/Action Images

TOP TEN DRIVERS

Chosen by the Editor, Paul Fearnley

Trevor Davies/Shutterspeed Photografik

LAT Photographic

1

The Swiss heads this list for a simple reason: I believe he is the only man who would have beaten John Cleland given the same equipment. In the early part of the season he won races when the Renault was far from easy to drive – to coax home even, as evinced by his team-mate's troubled performances. But by the season's end it was the class of the field and he was its gloss. Seven wins, eight fastest laps, 162 laps led – all season highs – plus six pole positions bear testament to his speed and racing nous. He also eradicated the unnecessary off that has sometimes coloured his past efforts, while retaining his edge over the rest when it comes to that initial burst on cold tyres. A hard yet fair racer, who but for the frustrations of a fiddling gearbox failure at Knockhill and a steamed-up windscreen at Silverstone might have gone one better and taken the title. With Williams now well and truly into the touring car swing of things, he must start next season as the bookies' favourite. The complete article.

2

At 43 there appears to be no decline in the Scot's pace, commitment and will to win. He momentarily appeared fazed by the early-season speed of the Volvos – even that of his team-mate – but regrouped after his April Brands Hatch debacle to press home the advantage with four consecutive wins in the middle of the year. However, it was 18 podium finishes that were the key to his successful title bid, matching his car's reliability to an uncanny knack of keeping out of trouble. But this is not to say that he won by consistency alone – for my money, only Menu is quicker on a lap-for-lap basis. Blend his blazing speed with a wealth of experience and dogged determination, and you have a very hard man to beat. Blessed with the best chassis of the season, he reached within himself to up his qualifying performance and, as he zeroed in on the championship, extracted just the amount he needed to from his beloved Cavalier. And there's plenty more to come from this garrulous Borders man.

Gavin Lawrence/Sutton Photographic

3

It was sad to see the New Zealander's season rely upon his ability to nail a lap on qualifiers, and then revolve around a series of cussed and generally futile defences of a decent position in the opening exchanges of a race. By the middle of the season he appeared demotivated, understandably, but if his style looked ragged, almost desperate, it was only because the wayward Ford demanded it be so. Silverstone National was the only circuit where it was a potential race-winner, and he took a first and second there in May. The frequent wet races also allowed him to show his mettle. So there is no reason to suggest that he is not the driver he was in the latter half of 1993. Drop him into a Renault, Vauxhall or Volvo, and he would have been a serious threat for the title. And given the right circumstances, his fatalistic demeanour will allow him to put the disappointments of the last two seasons behind him as quickly as he burst onto the scene.

LAT Photographic

4

It is too easy to hang a label upon a driver. Does this Stockholm man's quiet manner leave him unprepared for the rough and tumble of Super Touring? In terms of paddock sightings he is positively nocturnal, but behind the wheel he is the focus of attention, extracting lap after dramatic lap from the Volvo in qualifying. There are no square edges to his driving, and the resultant speed from this one-lap high-wire act cannot be questioned. Yet the label may have stuck. Had he converted his myriad pole positions into something like, he would have romped away with the title. There was more to it than just a hesitant driver, but the problem occurred too often for him to be exonerated. Remember also, though, that two brake failures and two steamed-up windscreens cost him a hatful of points, while the fizzling out of his title bid should be linked more to the tyre war than a lack of self-belief.

LAT Photographic

5

After an iffy start, the man with a single Formula One point to his name dropped back into the groove. And when the TOM'S-built Toyota at last gave him an opportunity to run at the front, he looked as though he'd never been away – only misfortune kept him off the podium. To race in the middle of the BTCC pack is no bed of roses, but with the minimum of fuss this deceptively quick pilot regularly prevails in the multi-car battles that abound in this form of racing – a sure sign of a finely honed racecraft. Unfortunately, his almost couldn't-care-less demeanour can mislead outsiders – even insiders – but it is a poor front for a man who desperately wants to win. Just one victory in three years with Toyota has lowered his stock with some, but potentially here is a regular race-winner – perhaps a champion.

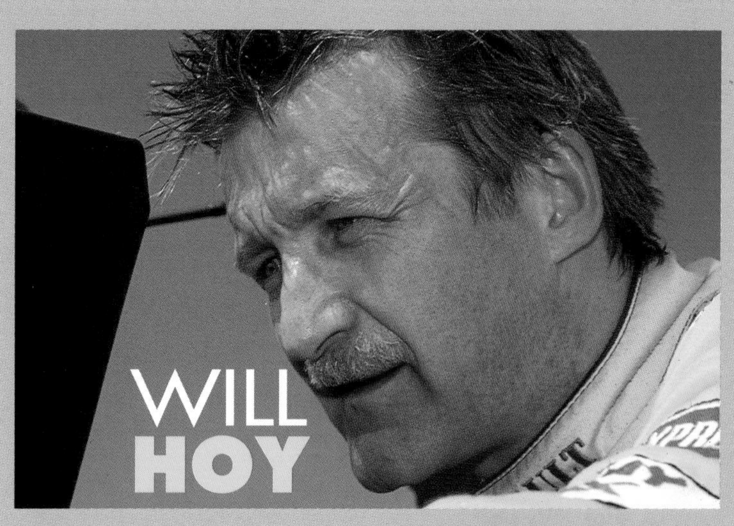

John Marsh/Action Images

What had looked to be the beginning of the end became a rebirth for the 1991 BTCC champion. A string of niggling problems and retirements, plus the unflattering pace and success of his team-mate, had the vultures circling. Suggestions that two winless years at Toyota had blunted his winning instinct were rife, and his hangdog expression gave little outward hope of change. Thus he deserves great credit for displaying the character to turn this state of affairs around. Given a new race engineer, a switch to the T-car and a set-up that suited his slow-in fast-out style, he was back on the pace, ending his drought in fine style at Brands Hatch. Even his luck changed, inheriting a victory at Snetterton when Rydell spun out. A natural? Perhaps not. But if he is confident of his car, he has shown that he can string the victories together – a precious commodity in this highly competitive form of racing.

LAT Photographic

KELVIN BURT

7

The unwieldy Mondeo must have come as a huge shock to this ex-British Formula Three champion, but he coped manfully. Unable to match his more experienced team-mate in the one-lap banzai stakes, his qualifying performance suffered by comparison. Yet this laid-back driver outraced Radisich – wet or dry – in the second half of the season, appearing more willing to drive around the car's inadequacies. His win at Snetterton came via an inspired tyre choice, and it is the contrary nature of this sport that his year will be principally remembered for what was one of his easier drives. But a couple of earlier dices with Rydell had already marked him out as a front-wheel drive adaptee. If he ever gets his hands on a new-generation Super Touring car he will be a match for anybody.

JAMES THOMPSON

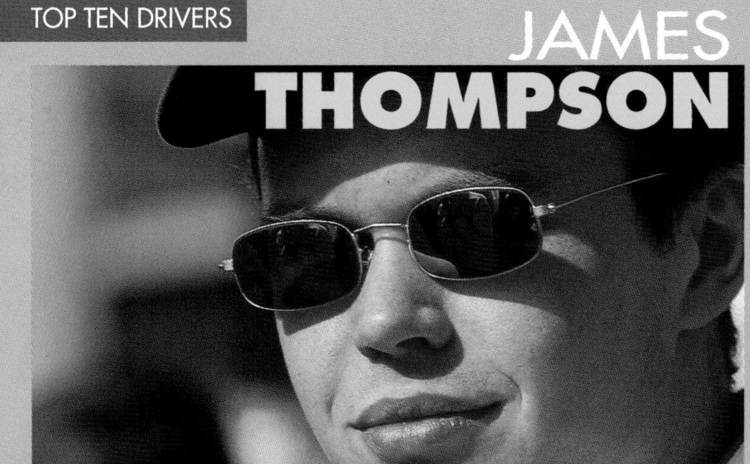

LAT Photographic

8

Before his horrifying testing shunt at Knockhill, this 21-year-old Yorkshireman had impressed everyone with his speed and maturity. Critics point to the fact that he had the 'car of the season' at his disposal, but forget that this brings with it further attendant pressures for one so young. His sensational qualifying pace undoubtedly acted as a spur to Cleland, as did his controlled drive into second place in the streaming wet at Brands Hatch in April. His first win appeared to be only a matter of time, and it duly came at Thruxton after another calm drive. Following this victory, however, Cleland turned the screw, the novelty wore off, and it became clear that James still had a lot to learn. He was inclined towards the odd impetuous move, and could be outfumbled on the opening laps. But all this will smooth out with time which, along with speed, he has plenty of.

Trevor Davies/Shutterspeed Photografik

JAMES KAYE

9

This choice will come as a surprise to many. David Leslie, his Honda team-mate, often drove excellently and tended to score the headline-grabbing results for Honda, but it was clear that the Yorkshireman had been handed the short straw in terms of testing time and tyres. In this respect he found himself caught in a mind-trap, being desperate to impress in his first year as a works driver, yet unwilling to speak out against the team that had given him the opportunity. At times this scenario wore him down and affected his performance. This changed at Knockhill, where he set the fastest time in morning warm-up before winning a tough battle with Cleland to be fifth. Afterwards, his smooth, unhurried style never quite brought the result it deserved. Certainly, the decision to lumber him with the next-to-useless Yokohama wets at Snetterton was perhaps the biggest missed opportunity of the year, for he is a win away from being a major player.

LAT Photographic

DAVID BRABHAM

10

At the start of the season this affable Aussie looked to have one of the season's toughest assignments: Johnny Cecotto is not the team-mate most would choose for their first season of touring car racing, for not only is the Venezuelan fast, he is BMW's chosen man and renowned for an Ayrton Senna-like ability to get the team wholly behind him. Yet, in his own quiet way, Brabs did more than match his illustrious colleague. It is perhaps not surprising that he was more prepared to take the rough with the smooth – Cecotto is very used to winning with BMW – bringing his car home more often that not, while Johnny had his fair share of shunts. It was also typical of this praiseworthy attitude that he should score his best dry-race result – fourth at Knockhill – after the trauma of rushing his young son to hospital with a bad scald.

JEFF ALLAM
The Epsom car dealer made a brief return to the championship with a one-off Vauxhall drive at Knockhill, replacing the injured James Thompson. After a reasonable run in testing, he struggled with an unfamiliar qualifying set-up. Then in the races he produced two measured performances to pick up places and finish in the points. He knew, though, that this was hardly the derring-do he had hoped might put him back on the BTCC shopping list.

MIKE BRIGGS
The recently crowned South African Touring Car champion was a regular points-finisher in his eight races as John Cleland's team-mate, but there was no hiding the fact that he had been unprepared for the pace and close competition of the BTCC. A hard and aggressive racer, he was not backward in coming forward, but an inability to extract the last tenth from the Vauxhall in qualifying on unfamiliar circuits often forced him to battle through the pack. Desperate to race in Europe, he may have cause to rue his last-lap loss of second place at Snetterton to an out-of-order David Leslie.

JOHNNY CECOTTO
There were several occasions when this urbane Venezuelan appeared to be going through the motions. It wasn't until the championship reached Knockhill that we saw the best of him. In his long association with BMW this was the first time he knew victory was an unrealistic proposition, and it hit him hard. It was a scenario worsened by the fact that his renowned ability to get what he wants from the Munich manufacturer also failed him on this occasion. A season littered with shunts, a surprising number of which were unassisted, it was not a campaign he will look back on with great fondness.

SIMON HARRISON
Anyone able to out-qualify Patrick Watts in the same car is blessed with plenty of speed. The 26-year-old's smooth style one-lap was perhaps better suited to the bewinged Peugeot than his team-mate's, but his racecraft still displays some holes that must be plugged. As James Thompson took the 'new star' plaudits in the vastly superior Vauxhall, Simon put his head down and worked commendably hard in the middle of the braying pack, where he was singled out for his fair share of bullying. Rarely able to break out from this cloying environment, what was a promising first year was generally shielded from view.

TIM HARVEY
At the first Brands Hatch meeting, the 1992 champion passed his highly-rated team-mate in the dry and the wet. He went on to win both races – again showing his proficiency in the rain. But thereafter his season was punctuated by several no-more-than solid drives and some dramatically poor qualifying performances. Whereas Rydell appeared in total harmony with his Volvo, the Englishman floundered in a sea of uncertain set-up. A switch to the T-car helped temporarily, but it wasn't enough to turn around what was a disappointing season. Even his wet weather prowess deserted him at Silverstone. This may sound harsh on the man who finished fifth in the points, but there is no getting away from the fact that at times he was unconvincing.

Photos: LAT Photographic and Diana Burnett (Cecotto)

Photos: LAT Photographic

DAVID LESLIE

The Scot has a rare ability to set bang-on-the-button qualifying times that go unnoticed. His smooth, fingertip style was ideally matched to the impressive Honda, and a host of excellent qualifying performances was the result. It was a slightly different story in the races, where a fascination with little looks around the outside of an opponent could lead to an accident or cost him places. There is no question that he is capable of winning if he gets out front, but doubt remains about his ability to soak up pressure in a dice situation. Also, his extra track time in the Accord should perhaps have ensured a bigger performance gap between himself and his team-mate.

GIAMPIERO SIMONI

His speed remained intact and his feedback was reportedly much improved, yet by the middle of the season the little Italian was unemployed. His familiarity with the Alfa Romeo usually allowed him to get the better of Derek Warwick, and also left him better placed to confirm it as a backward step from the pacesetter of '94.

TIM SUGDEN

A purveyor of brilliant starts, he will no doubt be cursing himself for throwing a couple of them away. At the beginning of the season he was more than a match for Julian Bailey in qualifying, yet the results never quite came his way. He had a brief glimpse of what might have been with an encouraging run in the TOM'S-built Carina at Snetterton. But the lot of a 'number two' is not a happy one, and the car was handed over to his team-mate for the last four races of the year. Ironically, the Yorkshireman's qualifying and race performance in the final round was perhaps his best of another 'nearly' season.

GABRIELE TARQUINI

Not even the reigning champion could coax the disappointing Alfa Romeo onto the podium. And here lies the problem with such a subjective list. Is he any less of a driver than he was last year? Palpably not. At Brands Hatch and Oulton Park he gave object lessons in opportunism, and the string of fourth places he garnered late in the season were cameos of the touring car art. The number of incidents he was involved in merely emphasised that battling in the middle of the pack is no picnic. Had he contested the entire season he would have been ranked high in the Top 10.

DEREK WARWICK

In terms of speed the Hampshire man was a breath away from Gabriele Tarquini and Giampiero Simoni – drivers held up to be two of the fastest in '94. Yet this regularly relegated him to the far reaches of the grid, which set him upon a slippery slope. Instead of settling into a race-winning mode as he had hoped, he found himself leading a major redevelopment of the car – no way to get to grips with such a specialised formula. His season degenerated into a litany of set-up gambles and dodgy early-lap moves in an effort to grab the odd point or two. He can be criticised for trying too hard on occasions, but you have to feel for him. It would be a brave man, though, to suggest that he will never make a success of this touring car lark.

PATRICK WATTS

The behind-the-wheel pyrotechnics of this Kentish driver could no longer hide the defects in the Peugeot's chassis. He remains one of the best seat-of-the-pants pilots in the field, but he seemed unwilling to pare away the rougher edges of his style that the wings demanded. The arrival of the new 406 may be his final chance to convert his sheer speed into race-winning form. At the moment, the lack of a BTCC victory is perhaps beginning to wear down this chirpy natural talent.

KIETH O'DOR

An appreciation by Paul Fearnley

In a single day Kieth O'dor's family and friends experienced the ecstasy and tragedy so inextricably linked with motorsport.

On 10 September at Avus, Berlin, the 33-year-old's Nissan Primera secured a 'sprint' race victory in the penultimate round of the ADAC *Supertourenwagen* Cup. Just hours later, during the 'main' race, while sitting stationary in the middle of the track, it was struck amidships by another car. It was a huge impact. However, the initial reports of Kieth's condition were hopeful. Then early on Monday morning, the touring car world was rocked back on its heels when the Salisbury driver was declared dead.

I wasn't there, but I know just how much joy his father would have received from Kieth's victory in Germany. It was his first win since a cool and determined performance in the 1993 British Grand Prix support race at Silverstone had enabled him to hold off the BMW of touring car benchmark, Steve Soper. On that occasion Jan almost burst with pride; that the first BTCC win for his Janspeed team should be scored by his son was the realisation of a dream. That day his was an infectious spirit. And, for a short while, Avus would have been no different.

That Silverstone success was the one which quelled suggestions of sheer nepotism. Of course Jan was protective of his progeny, keen to help him succeed; but equally his son proved himself a winner at the highest level of his chosen category.

There is no doubt that Kieth O'dor was an underrated racing driver. Sadly, he will never now shake off the 'favoured driver' tag he was labelled with at Janspeed, but the likes of Win Percy and Eric van de Poele – former Nissan team-mates – can testify to this quiet man's pace.

Shy, and naturally extremely keen to show Janspeed off in a good light, he could be hard work for a journalist. Some called him diffident. He wasn't great for quotes, certainly, but I had a sneaking regard for the Wiltshireman. In 1993, my first year of covering the BTCC, he finished sixth overall, scored that famous victory, set pole positions and raced determinedly. He wasn't the greatest door-handler the saloon car world had ever seen, and sometimes his racecraft would be called into question by his more experienced colleagues, but he shut up plenty of his critics that season.

It was ironic, however, that this most undemonstrative of men should be remembered for the severity and frequency of his accidents: his fence-clearing roll in the 1992 TOCA Shoot-Out at Donington Park was startling; during the morning warm-up for the 1993 FIA Touring Car World Cup at Monza he collected his team-mate, Mark Skaife; his 1994 BTCC campaign was stymied by a run of unavoidable shunts, few of which were of his own making. Even at Avus he was forced to drive a 1994 Primera having rolled the latest example at the Salzburgring a few weeks earlier.

Yet it never crossed my mind that one day he wouldn't simply step out of his damaged car unhurt. For here was no madman battling out of his depth. His was a name rarely mentioned in another driver's post-accident rant. In fact, in a dice situation he tended to err on the cautious side.

And yet. And yet.

This year was billed as a watershed for him. Contesting a season outside Great Britain for the first time, away from the overtly protective Janspeed umbrella, he was proving more than a match for his BMS-Scuderia Italia team-mates, Ivan Capelli and Sascha Maassen. His win at Avus should have been a turning-point for both himself and the team – it was Nissan's first in Germany. Instead, it will remain always as a bitter-sweet tribute.

Photos: LAT Photographic

KIETH O'DOR

5 April 1962 – 10 September 1995

Career:

Began in rallying, contesting the Lada Challenge, before switching to production car racing with a Janspeed-prepared Peugeot 205 GTI. The following year he graduated to a Ford Sierra RS Cosworth.

1989: Firestone Production Saloon Champion (Ford Sierra RS Cosworth). Eleven wins.

1990 Esso Group N Champion (Nissan Skyline GT-R). Nine wins. Won Spa 24-Hours Group N category.

1991 Contested BTCC (Nissan Primera). Best result sixth. Won Spa 24-Hours Group N category in Nissan Skyline GT-R.

1992 Contested BTCC (Nissan Primera). Best result sixth.

1993 Contested BTCC (Nissan Primera). Finished sixth overall – one win, two seconds, a fourth and three fifth places.

1994 Contested BTCC (Nissan Primera). Best result fourth.

1995 Contested ADAC *Supertourenwagen* Cup (Nissan Primera). One win.

BTCC CHAMPION PROFILE

CLELAND OF PLENTY

by Paul Fearnley

He speaks of 'The Chicken' with great affection. If it is within reach, he will pat it for emphasis. For theirs has been a long and productive friendship.

For those of us not so well acquainted with the said fowl, I should explain: John Cleland has been a Vauxhall driver for so long that he's on nickname terms with the Luton marque's famous standard-bearing gryphon logo. During the six seasons that the hugely successful two-litre touring car formula has been in existence, it's only constant on-track factor has been the Scot and his 'ultimate repmobile'.

And before the Cavalier came the BTCC Astra, the mighty Thundersaloons – Senator and Carlton – and a host of GM-sourced production saloon racers stretching back in an unbroken line to 1980. This is a loyalty that is rare in a sport of one-year contracts and uncertain winter off-seasons; a loyalty that could have led this father-of-four down a career cul-de-sac.

As is usual with all long-term relationships, there have been highs and lows, but this season the Cleland/Cavalier combo has enjoyed an Indian summer. Any driver would be rightly proud of the 43-year-old's achievements in 1995, but few, if any, can say that they have nurtured such a long-lived and so successful a racing car from its genesis to revelation. Two constructors (Dave Cook and Ray Mallock) and three makes of tyre (Dunlop, Yokohama and Michelin) have come and gone, and so it is the common thread of Cleland that strings together the Cavalier's remarkable story. In 1990 he took on the might of BMW with an untried car and finished runner-up in the inaugural two-litre category; by common consent a lack of Yokohamas denied him the title in 1991; in 1992 it was an incensed Steve Soper at Silverstone; 1993 was a blip with just one victory; 1994 was a learning year with Mallock.

Of course, Cleland had already won the championship. Yet it had always niggled him that his success in 1989 – at the wheel of a Cook-built Astra – had sunk in a morass of class confusion. The flame-spitting Sierra Cosworths naturally grabbed the attention while the Scot blitzed a depleted class. The first-past-the-post format introduced in 1991 was far more suited to his clan-like fighting qualities. He just had to win it.

And his TV interview after doing just that at Oulton Park this year was a clear indication of what it meant to him. I'd never seen him lost for words before! Usually, a conversation with him is a draining experience. His self-belief is unwavering, remorseless. He's a Muhammed Ali without the poetry. And for those of a nervous disposition, a head-to-head once a fortnight would suffice. In a world where a manufacturer's image is paramount,

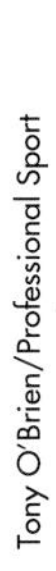

Career highlights:

1986 Thundersaloon Champion (Vauxhall Senator)

1987 Thundersaloon Champion (Vauxhall Senator)

1989 BTCC Champion (Vauxhall Astra). Eleven class wins from 13 starts.

1989 Thundersaloon Champion (Vauxhall Carlton)

1990 Runner-up BTCC two-litre category (Vauxhall Cavalier)

1991 Runner-up BTCC (Vauxhall Cavalier). Three wins.

1992 Third BTCC (Vauxhall Cavalier). Three wins. *Also wins TOCA Shoot-Out.*

1993 Fourth BTCC (Vauxhall Cavalier). One win. *His victory at Knockhill is his first success on home ground in a career that stretches back to 1972. Finishes third in first heat of FIA Touring Car World Cup at Monza.*

1994 Fourth BTCC (Vauxhall Cavalier). Two wins. *Leads FIA Touring Car World Cup at Donington Park.*

1995 BTCC Champion (Vauxhall Cavalier). Six wins.

Below left: **The promise of 1992 was infamously wiped out by an errant Steve Soper in the Silverstone finale.**

his candour can shock. He speaks his mind, rarely bullshits and is never short of an opinion. His defeat of Rickard Rydell in the '95 title battle cost this writer a £500 dividend with Ladbrokes, but ensured that the champion's interview would be a breeze, as opposed to a blood letting/stone-type operation with a quiet Swede carefully coached by the TWR 'secret service'.

Cleland is not averse to a bit of mischief, has a host of one-liners, and always provides good copy . . .

'The age side doesn't bother me. I've just proved that you don't have to be able to run marathons to do this job. I quite honestly do nothing to keep fit. Nothing at all. Not a bloody thing. And I think that's quite funny. I couldn't run a mile if I tried!'

A chuckle burbles down the phoneline. Just two days have elapsed since he captured the title. He's buoyant. I'm glad there's a 90-minute tape whirring away in my recorder.

He also enjoys alluding to the struggles endured by F1 stars Derek Warwick and Nigel Mansell in their short – and shorter – touring car careers. For the man in the street the latter's 'crashing' failure in the 1993 TOCA Shoot-Out at Donington Park plainly illustrated that racing a 300 bhp front-wheel drive touring car is not the most straightforward of exercises. It is this that provides the most remarkable aspect of Cleland's career: his instant adaptation to front-wheel drive, allied to the honing of his style commensurate with the car's six-season metamorphosis – from white knuckles to fingertips. He may not be able to run a mile, but when it comes to BTCC survival, he's one of the fittest.

'The early Cavalier was fast through the quick corners, but if you lifted off it was gone,' he remembers. 'So you had to have the balls to stay on it no matter how far out of shape it got. But in the last two or three years I've really started to drive the thing with my fingertips. You have to be kind to it; if you root the tyres early then you've gone.'

Was this a conscious decision, or a gradual process?

'It was a gradual thing. It's the same bodyshell but everything else has changed – it's been an evolution for me as much as the car. I've learned all the time.'

The preceding two championships had provided frustration, with just three victories to his name. So what made this Cavalier that little bit special?

'Before the season started, I thought, "It's the sixth year of the old dog and, okay, we'll win some races . . ." And then I drove the car Ray [Mallock] had built for the Spanish team. It was just unbelievable. I came away saying, "We're going to win this thing." '

As a car dealer – Volvos and Mazdas – he was not enamoured of the non-standard look bestowed on the race cars by the newly introduced rear wings and front splitters, but he will admit that they were the penultimate pieces in the Cavalier's jigsaw.

'The wings, for sure, made a massive difference to a car that has always worked quite well. They give it stability through some of the medium-speed corners. The Cavalier's always been very good through the faster corners. Strangely enough, Ray's cars have never been as good through the high-speed corners as Cookie's cars, but it comes out of the slower corners much better. So that combination, with the addition of wings, made the car so effective.'

Did the wings make a bigger difference than he'd anticipated?

'Yes, but then I didn't come from a single-seater background. I think if you'd asked Rickard [Rydell] or Alain [Menu], they would have said, "Yes, that's what I expected." But never having been in a single-seater, I was amazed by the downforce. We'd played around a lot during their development. We had some massive rear spoilers that gave it so much downforce that it took 30 mph off our top speed. Then we put some huge front splitters on that made it evil at the rear. We had to find a balance.'

This was a very worrying time for teams as the homologation deadline loomed, for once the wing templates had been delivered to the FIA there would be no chance of recourse. So was Cleland worried by his lack of experience of aerodynamic downforce?

Nope.

Stupid question, really.

'We had some major panics because of the weather but, at the end of the day, I've done more laps in a Cavalier than anyone else in the world, and I know what that car feels like when it's out of control. If a bolt was loose I'd be able to tell you. It was a seat-of-the pants feel for, "No, that's too much. No, that's too little." It worked well as the car was beautifully balanced this year.' Truly, its rivals could only marvel at its frugal use of that most precious of BTCC commodities – the six slicks allowed for qualifying and racing.

Plus there is nobody better than the Borders man at striking that delicate balance between the need to qualify on the front row, to push hard to establish an early lead, or to battle through the pack, while ensuring that the latter stages of a race do not dissolve in a sea of wash-out understeer. But it has been a standing joke among his rivals that, for Cleland, the rubber is always leaner and meaner on the other side. Not any more it's not.

'Michelin is the most professional company I have ever worked with in motor racing. The first time I worked with them was at Nogaro, and the controlled environment they created to do slick testing and wet testing was so meticulous. They would never tell you what they were using; they would start you on a control tyre, give you a couple of new ones and then put the control tyre on again. Fortunately, I could feel the difference. But they took nothing for granted; if I said that the car did XYZ when that tyre was on, they would check the data-logging, check the wheelspin, check the lateral movement, check the G-forces, to substantiate what I was saying.

'That has been the benchmark this year. Previously, Dunlop had tried very hard – obviously, they've made a pretty good job of it this year – but we knew that if Alfa Romeo, Ford and Renault were on Michelins, should we go to a circuit and be off the pace, we would know that it wasn't the tyres.'

Cleland's only tyre problem was keeping abreast of the raft of development tyres the French manufacturer submitted in the second half of the season.

'I was just getting to the stage where I was learning the compounds, and they'd change all the bloody names again,' he sighs. 'It was confusing. It was a case of learning to trust them. And it helped that most of the things Michelin produce are a step forward.' Jigsaw complete.

'The only thing we never got to work was a Q [a softer tyre used purely for qualifying purposes]. That's something we will have to

Top photo: Shutterspeed Photografik, *Centre photos:* LAT Photographic

***Inset:* Opposites interact: Cleland and Mallock optimised their sometimes awkward relationship this season.**
***Right:* Oulton Park is one of the Scot's favourite circuits.**

look at for next year, because I'm sure it will get more competitive.'

It will. It certainly did this year. After the season opened with two processional races at Donington Park – Cleland winning one and Rydell the other, both leading from start to finish – it was obvious that a front-row spot was vital if races were to be won. The introduction of wings had shortened braking distances and increased tyre life, putting overtaking at a premium.

In the days when a car had to be grabbed by the scruff of the neck to shake a time out of it, Cleland was a pole position regular. But when he claimed two consecutive poles at Donington Park in June this year, they were his first since the middle of 1993. One of his previously well-worn motifs had been that, given a spot on the first three rows, he could win the race. There is no doubt that he's one of the best racers out there, but this was one belief that no longer held true. To win – in the dry at least – you had to reach the first corner in the lead. The dazzling one-lap form of Rydell kept him off the top spot more often that not, but Cleland definitely upped his game in qualifying this season.

'I suppose I did.' Oh, come on. 'There was no point being in the middle of the grid. It got to the stage where even the second row was not the place to be. Yeah, I think I did try harder.' Like I said. With the raw speed of James Thompson, his new 21-year-old team-mate, acting as a spur, and the Cavalier's superb balance allowing him to string together several fast laps without unduly compromising its race rubber, the Scot regularly manoeuvred himself into race-winning positions. He grabbed the opportunities, too.

'This year I've made some of the best starts of my career. I don't know how I do it – it's just a feel. It may be that the tyre has a little bit better grip to begin with. That is where Rickard lost out this season; he had 13 or 14 pole positions and converted them into bugger all. He was just going backwards into fourth or fifth, even worse sometimes. I think if I had a car/tyre combination that was capable of getting me onto pole position that many times, I would go and find out why the hell it wouldn't get off the line properly. The gearbox? The clutch? Weight transfer? The driver?'

The driver? In purely psychological terms, the personable but introspective Swede would appear to be no match for the bombastic Cleland, although they are good friends off the track. Menu is perhaps more capable of taking the fight to Cleland. It is impossible to imagine, however, either rival questioning the roles of Tom Walkinshaw or Frank Williams in print. But the man from Galashiels always grasps the nettle. At the moment he is as close to being indispensable to a touring car team as a driver can be. Vauxhall has learned that having the biggest personality in the championship under its wing brings with it the rough and the smooth; he says that his age doesn't bother him, yet Cleland acts and speaks like a man who knows that time is not on his side. Niceties and kow-towing are for drivers with 20 years ahead of them. Politicking for him means a selfish desire for number one status, not back-scratching or mealy-mouthed platitudes. When, in early 1993, a parallel Ecurie Ecosse Vauxhall outfit was mooted, he stamped on it – Mallock's long-term association with David Leslie being deemed too much of a threat and a drain on rescources. And when he didn't want Ray Mallock to engineer his car on race weekends, he said so. The latter is a superbly able, inventive engineer, without whom Vauxhall would not have won the championship. But on a short-term, race-to-race basis he and his number one driver did not always see eye to eye.

'The biggest factor for me this year was that I had a new race engineer in Phil Barker.' An ex-Tyrrell man, Barker first worked with Cleland in the 1994 FIA Touring Car World Cup at Donington Park, where he engineered him into a brief lead. 'We speak the same language. He doesn't suffer fools either, and if people don't mess him about he will cure the problem. He's got nothing radical that he will attempt to change. Basically, we go for a set-up early; for instance, we don't go for a change of springs or dampers on a race weekend. We find a good set-up in the TOCA test, go straight into qualifying and, unless we have a drama, we don't change it. I would hold my hands up to perhaps making a mistake in the morning, and get down to it in the second session.'

From the off Cleland was adamant that all the necessary pieces were in place. He now demanded consistency – something he felt had been denied him in 1994.

'With Ray I was always working with the bossman of the company, who maybe had different views or reasons for why he was or wasn't going to change something – whether it be for a financial reason or a fundamental design reason. Last year it was, "Yeah, let's try that." He was trying to engineer my car, the other car, run a workshop, design a new car and do everything else.'

Alike they are not. Mallock is reserved and quiet. Certainly, he will wince when he reads this – preferring to keep his thoughts on the matter out of the press – but there is no doubt that the pair's working relationship has improved this season. Mallock may even have been hardened by Cleland's attitude.

Even so, look away now, Ray.

'He [Mallock] really didn't like being told that he would have to have two drivers that were paid by Vauxhall. Previously, everything Ray Mallock did was with Ray Mallock Limited-employed people. And for Ray to build his cars – his babies – for them to be then driven by a couple of hoodlums was maybe not on for him. I probably wasn't his favourite person, I don't know.' I do. 'He loves guys who don't argue back, who don't buck the system and give him written reports about this, this, this and this. I'm not like that.' Tell me. 'I enjoy my sport, but I work harder than anybody at it. I don't have to tell Ray that it needs to be three pounds more on the front springs, to change the pre-load on the diff by XYZ, and "Give it a re-spray while you're at it," and I think he's realised that now. Sometimes they won't like what I say but, to be honest, I think that has been one of the helps. And to be fair to him and everyone in the team, they have given 100 per cent this year.

'The car was fantastic this season. I think the six-year development has helped. And when Ray got his hands on it he changed it a little bit in that he's got some very clever people around him now, and he uses a degree of his sportscar and single-seater experience to produce a chassis that really works well. It just does everything well – it gets off the line properly, the traction's good, the engine's mid-range torque is better than anybody's. And it was all just so reliable.'

This is borne out by the fact that John suffered just two retirements during the regular season. Neither was the fault of the car. Ahem.

Ironically, the disaster at Brands

Main photo: Mark Bothwell/Bothwell Photographic, Inset photo: LAT Photographic

Hatch in April – when he led the pack into Paddock Hill Bend on no less than four occasions, only to plunge deep into the gravel twice – was perhaps the turning-point of his year.

'I accept the blame for that. It would've been even more galling to lose the championship for the want of a few points that could've been gained that day. I learned, even at the age of 43, that it wasn't a clever thing to do.'

The second incident came after a first-lap clash with Rydell. In the immediate aftermath, the Vauxhall man chose to race the new leader, Rickard's team-mate Tim Harvey, into Paddock Hill Bend, even though he was a lap down. Yet he insists that he was not suffering from 'red mist'.

'In the first race I'd made a very poor choice of tyre; in the second I felt that I could still do the business and was gambling on something. Red mist or otherwise – a few years ago it would've been, but I like to think that I've calculated things out a bit better this year – I had a long journey home thinking, "That was stupid." The ensuing press reports that week ripped me to bits for it. Maybe I deserved it. But they didn't know that I had no brakes as I approached Paddock for the second time.'

But the pattern set by the preceding champions, Joachim Winkelhock and Gabriele Tarquini, i.e. a spate of early wins backed by consistent podium finishes, made it clear to Cleland that he could not afford any more errors. There were none.

'At the start of the year I thought I would have to win at least six races. But most of all you have to consistently store up points. And that's exactly what happened. I reckon I've used my head more this year than any other year. I reckon I understand all these guys better than anybody else, and I know who I can push where and when, and I know the ones who I can pull a stroke on.'

Four consecutive mid-season wins – two in the wet and two in the dry – at Brands Hatch, Donington Park and Silverstone, were the crux of his title bid.

'I like to think that we won it all year. But to take four wins on the trot was the point at which it was sealed. I would have been disappointed to have then lost it. But perhaps the most important thing I did this year was that I stuck a general manager in my dealerships. This allowed me to be more focused than ever before. I committed everything. And I don't see why I can't commit it for the next handful of years.

'I think that Vectra [the Cavalier's replacement for '96] has got amazing opportunities. That was the reason I did a two-year deal with Vauxhall: to see the old car out and see the new car in, to be part of the development of that. I'm happy that the Vectra's looking good, and that it's a potential race- and championship-winner.'

This year was no parting shot from the oldest works driver in the BTCC . . .

THE THOUGHTS OF CHAIRMAN GOW

by Paul Fearnley

LAT Photographic

For the more reactionary members of this country's motoring hierarchy, it must have been the thin end of the wedge. In 1991, an independent commercially based company was set up with the express intention of running the British Touring Car Championship – the RAC British Touring Car Championship. Further, this independent commercially based company was to be fronted by . . . an Australian. How the broadsheets must have twitched in the RAC's sumptuous Pall Mall club.

Along with Dave Cook, Dave Richards and Andy Rouse – then running Vauxhalls, BMWs and Toyotas in the BTCC – Melbourne's Alan Gow formed TOCA. Under its tutelage the championship has experienced unparalleled growth during the past four seasons, a success so staggering that it convinced the FIA to give its mandate to the regulations in 1993, and triggered off a wave of sister series in France, Italy, Germany, Spain, Portugal, Scandinavia, South Africa, Australia, and perhaps now even America. The antics of John Cleland *et al.* are today watched by a worldwide audience that numbers in the hundreds of millions; trailers pulled by Ford Transits have been replaced in the paddocks by the teams' gleaming articulated lorries, as manufacturers have flooded into the most competitive series of its type. Yet TOCA still has its critics.

'Absolutely, absolutely. We are not universally liked . . .' Gow gives a slightly crooked, mischievous grin that suggests he is not overly bothered by whatever resentment there may be.

He's not.

'I would imagine that most of it is motivated by jealousy. When we took over the championship we restructured entirely the way it was run and, in fact, how a race meeting was run. There's always an element of – and it's not just in motor racing – "Oh, we've never done it like that before." I don't pretend for a minute that there's 100 per cent support out there for our company. There are certain factions within the sport that would like to see us curl up and die, and it must be a huge annoyance to them to see our success. But that's their problem and not ours.'

There came an inkling of this 'success' via the strong reaction to the series when it was first televised on *Grandstand* in 1989. But Gow's experiences in Australia, where he worked with the legendary Peter Brock (a saloon car hero with the height of profile Nigel Mansell enjoys over here) had already proved to him just how popular the BTCC could be, especially with the public perception-friendly single-class system that was introduced for the start of 1991.

'Touring cars have always been the absolute pinnacle of Australian motorsport,' explains Gow. 'People who run touring cars over there are household names; Dick Johnson or Peter Brock can go to a supermarket and get swamped. So I could see that you didn't have to be a Formula One driver to have a public following.

'But people didn't know what our agenda was to start off with. Some thought that we were looking at ways of taking over control of national motor racing here. We're not. If other opportunities come along – like Australia and America [where TOCA has advised on the creation and running of Super Touring series] – then we get involved in it, providing it doesn't disrupt what we are doing here. The BTCC is our core business and we are not about to let our success in it slide in exchange for us doing something else within the sport.'

His focus is understandable. Any sport that can play second fiddle to the Rugby World Cup in the TV ratings war, squeezing out the US Open Golf and Stella Artois tennis tournaments to do so, must be viewed as a big hitter. But outside of Formula One, the backers of motorsport are notoriously fickle, and there has been a legion of once-strong championships which collapsed in the flutter of a chequered flag. So is Gow worried that this is a classic case of too much too soon?

'In general terms, it would be impossible to sustain the growth that we've had for the last three years,' he acknowledges.

The Aussie has had to preside over at least nine manufacturers during the past three seasons – a daunting juggling act.

So has its zenith been reached? The rain that followed the series around this season capped the recent growth of crowds, but the TV figures, which Gow admits the BTCC 'lives and dies by', have increased substantially.

'If you look back at anything I've said over the last four years, I've always maintained the same stance: we wish to see the BTCC become a self-perpetuating entity, not something that balloons and then implodes. For that reason we are quite happy with the way it is going.'

It may sound like a dose of reverse logic, but he does harbour a niggling worry over the high number of manufacturers involved – ten two years ago, and nine each in 1993 and '95.

Gow: 'If you have too many manufacturers there is a greater chance of them pulling out at the same time.'

Six, running three cars each, is his ideal scenario, with manufacturers giving a longer commitment and thus providing the championship with a greater stability. And he believes that the series will eventually reach that level. He then stresses that he has been making the same point for the past three years!

It's a nice problem to have, but it's a problem all the same. Clearly, the current composition of the BTCC makes it impossible for each manufacturer to reap the same benefits from it. A works car is always going to qualify 18th, which is of little use to their marketing departments, and hardly image-enhancing. And the worry of this manufacturer exodus was close to becoming a reality at the time of writing, with Alfa Romeo, BMW and Toyota teetering on the brink. But such is the accessibility of this form of racing to the manufacturers, the likes of Audi, and a little further into the future, Hyundai, look set to plug any gaps. The kudos of winning the BTCC is a strong draw. It may even persuade the 1995 hedgers to return . . .

Gow: 'We always look at the manufacturers to increase their support of the championship, particularly in the way they go about marketing their involvement; some manufacturers are fantastic at it, some you do wonder why they are in it, because they don't support it in any other way. But they must all be getting some value out of it, otherwise they wouldn't be doing it.'

The fact that they are all jostling for the biggest piece of 'value' leaves Gow with the ticklish problem of keeping his – what's the collective noun for manufacturers? – happy. In this respect, he is determined to maintain a united front. This year, the BTCC's undercurrents only once caused any ripples – the £10,000 fine and dire warning that Volvo 850 Racing received for a breach of TOCA's Sporting Regulations at Snetterton. The journalists could gather little more than hearsay, and the boat was quickly steadied. This is how Gow likes it . . .

'It's in everyone's interests for any political, or technical, arguments to be kept out of the public eye. As a journalist, you might say that people like to read about the Hill/Schumacher affair, but that's a different area. If there's a problem between any of the manufacturers or teams, we prefer to sort it out between ourselves. Of course, there was the public dispute regarding Alfa Romeo last year, but that was an FIA thing.

'We have a very good relationship with the manufacturers and the teams. All the manufacturers and teams in this championship know the way we operate – we don't do secret deals, we treat each manufacturer and team equally.

'They haven't got genuine cause for complaint. They are realistic: we come from a competitive background; we're not some old bunch of farts that postulate about the way things should be done, but aren't in touch with reality.' (Has anyone got the phone number of Will Carling's lawyer?) 'All TOCA's directors have been involved in motor racing for a very long time on the other side, so we know what it's like to be a competitor. We know what it's like to run teams, to get involved in championships, and we know the frustrations that go hand-in-hand with it. We are very much aware of those sorts of areas and we are responsive to them. I don't think that there's one team out there that feels that it's been unfairly dealt with by TOCA.'

That's not the case elsewhere. Motorsport in the United Kingdom is hugely diverse and prolific, and the TOCA race package bestrides it like a Colossus. But Gow insists that he has no intention of totally blocking out the lower lights of the sport. This is not a philanthropic stance – there's nothing out there he wants. For him, TOCA is reacting to a market demand and, outside Formula One, only touring cars have the necessary mass appeal.

'The problem with British motorsport is that, if you take away our thirteen race meetings of the year, the rest of the motor racing that is going on around this country is not special. It has no presence about it. There is nothing exciting about it. There's no reason to be there. There are very few personalities involved.'

At this point many of you will turn the page, even put the book down, but there can be no escaping the fact that the TOCA package dominates the racing scene in this country – and provides the bulk of the copy for this book. Rightly or wrongly, public perceptions of any sport are always moulded by the top few per cent of its participants. And this is Gow's point.

He continues: 'John Cleland has not become a personality because TOCA has promoted him, but because the team and the man himself have promoted him as a jovial Scotsman who's good for a one-liner. Very few people within British motorsport have sought to improve their public profile in the way that a lot of the touring car drivers have.

'There is no reason for people to get angry about what I am saying. They should take it on board and look at the way they go about promoting their own participation in motorsport. But, as I said, TOCA didn't promote those people, we just gave them the opportunity to promote themselves.'

But Cleland's public profile still falls a long way short of Peter Brock's . . .

'Yeah, but he's a lot closer to it than he was four years ago.'

Touché.

LAT Photographic

WHAT'S IN A NAME?

My initial reaction was that he was being purposely vague. When I'd asked if the team had made any great strides with the Renault Laguna during the season, I was searching for specifics – different shock absorbers, a change of differential and the like.

'Knowledge,' was Ian Harrison's succinct reply. I laughed, understanding this to be the team manager/journalist word game so prevalent in a championship where hard-fought battles for tenths ensure a walls-have-ears approach.

I have since realised that he was deadly serious.

In motorsport it doesn't come much bigger than Williams. Over the past 18 years we have been ingrained by its Formula One success: Williams means victories, 1-2s, World Champions and a host of Constructors' awards. Consequently, when this Didcot-based concern branched into touring car racing, dominance was predicted – even expected. And this was achieved by Williams Renault Dealer Racing in the final two meetings of the season, three 1-2s from four races sufficient to swipe the manufacturers' championship from under Vauxhall's nose. But it is wildly wrong to suggest that this performance came about purely because of a name.

Yes, the team had a decent budget and a proven car. But it's been a case of perpetual motion since 7 November 1994, the day it moved into its new premises. The title and a season-high ten victories have been the result of serious hard graft. The BTCC is too competitive to expect something for nothing.

'The general feeling along the pit lane is that this has been the most competitive season there's ever been. And, typically, we're involved in it,' smiles Harrison. 'It's been bloody tight, and there's been no let-up. All the crew's had enough. They've been flat out since November, with very little time off, and they are getting a bit jaded.'

Yet for two seasons Harrison had the plum job of team manager for Williams Grand Prix Engineering. Wasn't that challenging enough? Did he need the extra aggravation?

For it was he who mooted the idea of going touring car racing: Patrick Head was keen, but Frank Williams took some persuading, fearing that it might take away impetus from his beloved Formula One. Harrison insisted, however, that it would be a totally separate company, and that he could handle it. He'd put his reputation on the line. And so, when Alain Menu's '95 race car turned its first wheel just one day before the opening race of

Photos: Shutterspeed Photografik

IAN HARRISON INTERVIEW *by Paul Fearnley*

Harrison is a self-confessed motorsport 'bobble hatter'. Here's the proof.

the season, the man from County Durham did wonder whether he'd bitten off more than he could chew. Vitally, the Swiss qualified on the front row, and came away from Donington Park in April with a solid haul of points. Harrison's relief was tangible. Time had been his biggest enemy.

'When we started the project off we wanted to change about 20 per cent of the car, but we ended up fiddling with about 80 per cent of it. There were a few items which we felt needed serious attention, and there are still things on the car that need serious attention, but we won't be doing that until next season.

'The cars have been running on a knife-edge, which is a legacy of not having the time to do it in the first place. Plus finding ourselves in a position, quite surprisingly really, that we could actually win the thing and having to make the car go quicker every fortnight. If you haven't got it right before you start, you're history. There's no time to do retro work on parts that are marginal. What you have got to do is be as intense as you can be with the husbandry, and give it a lot of TLC to try and keep the thing in one piece for the weekend. In that respect, the lads have done a good job, a very good job. We had a few failures during the year but, in general, the mechanics have managed to keep on top of it.'

Two 'failures' in particular will come back to haunt him: the broken gearbox that cost Menu a win at Knockhill, and the steamed-up windscreen that forced the Genevois to pit at Silverstone. Harrison puts it all down to 'knowledge'. Initially, this suggestion clashes with the idea of Williams going motor racing, but it's an absolutely fair assessment; this season has been a fantastic effort by what is a fledgling team. It doesn't matter how much experience you draft in, it still takes time for 38 people to gel, especially when faced with a series of fortnightly deadlines. Harrison, who had just one season of the BTCC behind him, masterminding the Prodrive BMWs in '92, must take much of the credit for this. Mainly because he is also prepared to take the punches on the chin.

'Low points? The first race at Knockhill when both cars didn't finish. And then the first race at Snetterton, when we made a total cods of it; we just didn't stick our necks out enough. It was our lack of experience, to be honest; we took a gamble at Brands Hatch, it went the wrong way and we got our fingers burnt, and from then on I think we became a bit conservative.

'The windscreen? For most of us, it's the first time that we've had to worry about windscreen wipers and rubbish like that. A windscreen is usually a one-and-a-half-inch high piece of perspex, that's fastened with six bolts – that's a windscreen. Again, that's our lack of experience, and we've had to learn from it.

'There's always room for improvement. We make drop-offs every time we go out. But I think that's the same with any sort of racing; it doesn't matter how long you've been doing it and what it is, the secret is to take the necessary action to make sure it doesn't happen again. And there have been times this year when we've had the same failure, so that means that we haven't done the job properly.'

A job. That's exactly what it has been. No fuss. No fanfares. The idea of McLaren, Ferrari or Benetton stepping down in such a low-key manner is inconceivable. There is a down-to-earth attitude that filters through Williams. For such a successful outfit, that operates in such a rarefied atmosphere, it works hard to retain its human touch. In this way it quickly assimilated itself into the BTCC paddock. Harrison has strong views on the championship, but wore 'kid gloves' throughout the year, for he was very conscious of his team's image. And it paid off. Barring the odd grumble about bigger budgets, his rivals had nothing but compliments and respect for the Williams effort.

'I like to think that we play by the rule book, and I think it's important that the team is seen to do that. I don't have a problem with the other teams. I don't know if they have a problem with us. I don't think that they view us as this big outfit that's come in to steamroller their way into it – I just don't see that. And I don't think that we've done that – we've struggled just like everybody else has.'

The decision to concentrate on a single championship, however, has caused some complaints from manufacturers, like BMW, which choose to spread the gospel. The efforts of TWR and Williams have stepped up the level of BTCC competition, and only Vauxhall and Honda appear able to match them at the moment. Super Touring has become more specialised this year; talk of 'packaging' and 'aerodynamics' is reminiscent of the sweeping changes that affected F1 during the ground-effects era of the late Seventies – a period when Williams came to the fore.

Harrison: 'If they [BMW] want to tackle more than one series, that's exactly their problem. I don't say that one or the other is right, it's just how it's worked out. You have to look at the philosophy between the way they do it and the way we do it, and weigh up the pros and cons. It's as simple as that. But they can't come into a championship, like the British Touring Car Championship, where there are class acts like ourselves and TWR that just build specialised sprint cars for Super Touring, and expect to win with a car that could do a 24-hour race. They have done in the past, but those days have gone. They've got to wise up to the fact that they've got to build a specialised sprint car, or go and do something else.'

But hasn't Max Mosley, President of the FIA, stated that he wants Super Touring to be left to the privateers, while manufacturers should concentrate on the ITC? Does he really want the likes of Williams to move in on the national Super Touring scene? Harrison thinks so . . .

For a while it looked as though Will Hoy would stay in the background. But as Damon Hill has discovered to his cost, it's not the Williams way to favour one car. Here Harrison plots with Alain Menu.

LAT Photographic

WHAT'S IN A NAME?

'My own understanding of it is that he views us as the archetypal privateer team.' Stretching belief? Perhaps. 'We don't produce cars, we are just a chassis tuner. We tune racing cars, much along the same lines as TWR do. And I think that's what he perceives to be the right sort of team to be involved in Super Touring. Now if Renault Sport as a company were to get involved in touring car racing then, from my understanding, it means that they will be encouraged to go into ITC.

'Don't forget, the BTCC programme is not sponsored by Renault, or Renault Sport, it's sponsored by Renault UK. It's purely a nationally sponsored programme.'

However, Harrison is opposed to what he perceives to be an insularity of credo within the BTCC.

'I don't think there's enough money in this series. For what is supposed to be the best championship in the world – people keep telling me it is, anyway – I think we need a bigger profile series sponsor to put more money into it. This will raise the profile of the series, and that will attract more finance into it.

Shutterspeed Photografik

Shutterspeed Photografik

There's enough teams in it now, ourselves included, that have got experience in other formulae, and can contribute to this championship to make it better and improve everybody's lot. But teams don't seem to be taken very seriously in this championship, yet at the end of the day we, along with the manufacturers, are the people who are putting the show on.

'We are not in the job of coming in here and saying, "Well, in Formula One we did it like this." It's not applicable. It's just totally irrelevant. But I do believe that there are certain things that would help if people were prepared to listen.'

One change that Harrison is adamant *will* be a boon for 1996 is that Williams Renault Dealer Racing will be able to buy the T-shirt, having 'been there, done that'.

GUARDIAN OF SWEDEN

by Nick Phillips

Main photo: John Marsh/Action Images, *Top photo:* Bill Bothwell/Bothwell Photographic

There were plenty of smug faces among the TWR personnel at the pre-season press day. This wasn't because its four-square Volvo saloon was ripping around a chilly Donington Park, wowing the hacks and VIPs strapped into its temporary passenger seat. Or because it had managed more testing miles than any of its rivals in the winter off-season. It was because Ladbrokes had quoted Rickard Rydell and Tim Harvey at 25/1 and 20/1 for the championship. Every wallet in that garage had a neatly folded pink slip tucked away inside it. All except Rydell's. As is the case with most big-name drivers, he didn't have any cash on him!

When Volvo signed a three-year contract with Tom Walkinshaw's highly successful team, it knew exactly what to expect. In the mid-Eighties the sturdy Scot's Rover V8s represented the enemy on the track – and in the courtroom – as its 240 Turbos took to the tracks in the European Touring Car Championship. A wry grin crept across Walkinshaw's face when this was mentioned during the launch of Volvo 850 Racing at the 1994 Stockholm Motorshow.

On the surface it appeared a strange liaison: the purveyors of sensible cars to genteel people lining up with the biggest, baddest team in the pits. If it was a change of image the Gothenburg-based manufacturer wanted, it had come to just the right place. Walkinshaw's team gets results. In the process it may tread on a few toes, upset the odd sensibility and flex a regulation or two towards breaking point, but give it three years and it should get you what you want . . .

At a snowy Stockholm two years ago, Walkinshaw laid out the itinerary: Year One was for learning and perhaps the odd podium finish; Year Two was for winning races; Year Three was for the championship.

Year One proved a disappointment with the outrageous 850 Estates. But Year Two's plan was almost by-passed as the new saloon provided a consistent threat to John Cleland's Vauxhall throughout the season.

And as the torn pink slips blow around the garage TWR used at Oulton Park, the team can look ahead to Year Three.

I bet Walkinshaw had Rydell each-way . . .

Ultimately, Volvo and Rickard were pushed back to third in their respective championships by a sparkling end-of-season burst from Renault and Alain Menu. Yet . . .

'It was a very successful year,' stresses TWR's Andy King. 'With a brand new car, we had 13 poles, six wins and 19 podium positions. I think if we'd been offered that pre-season, we would have been delighted to take it. The BTCC was more competitive than ever and we played a major part in the success of the championship and its competitiveness.'

A busy winter of testing allowed the Volvos to hit the ground running at the start of the season. The form of the Vauxhall Cavalier at Donington Park had John Cleland pencilling in a couple of wins in his diary, but the Scot was to be surprised by the pace of Rydell, who began an amazing sequence with two pole positions. He began another sequence when he muffed his start in the first race. He made amends by winning the second.

Rickard registered two more poles at Brands Hatch, but it was Tim who scored Volvo's two wins in the streaming conditions. Moreover, Cleland had twice parked his Cavalier untidily in the gravel at Paddock. He was under pressure. Harvey and Rydell were first and second in the championship, and it was conceivable that Volvo might dominate the season in the way BMW and Alfa had in '93 and '94, i.e. hit the front, build a lead, consolidate.

It never quite happened. Fortunes ebbed and flowed. Rydell – with wins at Silverstone and Oulton Park – held the series lead for a month between May and June. Then Cleland struck a rich vein of form, four consecutive wins giving him an advantage he would never cede.

'I don't think we lost it. I think Vauxhall went out and won it,' says King, cutting the TWR critics off at the pass. Vauxhall's effort should

Left: The forthright Scot's 850s dominated at a wet Brands Hatch in April.
Below: TWR's standard of preparation and attention to detail are second to none.

not be underestimated; any team that beats TWR and Williams in the same season deserves to give itself a pat on the back. But TWR's numerous successes have ensured that thirds will always be looked upon as failures. Yes, I know it was only the team's second year with front-wheel drive. Ditto for Rydell. And the first year for the saloon . . .

Out of the car Rydell wouldn't say boo to a goose – inside it he's a demon – but he will calmly cite the glitches that perhaps cost him his chance. He is not angry. He knows how tough the BTCC is, and that even though TWR is the most professional team he has ever been involved with, everything and everybody needs a little time to succeed. He is confident that in '96 there will be no repeat of the misted-up windscreens at Brands Hatch in May and Silverstone in July, the brake failures at Brands Hatch in June and Snetterton in September, the error that left him with two fifth gears for qualifying at Oulton Park in September and the engine failure of the final round.

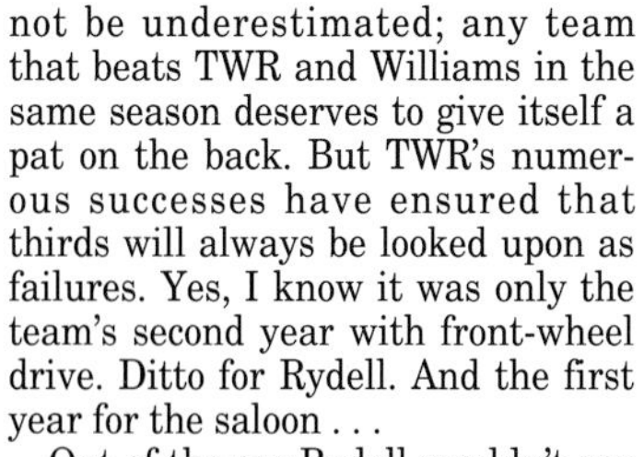

With six years of development and years of saloon car experience behind its wheel, the Cavalier of Cleland retired just twice. Perhaps surprisingly, given the preceding paragraph, Rydell recorded the second-highest number of finishes. Too often, however, he was on the outskirts of the points.

The sceptics will motion to the contract for '96 sticking out of his back pocket, and recall the places lost by his history of tardy starts, when the Stockholm florist's son proffers his softly-softly review of the year.

King is more forthright: 'If you look at the statistics, as a manufacturer, we had as many finishes as anyone – 44. It was, I suppose, a combination of bad luck, mechanical problems and driver errors.' Some of this has been put down to experience; King points out that both Volvo 850 Racing and Williams Renault Dealer Racing had problems with demisting. 'We were the two teams who didn't have experience of running those cars in the wet.

'After six years I'd have been surprised if Cleland did have any mechanical problems. We certainly weren't sitting in the pits while Vauxhall ran away with it.'

Rydell, though, will admit that his poor early-season starts cost him a couple of victories. His form away from the line improved in the second half of the season – a turnaround he credits to a chat with his 1994 team-mate, Jan Lammers. It is ironic that when he made two fantastic starts from pole position at Snetterton, he came away from Norfolk with zero points.

There was a further irony in that the Volvo had lost its advantage by this time. The last four meetings provided a meagre haul of points for the one-time leader of the championship . . .

'We managed to keep the development and the speed of the car going right up until the last race,' suggests King. 'At Brands Hatch there was the incident with Cleland [the Vauxhall nosed Rickard into a half-spin and out of the lead], which was unfortunate. At Snetterton, Rickard was on pole for both races and he was leading comfortably before the problem [brake failure which saw him narrowly miss an ambulance]. At Oulton Park he should have been on pole for the second race – Tim was fourth fastest, which I think shows the car was good enough.

'At the same time, some of the other teams raised their game: Ford, Honda, Toyota, even Alfa and BMW made great progress. That meant it was even more important not to slip up in qualifying, because the pack behind was that much more competitive . . .'

But what about the Silverstone finale, when it was left to the privateer Ford Mondeo of Matt Neal to fly Dunlop's flag in the second session?

'It's sad that because it was the last meeting, that's what some people will remember. But you mustn't lose sight of the major success the season has been,' urges King.

He's right. There were so many strengths: in those early races the 850 looked significantly more composed on the track than its rivals, with the notable exception of the Cavalier; it was powerful, though not slippery-quick along the straights; it was fantastic on the brakes; it was well-sorted and raceable. In Rydell's hands it was a sensation in qualifying. The downhill plunge of Duffus Dip, McIntyres and the Chicane at Knockhill are daunting, and this Swedish combination was head and shoulders quicker than anybody else here – the Volvo's superb chassis glueing it to the deck as the rest hopped, skipped and jumped.

Up the hill, however, Menu would haul the Volvo in and, but for a gearbox failure, the Renault ace would have won both races.

After this lucky win, it was the season that went downhill for Volvo and Rydell. It is no coincidence that this coincided with a big push from Michelin. Until Knockhill, Dunlop had matched Michelin every step of the way. And at the Scottish circuit it provided a new tyre for the Swede to dominate testing and finish first and second. But thereafter Michelin, who had set its ball rolling at the Silverstone GP meeting, had a new tyre for just about every remaining meeting. It was a daunting display.

But this was not the whole reason for the reversal of fortune, and certainly Rydell never hid behind the tyre war: as far as he's concerned, Dunlop provided him with a superb tyre for qualifying, and he gave no indication that their performance over a race distance was any less consistent than the Michelins.

The problems that lost him the championship were much more transient than that. It could've been won. It wasn't. But it will be.

'We'll come back better and stronger. We'll have all the positives of this year and we'll eliminate the negatives,' says King. 'The new [Opel] Vectra will be very strong and so will the Honda. I'm sure the Renault will be quick again, too, and there will be the Audi as well. So it won't be any easier, but we'll be better equipped than we were this year. My prediction is that we'll win.'

Here beginneth Year Three.

What odds on Rydell now?

Gavin Lawrence/Sutton Photographic

IN THE LAST CHANCE SALOON?

by Paul Fearnley

Main photo: LAT Photographic, Inset: Mike Cooper/Allsport

Is this the man who passed over the Holy Grail, and accepted a poisoned chalice?

Derek Warwick will hear none of it. But there is no denying that the Hampshire driver once turned down Williams to stay at soon-to-disappoint Renault, thus allowing Nigel Mansell his final chance to succeed. Or that he joined Alfa Romeo just as the cream of touring cars turned sour.

Usually possessed of an upbeat outlook, he was positively buoyant during a meet-the-press wine-and-dine at the start of the year. He had just returned from a two-day test in last year's all-conquering 155TS at Mugello. He'd been quick. As quick as Gabriele Tarquini, the recently crowned British Touring Car champion.

'I have to say that I started the season full of expectations,' Warwick admits. 'I signed for Alfa because they won everything last year, and anybody that had to make a fresh decision for '95 would possibly have made the same one I did. The car looked like it probably wasn't going to win everything, but certainly win a few races, which would have given me a good footing and credibility to build on.'

Of the recent British Formula One stars, he was the one most would have picked to succeed in the BTCC: fast, adaptable, aggressive, massively determined – and with a strong stock car background that was deemed to be the ideal preparation for the regular saloon door-banging fare. So when he spoke of victories, a possible championship even, nobody doubted him for a minute.

Much to his annoyance, there are plenty of doubters now.

By his own admission, this has been the toughest season of an illustrious career. Good results have been hard to come by, retirements have abounded and his good humour has worn thin. Certainly, I touched a nerve during this interview.

'I have to say that, from about mid-season on, I was sick and tired of explaining to people why the car was slow this year and yet won everything last year. Why didn't they just say, "Why are you slow, Derek?" because that's what it felt like to me. I had to justify myself all the time. In the end . . . sod it, make your own decision.'

I'd put it to him that some of his rivals felt he'd been over-driving.

'It's sad for me to hear that from people like yourself. But you are obviously speaking from a small sector of people that keep their ear to the ground, and they seem to think that I am doing a bad job. Maybe I've been kidding myself; I thought I'd been doing not too bad – not a good job, but not a bad job.'

Over-driving is a problem that faces any driver in their first year of touring car racing. Warwick discovered that, unlike a Grand Prix car where the harder you drive the faster you go, with a touring car the harder you drive the slower you go. And he admits that this was especially difficult for him when he went for the ultimate lap in qualifying, a task made no easier by the nervous 155's love-hate relationship with qualifying tyres.

For those on the outside looking in, however, the reappearance of Tarquini with the third Alfa Romeo at Oulton Park in May was a more damning indictment of Warwick's performance. Howsoever it was

The BTCC's unseemly midfield scrum gave the Jersey-based Hampshire driver plenty of food for thought.

dressed up, the presence of the champion and his Italian Superturismo spec car put the Englishman under the sort of pressure he didn't need during a torrid start to the season. To all intents and purposes, it appeared that the rabid AC Milan fan was there purely to act as a benchmark for the UK-run car and its driver. And Gabriele struggled like hell; outqualified by Warwick and Giampiero Simoni in both sessions, he finished his Sunday jammed uncharacteristically in the gravel after less than half a lap of the second race.

The conclusion: the new Alfa was dreadful; the Prodrive developments Warwick had been working on made it a little more bearable; the man himself was extracting pretty much the maximum from it.

'The new car is not nice. It's very nervous at the back end; it jacks up and makes the rear go light all the time, and I am not an oversteering type of driver. I like a fairly neutral car, and in this respect we had a very small window to work within; it was like balancing the car on the edge of a sheet of paper, and if it fell off down either side we lost a lot of its performance. A couple of times this year the car has been perfect – at Donington and at Brands – and I've been blisteringly quick. I've been quicker at times like that because the car is predictable, and I've got something to build on. But when a car floats from the rear, and is not talking to the front end at all, it's difficult to build your confidence up.'

It soon became clear that the car had dominated last season mainly through its aerodynamic advantages. Alfa Corse had stayed one step ahead of its opposition throughout 1994 – it had out-thought and out-planned its rivals. Now it was simply out of step. The news that the FIA was to give the green light to a Class 1 International Touring Car series, plus the speed of the fantastic Mercedes C-Class in this hi-tech category, saw Alfa Romeo working flat out to match the input, both technical and financial, of the Three-Pointed Star. Class 1 was everything; its Italian Superturismo programme was axed, and in June Prodrive was cleared to lead the development of the 155TS. This was not what Warwick had had in mind at the start of the year.

'I am disappointed about the commitment of Alfa Romeo Italy. I believe that they rested on their laurels. I came in as a big Grand Prix driver and, I suppose, I expected a little bit more from them. With hindsight, I have to say that Alfa Romeo are committed to ITC, and not committed in the slightest to British touring cars.

'Because they won it last year, I think that they really didn't take their testing too seriously. They followed the route of one driver, and although Gabriele is a very good driver – quick and a good tester – I think you can get very confused by just following the leads of only one driver. You always need to be able to bounce ideas off other people, otherwise you end up developing a car for one driver's way of driving. You see it with Benetton.

'Everything about the Alfa Romeo, say compared to the Honda, is wrong: the rear suspension, the engine is only 275 bhp, although we made some big steps forward on the engine, the aerodynamics are crap, we can't get the car low enough, it doesn't ride the bumps – our car is not a good car.'

But he sets great store by the fact that Tarquini, who replaced Simoni for the second half of the BTCC, ran Prodrive's front dampers, rear dampers, rear leg, lower ride height and engine.

'We don't seem to get any kudos for that at all. I have to say that Prodrive took two or three months to weed out the bits that affected the performance of the car, because they had to get a lot of things passed by Turin. For a brand new team, they've moulded a great team, and we have made progress.'

But wasn't it Tarquini who used these developments to best effect, securing three fourth places towards the end of the season?

'Gabriele is quick, there's no doubt about that. But if you look at the races at Brands, for instance, I finished eighth and he didn't finish in the first race. Then he finished fourth in the second one. But if you actually look at what happened, a lot of the front-runners went out, and so he had a much easier race than mine, when all the front-runners kept going until the end.

'At Knockhill he did a bloody good job to finish eighth, I have to say, because I couldn't have finished eighth if I'd raced there for another 20 years. At Oulton Park he made a couple of nice moves, passed Rydell and capitalised on a few other people's mistakes . . .

'Okay, Gabriele's taken a flier on me a couple of times, but I'm quicker than him when my car's right. But people have very short memories. If we'd have both been running at the front, say he'd been on pole and I was fourth, two-tenths behind him, everybody would have been saying, "What a great job Derek's doing." But if I'm two-tenths behind him in 17th, it's a disaster.

'If you look at Tim Harvey's performance and, early on, Will Hoy's performance, in many ways they have done a much worse job. They are half a second slower than their team-mate, and it's still good enough to put them fifth and sixth on the grid.'

Derek admits that there have been gambles on set-up and dicey manoeuvres on the first lap – but then he's not designed to finish 15th. He left his beloved F1 to get away from running around at the back in uncompetitive machinery.

Maybe he's been too impatient with himself. But his situation was always going to deny him a settling-in period; he chose to drive last year's dominant car, and a man with his record was expected to win races from the off.

Ironically, this year has probably taught him more about touring car racing than if he had shared in Tarquini's 1994 glories. But has he now been labelled 'unclean' by the touring car paymasters?

'I've had a dreadful year. I couldn't have picked a worse situation to try and build on. I think that if a few situations could have just rolled the other way, I could have had better results. I think the team will be the first to back me up as far as the testing and PR is concerned, because I think I've done quite well.

'I am big enough and strong enough to listen to all the criticism, and I just hope that I can come through it and race a car that can prove to all of you that I can still drive.'

His unabashed confidence and determination are the keys to his survival.

'I want to stay in British touring cars. Yes, I'd love to do ITC because it's a "world" championship, but this is unfinished business now. This has pissed me off big time. I think that if I get a good drive for next year we are going to be sitting here having a completely different conversation. All I am going to say to you is, "I told you so." '

No, he won't. He won't stop rubbing it in until he touches a nerve. And I've got a feeling he's going to get his own back.

Above: But for a poor first start of the season, Rickard Rydell's impressive Volvo might have won both races.

Renault 'new boy', Will Hoy *(right)*, survived an exclusion scare to score points in both races.

Main photo: John Cleland left Leicestershire in the lead of the championship.

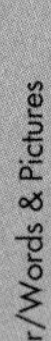

LAT Photographic

Below: **James Kaye leads David Brabham's BMW on his way to scoring the Honda Accord's first BTCC point.** ***Below centre:*** **Paul Radisich made a solid start to his campaign.** ***Bottom:*** **Pondering a 'not so safe journey' is Derek Warwick.**

Colin McMaster/Words & Pictures

LAT Photographic

LAT Photographic

DONINGTON PARK

The problem was plain for all to see: Rickard Rydell had dominated both qualifying sessions on Saturday, annexing pole position each time by a comfortable margin, yet a tardy start stranded his Volvo in fourth from beginning to end of the season's opening encounter. The FIA-approved addition of rear wings and front splitters, plus careful reworking of the cars' underbodies over the winter, had transformed natural saloon car lift into semi-serious racing car downforce: braking distances were shorter, tyre wear was reduced and the usual touring car pyrotechnics had been extinguished. The top four – John Cleland, Alain Menu, Paul Radisich and Rydell – remained static throughout.

The softly spoken Swede made no mistake later in the day, bursting from the inside of the front row to lead into Redgate. Next time around he set the fastest lap of the race by over a second. He was gone. Afterwards he joked that he was relieved not to have won the first race of the year – he had done so on three previous occasions in the UK, only for his title aspirations to dwindle. He knew, however, that two good starts would have netted him two wins. Having done more worthwhile testing than any of their rivals, the TWR-built and -run Volvos had hit the ground running to score the first BTCC win for the Swedish manufacturer.

This provided Cleland with a win-win situation. This beautifully smooth circuit has always suited Ray Mallock's Vauxhall Cavaliers, and when Rydell hesitated he lost, for the talkative Scot grabbed the opportunity to lead from lights to flag and open his account in style. However, a minor gearchange problem in afternoon qualifying forced him to start from the outside of the third row in the second race, and even he would have to play a patient game in order to work his way through to second. But whether he chose to wear his 'Vauxhall racer' or 'Volvo dealer' hat, the series leader did so with a smile.

So the BTCC's 'V Formation' had set out its stall. But who was on its tail? Renault.

Alain Menu had surprised himself and the newly formed Williams Renault Dealer Racing team by qualifying third and second on Saturday. Both he and team-mate, Will Hoy, had had very little time in its new Lagunas, yet they bagged a second, fourth, fifth and sixth between them on Sunday.

It is hazardous to suggest that a season's pattern has been established on its opening day, but that's how it appeared: the wings had seemingly taken the guesswork out of the BTCC. Teams hoping to recover from early setbacks looked set to remain disappointed.

This was a worry for Derek Warwick and Alfa Romeo. The championship's highest profile winter signing was struggling. Undoubtedly, his car had been left behind in the development stakes, but adapting to front-wheel drive was causing him some headaches. He stuck his 155TS in the gravel in race one, and was nerfed into a spin and straightlined the Esses in the second before calling it a day. This media-friendly driver left the circuit with nary a word. He would later admit that it was the first time in his illustrious career that he'd felt embarrassed.

SNIPPETS

. . . It snowed during the Thursday TOCA test, yet Sunday's race is run in a heatwave. • Paul Radisich, a winner here of the FIA Touring Car World Cup the previous October, can only manage third and sixth places for Ford. • His new team-mate, Kelvin Burt, starts his first BTCC race for Ford from the back of the grid after missing the pit lane closure. • James Thompson marks his debut as a works Vauxhall driver by qualifying his Cavalier third in the second session – three places ahead of Cleland. The 20-year-old Yorkshireman finishes seventh in both races. • Peugeot's 'young gun' Simon Harrison outqualifies his experienced team-mate, Patrick Watts, thanks to tenth position in the second session. • James Kaye scores Honda's first BTCC point when he finishes tenth in the second race. • David Leslie qualifies the impressive Accord ninth for the first race, and is fourth fastest in the morning warm-up. Unfortunately, he slides off in the first race when a tie-rod breaks. • Hoy is excluded from the first race for pushing Julian Bailey's Toyota off. He is later reinstated to sixth place – it's his birthday! • In the Total Cup Matt Neal scores two pole positions and two wins with his Team Dynamics Ford Mondeo.

RESULTS • ROUND 1

1 JOHN CLELAND Vauxhall Cavalier 16V
2 ALAIN MENU Renault Laguna
3 PAUL RADISICH Ford Mondeo Ghia
4 RICKARD RYDELL Volvo 850 20v
5 JOHNNY CECOTTO BMW 318iS
6 WILL HOY Renault Laguna
TOTAL CUP
1 MATT NEAL Ford Mondeo Ghia

RESULTS • ROUND 2

1 RICKARD RYDELL Volvo 850 20v
2 JOHN CLELAND Vauxhall Cavalier 16V
3 TIM HARVEY Volvo 850 20v
4 ALAIN MENU Renault Laguna
5 WILL HOY Renault Laguna
6 PAUL RADISICH Ford Mondeo Ghia
TOTAL CUP
1 MATT NEAL Ford Mondeo Ghia

BRANDS HATCH *Indy*

LAT Photographic

LAT Photographic

LAT Photographic

Allsport UK

It's a mixed metaphor, but it took a splash of rain to spark the BTCC into life. If Donington Park was dry and dull, then Brands Hatch was wet and wild. So was John Cleland. The Vauxhall man had one of his rare off-days, leading the pack into Paddock Bend on four occasions only to crash out twice. In contrast, Tim Harvey – who shows a deftness of touch in the wet that he sometimes lacks in the dry – kept his cool, took his luck and scored two wins for Volvo to supplant the Scotsman at the head of the points table.

The fun began when the rain arrived as the cars were sitting on the grid awaiting a restart. This was delayed further to allow the drivers to switch from slicks if they so desired. Amazingly, only the Volvos, the works Fords, the BMW of David Brabham and the privateer Ford of Charlie Cox bolted on full wets . . .

Rickard Rydell had added two more pole positions to his collection on Saturday, and by the end of the second lap he and Harvey had carved out a seven-second lead over the rest! But there was to be more disappointment for the Swede: his windscreen misted up, and the resultant pit stop dropped him out of the points. To be fair to Tim, however, he had passed his team-mate to take the lead in the dry just moments before the first red flag.

The Mondeos had been dire during the dry qualifying sessions. Paul Radisich started from his lowliest BTCC grid position (18th), but he and Kelvin Burt stormed through the field to take second and third for Ford, ahead of Brabham and Cox.

The latter's drive was remarkable. Stepping up after two class-winning years in the National Saloon Car Championship, the amiable Australian had never driven his Ford in the wet, yet he had the crowd on its feet. He had worked his way up to fifth by lap four, spun four laps later, but repeated his earlier progress to regain fifth spot and equal the best-ever result for a privateer.

The second race of the day was a little more staid, with everybody now on wets. But Cleland did his best to liven it up, squeezing through from the second row to lead at both starts. His first effort was cancelled out when Radisich and Patrick Watts's Peugeot scattered themselves along the pit straight; his second was nullified when Rydell attempted to run around the outside of him at Surtees. They touched and spun. Menu was baulked and Harvey was through.

The first race winner had been relegated to the back of the grid for the original start of this race, when a faulty starter motor caused him to miss the pit lane closure. For the restart, however, he was able to take up his original third-row slot. The sun wasn't shining, but the gods were smiling.

The marooned Cleland eventually selected reverse – not the easiest of operations with a sequential gearbox – and gathered his car together. Sadly, he did not gather his thoughts. In peevish fashion he rejoined directly in front of the new leader and chose to race him into Paddock. It was only then that he discovered his brakes had been damaged in his clash with Rydell . . . If he wanted to win this title, he'd had his red mist for the season.

In contrast, his young team-mate drove with great maturity to take second. James Thompson put aside the disappointment of missing the start of the first race because of a faulty alternator to keep the pressure on Harvey throughout.

And Rydell? He recovered to win a hectic battle with Burt for third. Four poles, one win – an imbalance that had to be redressed.

SNIPPETS

. . . Both Honda Accords have their times from the second session disallowed: James Kaye for refuelling in the pit lane, David Leslie for failing the ride-height check at the end of the session. Kaye is sixth in the first session. Both men are advised to choose slicks for the first race restart! • Thompson starts his fourth race for Vauxhall from the front row. • Radisich races with sore ribs sustained during a physical training session. He sets the fastest lap in the first race. Ford team-mate, Burt, takes this honour in the second. • Derek Warwick notches up his first BTCC finish with 12th place in the first race. He does so having started from the back of the grid after a last-minute decision to change from slicks to intermediates. In the second race he is shunted into retirement at the start by his Alfa Romeo team-mate, Giampiero Simoni. • In the second race Matt Neal makes it three Total Cup wins from four starts. • The first race is stopped after one lap because of a clash between Richard Kaye's Ford Mondeo and Nigel Smith that leaves the latter's Vauxhall Cavalier beached on the inside kerb at Druids.

RESULTS • ROUND 3

1 TIM HARVEY Volvo 850 20v
2 PAUL RADISICH Ford Mondeo Ghia
3 KELVIN BURT Ford Mondeo Ghia
4 DAVID BRABHAM BMW 318iS
5 CHARLIE COX Ford Mondeo Ghia
6 JULIAN BAILEY Toyota Carina E

TOTAL CUP

1 CHARLIE COX Ford Mondeo Ghia

RESULTS • ROUND 4

1 TIM HARVEY Volvo 850 20v
2 JAMES THOMPSON Vauxhall Cavalier 16V
3 RICKARD RYDELL Volvo 850 20v
4 KELVIN BURT Ford Mondeo Ghia
5 JOHNNY CECOTTO BMW 318iS
6 DAVID BRABHAM BMW 318iS

TOTAL CUP

1 MATT NEAL Ford Mondeo Ghia

Gavin Lawrence/Sutton Photographic

Below: **First race stories: Charlie Cox was the undoubted star, his privateer Ford finishing fifth; James Kaye qualified sixth, but was sent out on slicks . . . David Brabham was the last unlapped runner – in fourth!**

Bryn Williams/Words & Pictures

Anton Want/Allsport

LAT Photographic

Opposite page, from the top: **Paul Radisich's day started promisingly, but ended violently when he clipped the already crashed Peugeot of Patrick Watts.**

John Cleland and Rickard Rydell exit stage left at Surtees. The Scot rejoined last and promptly stuck his Vauxhall in the Paddock gravel for a second time.

Above: **The Dunlop-shod Volvos were untouchable in the first race; here Rydell holds the lead over Harvey that would eventually succumb to a misted windscreen.**

Right: **Memories of the Donington Park processions were washed away by two frenetic races in Kent; Tim Sugden's Toyota and the Renault of Alain Menu would eventually clash.**

LAT Photographic

Bryn Williams/Words & Pictures

Tony O'Brien/Professional Sport

Tony O'Brien/Professional Sport

Bryn Williams/Words & Pictures

Bruce Grant-Braham

Gavin Lawrence/Sutton Photographic

LAT Photographic

LAT Photographic

Giampiero Simoni gave Alfa Romeo hope with a sixth place. After his Brands Hatch heroics, Charlie Cox cartwheeled his Ford to destruction. Outpaced by Matt Neal's Ford in qualifying, Nigel Smith took two Total Cup wins in his Vauxhall. James Thompson grabbed the headlines by becoming the youngest winner of a BTCC race.

Left: **Rickard Rydell, Tim Sugden and Paul Radisich attack the chicane; the Volvo and Ford clashed here in the first race, while the Toyota soldiered on to finish fourth.**

Below: **Meanwhile, John Cleland paid close attention to Alain Menu, to no avail.**

THRUXTON

Bryn Williams/Words & Pictures

Accepted theory: experience is the key to a top-notch touring car driver. Exception to the rule: James Thompson.

At just turned 21, the York driver became the youngest-ever BTCC pole position-sitter when he topped out the most competitive session for years on Saturday. Then, on Monday, in only his sixth race as a works driver, he maintained his composure at the start, and a restart, to lead his more experienced colleagues home. His success did not mark the end of an era, but it was a breath of fresh air. And to think that the sceptics had been tutting in disapproval after his third place in the first race fell victim to a puncture on this abrasive track . . .

Thompson shared the spoils – but not the headlines – with Alain Menu, who became the third championship leader in as many meetings. Thruxton had been expected to be a John Cleland stronghold, yet the Swiss took pole position for the first race, and then held off the Scot's persistent Cavalier for its entirety. The fastest track on the calendar is also the hardest on tyres, and so the Vauxhall's carefully rationed use of its rubber was supposed to be a trump card. But the six-race-old Williams outfit gave further notice that experience is not everything.

And so the 'V Formation' was broken.

The lack of testing at the Hampshire venue – just two 55-minute sessions because of noise restriction – nullified Volvo's early-season advantage. In plain language, the TWR 850s were a handful over the fast bumps that pepper Thruxton and lacked straightline speed.

Rickard Rydell clashed with Paul Radisich's Ford in the first race and dropped back to ninth, and Kelvin Burt's Mondeo restricted him to fourth in the second. It says something for the situation that the Swede was relatively happy with his results. Meanwhile, his team-mate lost the championship lead in a flurry of oversteer and a missed pit lane weighbridge. The latter infringement saw Tim Harvey start from the back of the grid with a ten-second penalty in the first race. A second-race seventh place was the 'highlight' of his weekend.

The scorching weather exacted a heavy toll, but Patrick Watts and Tim Sugden stayed cool to lift Peugeot and Toyota into the respectability zone with a third and fourth in the first race. The former had missed the official test as his Peugeot was being reshelled in the aftermath of its Brands Hatch race-stopping shunt. He was almost half a minute behind the leading two in the first race, yet still put the Coventry team back on the podium. He clashed with Cleland in the second race, broke a wheel and spun off.

Following his kamikaze display at Brands Hatch, the latter found himself cast as the miserly Scot, an unusually cautious first lap in the second race dropping him down to ninth. He eventually battled through to finish fifth, but having followed Thompson and seen the Cavalier's four-square road holding, Menu for one was surprised that the more experienced Vauxhall man hadn't won both races . . .

Tony O'Brien/Professional Sport

Above: **Patrick Watts scored Peugeot's first podium finish of the season.**

Left: **Menu gave Williams its first BTCC win, at only its fifth attempt.**

SNIPPETS

. . . An Alfa Romeo qualifies in the top ten: Giampiero Simoni is ninth fastest in the first session. He is a fighting sixth in the corresponding race. • The top five cars in the second session are separated by just 67/1000ths of a second. • Will Hoy is second fastest in this session, but is unable to take up the front-row position after his Renault Laguna's steering rack, replaced following an accident in the first race, begins to leak. He makes the restart without power steering, but retires at the end of the first lap. • Total Cup runner Matt Neal stars in qualifying, his Ford Mondeo securing seventh and tenth places for the races. His foray among the works cars brings its problems, however, and he is nerfed off in the early stages of both. • Neal's misfortunes allow the Vauxhall Cavalier of Nigel Smith to take two well-judged Total Cup victories. • After his first race victory, Menu reveals that his Renault Laguna's gearchange was repaired as he waited on the startline. • The second race is stopped following a huge accident for Charlie Cox. The hero of Brands Hatch has the rear brakes of his Ford Mondeo lock up as he approaches the chicane for the first time, launching the car into a series of horrifying rolls. Its driver suffers a fractured skull, haemorrhaging of the eyes and severe bruising. He will be out of action for the next three months. • Burt has a narrow escape in the first race when his Ford Mondeo suffers a front-left puncture as it rounds Church Corner. It ploughs on across the grass for 250 yards before its flight is arrested by a sturdy bush.

RESULTS • ROUND 5

1 ALAIN MENU Renault Laguna
2 JOHN CLELAND Vauxhall Cavalier 16V
3 PATRICK WATTS Peugeot 405
4 TIM SUGDEN Toyota Carina E
5 DAVID BRABHAM BMW 318iS
6 GIAMPIERO SIMONI Alfa Romeo 155TS

TOTAL CUP

1 NIGEL SMITH Vauxhall Cavalier 16V

RESULTS • ROUND 6

1 JAMES THOMPSON Vauxhall Cavalier 16V
2 ALAIN MENU Renault Laguna
3 KELVIN BURT Ford Mondeo Ghia
4 RICKARD RYDELL Volvo 850 20v
5 JOHN CLELAND Vauxhall Cavalier 16V
6 PAUL RADISICH Ford Mondeo Ghia

TOTAL CUP

1 NIGEL SMITH Vauxhall Cavalier 16V

Right: **The Fords wanted to play at Silverstone. Rickard Rydell holds a temporary lead from Paul Radisich and Kelvin Burt at one of the three starts.**

Below: **But it was the New Zealander's Mondeo that led for most of the day. This battling pair shared the wins.**

Opposite page, top to bottom: **Alain Menu, here with race engineer Mark Ellis, salvaged fourth for Renault in the second race. Burt's excellent qualifying performance was negated when the fast-starting Toyota of Tim Sugden took him out on the first lap of the day. After his Thruxton win, Vauxhall's James Thompson struggled in qualifying and retired from the second race. He was a fighting fourth in the first, however. The weight-penalised BMWs hated the stop-go nature of the track. For the second meeting in succession, David Brabham clashed with Derek Warwick's Alfa Romeo.**

LAT Photographic

SILVERSTONE *National*

Two more pole positions, three more iffy starts, but a healthy haul of points gave Rickard Rydell the championship lead.

This time Ford wanted to play; on the pace during testing and qualifying, Paul Radisich proved to be the fly in Volvo's ointment throughout the weekend, scoring his first BTCC win for nine months in the process.

The Mondeo suits this track, and when its waywardness under braking and reluctance to change direction were improved, it became the threat many had anticipated pre-season. It was still no match for Rydell's Volvo in the one-lap stakes, however, the Swede being the only man to dip under the 61s barrier in either session.

However, Rickard found it harder to get his 850 off pole position than he had putting it there, and when Radisich reached the complex in the lead at the end of the first lap, eyebrows were raised – the Stockholm driver's standing within his team hung in the balance. To his credit he stayed calm, tracked the Mondeo and made a decisive pass with three laps to go. TWR breathed a collective sigh of relief. Its man did not have a glass jaw.

At the second start both Fords – Kelvin Burt had also shone in qualifying – passed Rydell on the run to Copse, where the race was red-flagged because of a multiple shunt.

Third time lucky for Rickard? No.

Radisich again hit the front at the green light, and this time there was to be no face-saving, late-race pass. Indeed, Rydell never looked like making a move. Still, he had added some mid-season weight to his championship bid, becoming the fourth points-leader in as many meetings.

Rydell notched up his 100th point at this meeting, while the opening race marked John Cleland's 100th BTCC start. The Vauxhalls were steady rather than startling here, finding the two 90-degree rights at Luffield an unfathomable mystery. Yet the Scot found his racing touch and pounced at every available opportunity in the first race to lead his team-mate, James Thompson, home in third. In the second he was fifth and left Silverstone contemplating a 12-point gap to Rydell.

A broken output shaft ended Alain Menu's first race, but a fighting fourth in the second allowed him to maintain his title challenge, as did a third for Tim Harvey, who had swapped to Volvo's T-car, having given up on his race car's balance.

Photos: LAT Photographic

SNIPPETS

. . . The Honda Accord uses a Yokohama qualifying tyre for the first time and David Leslie turns heads when he claims third position for the second race. He had been ninth fastest earlier in the day. He finishes ninth and eighth in the races, while team-mate, James Kaye, joins him in the points in the first race with tenth. • After his startling performance at Thruxton, Thompson is brought back down to earth when he qualifies eighth and 12th. He retires from the second race after a clash with Leslie. • Burt secures his inaugural front-row start for Ford on Saturday morning, but is taken out of the first race on the opening lap by Tim Sugden's Toyota Carina. He finishes seventh in the second race, one place behind Sugden. • Radisich sets the fastest lap in both races. • Julian Bailey's second race ends with his Toyota stuck in the Copse gravel, just as it was in last year's British Grand Prix support race. He had been put there by the Peugeot of Patrick Watts. • Will Hoy switches to Williams Renault Dealer Racing's T-car for this meeting, and finishes fifth in the first race. He does so with a malfunctioning clutch, which forces him to start from the back of the grid for the second race. • Derek Warwick's troublesome season hits a new low: he qualifies his Alfa Romeo 19th – and last works car – in both sessions, breaks a driveshaft in the first race and finishes last. In the second race he breaks a wheel in a clash with David Brabham's BMW before finishing next to last. • Matt Neal secures two more Total Cup pole positions and two more wins in his Ford Mondeo.

RESULTS • ROUND 7

1 RICKARD RYDELL Volvo 850 20v
2 PAUL RADISICH Ford Mondeo Ghia
3 JOHN CLELAND Vauxhall Cavalier 16V
4 JAMES THOMPSON Vauxhall Cavalier 16V
5 WILL HOY Renault Laguna
6 PATRICK WATTS Peugeot 405

TOTAL CUP

1 MATT NEAL Ford Mondeo Ghia

RESULTS • ROUND 8

1 PAUL RADISICH Ford Mondeo Ghia
2 RICKARD RYDELL Volvo 850 20v
3 TIM HARVEY Volvo 850 20v
4 ALAIN MENU Renault Laguna
5 JOHN CLELAND Vauxhall Cavalier 16V
6 TIM SUGDEN Toyota Carina E

TOTAL CUP

1 MATT NEAL Ford Mondeo Ghia

Bryn Williams/Words & Pictures

Bryn Williams/Words & Pictures

LAT Photographic

Clockwise from top right: **Paul Radisich took the lead of the first race from the third row, only for it to be red-flagged. His Ford was fifth in the second race. Simon Harrison attempts to save rubber, as Tim Harvey and the once pole-sitting James Thompson continue their first-race charge through the field. Alain Menu shines at the Cheshire track. Not so Derek Warwick. His Alfa Romeo was tapped into a high-speed accident by David Leslie's Honda. The Englishman had outqualified the returning Gabriele Tarquini, however. Thompson and Kelvin Burt collided at the first start, and diced in the second race, too. Bearing the scars of the first-start shunt, Rickard Rydell heads John Cleland to victory and the series lead. Once again the BMWs were off the pace, at a track where they used to dominate.**

Colin McMaster/Words & Pictures

Gavin Lawrence/Sutton Photographic

LAT Photographic

yn Williams/Words & Pictures

OULTON PARK

The title triumvirate of Rickard Rydell, Alain Menu and John Cleland laid down the bricks and mortar of their campaigns here. No one else set foot on the podium as they drove hard, calculating races to share a substantial haul of points. Consolidation was the watchword. In the early stages of the restarted first race, Cleland appeared quicker than the leading Rydell, while the third-placed Menu felt he was quicker than both of them, yet the tang of anticipation has been dulled by the wings. A pass was too much of a risk. Reach Old Hall Corner in the lead and the races were yours to be won or tossed away.

This might have been James Thompson's prerogative had his pole-sitting Vauxhall Cavalier not been turned around by the fast-starting and insistent Ford of Kelvin Burt. The melee allowed the meteoric Mondeo of Paul Radisich to grab the lead from the third row. But his opportunism was cancelled out by another first-lap shunt and the resultant red flag.

With no front-row opposition – the damaged Thompson started from the back of the grid – Rydell was unchallenged at the restart and took a lead he was never to cede. Cleland chased, as did Menu, but they stayed two and three throughout.

In the second race it was Menu's turn to lead all the way, Rydell content with second and the consequent buttressing of his position at the top of the standings. Burt delayed Cleland in the early stages, and by the time the Scot had found a way past, a closing third was as much as he could hope for.

Julian Bailey did his usual competent job to take fourth for Toyota in the first race, while Thompson followed Cleland dutifully in the second before dropping back with a smoky engine. But nobody could live with the top three: there had been no collusion between them, no pre-race carving up of the cake, but there clearly existed a tacit non-aggression pact. They were sparring. There were plenty more rounds in which the knock-out punch could be delivered.

In contrast, the reigning champion was floored in the first. Gabriele Tarquini returned to the BTCC to drive the third Alfa Romeo in Cheshire: he qualified 19th and 21st, finished 11th in the first race and spun off on the opening lap of the second. His presence merely served to illustrate the progress made by Renault, Vauxhall and Volvo.

Not every Volvo, however. Tim Harvey detached himself from the title race after a disastrous day of qualifying left him languishing in 17th and 19th. And it didn't get any better: he finished eighth in the first race, and was dumped out of seventh in the second when he was docked 20 seconds for straightlining the Knickerbrook Chicane.

And then there were three.

SNIPPETS

. . . A testing accident leaves Thompson's Vauxhall Cavalier five millimetres shorter on its nearside. He puts it on pole! • Alfa Romeo BTCC regulars, Giampiero Simoni and Derek Warwick, outqualify the returning Tarquini in both sessions. Simoni's fifth place in the first race is the best yet for the beleaguered 155TS. • Warwick is not so successful. He flies backwards into the armco on the opening lap of the first race after contact with David Leslie's Honda Accord, and is momentarily knocked unconscious. He is taken to hospital for a precautionary check-up. The Honda's data-logging system registers nine G upon impact, but Leslie is unharmed. His day, however, like Warwick's, is over.• BMW's Joachim Winkelhock scored three wins from four starts at Oulton Park in 1993 and 1994, yet the best the Munich marque can muster on this occasion is David Brabham's eighth place in the second race. • Simon Harrison outqualifies Patrick Watts, his Peugeot team-mate, in both sessions. The youngster is in the top ten in both. • Burt retires from round nine on the opening lap because of suspension damage picked up in his clash with Thompson. He misses the restart, but defies a broken exhaust manifold to finish sixth later in the day. • Tim Sugden is second for Toyota when the first race is stopped. He is fourth in the restarted race until he leaves the road at Lodge. In the second race he deliberately pushes team-mate Bailey past James Kaye's Honda for ninth place in the final few metres! • Nigel Smith (Vauxhall Cavalier) and Matt Neal (Ford Mondeo) share the Total Cup spoils.

RESULTS • ROUND 9

1 RICKARD RYDELL Volvo 850 20v
2 JOHN CLELAND Vauxhall Cavalier 16V
3 ALAIN MENU Renault Laguna
4 JULIAN BAILEY Toyota Carina E
5 GIAMPIERO SIMONI Alfa Romeo 155TS
6 JAMES THOMPSON Vauxhall Cavalier 16V

TOTAL CUP

1 NIGEL SMITH Vauxhall Cavalier 16V

RESULTS • ROUND 10

1 ALAIN MENU Renault Laguna
2 RICKARD RYDELL Volvo 850 20v
3 JOHN CLELAND Vauxhall Cavalier 16V
4 JAMES THOMPSON Vauxhall Cavalier 16V
5 PAUL RADISICH Ford Mondeo Ghia
6 KELVIN BURT Ford Mondeo Ghia

TOTAL CUP

1 MATT NEAL Ford Mondeo Ghia

LAT Photographic

Mark Bothwell/Bothwell Photographic

BRANDS HATCH
Grand Prix

Left: They went into Paddock two-by-two: Alain Menu leads one of the day's five starts.

Below from left: Hamish Irvine scored a surprise Total Cup victory in his venerable Peugeot.

'Are you standing uncomfortably . . . ?' The drivers receive their warning.

Patrick Watts tried all he knew, but there was to be no repeat of last year's podium finish at his home track.

Mark Bothwell/Bothwell Photographic

LAT Photographic

Like naughty schoolboys, the drivers were called up to the front and given a lecture. TOCA later insisted that no one was censured for their driving, merely that its Race Director, Pierre Aumonier, had informed them that one more restart – there had been three already that day – would lead to the cancellation of round 12. The drivers were incensed by this public dressing-down, however, pointing out that two of the race-stopping incidents were the result of drivers crashing without the assistance of a reckless colleague. And it was raining cats and dogs. And it was a race . . .

Whatever the rights or wrongs of this showdown, there can be no doubting that the Brands Hatch Grand Prix circuit provided a damp, hugely forgettable occasion. John Cleland scored a second and first place to retake the lead of the series, but even he admitted that it had been a confusing day.

Alain Menu shared the wins with the Scot, having taken both pole positions with the Renault Laguna. He won both sections of the first race to score an aggregate victory, but could only once beat the Vauxhalls of Cleland and James Thompson off the line in three attempts in the second race. At the last time of asking both Cavaliers got by him, forcing the Swiss to sit in their spray throughout the ten laps that remained.

Rain at Brands Hatch does not sit happily with Rickard Rydell's title hopes: his Volvo was pushed around in a fracas on the opening lap of the day, and seventh was the best the Swede could garner. This was topped when his throttle stuck open at Westfield on the first lap of the second race, causing the 850 to clang against the armco and flip over. Rickard stepped out unhurt, but he had slipped from first to third in the opening of a cloud.

As usual, his team-mate made the most of the rain. Tim Harvey had just passed Cleland for a challenging second place when the first race was stopped and the results were taken from the order on the previous lap. There was to be no repeat of his April double victory, although third and fifth were perhaps better than he might have hoped for had it stayed dry.

The works Fords, Harvey's nearest challengers here in April, missed out: Paul Radisich was tipped out of the first race and managed seventh in the second, while Kelvin Burt plunged into the Druids gravel before starting the second race from the back of the grid with a ten-second penalty picked up for missing the pit lane weighbridge in qualifying. He was 14th.

In contrast, Renault's Will Hoy had his most consistent meeting of the season to date, qualifying on the second and third rows and finishing fourth in both races.

Next!

SNIPPETS

. . . The Toyotas feature a new front suspension that endows the Carina with better turn-in. • The Honda Accords suffer their worst meeting of the season to date: James Kaye causes the second qualifying session to be stopped with a boot-crushing shunt at Dingle Dell, while David Leslie can manage no better than 12th. In the races, the Yokohama wets prove hopelessly inadequate, and the Hondas hold up the privateers for a time! • Matt Neal scores two more Total Cup pole positions with his Ford Mondeo, but his Sunday ends within seconds of its start when his steering rack is broken in a multi-car ruck at Graham Hill Bend. • Previously unsung Total Cup runner, Hamish Irvine, stars in the wet conditions. His elderly Peugeot scores a first and second place, only losing out in a last-gasp dash to the flag with Richard Kaye's Ford Mondeo in the second race. • Kaye benefits from a 1994 specification engine, but runs for the bulk of the races without a front spoiler. This had been lost during a brief trip through the gravel. • He also plays a part in the first stoppage of the day, tangling with Nigel Smith's Vauxhall Cavalier at Stirlings. • The second stoppage of the day is caused by Tim Sugden. Unsighted by a steamed-up windscreen, the Bradford driver's Toyota rolls gently in the gravel at Clearways. • Thompson, on the front row for both races, retires his Vauxhall from the first race with damaged suspension. He had punctured a tyre in a slight collision with Menu's Renault Laguna at Druids on the first lap of the first race. • Derek Warwick scores his first points of the season for Alfa Romeo when he finishes eighth in the first race. He is 11th later in the day.

RESULTS • ROUND 11

1 ALAIN MENU Renault Laguna
2 JOHN CLELAND Vauxhall Cavalier 16V
3 TIM HARVEY Volvo 850 20v
4 WILL HOY Renault Laguna
5 PATRICK WATTS Peugeot 405
6 JULIAN BAILEY Toyota Carina E

TOTAL CUP

1 HAMISH IRVINE Peugeot 405

RESULTS • ROUND 12

1 JOHN CLELAND Vauxhall Cavalier 16V
2 JAMES THOMPSON Vauxhall Cavalier 16V
3 ALAIN MENU Renault Laguna
4 WILL HOY Renault Laguna
5 TIM HARVEY Volvo 850 20v
6 JULIAN BAILEY Toyota Carina E

TOTAL CUP

1 RICHARD KAYE Ford Mondeo Ghia

Mark Bothwell/Bothwell Photographic

LAT Photographic

From top: **Simon Harrison's Peugeot nerfs Will Hoy sideways at Melbourne. Kelvin Burt, Alain Menu, Rickard Rydell and James Thompson give chase to the out-of-sight John Cleland. Vauxhall Sport *(right)* celebrates the Scot's virtuoso performance. Richard Kaye raced against doctor's orders . . . and won with a broken leg!**

Opposite top: **Paul Radisich kept his slim championship hopes alive with a fighting second place. *Below:* Both Honda Accords got among the points in the second race, James Kaye finishing just behind David Leslie in tenth.**

Tony O'Brien/Professional Sport

LAT Photographic

BTCC ROUNDS 13 & 14 • 25 June 1995

DONINGTON PARK

John Cleland is no shrinking violet. He will back himself to beat anybody in a straight fight on the track. Anywhere on the first three rows used to be enough to have him talking confidently of victory. Not any more. He denied it fervently, but his rivals were strong in the belief that the Scot had upped his qualifying game to score his first pole positions for two years. The Vauxhall Cavalier's form at the bump-free Leicestershire venue had marked these rounds down as bankers for the Borders man, and he cashed in on them – with interest. Two solid starts were followed by a couple of devastating bursts that drew him away from the pack, after which he controlled the remainder of each encounter with ease. Two fastest laps emphasised his dominance: the oldest works driver in the field, replete with a model in its sixth year of the BTCC, had provided the most complete performances of the season so far.

The efforts of Rickard Rydell and Alain Menu were mundane by comparison. Second and third respectively in the first race, with the Renault Laguna driver fighting might and main to hold off the Cavalier of James Thompson in the closing laps, was followed by sixth and fourth places in the second. Now Cleland was over a victory distant in the points race. Neither the Swiss nor the Swede had any major complaints about their mounts – the Vauxhall was simply too good on this occasion.

As in April, Donington Park provided two dull races, with Thompson being the only mover at the front. An initially long brake pedal prevented him from making the most of his front-row position in the first race of the day, although he was able to make up three places from his first-lap position to take fourth. But even he struggled to make any gains later in the day, and he finished fifth.

On this latter occasion, the Ford Mondeos of Paul Radisich and Kelvin Burt proved insurmountable obstacles. The Englishman was using a brand new car, which he put on the front row after a morning-ruining brake balance problem had been cured, only to be beaten into Redgate by his New Zealand team-mate. They stayed this way – second and third – to the end, a result that ensured the reigning World Touring Car Champion could still harbour vague hopes of making a bid for that elusive BTCC title.

The best story of the day, however, was provided by a Total Cup runner. Richard Kaye had broken his right leg in a cycling accident the week prior to the meeting, and arrived at the track sporting a sturdy knee brace. He spent the Saturday qualifying sessions acquainting himself with the intricacies of left-foot braking, and in this manner was able to finish second privateer in the first race. Incredibly, he went one better in the second to draw level with Matt Neal in the title chase.

SNIPPETS

. . . David Leslie matches his '95 qualifying best with a third place for the first race. He makes a good start to be second behind Cleland on the opening lap, but when he looks down the outside of the Vauxhall at Goddards his Honda Accord is pushed onto the grass and he loses a number of places. He eventually finishes seventh. He follows this with ninth in the second race, just ahead of team-mate, James Kaye. Both men are using the latest 650-mm diameter Yokohama slick • Only in the second race does it become apparent that Tim Harvey's Volvo is suffering from an ailing diff. He finishes 10th and 12th. • Derek Warwick's eighth place in the morning session is the first time his Alfa Romeo has broken into the top ten on the grid. He collects no points, however, finishing 13th in the first race and retiring from the second after a clash with Patrick Watts's Peugeot. • This latter incident also claims the Hampshire man's Prodrive team-mate, Giampiero Simoni. This marks the end of a dreadful day for the little Italian, who had retired from the first race with a broken steering rack. • Watts is also sidelined in this three-way shunt. Donington Park has never been a happy hunting ground for the 405; Watts is 15th in the first race, while Simon Harrison retires the second works Peugeot from both races with, respectively, a severe vibration and an underbonnet fire. • Johnny Cecotto survives for just two laps in both races. In the first he clashes with Matt Neal's Ford Mondeo at McLeans, and in the second he goes off all by himself at Coppice. The best BMW can manage is two 11th places for David Brabham. • Neal also crashes out of the second race, when a long brake pedal sees him collide with the Vauxhall Cavalier of first-race Total Cup winner, Nigel Smith. However, yet two more pole positions for the lanky Midlander assure him of an unassailable lead in the £5,000 Total Cup Flyer award.

RESULTS • ROUND 13

1 JOHN CLELAND Vauxhall Cavalier 16V
2 RICKARD RYDELL Volvo 850 20v
3 ALAIN MENU Renault Laguna
4 JAMES THOMPSON Vauxhall Cavalier 16V
5 PAUL RADISICH Ford Mondeo Ghia
6 JULIAN BAILEY Toyota Carina E

TOTAL CUP

1 NIGEL SMITH Vauxhall Cavalier 16V

RESULTS • ROUND 14

1 JOHN CLELAND Vauxhall Cavalier 16V
2 PAUL RADISICH Ford Mondeo Ghia
3 KELVIN BURT Ford Mondeo Ghia
4 ALAIN MENU Renault Laguna
5 JAMES THOMPSON Vauxhall Cavalier 16V
6 RICKARD RYDELL Volvo 850 20v

TOTAL CUP

1 RICHARD KAYE Ford Mondeo Ghia

VOLVO
Mondeo
Ford
Valvoline
ICS plc
Bailey ICS plc.
Ford
ELECTRONICS
Valvoline

HONDA
Kaye
Enny
clarion
CAR AUDIO
YOKOHAMA
ACCORD

Right: John Cleland and Will Hoy simultaneously pass Paul Radisich for first and second. The opening laps provided some of the best racing of the season.

Hoy finished second, but Renault team-mate Alain Menu *(lower right)* had his windscreen mist up.

Bottom right: Derek Warwick leads his Alfa Romeo team-mate; this was Giampiero Simoni's last BTCC race for the foreseeable future.

His tyres deteriorating, Radisich *(below)* is passed by James Thompson and Ford team-mate, Kelvin Burt. Julian Bailey follows, and the Toyota man set the fastest lap while passing both Fords to finish fourth.

Gavin Lawrence/Sutton Photographic

SILVERSTONE
Grand Prix

John Marsh/Action Images

Darren Heath

The only gripe emanating from John Cleland was that he had chosen the only singleton race of the season to give another consummate performance. The Peebleshire driver fought off a determined challenge from Paul Radisich's Ford Mondeo in the early part of this wet race, before stretching away to score his fourth – two in the wet, two in the dry – consecutive win.

In contrast, his title running-mates suffered a severe case of Scotch mist: Alain Menu and Rickard Rydell were third and fourth as the pack streamed onto Hangar Straight for the first time, yet the windscreens of both the Renault and Volvo were already opaque with condensation. This difficulty forced both men to pit, so that neither was to score any points on this occasion. For such big-budget, experienced outfits as Williams and TWR, these were unforgivable occurrences.

Further, had Will Hoy not lost his windscreen wiper on the first lap, his Laguna might have offered a more serious threat to Cleland. As it was, the 1992 BTCC champion was left to contemplate what might have been in the aftermath of his season-best second place.

Cleland had no such worries.

Vauxhall Sport had suffered a minor hiccough, however, James Thompson losing his overnight pole position on Friday evening when his Cavalier was discovered to be four millimetres too wide. The Yorkshire youngster had been half a second quicker than the rest, but eventually had to make do with fourth on the grid and third in the race.

The Saturday half-hour proved the quicker of the two sessions, as the drivers had to readjust to the old qualifying format of eking out two 30-minute sessions from just six tyres. And Cleland – on his 43rd birthday – proved the master of this with his third pole position in a row, ahead of Menu and Radisich's Ford.

The latter plumped for Michelin's softest wet for the race, and twice passed Cleland in the first three laps. But once the Scot and the closing Hoy – his Laguna on a mixture of 19-in. and 18-in. Michelin wets – passed the Mondeo in one fell swoop on lap four, the New Zealander plunged down to sixth.

An inspired choice of the older 18-in. wets all round allowed Julian Bailey to set the fastest lap of the race, as his Toyota Carina E finished a closing fourth place to Thompson – from 19th on the grid. Kelvin Burt was fifth, having survived an outbraking contest that saw Tim Harvey's Volvo plunge into the Club gravel.

This was a rare error in the testing conditions, as the BTCC brigade laid to rest the ghost of the crash 'n' smash of last year's showpiece event.

SNIPPETS

. . . Michelin creates a stir by making its latest tyre – designated the T – available to Vauxhall, Ford and Renault only. The French rubber manufacturer openly admits that it has chosen those teams most likely to give it a victory, but insists that the tyre will be made available to all its users at Knockhill. Each of the above teams gets four Ts apiece, but this is of little consequence when the heavens open just minutes before the race is due to start. • This is Giampiero Simoni's last BTCC race for the foreseeable future, as Alfa Romeo announces that he will be replaced by reigning champion, Gabriele Tarquini, for the remainder of the season. Giampiero finishes 11th from the corresponding position on the grid. • Hoy switches to Williams Renault Dealer Racing's spare Laguna for this meeting. He qualifies it sixth. • Bailey's Toyota Carina E features a new specification engine. • Johnny Cecotto mistakenly drives his BMW into the Grand Prix pits at the start of Friday's session, and has to charm a marshal into letting him back out on the track! The Venezuelan had not realised that the BTCC field was to use the support race pits on the outside of the Brooklands/Priory complex! He qualifies 12th, only to retire with a blown clutch. David Brabham is seventh in the other 318iS. • Like Bailey, Tim Sugden chooses 18-in. wets for his Toyota Carina E, and finishes eighth from 18th on the grid. • Yokohama's wet tyre is still uncompetitive, and David Leslie languishes in 12th with the Honda Accord. James Kaye's electrics are swamped by the conditions. • Simon Harrison suffers a dreadful weekend. A misfire and a broken wheel bearing limit his Peugeot to just one flying lap in qualifying, and an oil leak forces him to start from the back of the grid. He eventually finishes 15th. Patrick Watts salvages a point for the team with tenth. • Robb Gravett makes a victorious return to the Total Cup. After just two hours' testing with his new Ford Mondeo, the former champion passes Matt Neal's similar car for the lead on lap seven. The latter's second place gives him the lead in the series, however, as Richard Kaye slides off into the Stowe gravel.

RESULTS • ROUND 15

1 JOHN CLELAND Vauxhall Cavalier 16V
2 WILL HOY Renault Laguna
3 JAMES THOMPSON Vauxhall Cavalier 16V
4 JULIAN BAILEY Toyota Carina E
5 KELVIN BURT Ford Mondeo Ghia
6 PAUL RADISICH Ford Mondeo Ghia

TOTAL CUP

1 ROBB GRAVETT Ford Mondeo Ghia

Mark Bothwell/Bothwell Photographic

Clockwise from above:
A winner in Scotland for Toyota in '93, Julian Bailey scored two more points-scoring finishes in the Carina.

Alain Menu shook up the testing-dominant Volvos and should have scored two wins for Renault.

Tim Harvey was back on the pace and gave strong support to his Volvo team-mate.

Rickard Rydell celebrates a victory, a slice of luck and the series lead.

David Brabham missed the first race in order to take his young son to hospital, but returned to finish fourth later in the day.

John Cleland was disappointed by his Knockhill performance, but not as disappointed as his thousands of fans at the track.

Mark Bothwell/Bothwell Photographic

LAT Photographic

LAT Photographic

LAT Photographic

Trevor Davies/Shutterspeed Photografik

KNOCKHILL

It was a great irony that John Cleland's title bid should falter in front of his home fans: Vauxhall's week-long preparation stuttered when James Thompson was injured in a massive testing shunt on Tuesday; Cleland was furious that his regular Michelin tyre man had missed Saturday's qualifying sessions because he was away on the Ulster Rally; the usually stable Cavalier was unwilling to bounce over the kerbs at this demanding little track. It all added up to disappointment.

In contrast, Rickard Rydell's Volvo appeared to have been built especially for this circuit's swoops and plunges. The Swede was half a second quicker than anyone else on Saturday morning, having dominated testing. But Alain Menu was not unduly worried. A leaking brake seal had limited his Renault Laguna to just one flying lap in the same session, and yet this was enough for him to join the 850 on the front row. In the afternoon he was just a tenth adrift of the Swede, and was quick to point out that he had been faster than his rival over a simulated race distance . . .

And when he reached Duffus Dip in the lead, the Genevois looked all set to prove his point. Rydell barged his way past Paul Radisich's intervening Ford on the second lap, and gave chase to Menu. But had it not been for a broken weld on the Laguna's gear selector barrel – an unheard-of failure – the Volvo would have remained second.

It did so later in the day. Another poor start again saw it beaten into Duffus Dip by Menu, and this time there was no stopping the Laguna. His runner-up spot, however, still enabled Rydell to move to the head of the chase of Cleland, who was now just 32 points to the good.

The Scot had made a reasonable fist of a damage-limitation exercise, staying out of trouble and accepting any opportunities when they arose to be fifth and sixth. In this respect, Tim Harvey had backed up Rydell well, finishing second and third to provide a points buffer between his team leader and the struggling Cavalier.

Kelvin Burt suffered a mixed day. In the first race he scored his fourth third place of the season for Ford, and then survived a worrying moment when his brakes failed on the approach to Duffus Dip.

BMW was benefiting from the FIA-agreed 25 kg reduction in its base weight, and Johnny Cecotto and David Brabham took turns to finish fourth. The latter's effort was particularly praiseworthy, as he had missed the first race when his young son was rushed to hospital with scalds. The now-tigerish Cecotto spun out of the second race when his foot missed the brake pedal!

SNIPPETS

. . . TOCA's Safety Car makes its debut. Thankfully, it stays put on this occasion. • Will Hoy retires from the second race with a repeat of the gearbox failure that had sidelined Menu. In the first race he had clashed with Radisich on the penultimate lap. • It is not a good day for the New Zealander, who scores no points from third and fourth on the grid. In the second race he loses a solid third place with a puncture, just two laps from home. • Dunlop provides a new compound for the Volvos. • Jeff Allam is called in by Vauxhall as a last-minute replacement for the injured Thompson. The Epsom car dealer struggles in qualifying to be 18th and 20th, before finishing eighth in the first race, and 12th later in the day, minus second gear. • For the first time both Hondas qualify in the top ten for both races. James Kaye has his best weekend of the year, lining up sixth for the second race, setting the fastest time in the morning warm-up and beating Cleland to take fifth in round 17. David Leslie runs as high as fourth in the same race before dropping back to seventh when his tyres go off. • Once again the Toyotas are solid if not spectacular, Julian Bailey and Tim Sugden finishing in the points in both races. • Gabriele Tarquini loses a front wheel in the first race, but brings his Alfa Romeo home eighth in the second race. • Alfa Romeo's Derek Warwick has his licence endorsed for his part in a collision with Simon Harrison's Peugeot on lap two of the opening encounter. A lap later he goes off on his own. Another grassy moment limits him to 16th in the second race. He is also fined for leaving the circuit before speaking to TOCA's Race Director. • Peugeot has a disastrous day: in both races Harrison winds up in the gravel at the hairpin; Patrick Watts qualifies last and 16th respectively after engine problems, and can only manage 11th place in the second race, having broken a driveshaft on the green flag lap of the first. • The Total Cup provides its most competitive races to date. Robb Gravett takes pole position away from Matt Neal in the morning session. This situation is reversed as Richard Kaye provides a three-way Mondeo battle in the afternoon. Neal wins both races, however, as he and Gravett annex the final two places in the first-race points.

RESULTS • ROUND 16

1 RICKARD RYDELL Volvo 850 20v
2 TIM HARVEY Volvo 850 20v
3 KELVIN BURT Ford Mondeo Ghia
4 JOHNNY CECOTTO BMW 318iS
5 JOHN CLELAND Vauxhall Cavalier 16V
6 JULIAN BAILEY Toyota Carina E
TOTAL CUP
1 MATT NEAL Ford Mondeo Ghia

RESULTS • ROUND 17

1 ALAIN MENU Renault Laguna
2 RICKARD RYDELL Volvo 850 20v
3 TIM HARVEY Volvo 850 20v
4 DAVID BRABHAM BMW 318iS
5 JAMES KAYE Honda Accord
6 JOHN CLELAND Vauxhall Cavalier 16V
TOTAL CUP
1 MATT NEAL Ford Mondeo Ghia

BRANDS HATCH *Indy*

Gavin Lawrence/Sutton Photographic

LAT Photographic

The various parties in a motor racing accident rarely agree when it comes to the apportioning of blame. Usually, however, there is a consensus that contact was made. Not so on this occasion. Rickard Rydell rolled his eyes skywards when John Cleland, a close off-track friend of the Swede, explained that his Vauxhall Cavalier had not touched the Volvo. Rydell had led the second race around the Kentish speed bowl from its start, but he was under severe pressure from the championship leader when his car snapped sideways at Clearways. In a trice the Scot was through and on his way to a sixth win of the season.

However, as protest was met by appeal was met by counter-protest, a title by jury appeared to be in the offing.

Cleland had made contact, albeit it very lightly. If he had meant it, he could not have been more subtle. Certainly, he was incredulous that he would have to wait two weeks to discover whether his victory would stand. Rydell, meanwhile, gathered the resultant moment up quickly enough to finish third, but left the track hoping that the 40-point gap to Cleland was only a temporary state of affairs. The Stockholm man's case was not watertight, however.

Having squandered yet another pole position – he had been quickest in both sessions – he had tipped Cleland into a sideways moment at Druids that let Will Hoy's Renault through into a first-race lead it would never relinquish. A lead that was given substance when Rickard eventually barged past the not-laughing Cavalier at Clearways later the same lap. An eye for an eye?

As the muttering Volvo and Vauxhall contingents gathered at either end of the press conference tent, Hoy played piggy in the middle. A new engineer, plus a radically different set-up and tyre choice had enabled the Chelsea-based driver to score his first BTCC win since 1992. Cleland was too quick in the second race, but he was happy to follow the Vauxhall home. Williams Renault Dealer Racing was pleased for its man – but it was the wrong man . . .

In a brand new Laguna, Alain Menu's title hopes took a dive with his worst qualifying performances of the season – seventh and eighth. He salvaged fourth in the first race, but lost 12 laps in the pits with a jammed throttle slide in the second. He would be a more-than-interested observer when TOCA made public its Cleland/Rydell judgement at Snetterton.

Above: 'And then you went like this . . .' John Cleland took the lead away from Rickard Rydell in controversial circumstances.

Right: Gabriele Tarquini finished a fine fourth for Alfa Romeo.

Below: Will Hoy celebrates his first BTCC win since '92.

Bottom: South African Mike Briggs made an impressive – and rumbustious – BTCC debut for Vauxhall.

Opposite page: Hoy was impressively cool under severe pressure from the title contenders – Rydell, Cleland and Renault team-mate Alain Menu – throughout the first race.

LAT Photographic

LAT Photographic

LAT Photographic

SNIPPETS

. . . Just days after winning the South African Touring Car Championship for Opel, Port Elizabeth's Mike Briggs makes his BTCC debut as James Thompson's replacement at Vauxhall Sport. Ninth and tenth on the grid, he kicks off his BTCC career with sixth and fifth places. • Charlie Cox returns to the BTCC, three months after his severe Thruxton shunt. The Australian does so at the wheel of a hatchback Ford Mondeo which, but for the quick thinking of some Renault mechanics, might have succumbed to an underbonnet fire after just one lap of the official TOCA test. It finishes both races: 21st in the first, after being black-flagged for a loose piece of bodywork, and 15th in the second, with a blowing exhaust. • A sickly Matt Neal scores two more Total Cup pole positions and two more wins in the Team Dynamics Ford Mondeo. The Midlander uses Dunlops for the first time this season, but is made to work hard for his victories by Nigel Smith's Cavalier and the Mondeo of Robb Gravett. • The works Fords have a dreadful time in the races, as chronic understeer plagues both Paul Radisich and an unwell Kelvin Burt. Neither of them scores a point. The former retires from the second race after a clash with Julian Bailey's Toyota. • Derek Warwick is just three-tenths off pole position during the first session – in eighth – as Alfa Romeo makes progress. The Hampshire man finishes eighth in the corresponding race, but it is Gabriele Tarquini who gives Prodrive its biggest boost to date, surprising Rydell with the 155's pace as he chases the Volvo home to take fourth later in the day. • The Hondas run on 19-in. rims for the first time. James Kaye is eighth in the second race on a mixture of 18-in. and 19-in. • Johnny Cecotto is a competitive fifth in the first race, only for his BMW to be pushed around by Menu in the second. David Brabham retires from both races, having helped his team-mate sew up the third row for the Munich marque in the second session. • A do-or-die qualifying lap and a bout of first-lap opportunism allow Patrick Watts to salvage a second-race sixth place for Peugeot on his home track. This follows an 11th in the first race, during which team-mate Simon Harrison suffers an engine problem that will prevent him starting the second race.

RESULTS • ROUND 18

1 WILL HOY Renault Laguna
2 RICKARD RYDELL Volvo 850 20v
3 JOHN CLELAND Vauxhall Cavalier 16V
4 ALAIN MENU Renault Laguna
5 JOHNNY CECOTTO BMW 318iS
6 MIKE BRIGGS Vauxhall Cavalier 16V

TOTAL CUP

1 MATT NEAL Ford Mondeo Ghia

RESULTS • ROUND 19

1 JOHN CLELAND Vauxhall Cavalier 16V
2 WILL HOY Renault Laguna
3 RICKARD RYDELL Volvo 850 20v
4 GABRIELE TARQUINI Alfa Romeo 155TS
5 MIKE BRIGGS Vauxhall Cavalier 16V
6 PATRICK WATTS Peugeot 405

TOTAL CUP

1 MATT NEAL Ford Mondeo Ghia

KALIBER
elf
2
KALIBER
RENAULT
VAUXHALL
CAVALIER
4
Mobil 1
VAUXHALL
MICHELIN
VOLVO
850
15
Q8
Q8
TWR
DUNLOP
KENWOOD
DUNLOP
KALIBER
elf
elf
Renault Fin cial Services
elf
22
KALIBER
RENAULT

Right: Paul Radisich was in contention initially, but dropped away when his tyres went off. The following Vauxhall of Mike Briggs might have finished second but for a last-lap incident with David Leslie.

Below: Fourth place in the second race emphasised that Matt Neal's qualifying performance was no fluke.

John Overton

Darren Heath

Right: An inspired tyre choice, plus the patience to wait for them to come into their own on a drying track, saw Kelvin Burt prevail for Ford.

Below centre: John Cleland finished 13th in the first race, but, crucially, just ahead of Rickard Rydell.

Below: Grand Prix tactics – a pit stop to switch to slicks – allowed Johnny Cecotto's BMW to set the fastest lap. Richard Kaye's two-year-old Mondeo, here sandwiched by the BMWs, finished a fine fifth in this day of days for the Total Cup runners.

Colin McMaster/Words & Pictures

Julian Bailey's Toyota *(below)* staged an early charge in the first race before its tyres went off.

Centre right: **Smiles on the podium: David Leslie's soon disappeared, however, when he learned of his penalty, which elevated Patrick Watts *(above)* to a fine second place. And Robb Gravett's privateer Mondeo *(bottom)* to a record-breaking third.**

LAT Photographic

SNETTERTON

When the breathless mechanic returned to explain that his brief foray up the grid had confirmed that nobody in front had plumped for intermediates, Kelvin Burt was confident of success – even from the inside of the fifth row. It was raining at the start, but Snetterton is open and windswept, giving it a reputation as a quick-drying track. And the Tamworth driver played the conditions to perfection. On lap nine his Ford Mondeo swept past the leading, wet-tyred battle of John Cleland and team-mate Paul Radisich in one fell swoop, and he promptly galloped away to score his first BTCC victory.

Even more remarkably, Patrick Watts finished second after having dived into the pits at the end of the green flag lap to have slicks bolted onto his Peugeot. Initially, this position looked to have gone to the Yokohama intermediate-shod Honda of David Leslie, only for the Scot to be stripped of the Accord's first BTCC podium finish when a ten-second penalty was levied for his part in a last-lap clash with the Vauxhall of Mike Briggs. This dropped Leslie to eighth.

This allowed Robb Gravett to create a bit of history by becoming the first Total Cup runner to stand on the podium. The former champion had qualified an excellent eighth before gambling on slicks to finish third.

On a mixture of slicks and intermediates Gabriele Tarquini scored another fourth for Alfa Romeo, just nipping by the slick-shod privateer Ford of Richard Kaye on the run to the line. This pair had started from 20th and 19th on the grid.

Clearly, it was a topsy-turvy affair, and rarely can Cleland have been so delighted with 13th place. Had Rickard Rydell fitted castors to the back of his Volvo, the Vauxhall man would have followed suit. He had no reason to gamble. Both men went for wets, and the Cavalier finished two-tenths ahead of its nearest series rival.

In the dry second race Cleland was prepared to hold a watching brief in fourth, while Rydell made the most of his second good start of the day to lead from pole. The Scot, meanwhile, was unwilling to stick his neck out in an effort to pass Rydell's team-mate, Tim Harvey, for third. And his caution was rewarded. With six laps remaining the leader's brakes failed entering the very fast Riches corner and he spun into retirement, narrowingly missing an ambulance in the process. At the start of the weekend Vauxhall and Volvo had, surprisingly, agreed to a cessation of their Brands Hatch hostilities, and so now Cleland was 52 points to the good in the title race.

In the midst of all this Will Hoy had scored his second win in four races, though once again the Williams outfit's celebration was muted: Alain Menu's title hopes had ended here in Norfolk because of two clashes with Harvey, an ex-Renault team-mate.

And then there were two . . .

SNIPPETS

. . . Rydell records his 12th and 13th pole positions of the season for the TWR Volvo team, and promptly announces that he has signed another two-year contract. • Menu's Renault Laguna is second fastest in both sessions, but leaves the Norfolk venue with just a single point to its credit. • Tim Sugden debuts a right-hand drive version of the Toyota Carina E and uses the TOM'S GB-built car to good effect, finishing sixth and seventh. He is just pipped by team-mate Julian Bailey in the second race. • Johnny Cecotto sets the fastest lap in the first race after pitting for slick tyres. He finishes tenth. Later in the day his BMW is taken out by Derek Warwick, for which the Alfa Romeo driver has his licence endorsed. • Burt slips to 12th in the second race after a collision with Simon Harrison's Peugeot. • Burt and Radisich use a Ford Mondeo with a floor-mounted pedal box and pushed-back driving position for the first time. Paul is ninth in the first race, having pitted for slicks, but retires from the second with a blistered front-left Michelin. • James Kaye qualifies his Honda sixth for the first race, only for MSD to lump him with the next-to-useless Yokohama wets. The Yorkshireman stalls at the second start, but charges back up to ninth, one place behind Leslie. • Watts and Gravett, second and third in the first race, are both eliminated from the second race on the first lap, by a broken fuel rail and startline accident respectively. • Matt Neal creates a sensation by qualifying his Total Cup Ford Mondeo fifth for the second race. He follows this up with a confident showing on his way to fourth place.

RESULTS • ROUND 20

1 KELVIN BURT Ford Mondeo Ghia
2 PATRICK WATTS Peugeot 405
3 ROBB GRAVETT Ford Mondeo Ghia
4 GABRIELE TARQUINI Alfa Romeo 155TS
5 RICHARD KAYE Ford Mondeo Ghia
6 TIM SUGDEN Toyota Carina E
TOTAL CUP
1 ROBB GRAVETT Ford Mondeo Ghia

RESULTS • ROUND 21

1 WILL HOY Renault Laguna
2 TIM HARVEY Volvo 850 20v
3 JOHN CLELAND Vauxhall Cavalier 16V
4 MATT NEAL Ford Mondeo Ghia
5 MIKE BRIGGS Vauxhall Cavalier 16V
6 JULIAN BAILEY Toyota Carina E
TOTAL CUP
1 MATT NEAL Ford Mondeo Ghia

OULTON PARK *Fosters*

He knew what he needed to do, but he wasn't quite sure how best to go about it. In the first race he had begun too cautiously, let people by too easily and lost his rhythm before finishing third. Now he was on the verge of securing his second British Touring Car Championship – his only title rival powerless, stuck fast on the outskirts of the top ten – and yet he was keen to maintain his race pace in a closely fought battle for second. That David Leslie – not a man who features high on his Christmas card list – had his Honda tucked right in behind him was no doubt a spur to John Cleland, but for one fleeting moment the champion-elect was to have cause to regret this more aggressive approach. On the penultimate lap his Cavalier lurched sideways at a greasy Cascades . . .

But it matters not now. The moment was gathered up by its driver. In fact, even a trip into the armco wouldn't have prevented him from taking the title, but a bent Cavalier would have put a dampener on the occasion. Instead, there were to be nothing but celebrations in the Vauxhall camp.

The ball had been put well and truly into the Scot's court the day before: Rickard Rydell had struggled in the morning to qualify sixth. Fifty-two points behind Cleland going into the weekend, he needed to recover his fantastic qualifying form in the afternoon half-hour if he was to stand any chance of extending his title challenge into the Silverstone finale. Instead, he spent fully 11 seconds on the rev limiter while he qualified the Volvo 18th – his worst showing of the season – minus sixth gear. And there was to be no redeeming charge in the races, fifth and tenth providing an anti-climactic end to his championship bid.

There was no doubt that Volvo and Dunlop's attack had been blunted by yet another wave of new Michelins. Alain Menu gambled on these for the first race and won at a canter. Mind you, he did so later in the day on their predecessors. The Swiss has a beautiful relationship with this Cheshire parkland track, and with a new specification engine in the Laguna he was untouchable, setting two pole positions and two fastest laps as well as claiming his wins. In the first race he was followed home by team-mate, Will Hoy, to give Williams its first touring car 1-2. Cleland was out of reach but, thanks to this performance, Renault and Menu still had their sights on the manufacturers' championship and runner-up spot in the driver standings.

The Total Cup was also won at Oulton Park, Matt Neal's red Mondeo securing two more pole positions, from where he scored two victories to claim the £25,000 first prize.

SNIPPETS

. . . Volvo's weekend begins badly when TOCA levies a £10,000 fine – five times larger than the previous highest – for a breach of its Sporting Regulations by TWR at Snetterton. The team admits that a 'sticky substance' was discovered on the lens of Tim Harvey's 'bumper cam' after the first race, otherwise all parties are tight-lipped about the matter. • Harvey qualifies ninth and fourth, retires from the first race with a broken cambelt, and finishes fifth in the second minus his power-steering. • Leslie scores the first 'official' BTCC podium finish for Honda when his Accord is third in the second race. Fitted with new high-torque engines, both he (fifth and third) and James Kaye (seventh each time) qualify in the top ten for both races. They finish in both top tens, too – third, sixth, seventh and ninth being their eventual haul. • Renault's hopes of a second 1-2 on the day are dashed when Hoy retires from the second race with damaged suspension and a broken engine mount after a first-corner clash with Harvey. • Julian Bailey switches to the TOM'S-built, right-hand drive Toyota and qualifies it third and fifth. He is third in the first race when he spins because of a power-steering failure, but finishes fourth in the second. By way of contrast, Tim Sugden – in Bailey's old car – is knocked out of both races on the first lap. • The latter incident brings out the Safety Car for the first time. As it pulls into the pits it begins to rain. • Gabriele Tarquini uses the latest Prodrive rear suspension and engine to score a fourth place in the first race for Alfa Romeo. Derek Warwick is eighth in this race, but crashes out of the second. Tarquini is 12th after pitting because of a first-corner incident. • Paul Radisich's Ford qualifies 19th for the second race, and is outpaced by Neal's privateer car on his way to a dispiriting 12th place. Earlier in the day he had attempted to pass team-mate, Kelvin Burt, only to go off and damage an oil line. Burt salvages some respectability with seventh place in the second race. • The high point for Peugeot is Simon Harrison's ninth place in the first race. In the second he retires with a severe misfire, while Patrick Watts suffers two engine failures – the latter occurring while he is running behind the Safety Car. • Nigel Smith's Vauxhall Cavalier is second in both Total Cup races, closing to within two points of Richard Kaye's second place with two rounds remaining.

RESULTS • ROUND 22

1 ALAIN MENU Renault Laguna
2 WILL HOY Renault Laguna
3 JOHN CLELAND Vauxhall Cavalier 16V
4 GABRIELE TARQUINI Alfa Romeo 155TS
5 RICKARD RYDELL Volvo 850 20v
6 DAVID LESLIE Honda Accord

TOTAL CUP

1 MATT NEAL Ford Mondeo Ghia

RESULTS • ROUND 23

1 ALAIN MENU Renault Laguna
2 JOHN CLELAND Vauxhall Cavalier 16V
3 DAVID LESLIE Honda Accord
4 JULIAN BAILEY Toyota Carina E
5 TIM HARVEY Volvo 850 20v
6 JOHNNY CECOTTO BMW 318iS

TOTAL CUP

1 MATT NEAL Ford Mondeo Ghia

Gavin Lawrence/Sutton Photographic

Left: Rickard Rydell collected autographs as well as signed them at Oulton Park – Cleland obliging the Swede.

Below: Alain Menu was never headed on his way to a double success.

Colin McMaster/Words & Pictures

LAT Photographic

Bill Bothwell/Bothwell Photographic

TWR was in the wars: Rydell's second session was ruined by a gearbox preparation error, while the team picked up a record fine for apparently tampering with Tim Harvey's 'bumper cam' at Snetterton.

Below: Leaning or squeezing? Kelvin Burt and Mike Briggs dispute Fosters.

Gavin Lawrence/Sutton Photographic

SILVERSTONE
National

A shiver must have run down the opposition's back at Silverstone. Ian Harrison, the Team Director of Williams Renault Dealer Racing, had always insisted that this would be a learning year for his new outfit, that its illustrious name did not automatically confer upon it the status of touring car 'steamroller'. Yet his Lagunas flattened the opposition on this occasion, to secure the manufacturers' championship for Renault.

His drivers, Alain Menu and Will Hoy, played the occasion to perfection and John Cleland could only smile at his predicament. Twice the Safety Car made an appearance and twice the Lagunas stitched him up like a kipper, for as the lights flashed green to restart the races, so one Laguna lagged as the other grabbed an unassailable lead. It wasn't subtle. But then neither was their advantage on the day, as they took turns to head the first double 1-2 of the season. The newly crowned champion had done his utmost to secure a title clean sweep for Vauxhall, but he had had to make do with the team prize only.

Cleland shook up the Renaults briefly on Saturday, though, by grabbing a late-session pole position in the morning, on a track that has not suited the Cavalier in the past. In the afternoon, however, he slipped to sixth. And so Vauxhall's chance disappeared in a flurry of wheelspin as he made a rare bad start to squander his pole position. Thereafter, he harried Hoy in the first race, was passed by and re-passed Kelvin Burt's Ford, and eventually took third. Later, he battled past Julian Bailey's Toyota and the Honda of David Leslie to be third again. But, for once, he seemed happy to stand on the bottom steps of the podium. Indeed, he was keener to talk of a forthcoming holiday on the Great Barrier Reef, or to organise a drivers' night out for a few days before the FIA Touring Car World Cup, than speak of the races.

Leslie again gave notice of the increasing Honda threat, the Scot heading the times in Friday's TOCA test and finishing strongly in fifth and fourth. The latter result included temporarily passing Menu for second when the track was damp. Afterwards he was seen rubbing his hands in glee with the news that he would be using Michelins at the World Cup.

He had good reason to be pleased. Truly, the input and effort of Michelin in the second half of this season can only be marvelled at, as yet again it made available a new tyre that provided its users with an advance in grip and longevity.

Certainly, this went some way towards explaining the relatively poor performance of the Dunlop-shod Volvos. The 850s' season fizzled out, with both Rickard Rydell and Tim Harvey curiously off the pace in qualifying. Harvey managed tenth in the first race, but had his licence endorsed for his part in a shunt that included Simon Harrison and Matt Neal. Later, he equalled Rydell's first-race seventh place, while the Swede retired with an engine failure – an undeserving end to a very impressive year.

SNIPPETS

. . . Harrison's Peugeot is too badly damaged in the above accident to start the second race. Team-mate Patrick Watts salvages eighth, however, having started 18th. • Neal loses 12 laps in the pits and finishes 17th, but is able to score another Total Cup victory with 11th in the second race. His most startling achievement, however, is his ninth place in second qualifying, making him the fastest Dunlop runner. • Once again the works Fords run well at this track, Paul Radisich qualifying third and fourth. He is shunted off at the first corner by Hoy, however, and so it is Kelvin Burt who shines, briefly taking third from Cleland, before finishing fourth. In the second race the works Fords clash at Copse! Burt is out, while Radisich finishes 12th after being black-flagged for a loose rear bumper. • Julian Bailey again demonstrates the potential of the TOM'S-built Toyota Carina. He qualifies fifth and seventh, and finishes fifth in the second race. Having run comfortably in fourth earlier, he retires after damaging the splitter on a kerb. Tim Sugden does an excellent job in the older car, finishing sixth behind his team-mate in the second race. • The BMWs are off the pace, David Brabham and Johnny Cecotto both ending their day stuck fast in the gravel. • Derek Warwick scores points in both races – eighth and tenth – in spite of suffering a collapsed shock absorber in the second encounter. His Alfa Romeo is running 15 mm lower than usual. In his last UK Super Touring race Gabriele Tarquini finishes last after gambling on a pit stop for intermediates. • In the Total Cup Richard Kaye is handed second place on a plate when Nigel Smith's Vauxhall is squeezed into the gravel at Copse on the second lap of the day. This also precludes him from taking the second start. • Kaye's Mondeo wins the first race when Robb Gravett takes Charlie Cox out of the lead at Becketts. • Rain affects the middle section of both races.

RESULTS • ROUND 24

1 ALAIN MENU Renault Laguna
2 WILL HOY Renault Laguna
3 JOHN CLELAND Vauxhall Cavalier 16V
4 KELVIN BURT Ford Mondeo Ghia
5 DAVID LESLIE Honda Accord
6 MIKE BRIGGS Vauxhall Cavalier 16V

TOTAL CUP

1 RICHARD KAYE Ford Mondeo Ghia

RESULTS • ROUND 25

1 WILL HOY Renault Laguna
2 ALAIN MENU Renault Laguna
3 JOHN CLELAND Vauxhall Cavalier 16V
4 DAVID LESLIE Honda Accord
5 JULIAN BAILEY Toyota Carina E
6 TIM SUGDEN Toyota Carina E

TOTAL CUP

1 MATT NEAL Ford Mondeo Ghia

Mark Bothwell/Bothwell Photographic

Colin McMaster/Words & Pictures

LAT Photographic

It was Renault all the way at Silverstone – almost. *Top:* Williams celebrates its manufacturers' title. *Right:* As do Alain Menu and Will Hoy. However, David Leslie's Accord *(left)* was a serious threat, passing Menu briefly for second. *Above:* The Swiss put this situation to rights, however, so that Williams could score its third 1-2 in four races.

Bill Bothwell/Bothwell Photographic

AUTO TRADER RAC BRITISH TOURING CAR CHAMPIONSHIP • ROUNDS 1 & 2

Donington Park, 2 April, 2 x 18 laps, 57.78 miles/92.96 km

RACE 1										RACE 2					
Pos.	Name (Nat.)	No.	Entrant	Car	Tyres	Q Time	Q Pos.	Time/Status	Fastest lap	Pos.	Name	Q Time	Q Pos.	Time/Status	Fastest lap
1	**John Cleland (GB)**	**4**	**Vauxhall Sport**	**Vauxhall Cavalier 16V**	**M**	**1m38.65s**	**2**	**30m30.49s** **89.73 mph/** **144.40 km/h**	**1m40.30s**	**1**	**Rydell**	**1m38.71s**	**1**	**30m26.66s** **88.68 mph/** **142.72 km/h**	**1m39.80s**
2	**Alain Menu (CH)**	**2**	**Williams Renault Dealer Racing**	**Renault Laguna**	**M**	**1m38.77s**	**3**	**30m36.43s**	**1m40.90s**	**2**	**Cleland**	**1m39.76s**	**6**	**30m33.75s**	**1m41.16s**
3	**Paul Radisich (NZ)**	**3**	**Valvoline Team Mondeo**	**Ford Mondeo Ghia**	**M**	**1m38.78s**	**4**	**30m39.13s**	**1m41.02s**	**3**	**Harvey**	**1m39.57s**	**5**	**30m35.69s**	**1m41.06s**
4	**Rickard Rydell (S)**	**15**	**Volvo 850 Racing**	**Volvo 850 20v**	**D**	**1m38.50s**	**1**	**30m39.86s**	**1m41.14s**	**4**	**Menu**	**1m39.41s**	**2**	**30m38.50s**	**1m41.16s**
5	**Johnny Cecotto (YV)**	**16**	**BMW Team Motorsport**	**BMW 318iS**	**M**	**1m39.23s**	**6**	**30m40.63s**	**1m40.82s**	**5**	**Hoy**	**1m39.90s**	**9**	**30m40.61s**	**1m40.98s**
6	**Will Hoy (GB)**	**22**	**Williams Renault Dealer Racing**	**Renault Laguna**	**M**	**1m39.84s**	**11**	**30m43.87s**	**1m40.56s**	**6**	**Radisich**	**1m39.56s**	**4**	**30m44.94s**	**1m41.28s**
7	**James Thompson (GB)**	**14**	**Vauxhall Sport**	**Vauxhall Cavalier 16V**	**M**	**1m39.23s**	**7**	**30m44.26s**	**1m41.01s**	**7**	**Thompson**	**1m39.48s**	**3**	**30m46.44s**	**1m40.86s**
8	**Tim Harvey (GB)**	**9**	**Volvo 850 Racing**	**Volvo 850 20v**	**D**	**1m39.11s**	**5**	**30m44.63s**	**1m40.91s**	**8**	**Cecotto**	**1m39.86s**	**7**	**30m49.11s**	**1m41.29s**
9	**Tim Sugden (GB)**	**12**	**Team Toyota GB**	**Toyota Carina E**	**M**	**1m39.54s**	**8**	**30m48.75s**	**1m41.25s**	**9**	**Simoni**	**1m40.11s**	**12**	**30m51.59s**	**1m41.74s**
10	**Giampiero Simoni (I)**	**5**	**Alfa Romeo Old Spice Racing**	**Alfa Romeo 155TS**	**M**	**1m39.94s**	**13**	**30m50.04s**	**1m41.03s**	**10**	**J.Kaye**	**1m40.50s**	**17**	**30m55.03s**	**1m41.66s**
11	James Kaye (GB)	21	Honda Team MSD	Honda Accord	Y	1m40.39s	19	30m53.39s	1m41.47s	11	Watts	1m40.18s	14	30m56.10s	1m41.54s
12	David Brabham (AUS)	17	BMW Team Motorsport	BMW 318iS	M	1m40.06s	15	30m57.66s	1m41.77s	12	Brabham	1m40.53s	18	30m56.49s	1m41.38s
13	Patrick Watts (GB)	8	Total Team Peugeot	Peugeot 405	M	1m39.86s	12	30m59.11s	1m41.23s	13	Burt	1m40.21s	15	31m03.87s	1m41.98s
14	Simon Harrison (GB)	18	Total Team Peugeot	Peugeot 405	M	1m40.08s	16	31m11.24s	1m42.20s	14	Neal	1m40.22s	16	31m13.19s	1m42.39s
15	Matt Neal (GB)	77	Team Dynamics	Ford Mondeo Ghia	M	1m40.35s	18	31m14.33s	1m41.99s	15	Gravett	1m42.79s	22	31m20.09s	1m42.30s
16	Nigel Smith (GB)	25	Team HMSO	Vauxhall Cavalier 16V	M	2m02.46s	23	31m19.62s	1m42.81s	16	Smith	1m43.36s	23	32m15.20s	1m43.52s
17	Richard Kaye (GB)	23	Mint Motorsport	Ford Mondeo Ghia	D	1m41.52s	20	31m20.71s	1m42.96s	17	Harrison	1m39.93s	10	@ 3 laps	1m41.83s
18	Charlie Cox (AUS)	19	Thames Ford Dealer Team	Ford Mondeo Ghia	D	1m43.50s	22	31m25.78s	1m43.14s	18	Irvine	1m47.28s	24	@ 5 laps	1m47.03s
19	Robb Gravett (GB)	30	Robb Gravett	Vauxhall Cavalier 16V	D	1m43.33s	21	31m30.30s	1m43.23s	19	Cox	1m40.88s	20	15 laps-accident	1m42.08s
20	Kelvin Burt (GB)	33	Valvoline Team Mondeo	Ford Mondeo Ghia	M	1m39.94s	14	8 laps-clutch	1m41.43s	20	Bailey	1m39.88s	8	15 laps-accident	1m41.03s
21	Hamish Irvine (GB)	26	SCB Motorsport	Peugeot 405	M	No Time	24	7 laps-engine	1m46.78s	21	Leslie	1m40.15s	13	10 laps-gearbox	1m41.27s
22	Derek Warwick (GB)	55	Alfa Romeo Old Spice Racing	Alfa Romeo 155TS	M	1m40.20s	17	6 laps-accident	1m42.22s	22	R.Kaye	1m42.38s	21	9 laps-engine	1m43.07s
23	Julian Bailey (GB)	11	Team Toyota GB	Toyota Carina E	M	1m39.65s	10	3 laps accident	1m40.83s	23	Sugden	1m40.01s	11	8 laps-engine	1m41.29s
24	David Leslie (GB)	20	Honda Team MSD	Honda Accord	Y	1m39.64s	9	2 laps-steering	1m49.78s	24	Warwick	1m40.77s	19	8 laps-brakes	1m42.68s

Fastest lap: Cleland 1m40.30s, 89.73 mph/144.40 km/h

Fastest lap: Rydell 1m39.80s, 90.18 mph/145.13 km/h

Championship positions: **1** Cleland 42; **2** Rydell 34; **3** Menu 28; **4** Radisich 18; **5** Harvey 15; **6** Hoy 14; **7** Cecotto 11; **8** Thompson 8; **9** Simoni 3; **10** Sugden 2 etc.

Total Cup: **1** Neal 48; **2** Smith 30; **3** Gravett 26; **4** R.Kaye 12; **5=** Cox, Irvine 10

AUTO TRADER RAC BRITISH TOURING CAR CHAMPIONSHIP • ROUNDS 3 & 4

Brands Hatch Indy, 17 April, 25 & 27 laps, 30.77 & 33.23 miles/49.51 & 53.47 km

RACE 1										RACE 2					
Pos.	Name (Nat.)	No.	Entrant	Car	Tyres	Q Time	Q Pos.	Time/Status	Fastest lap	Pos.	Name	Q Time	Q Pos.	Time/Status	Fastest lap
1	**Tim Harvey (GB)**	**9**	**Volvo 850 Racing**	**Volvo 850 20v**	**D**	**46.10s**	**4**	**23m45.55s** **75.98 mph/** **122.29 km/h**	**55.88s**	**1**	**Harvey**	**46.50s**	**6**	**24m56.63s** **79.14 mph/** **127.36 km/h**	**54.75s**
2	**Paul Radisich (NZ)**	**3**	**Valvoline Team Mondeo**	**Ford Mondeo Ghia**	**M**	**46.41s**	**10**	**23m51.49s**	**55.44s**	**2**	**Thompson**	**46.08s**	**2**	**24m58.32s**	**54.53s**
3	**Kelvin Burt (GB)**	**33**	**Valvoline Team Mondeo**	**Ford Mondeo Ghia**	**M**	**46.69s**	**16**	**23m54.65s**	**55.73s**	**3**	**Rydell**	**45.94s**	**1**	**25m01.21s**	**54.66s**
4	**David Brabham (AUS)**	**17**	**BMW Team Motorsport**	**BMW 318iS**	**M**	**46.52s**	**14**	**24m05.17s**	**56.08s**	**4**	**Burt**	**46.43s**	**5**	**25m02.09s**	**54.15s**
5	**Charlie Cox (AUS)**	**19**	**Thames Ford Dealer Team**	**Ford Mondeo Ghia**	**D**	**47.37s**	**21**	**@ 1 lap**	**57.30s**	**5**	**Cecotto**	**46.55s**	**8**	**25m03.79s**	**54.36s**
6	**Julian Bailey (GB)**	**11**	**Team Toyota GB**	**Toyota Carina E**	**M**	**46.46s**	**12**	**@ 1 lap**	**57.58s**	**6**	**Brabham**	**46.68s**	**15**	**25m04.58s**	**54.63s**
7	**Alain Menu (CH)**	**2**	**Williams Renault Dealer Racing**	**Renault Laguna**	**M**	**46.23s**	**5**	**@ 1 lap**	**57.24s**	**7**	**Hoy**	**50.19s**	**23**	**25m11.50s**	**54.39s**
8	**Patrick Watts (GB)**	**8**	**Total Team Peugeot**	**Peugeot 405**	**M**	**46.33s**	**7**	**@ 1 lap**	**57.46s**	**8**	**Bailey**	**46.71s**	**16**	**25m12.69s**	**54.89s**
9	**Will Hoy (GB)**	**22**	**Williams Renault Dealer Racing**	**Renault Laguna**	**M**	**46.41s**	**11**	**@ 1 lap**	**57.35s**	**9**	**Menu**	**46.32s**	**4**	**25m14.66s**	**54.73s**
10	**Giampiero Simoni (I)**	**5**	**Alfa Romeo Old Spice Racing**	**Alfa Romeo 155TS**	**M**	**46.70s**	**17**	**@ 1 lap**	**57.57s**	**10**	**Sugden**	**46.51s**	**7**	**25m25.75s**	**55.49s**
11	Johnny Cecotto (YV)	16	BMW Team Motorsport	BMW 318iS	M	46.38s	9	@ 1 lap	57.88s	11	Harrison	46.58s	9	25m26.80s	55.47s
12	Derek Warwick (GB)	55	Alfa Romeo Old Spice Racing	Alfa Romeo 155TS	M	46.61s	15	@ 1 lap	57.93s	12	Simoni	46.64s	12	25m28.09s	55.56s
13	Rickard Rydell (S)	15	Volvo 850 Racing	Volvo 850 20v	D	45.89s	1	@ 1 lap	55.82s	13	Neal	47.01s	18	25m28.50s	55.39s
14	Tim Sugden (GB)	12	Team Toyota GB	Toyota Carina E	M	46.38s	8	@ 1 lap	58.21s	14	J.Kaye	46.63s	11	25m34.36s	55.15s
15	Simon Harrison (GB)	18	Total Team Peugeot	Peugeot 405	M	46.51s	13	@ 1 lap	59.44s	15	Cox	47.55s	21	25m48.04s	56.38s
16	Matt Neal (GB)	77	Team Dynamics	Ford Mondeo Ghia	M	47.38s	22	@ 2 laps	59.36s	16	Smith	47.36s	20	25m48.68s	55.57s
17	David Leslie (GB)	20	Honda Team MSD	Honda Accord	Y	46.91s	18	@ 3 laps	59.92s	17	Leslie	46.97s	17	@ 1 lap	55.55s
18	Nigel Smith (GB)	25	Team HMSO	Vauxhall Cavalier 16V	M	47.37s	20	@ 3 laps	58.92s	18	Irvine	50.08s	22	@ 3 laps	57.61s
19	James Kaye (GB)	21	Honda Team MSD	Honda Accord	Y	46.31s	6	@ 3 laps	57.18s	19	R.Kaye	47.13s	19	@ 11 laps	56.74s
20	Richard Kaye (GB)	23	Mint Motorsport	Ford Mondeo Ghia	D	47.22s	19	@ 6 laps	57.77s	20	Warwick	46.66s	13	1 lap-accident	1m26.97s
21	James Thompson (GB)	14	Vauxhall Sport	Vauxhall Cavalier 16V	M	46.10s	3	@ 14 laps	58.21s	21	Cleland	46.22s	3	1 lap-accident	2m00.19s
22	Hamish Irvine (GB)	26	SCB Motorsport	Peugeot 405	M	49.92s	23	4 laps-accident	1m02.11s	22	Watts	46.59s	10	0 laps-accident	
23	John Cleland (GB)	4	Vauxhall Sport	Vauxhall Cavalier 16V	M	46.07s	2	1 lap-accident	1m09.28s	23	Radisich	46.66s	14	0 laps-accident	

Fastest lap: Radisich 55.44s, 78.15 mph/125.77 km/h

Fastest lap: Burt 54.15s, 80.01 mph/128.77 km/h

Championship positions: **1** Harvey 63; **2** Rydell 46; **3** Cleland 42; **4** Radisich 36; **5** Menu 34; **6** Thompson 26; **7** Burt 22; **8** Hoy 20; **9** Cecotto 19; **10** Brabham 16 etc.

Total Cup: **1** Neal 90; **2** Smith 54; **3** Cox 52; **4** R.Kaye 30; **5** Gravett 26; **6** Irvine 20

AUTO TRADER RAC

BTCC ROUND-BY

AUTO TRADER RAC BRITISH TOURING CAR CHAMPIONSHIP • ROUNDS 5 & 6

Thruxton, 8 May, 20 & 17 laps, 47.12 & 40.05 miles/75.81 & 64.44 km

RACE 1										RACE 2					
Pos.	Name (Nat.)	No.	Entrant	Car	Tyres	Q Time	Q Pos.	Time/Status	Fastest lap	Pos.	Name	Q Time	Q Pos.	Time/Status	Fastest lap
1	**Alain Menu (CH)**	**2**	**Williams Renault Dealer Racing**	**Renault Laguna**	**M**	**1m18.262s**	**1**	**26m39.08s** 106.08 mph/ 170.72 km/h	**1m18.61s**	**1**	**Thompson**	**1m18.229s**	**1**	**22m38.48s** 106.13mph/ 170.81km/h	**1m18.84s**
2	**John Cleland (GB)**	**4**	**Vauxhall Sport**	**Vauxhall Cavalier 16V**	**M**	**1m18.334s**	**2**	**26m39.41s**	**1m19.00s**	**2**	**Menu**	**1m18.258s**	**3**	**22m41.33s**	**1m19.10s**
3	**Patrick Watts (GB)**	**8**	**Total Team Peugeot**	**Peugeot 405**	**M**	**1m19.284s**	**8**	**27m05.25s**	**1m19.77s**	**3**	**Burt**	**1m18.695s**	**7**	**22m45.38s**	**1m19.48s**
4	**Tim Sugden (GB)**	**12**	**Team Toyota GB**	**Toyota Carina E**	**M**	**1m19.964s**	**13**	**27m08.56s**	**1m19.75s**	**4**	**Rydell**	**1m18.269s**	**4**	**22m45.57s**	**1m19.10s**
5	**David Brabham (AUS)**	**17**	**BMW Team Motorsport**	**BMW 318iS**	**M**	**1m19.767s**	**12**	**27m09.63s**	**1m20.10s**	**5**	**Cleland**	**1m18.296s**	**5**	**22m52.16s**	**1m19.18s**
6	**Giampiero Simoni (I)**	**5**	**Alfa Romeo Old Spice Racing**	**Alfa Romeo 155TS**	**M**	**1m19.329s**	**9**	**27m09.98s**	**1m20.14s**	**6**	**Radisich**	**1m18.689s**	**6**	**22m53.38s**	**1m19.20s**
7	**Julian Bailey (GB)**	**11**	**Team Toyota GB**	**Toyota Carina E**	**M**	**1m20.608s**	**18**	**27m11.80s**	**1m20.66s**	**7**	**Harvey**	**1m19.254s**	**12**	**22m55.33s**	**1m19.03s**
8	**David Leslie (GB)**	**20**	**Honda Team MSD**	**Honda Accord**	**Y**	**1m20.578s**	**17**	**27m16.67s**	**1m20.40s**	**8**	**Bailey**	**1m19.875s**	**18**	**22m55.65s**	**1m19.61s**
9	**Rickard Rydell (S)**	**15**	**Volvo 850 Racing**	**Volvo 850 20v**	**D**	**1m18.833s**	**5**	**27m25.61s**	**1m20.09s**	**9**	**Harrison**	**1m19.082s**	**9**	**22m58.12s**	**1m19.34s**
10	**Simon Harrison (GB)**	**18**	**Total Team Peugeot**	**Peugeot 405**	**M**	**1m20.435s**	**16**	**27m26.41s**	**1m20.64s**	**10**	**Simoni**	**1m19.511s**	**15**	**22m59.62s**	**1m19.80s**
11	Nigel Smith (GB)	25	Team HMSO	Vauxhall Cavalier 16V	M	1m21.356s	19	27m29.97s	1m20.68s	11	Cecotto	1m19.355s	13	23m03.10s	1m20.02s
12	Derek Warwick (GB)	55	Alfa Romeo Old Spice Racing	Alfa Romeo 155TS	M	1m20.049s	14	28m00.67s	1m20.42s	12	Leslie	1m21.003s	19	23m08.53s	1m20.07s
13	Charlie Cox (AUS)	19	Thames Ford Dealer Team	Ford Mondeo Ghia	D	DQ	23	28m01.51s	1m20.77s	13	J.Kaye	1m19.847s	17	23m09.60s	1m20.04s
14	Richard Kaye (GB)	23	Mint Motorsport	Ford Mondeo Ghia	D	1m22.840s	20	28m04.03s	1m22.13s	14	Smith	1m21.032s	21	23m09.90s	1m20.08s
15	Tim Harvey (GB)	9	Volvo 850 Racing	Volvo 850 20v	D	DQ	22	@ 1 lap	1m19.36s	15	Neal	1m19.046s	10	23m30.60s	1m20.43s
16	James Kaye (GB)	21	Honda Team MSD	Honda Accord	Y	1m20.366s	15	@ 2 laps	1m20.53s	16	R.Kaye	1m21.679s	22	23m38.67s	1m21.55s
17	James Thompson (GB)	14	Vauxhall Sport	Vauxhall Cavalier 16V	M	1m18.811s	4	15 laps-puncture	1m18.63s	17	Warwick	1m19.769s	16	15 laps-handling	1m19.83s
18	Hamish Irvine (GB)	26	SCB Motorsport	Peugeot 405	M	1m25.446s	21	14 laps-engine	1m23.47s	18	Brabham	1m19.480s	14	13 laps-accident	1m20.10s
19	Johnny Cecotto (YV)	16	BMW Team Motorsport	BMW 318iS	M	1m19.516s	11	10 laps-engine	1m20.63s	19	Watts	1m18.927s	8	8 laps-accident	1m19.25s
20	Kelvin Burt (GB)	33	Valvoline Team Mondeo	Ford Mondeo Ghia	M	1m19.076s	6	9 laps-accident	1m20.04s	20	Sugden	1m19.248s	11	3 laps-engine	1m20.03s
21	Paul Radisich (NZ)	3	Valvoline Team Mondeo	Ford Mondeo Ghia	M	1m18.761s	3	7 laps-steering	1m19.79s	21	Hoy	1m18.246s	2	0 laps-steering	
22	Will Hoy (GB)	22	Williams Renault Dealer Racing	Renault Laguna	M	1m19.428s	10	6 laps-steering	1m19.21s	22	Cox	1m21.029s	20	DNS-accident	
23	Matt Neal (GB)	77	Team Dynamics	Ford Mondeo Ghia	M	1m19.244s	7	2 laps-accident	1m20.62s	23	Irvine	1m25.177s	23	DNS-engine	

Fastest lap: Menu 1m18.61s, 107.89 mph/173.63 km/h

Fastest lap: Thompson 1m18.84s, 107.57 mph/173.13 km/h

Championship positions: 1 Menu 76; **2** Cleland 68; **3** Harvey 67; **4** Rydell 58; **5** Thompson 50; **6** Radisich 42; **7** Burt 34; **8** Brabham 24; **9** Hoy 20; **10** Cecotto 19 etc.

Total Cup: **1** Neal 116; **2** Smith 102; **3** Cox 70 ; **4** R.Kaye 54; **5** Gravett 26; **6** Irvine 20

AUTO TRADER RAC BRITISH TOURING CAR CHAMPIONSHIP • ROUNDS 7 & 8

Silverstone National, 13 May, 25 & 22 laps, 41.05 & 36.12 miles/66.05 & 58.12 km

RACE 1										RACE 2					
Pos.	Name (Nat.)	No.	Entrant	Car	Tyres	Q Time	Q Pos.	Time/Status	Fastest lap	Pos.	Name	Q Time	Q Pos.	Time/Status	Fastest lap
1	**Rickard Rydell (S)**	**15**	**Volvo 850 Racing**	**Volvo 850 20v**	**D**	**1m00.954s**	**1**	**25m58.88s** 94.79mph/ 152.56 km/h	**1m01.46s**	**1**	**Radisich**	**1m01.116s**	**2**	**22m51.41s** 94.82mph/ 152.60km/h	**1m01.50s**
2	**Paul Radisich (NZ)**	**3**	**Valvoline Team Mondeo**	**Ford Mondeo Ghia**	**M**	**1m01.184s**	**3**	**26m00.38s**	**1m01.29s**	**2**	**Rydell**	**1m00.786s**	**1**	**22m51.84s**	**1m01.62s**
3	**John Cleland (GB)**	**4**	**Vauxhall Sport**	**Vauxhall Cavalier 16V**	**M**	**1m01.459s**	**5**	**26m06.52s**	**1m01.91s**	**3**	**Harvey**	**1m01.425s**	**6**	**22m58.70s**	**1m01.92s**
4	**James Thompson (GB)**	**14**	**Vauxhall Sport**	**Vauxhall Cavalier 16V**	**M**	**1m01.559s**	**8**	**26m07.21s**	**1m01.99s**	**4**	**Menu**	**1m01.310s**	**5**	**23m00.16s**	**1m01.94s**
5	**Will Hoy (GB)**	**22**	**Williams Renault Dealer Racing**	**Renault Laguna**	**M**	**1m01.532s**	**6**	**26m10.60s**	**1m01.88s**	**5**	**Cleland**	**1m01.426s**	**7**	**23m02.13s**	**1m01.90s**
6	**Patrick Watts (GB)**	**8**	**Total Team Peugeot**	**Peugeot 405**	**M**	**1m01.565s**	**9**	**26m11.71s**	**1m02.14s**	**6**	**Sugden**	**1m01.443s**	**8**	**23m02.83s**	**1m01.98s**
7	**Tim Harvey (GB)**	**9**	**Volvo 850 Racing**	**Volvo 850 20v**	**D**	**1m01.613s**	**11**	**26m15.51s**	**1m02.09s**	**7**	**Burt**	**1m01.303s**	**4**	**23m03.46s**	**1m01.65s**
8	**David Brabham (AUS)**	**17**	**BMW Team Motorsport**	**BMW 318iS**	**M**	**1m01.941s**	**16**	**26m15.78s**	**1m02.21s**	**8**	**Leslie**	**1m01.290s**	**3**	**23m04.02s**	**1m01.94s**
9	**David Leslie (GB)**	**20**	**Honda Team MSD**	**Honda Accord**	**Y**	**1m01.565s**	**10**	**26m18.17s**	**1m02.05s**	**9**	**Simoni**	**1m01.539s**	**13**	**23m04.45s**	**1m01.96s**
10	**James Kaye (GB)**	**21**	**Honda Team MSD**	**Honda Accord**	**Y**	**1m01.898s**	**15**	**26m20.53s**	**1m02.15s**	**10**	**Watts**	**1m01.477s**	**10**	**23m04.93s**	**1m01.87s**
11	Johnny Cecotto (YV)	16	BMW Team Motorsport	BMW 318iS	M	1m02.072s	18	26m23.95s	1m02.46s	11	Brabham	1m01.806s	17	23m07.81s	1m02.05s
12	Simon Harrison (GB)	18	Total Team Peugeot	Peugeot 405	M	1m01.977s	17	26m25.03s	1m02.57s	12	Cecotto	1m02.000s	18	23m08.84s	1m02.22s
13	Matt Neal (GB)	77	Team Dynamics	Ford Mondeo Ghia	M	1m01.639s	12	26m29.51s	1m02.42s	13	J.Kaye	1m01.723s	16	23m10.72s	1m01.98s
14	Richard Kaye (GB)	23	Mint Motorsport	Ford Mondeo Ghia	D	1m02.468s	21	26m47.53s	1m03.33s	14	Neal	1m01.566s	14	23m14.86s	1m02.28s
15	Hamish Irvine (GB)	26	SCB Motorsport	Peugeot 405	M	1m04.982s	22	@ 1 lap	1m05.11s	15	Hoy	1m01.477s	11	23m16.86s	1m02.37s
16	Derek Warwick (GB)	55	Alfa Romeo Old Spice Racing	Alfa Romeo 155TS	M	1m02.139s	19	@ 11 laps	1m02.50s	16	Harrison	1m01.665s	15	23m21.86s	1m02.50s
17	Tim Sugden (GB)	12	Team Toyota GB	Toyota Carina E	M	1m01.553s	7	24 laps-gearbox	1m02.19s	17	Warwick	1m02.105s	19	@ 1 lap	1m02.51s
18	Giampiero Simoni (I)	5	Alfa Romeo Old Spice Racing	Alfa Romeo 155TS	M	1m01.788s	14	23 laps-hub	1m02.09s	18	R.Kaye	1m02.691s	21	@ 6 laps	1m03.17s
19	Nigel Smith (GB)	25	Team HMSO	Vauxhall Cavalier 16V	M	1m02.339s	20	20 laps-electrics	1m02.62s	19	Irvine	1m04.993s	22	14 laps-engine	1m05.16s
20	Julian Bailey (GB)	11	Team Toyota GB	Toyota Carina E	M	1m01.726s	13	20 laps-engine	1m02.26s	20	Smith	1m02.204s	20	4 laps-engine	1m21.33s
21	Alain Menu (CH)	2	Williams Renault Dealer Racing	Renault Laguna	M	1m01.253s	4	3 laps-driveshaft	1m09.78s	21	Thompson	1m01.480s	12	3 laps-accident	1m02.50s
22	Kelvin Burt (GB)	33	Valvoline Team Mondeo	Ford Mondeo Ghia	M	1m01.134s	2	1 lap-accident		22	Bailey	1m01.454s	9	0 laps-accident	

Fastest lap: Radisich 1m01.29s, 96.44 mph/155.21 km/h

Fastest lap: Radisich 1m01.50s, 96.11 mph/154.68 km/h

Championship positions: 1 Rydell 100; **2** Cleland 88; **3** Menu 86; **4** Radisich 84; **5** Harvey 83; **6** Thompson 60; **7** Burt 38; **8** Hoy 28; **9** Brabham 27; **10** Watts 22 etc.

Total Cup: **1** Neal 156; **2** Smith 102; **3** R.Kaye 90; **4** Cox 70; **5** Irvine 32; **6** Gravett 26

ROUND RESULTS

AUTO TRADER RAC BRITISH TOURING CAR CHAMPIONSHIP • ROUNDS 9 & 10

Oulton Park, 29 May, 13 & 16 laps, 36.01 & 44.32 miles/57.94 & 71.31 km

RACE 1										RACE 2					
Pos.	Name (Nat.)	No.	Entrant	Car	Tyres	Q Time	Q Pos.	Time/Status	Fastest lap	Pos.	Name	Q Time	Q Pos.	Time/Status	Fastest lap
1	**Rickard Rydell (S)**	**15**	**Volvo 850 Racing**	**Volvo 850 20v**	**D**	**1m42.373s**	**2**	**22m39.09s** 95.55 mph/ 153.78 km/h	**1m43.85s**	**1**	**Menu**	**1m42.721s**	**2**	**27m47.01s** 95.88mph/ 154.31km/h	**1m43.07s**
2	**John Cleland (GB)**	**4**	**Vauxhall Sport**	**Vauxhall Cavalier 16V**	**M**	**1m42.503s**	**4**	**22m39.61s**	**1m43.63s**	**2**	**Rydell**	**1m42.626s**	**1**	**27m48.84s**	**1m43.40s**
3	**Alain Menu (CH)**	**2**	**Williams Renault Dealer Racing**	**Renault Laguna**	**M**	**1m42.533s**	**5**	**22m41.20s**	**1m43.61s**	**3**	**Cleland**	**1m42.990s**	**4**	**27m49.65s**	**1m43.37s**
4	**Julian Bailey (GB)**	**11**	**Team Toyota GB**	**Toyota Carina E**	**M**	**1m43.052s**	**9**	**22m49.00s**	**1m44.28s**	**4**	**Thompson**	**1m42.733s**	**3**	**28m02.10s**	**1m43.77s**
5	**Giampiero Simoni (I)**	**5**	**Alfa Romeo Old Spice Racing**	**Alfa Romeo 155TS**	**M**	**1m43.402s**	**13**	**22m51.84s**	**1m44.25s**	**5**	**Radisich**	**1m43.543s**	**7**	**28m05.08s**	**1m43.99s**
6	**James Thompson (GB)**	**14**	**Vauxhall Sport**	**Vauxhall Cavalier 16V**	**M**	**1m42.186s**	**1**	**22m52.34s**	**1m44.39s**	**6**	**Burt**	**1m43.461s**	**5**	**28m07.63s**	**1m43.97s**
7	**Simon Harrison (GB)**	**18**	**Total Team Peugeot**	**Peugeot 405**	**M**	**1m43.284s**	**10**	**22m53.43s**	**1m44.40s**	**7**	**Simoni**	**1m43.671s**	**9**	**28m12.52s**	**1m44.34s**
8	**Tim Harvey (GB)**	**9**	**Volvo 850 Racing**	**Volvo 850 20v**	**D**	**1m43.577s**	**17**	**22m56.09s**	**1m44.46s**	**8**	**Brabham**	**1m44.545s**	**18**	**28m12.71s**	**1m43.94s**
9	**Johnny Cecotto (YV)**	**16**	**BMW Team Motorsport**	**BMW 318iS**	**M**	**1m43.546s**	**15**	**22m56.60s**	**1m44.54s**	**9**	**Bailey**	**1m43.519s**	**6**	**28m20.47s**	**1m43.87s**
10	**David Brabham (AUS)**	**17**	**BMW Team Motorsport**	**BMW 318iS**	**M**	**1m43.715s**	**18**	**23m00.33s**	**1m44.56s**	**10**	**J.Kaye**	**1m43.894s**	**13**	**28m20.48s**	**1m44.61s**
11	Gabriele Tarquini (I)	1	Alfa Romeo Old Spice Racing	Alfa Romeo 155TS	M	1m43.811s	19	23m06.58s	1m44.75s	11	Sugden	1m43.834s	11	28m20.49s	1m44.11s
12	Nigel Smith (GB)	25	Team HMSO	Vauxhall Cavalier 16V	M	1m46.109s	22	23m13.14s	1m45.46s	12	Harrison	1m43.594s	8	28m21.95s	1m43.47s
13	Matt Neal (GB)	77	Team Dynamics	Ford Mondeo Ghia	M	1m43.552s	16	23m13.59s	1m45.71s	13	Watts	1m44.247s	15	28m27.93s	1m43.97s
14	James Kaye (GB)	21	Honda Team MSD	Honda Accord	Y	1m43.877s	20	23m14.86s	1m45.26s	14	Neal	1m44.486s	17	28m31.14s	1m45.29s
15	Richard Kaye (GB)	23	Mint Motorsport	Ford Mondeo Ghia	D	1m44.638s	21	23m24.73s	1m46.06s	15	Harvey	1m44.679s	19	28m31.98s	1m44.39s
16	Hamish Irvine (GB)	26	SCB Motorsport	Peugeot 405	M	1m52.153s	23	23m50.72s	1m48.67s	16	Smith	DQ	23	28m55.15s	1m45.96s
17	Will Hoy (GB)	22	Williams Renault Dealer Racing	Renault Laguna	M	1m43.303s	11	7 laps-engine	1m44.15s	17	R.Kaye	1m44.767s	20	29m07.51s	1m46.03s
18	Paul Radisich (NZ)	3	Valvoline Team Mondeo	Ford Mondeo Ghia	M	1m42.599s	6	1 lap-accident	1m51.23s	18	Hoy	1m44.346s	16	@ 1 lap	1m44.15s
19	Tim Sugden (GB)	12	Team Toyota GB	Toyota Carina E	M	1m43.049s	8	1 lap-accident	1m52.27s	19	Irvine	1m50.417s	22	9 laps-engine	1m48.49s
20	Patrick Watts (GB)	8	Total Team Peugeot	Peugeot 405	M	1m43.321s	12	0 laps-accident		20	Cecotto	1m43.837s	12	1 lap-suspension	
21	David Leslie (GB)	20	Honda Team MSD	Honda Accord	Y	1m42.819s	7	0 laps-accident		21	Tarquini	1m47.239s	21	0 laps-accident	
22	Derek Warwick	55	Alfa Romeo Old Spice Racing	Alfa Romeo 155TS	M	1m43.403s	14	0 laps-accident		22	Warwick	1m44.023s	14	DNS	
23	Kelvin Burt (GB)	33	Valvoline Team Mondeo	Ford Mondeo Ghia	M	1m42.500s	3	0 laps-accident		23	Leslie	1m43.728s	10	DNS	

Fastest lap: Menu 1m43.61s, 96.41 mph/155.17 km/h

Fastest lap: Menu 1m43.07s, 96.92 mph/155.98 km/h

Championship positions: **1** Rydell 142; **2** Menu 122; **3** Cleland 118; **4** Radisich 92; **5** Harvey 86; **6** Thompson 76; **7** Burt 44; **8** Brabham 31; **9=** Hoy, Bailey 28 etc.

Total Cup: **1** Neal 198; **2** Smith 144; **3** R.Kaye 114; **4** Cox 70; **5** Irvine 42; **6** Gravett 26

AUTO TRADER RAC BRITISH TOURING CAR CHAMPIONSHIP • ROUNDS 11 & 12

Brands Hatch Grand Prix, 11 June, 13 & 10 laps, 33.80 & 26.00 miles/54.38 & 41.83 km

RACE 1										RACE 2					
Pos.	Name (Nat.)	No.	Entrant	Car	Tyres	Q Time	Q Pos.	Time/Status	Fastest lap	Pos.	Name	Q Time	Q Pos.	Time/Status	Fastest lap
1	**Alain Menu (CH)**	**2**	**Williams Renault Dealer Racing**	**Renault Laguna**	**M**	**1m29.181s**	**1**	**22m34.60s** 89.83 mph/ 144.57 km/h	**1m42.22s**	**1**	**Cleland**	**1m29.220s**	**3**	**17m39.02s** 88.39mph/ 142.25km/h	**1m44.97s**
2	**John Cleland (GB)**	**4**	**Vauxhall Sport**	**Vauxhall Cavalier 16V**	**M**	**1m29.491s**	**5**	**22m35.95s**	**1m42.12s**	**2**	**Thompson**	**1m29.199s**	**2**	**17m39.64s**	**1m44.62s**
3	**Tim Harvey (GB)**	**9**	**Volvo 850 Racing**	**Volvo 850 20v**	**D**	**1m29.567s**	**8**	**22m40.06s**	**1m42.70s**	**3**	**Menu**	**1m29.062s**	**1**	**17m39.99s**	**1m44.45s**
4	**Will Hoy (GB)**	**22**	**Williams Renault Dealer Racing**	**Renault Laguna**	**M**	**1m29.431s**	**4**	**22m48.32s**	**1m42.38s**	**4**	**Hoy**	**1m29.451s**	**5**	**17m40.72s**	**1m44.49s**
5	**Patrick Watts (GB)**	**8**	**Total Team Peugeot**	**Peugeot 405**	**M**	**1m30.056s**	**9**	**22m59.82s**	**1m43.77s**	**5**	**Harvey**	**1m29.581s**	**7**	**17m41.24s**	**1m44.68s**
6	**Julian Bailey (GB)**	**11**	**Team Toyota GB**	**Toyota Carina E**	**M**	**1m30.359s**	**13**	**23m01.73s**	**1m43.19s**	**6**	**Bailey**	**1m29.788s**	**8**	**17m43.62s**	**1m44.67s**
7	**Rickard Rydell (S)**	**15**	**Volvo 850 Racing**	**Volvo 850 20v**	**D**	**1m29.401s**	**3**	**23m03.13s**	**1m43.22s**	**7**	**Radisich**	**1m29.577s**	**6**	**17m44.37s**	**1m44.60s**
8	**Derek Warwick**	**55**	**Alfa Romeo Old Spice Racing**	**Alfa Romeo 155TS**	**M**	**1m30.847s**	**18**	**23m03.97s**	**1m42.88s**	**8**	**Watts**	**1m29.879s**	**9**	**17m49.07s**	**1m45.15s**
9	**Giampiero Simoni (I)**	**5**	**Alfa Romeo Old Spice Racing**	**Alfa Romeo 155TS**	**M**	**1m30.585s**	**17**	**23m07.73s**	**1m43.48s**	**9**	**Cecotto**	**1m29.905s**	**10**	**17m52.38s**	**1m45.62s**
10	**Johnny Cecotto (YV)**	**16**	**BMW Team Motorsport**	**BMW 318iS**	**M**	**1m30.485s**	**16**	**23m18.96s**	**1m43.44s**	**10**	**Brabham**	**1m30.121s**	**13**	**17m55.55s**	**1m46.16s**
11	Simon Harrison (GB)	18	Total Team Peugeot	Peugeot 405	M	1m30.460s	15	23m35.10s	1m43.94s	11	Warwick	1m30.314s	14	17m56.06s	1m45.75s
12	David Leslie (GB)	20	Honda Team MSD	Honda Accord	Y	1m30.235s	12	23m35.23s	1m45.24s	12	Simoni	1m30.622s	17	17m57.14s	1m45.67s
13	James Kaye (GB)	21	Honda Team MSD	Honda Accord	Y	1m30.368s	14	23m41.90s	1m44.94s	13	Harrison	1m30.495s	16	17m59.12s	1m45.77s
14	Hamish Irvine (GB)	26	SCB Motorsport	Peugeot 405	M	1m34.395s	22	24m04.13s	1m47.21s	14	Burt	DQ	22	17m59.69s	1m45.40s
15	Richard Kaye (GB)	23	Mint Motorsport	Ford Mondeo Ghia	D	1m33.760s	21	24m15.01s	1m46.45s	15	R.Kaye	1m32.519s	19	18m21.48s	1m47.55s
16	Nigel Smith (GB)	25	Team HMSO	Vauxhall Cavalier 16V	M	1m30.976s	20	@ 2 laps	1m47.81s	16	Irvine	1m34.197s	20	18m21.50s	1m48.29s
17	Tim Sugden (GB)	12	Team Toyota GB	Toyota Carina E	M	1m30.086s	10	8 laps-accident	1m44.59s	17	Smith	1m31.277s	18	18m42.44s	1m50.20s
18	James Thompson (GB)	14	Vauxhall Sport	Vauxhall Cavalier 16V	M	1m29.336s	2	2 laps-accident	1m49.87s	18	Leslie	1m30.069s	12	18m45.27s	1m50.77s
19	Kelvin Burt (GB)	33	Valvoline Team Mondeo	Ford Mondeo Ghia	M	1m29.550s	7	1 lap-accident	1m53.50s	19	J.Kaye	1m50.297s	21	18m46.18s	1m50.74s
20	Paul Radisich (NZ)	3	Valvoline Team Mondeo	Ford Mondeo Ghia	M	1m29.501s	6	0 laps-accident		20	Rydell	1m29.421s	4	0 laps-accident	
21	David Brabham (AUS)	17	BMW Team Motorsport	BMW 318 iS	M	1m30.124s	11	0 laps-accident		21	Sugden	1m30.017s	11	DNS	
22	Matt Neal (GB)	77	Team Dynamics	Ford Mondeo Ghia	M	1m30.849s	19	0 laps-accident		22	Neal	1m30.395s	15	DNS	

Fastest lap: Cleland 1m42.12s, 91.66 mph/147.51 km/h

Fastest lap: Menu 1m44.45s, 89.61 mph/144.22 km/h

Championship positions: **1** Cleland 160; **2** Menu 158; **3** Rydell 146; **4** Harvey 106; **5** Radisich 96; **6** Thompson 94; **7** Hoy 48; **8** Burt 44; **9** Bailey 40; **10** Watts 33 etc.

Total Cup: **1** Neal 198; **2** Smith 168; **3** R.Kaye 156; **4** Irvine 84; **5** Cox 70; **6** Gravett 26

AUTO TRADER RAC

BTCC ROUND-BY

AUTO TRADER RAC BRITISH TOURING CAR CHAMPIONSHIP • ROUNDS 13 & 14

Donington Park, 25 June, 2 x 15 laps, 37.50 miles/60.34 km

RACE 1

Pos.	Name (Nat.)	No.	Entrant	Car	Tyres	Q Time	Q Pos.	Time/Status	Fastest lap
1	John Cleland (GB)	4	Vauxhall Sport	Vauxhall Cavalier 16V	M	1m37.730s	1	25m01.93s 89.88mph/ 144.65 km/h	1m39.02s
2	Rickard Rydell (S)	15	Volvo 850 Racing	Volvo 850 20v	D	1m37.934s	4	25m04.60s	1m39.59s
3	Alain Menu (CH)	2	Williams Renault Dealer Racing	Renault Laguna	M	1m38.215s	5	25m08.93s	1m39.62s
4	James Thompson (GB)	14	Vauxhall Sport	Vauxhall Cavalier 16V	M	1m37.786s	2	25m09.46s	1m39.27s
5	Paul Radisich (NZ)	3	Valvoline Team Mondeo	Ford Mondeo Ghia	M	1m38.402s	6	25m13.87s	1m39.56s
6	Julian Bailey (GB)	11	Team Toyota GB	Toyota Carina E	M	1m38.461s	7	25m14.36s	1m39.38s
7	David Leslie (GB)	20	Honda Team MSD	Honda Accord	Y	1m37.893s	3	25m19.89s	1m39.84s
8	Tim Sugden (GB)	12	Team Toyota GB	Toyota Carina E	M	1m38.745s	12	25m20.51s	1m40.27s
9	Kelvin Burt (GB)	33	Valvoline Team Mondeo	Ford Mondeo Ghia	M	1m38.616s	11	25m21.32s	1m39.50s
10	Tim Harvey (GB)	9	Volvo 850 Racing	Volvo 850 20v	D	1m38.585s	10	25m24.60s	1m40.19s
11	David Brabham (AUS)	17	BMW Team Motorsport	BMW 318iS	M	1m38.879s	13	25m24.87s	1m40.50s
12	Will Hoy (GB)	22	Williams Renault Dealer Racing	Renault Laguna	M	1m39.261s	19	25m26.23s	1m40.22s
13	Derek Warwick (GB)	55	Alfa Romeo Old Spice Racing	Alfa Romeo 155TS	M	1m38.465s	8	25m29.81s	1m40.04s
14	James Kaye (GB)	21	Honda Team MSD	Honda Accord	Y	1m38.572s	9	25m31.12s	1m40.20s
15	Patrick Watts (GB)	8	Total Team Peugeot	Peugeot 405	M	1m38.889s	14	25m37.96s	1m40.45s
16	Nigel Smith (GB)	25	Team HMSO	Vauxhall Cavalier 16V	M	1m41.255s	20	25m59.64s	1m41.62s
17	Richard Kaye (GB)	23	Mint Motorsport	Ford Mondeo Ghia	D	1m41.875s	21	26m06.60s	1m42.00s
18	Hamish Irvine (GB)	26	SCB Motorsport	Peugeot 405	M	1m42.199s	22	26m16.53s	1m42.67s
19	Simon Harrison (GB)	18	Total Team Peugeot	Peugeot 405	M	1m39.021s	18	9 laps-handling	1m40.20s
20	Johnny Cecotto (YV)	16	BMW Team Motorsport	BMW 318iS	M	1m38.951s	17	2 laps-accident	1m44.02s
21	Matt Neal (GB)	77	Team Dynamics	Ford Mondeo Ghia	M	1m38.898s	15	2 laps-accident	1m43.70s
22	Giampiero Simoni (I)	5	Alfa Romeo Old Spice Racing	Alfa Romeo 155TS	M	1m38.926s	16	2 laps-steering	1m52.44s

Fastest lap: Cleland 1m39.02s, 90.89 mph/146.27 km/h

RACE 2

Pos.	Name	Q Time	Q Pos.	Time/Status	Fastest lap
1	Cleland	1m38.044s	1	25m05.02s 89.69 mph/ 144.35 km/h	1m39.16s
2	Radisich	1m38.203s	3	25m11.03s	1m39.41s
3	Burt	1m38.139s	2	25m12.88s	1m39.80s
4	Menu	1m38.392s	6	25m14.27s	1m39.81s
5	Thompson	1m38.318s	5	25m16.21s	1m39.77s
6	Rydell	1m38.256s	4	25m16.85s	1m39.85s
7	Bailey	1m38.627s	8	25m17.03s	1m39.70s
8	Hoy	1m39.450s	17	25m21.18s	1m39.74s
9	Leslie	1m38.412s	7	25m23.55s	1m39.93s
10	J.Kaye	1m38.799s	10	25m23.93s	1m40.14s
11	Brabham	1m39.611s	19	25m24.32s	1m40.28s
12	Harvey	1m39.058s	12	25m28.51s	1m40.03s
13	Sugden	1m38.963s	11	26m04.60s	1m40.54s
14	R.Kaye	1m41.753s	21	26m04.72s	1m42.22s
15	Irvine	1m42.586s	22	26m06.07s	1m41.84s
16	Warwick	1m39.246s	14	8 laps-accident	1m40.11s
17	Simoni	1m39.289s	16	6 laps-accident	1m40.42s
18	Watts	1m39.239s	13	5 laps-accident	1m40.61s
19	Harrison	1m39.451s	18	4 laps-fire	1m40.82s
20	Smith	1m40.534s	20	4 laps-accident	1m41.47s
21	Neal	1m39.282s	15	3 laps-accident	1m41.33s
22	Cecotto	1m38.666s	9	2 laps-accident	1m41.30s

Fastest lap: Cleland 1m39.16s, 90.76 mph/146.06 km/h

Championship positions: 1 Cleland 208; **2** Menu 180; **3** Rydell 170; **4** Radisich 122; **5** Thompson 112; **6** Harvey 107; **7** Burt 58; **8** Hoy 51; **9** Bailey 50; **10** Watts 33 etc.

Total Cup: **1=** Neal, R.Kaye 198; **3** Smith 192; **4** Irvine 114; **5** Cox 70; **6** Gravett 26

AUTO TRADER RAC BRITISH TOURING CAR CHAMPIONSHIP • ROUND 15

Silverstone Grand Prix, 16 July, 15 laps, 47.13 miles/75.78 km

RACE 1

Pos.	Name (Nat.)	No.	Entrant	Car	Tyres	Q Time	Q Pos.	Time/Status	Fastest lap
1	John Cleland (GB)	4	Vauxhall Sport	Vauxhall Cavalier 16V	M	1m59.647s	1	33m47.70s 106.13mph/ 134.66 km/h	2m13.68s
2	Will Hoy (GB)	22	Williams Renault Dealer Racing	Renault Laguna	M	2m00.244s	6	33m55.27s	2m13.98s
3	James Thompson (GB)	14	Vauxhall Sport	Vauxhall Cavalier 16V	M	1m59.927s	4	33m56.96s	2m13.53s
4	Julian Bailey (GB)	11	Team Toyota GB	Toyota Carina E	M	2m01.577s	19	33m57.48s	2m13.39s
5	Kelvin Burt (GB)	33	Valvoline Team Mondeo	Ford Mondeo Ghia	M	2m00.514s	9	34m01.64s	2m13.76s
6	Paul Radisich (NZ)	3	Valvoline Team Mondeo	Ford Mondeo Ghia	M	1m59.910s	3	34m15.51s	2m15.20s
7	David Brabham (AUS)	17	BMW Team Motorsport	BMW 318iS	M	2m01.059s	13	34m23.28s	2m16.19s
8	Tim Sugden (GB)	12	Team Toyota GB	Toyota Carina E	M	2m01.363s	16	34m24.99s	2m15.22s
9	Derek Warwick (GB)	55	Alfa Romeo Old Spice Racing	Alfa Romeo 155TS	M	2m01.418s	17	34m31.63s	2m16.60s
10	Patrick Watts (GB)	8	Total Team Peugeot	Peugeot 405	M	2m01.168s	14	34m33.72s	2m16.16s
11	Giampiero Simoni (I)	5	Alfa Romeo Old Spice Racing	Alfa Romeo 155TS	M	2m00.655s	10	34m34.01s	2m16.45s
12	David Leslie (GB)	20	Honda Team MSD	Honda Accord	Y	2m.00.476s	8	34m41.74s	2m16.39s
13	Robb Gravett (GB)	19	Foesport	Ford Mondeo Ghia	M	2m02.986s	21	34m46.10s	2m16.67s
14	Matt Neal (GB)	77	Team Dynamics	Ford Mondeo Ghia	M	2m01.362s	15	34m48.72s	2m17.53s
15	Simon Harrison (GB)	18	Total Team Peugeot	Peugeot 405	M	2m01.439s	18	34m50.83s	2m17.35s
16	Alain Menu (CH)	2	Williams Renault Dealer Racing	Renault Laguna	M	1m59.805s	2	34m52.21s	2m14.97s
17	Rickard Rydell (S)	15	Volvo 850 Racing	Volvo 850 20v	D	2m00.045s	5	35m24.44s	2m14.54s
18	Hamish Irvine (GB)	26	SCB Motorsport	Peugeot 405	M	2m06.329s	23	35m59.77s	2m20.74s
19	Tim Harvey (GB)	9	Volvo 850 Racing	Volvo 850 20v	D	2m00.403s	7	11 laps-accident	2m14.24s
20	James Kaye (GB)	21	Honda Team MSD	Honda Accord	Y	2m01.027s	12	8 laps-electrics	2m17.59s
21	Nigel Smith (GB)	25	Team HMSO	Vauxhall Cavalier 16V	M	2m02.535s	20	7 laps-alternator	2m18.91s
22	Richard Kaye (GB)	23	Mint Motorsport	Ford Mondeo Ghia	D	2m03.170s	22	6 laps-accident	2m18.60s
23	Johnny Cecotto (YV)	16	BMW Team Motorsport	BMW 318iS	M	2m00.802s	11	0 laps-clutch	

Fastest lap: Bailey 2m13.39s, 84.79 mph/136.46 km/h

Championship positions: 1 Cleland 232; **2** Menu 180; **3** Rydell 170; **4** Radisich 128; **5** Thompson 124; **6** Harvey 107; **7** Hoy 69; **8** Burt 66; **9** Bailey 60; **10** Brabham 36 etc.

Total Cup: **1** Neal 216; **2** R.Kaye 198; **3** Smith 192; **4** Irvine 126; **5** Cox 70; **6** Gravett 50

ROUND RESULTS

AUTO TRADER RAC BRITISH TOURING CAR CHAMPIONSHIP • ROUNDS 16 & 17

Knockhill, 30 July, 31 & 32 laps, 40.30 & 41.60 miles/64.84 & 66.93 km

RACE 1										RACE 2					
Pos.	Name (Nat.)	No.	Entrant	Car	Tyres	Q Time	Q Pos.	Time/Status	Fastest lap	Pos.	Name	Q Time	Q Pos.	Time/Status	Fastest lap
1	**Rickard Rydell (S)**	**15**	**Volvo 850 Racing**	**Volvo 850 20v**	**D**	**53.463s**	**1**	**28m53.85s** 83.67 mph/ 134.66 km/h	**54.59s**	**1**	**Menu**	**53.902s**	**2**	**29m27.65s** 84.72 mph/ 136.34 km/h	**54.67s**
2	**Tim Harvey (GB)**	**9**	**Volvo 850 Racing**	**Volvo 850 20v**	**D**	**53.993s**	**4**	**29m00.82s**	**54.88s**	**2**	**Rydell**	**53.751s**	**1**	**29m30.51s**	**54.73s**
3	**Kelvin Burt (GB)**	**33**	**Valvoline Team Mondeo**	**Ford Mondeo Ghia**	**M**	**54.153s**	**5**	**29m01.79s**	**55.17s**	**3**	**Harvey**	**54.059s**	**3**	**29m46.84s**	**54.65s**
4	**Johnny Cecotto (YV)**	**16**	**BMW Team Motorsport**	**BMW 318iS**	**M**	**54.399s**	**12**	**29m02.79s**	**55.25s**	**4**	**Brabham**	**54.469s**	**10**	**29m52.20s**	**55.10s**
5	**John Cleland (GB)**	**4**	**Vauxhall Sport**	**Vauxhall Cavalier 16V**	**M**	**54.158s**	**7**	**29m03.51s**	**55.12s**	**5**	**J.Kaye**	**54.356s**	**6**	**29m53.55s**	**54.86s**
6	**Julian Bailey (GB)**	**11**	**Team Toyota GB**	**Toyota Carina E**	**M**	**54.157s**	**6**	**29m04.36s**	**55.27s**	**6**	**Cleland**	**54.418s**	**8**	**29m53.62s**	**54.99s**
7	**Tim Sugden (GB)**	**12**	**Team Toyota GB**	**Toyota Carina E**	**M**	**54.573s**	**17**	**29m06.35s**	**55.41s**	**7**	**Leslie**	**54.462s**	**9**	**29m55.77s**	**55.18s**
8	**Jeff Allam (GB)**	**10**	**Vauxhall Sport**	**Vauxhall Cavalier 16V**	**M**	**54.679s**	**18**	**29m07.32s**	**55.29s**	**8**	**Tarquini**	**54.758s**	**14**	**29m58.45s**	**55.23s**
9	**Matt Neal (GB)**	**77**	**Team Dynamics**	**Ford Mondeo Ghia**	**M**	**54.522s**	**16**	**29m12.55s**	**55.48s**	**9**	**Bailey**	**54.371s**	**7**	**30m00.02s**	**55.49s**
10	**Robb Gravett (GB)**	**27**	**Foesport**	**Ford Mondeo Ghia**	**M**	**54.511s**	**15**	**29m28.05s**	**55.67s**	**10**	**Sugden**	**54.589s**	**13**	**30m06.09s**	**55.61s**
11	David Leslie (GB)	20	Honda Team MSD	Honda Accord	Y	54.198s	8	29m38.17s	55.24s	11	Watts	54.805s	16	30m10.14s	55.61s
12	Nigel Smith (GB)	25	Team HMSO	Vauxhall Cavalier 16V	M	55.460s	21	@ 1 lap	56.57s	12	Allam	55.029s	20	30m12.56s	55.42s
13	Richard Kaye (GB)	23	Mint Motorsport	Ford Mondeo Ghia	D	54.957s	20	@ 1 lap	55.91s	13	Neal	54.834s	17	30m13.64s	55.69s
14	Hamish Irvine (GB)	26	SCB Motorsport	Peugeot 405	M	55.937s	22	@ 2 laps	56.71s	14	Gravett	55.000s	19	30m20.14s	55.94s
15	Paul Radisich (NZ)	3	Valvoline Team Mondeo	Ford Mondeo Ghia	M	53.958s	3	29 laps-accident	55.09s	15	R.Kaye	54.851s	18	30m21.52s	55.81s
16	Will Hoy (GB)	22	Williams Renault Dealer Racing	Renault Laguna	M	54.395s	11	29 laps-accident	55.39s	16	Warwick	54.794s	15	30m23.39s	55.74s
17	Gabriele Tarquini (I)	1	Alfa Romeo Old Spice Racing	Alfa Romeo 155TS	M	54.509s	14	25 laps-wheel	55.25s	17	Irvine	56.488s	23	@ 1 lap	56.73s
18	Alain Menu (CH)	2	Williams Renault Dealer Racing	Renault Laguna	M	53.949s	2	13 laps-gearbox	54.74s	18	Smith	55.933s	22	@ 4 laps	55.82s
19	James Kaye (GB)	21	Honda Team MSD	Honda Accord	Y	54.227s	9	6 laps-acc dam.	55.29s	19	Radisich	54.208s	4	30 laps-puncture	54.74s
20	Simon Harrison (GB)	18	Total Team Peugeot	Peugeot 405	M	54.479s	13	2 laps-accident	56.48s	20	Hoy	54.557s	11	18 laps-gearbox	54.90s
21	Derek Warwick (GB)	55	Alfa Romeo Old Spice Racing	Alfa Romeo 155TS	M	54.693s	19	2 laps-accident	56.67s	21	Harrison	55.250s	21	9 laps-accident	55.72s
22	Patrick Watts (GB)	8	Total Team Peugeot	Peugeot 405	M	58.743s	23	0 laps-gearbox		22	Cecotto	54.569s	12	6 laps-accident	55.23s
23	David Brabham (AUS)	17	BMW Team Motorsport	BMW 318iS	M	54.298s	10	DNS-personal		23	Burt	54.303s	5	4 laps-accident	55.16s

Fastest lap: Rydell 54.59s, 85.72 mph/137.96 km/h

Fastest lap: Harvey 54.65s, 85.63 mph/137.81 km/h

Championship positions: **1** Cleland 246; **2** Rydell 212; **3** Menu 204; **4** Harvey 137; **5** Radisich 128; **6** Thompson 124; **7** Burt 78; **8** Hoy 69; **9** Bailey 68; **10** Brabham 46 etc.

Total Cup: **1** Neal 264; **2** R.Kaye 220; **3** Smith 212; **4** Irvine 144; **5** Gravett 86; **6** Cox 70

AUTO TRADER RAC BRITISH TOURING CAR CHAMPIONSHIP • ROUNDS 18 & 19

Brands Hatch Indy, 13 August, 2 x 30 laps, 36.92 miles/59.40 km

RACE 1										RACE 2					
Pos.	Name (Nat.)	No.	Entrant	Car	Tyres	Q Time	Q Pos.	Time/Status	Fastest lap	Pos.	Name	Q Time	Q Pos.	Time/Status	Fastest lap
1	**Will Hoy (GB)**	**22**	**Williams Renault Dealer Racing**	**Renault Laguna**	**M**	**46.793s**	**3**	**23m51.57s** 90.80 mph/ 146.13 km/h	**47.04s**	**1**	**Cleland**	**46.680s**	**2**	**23m46.09s** 91.15mph/ 146.69km/h	**45.82s**
2	**Rickard Rydell (S)**	**15**	**Volvo 850 Racing**	**Volvo 850 20v**	**D**	**46.643s**	**1**	**23m52.03s**	**46.90s**	**2**	**Hoy**	**46.722s**	**3**	**23m53.93s**	**47.09s**
3	**John Cleland (GB)**	**4**	**Vauxhall Sport**	**Vauxhall Cavalier 16V**	**M**	**46.723s**	**2**	**23m52.27s**	**46.94s**	**3**	**Rydell**	**46.646s**	**1**	**23m55.72s**	**47.06s**
4	**Alain Menu (CH)**	**2**	**Williams Renault Dealer Racing**	**Renault Laguna**	**M**	**46.915s**	**7**	**23m52.75s**	**46.94s**	**4**	**Tarquini**	**47.018s**	**9**	**23m56.11s**	**47.23s**
5	**Johnny Cecotto (YV)**	**16**	**BMW Team Motorsport**	**BMW 318iS**	**M**	**46.844s**	**5**	**23m53.18s**	**46.91s**	**5**	**Briggs**	**47.067s**	**10**	**23m56.45s**	**47.09s**
6	**Mike Briggs (ZA)**	**24**	**Vauxhall Sport**	**Vauxhall Cavalier 16V**	**M**	**46.920s**	**9**	**24m01.27s**	**47.28s**	**6**	**Watts**	**46.979s**	**7**	**24m05.05s**	**47.58s**
7	**Tim Harvey (GB)**	**9**	**Volvo 850 Racing**	**Volvo 850 20v**	**D**	**46.868s**	**6**	**24m04.82s**	**47.52s**	**7**	**Harvey**	**47.076s**	**11**	**24m06.73s**	**47.29s**
8	**Derek Warwick (GB)**	**55**	**Alfa Romeo Old Spice Racing**	**Alfa Romeo 155TS**	**M**	**46.918s**	**8**	**24m09.08s**	**47.44s**	**8**	**J.Kaye**	**47.077s**	**12**	**24m10.72s**	**47.35s**
9	**Julian Bailey (GB)**	**11**	**Team Toyota GB**	**Toyota Carina E**	**M**	**47.051s**	**12**	**24m09.28s**	**47.06s**	**9**	**Sugden**	**47.312s**	**18**	**24m10.98s**	**47.42s**
10	**James Kaye (GB)**	**21**	**Honda Team MSD**	**Honda Accord**	**Y**	**47.009s**	**10**	**24m12.11s**	**47.19s**	**10**	**Leslie**	**47.106s**	**14**	**22m18.04s**	**47.31s**
11	Patrick Watts (GB)	8	Total Team Peugeot	Peugeot 405	M	47.122s	13	24m14.68s	47.54s	11	Burt	47.150s	15	24m20.08s	47.48s
12	Tim Sugden (GB)	12	Team Toyota GB	Toyota Carina E	M	47.391s	18	24m14.94s	47.75s	12	Neal	47.242s	16	24m20.49s	47.67s
13	Kelvin Burt (GB)	33	Valvoline Team Mondeo	Ford Mondeo Ghia	M	47.191s	14	24m21.67s	47.68s	13	Gravett	47.469s	19	24m20.77s	47.84s
14	Paul Radisich (NZ)	3	Valvoline Team Mondeo	Ford Mondeo Ghia	M	46.836s	4	24m22.78s	47.35s	14	Warwick	47.484s	20	24m22.44s	47.60s
15	Matt Neal (GB)	77	Team Dynamics	Ford Mondeo Ghia	D	47.304s	17	24m23.06s	47.81s	15	Cox	47.258s	23	24m30.84s	47.95s
16	Nigel Smith (GB)	25	Team HMSO	Vauxhall Cavalier 16V	M	47.587s	20	24m23.50s	47.82s	16	Smith	47.832s	22	24m31.10s	47.76s
17	David Leslie (GB)	20	Honda Team MSD	Honda Accord	Y	47.042s	11	24m28.06s	47.31s	17	R.Kaye	47.597s	21	@ 1 lap	48.51s
18	Richard Kaye (GB)	23	Mint Motorsport	Ford Mondeo Ghia	D	47.858s	21	24m36.11s	47.87s	18	Menu	46.997s	8	@ 12 laps	47.35s
19	Robb Gravett (GB)	27	Foesport	Ford Mondeo Ghia	M	47.523s	19	24m37.39s	47.92s	19	Radisich	46.802s	4	19 laps-accident	47.44s
20	Hamish Irvine (GB)	26	SCB Motorsport	Peugeot 405	M	49.221s	23	@ 2 laps	49.27s	20	Bailey	47.094s	13	13 laps accident	47.27s
21	Charlie Cox (AUS)	19	Thames Ford Dealer Team	Ford Mondeo Ghia	D	48.183s	22	@ 2 laps	48.03s	21	Brabham	46.973s	6	5 laps-oil line	47.49s
22	Gabriele Tarquini (I)	1	Alfa Romeo Old Spice Racing	Alfa Romeo 155TS	M	1m12.410s	24	27 laps-cooling	47.54s	22	Cecotto	46.895s	5	1 lap-accident	56.34s
23	David Brabham (GB)	17	BMW Team Motorsport	BMW 318iS	M	47.267s	16	26 laps-puncture	47.64s	23	Irvine	49.348s	24	0 laps-accident	
24	Simon Harrison (GB)	18	Total Team Peugeot	Peugeot 405	M	47.192s	15	12 laps-engine	47.75s	24	Harrison	47.293s	17	DNS	

Fastest lap: Rydell 46.90s, 92.38 mph/148.68 km/h

Fastest lap: Cleland 46.82s, 148.93 mph/92.54 km/h

Championship positions: **1** Cleland 282; **2** Rydell 242; **3** Menu 214; **4** Harvey 145; **5** Radisich 128; **6** Thompson 124; **7** Hoy 111; **8** Burt 78; **9** Bailey 70; **10** Brabham 46 etc.

Total Cup: **1** Neal 312; **2=** R.Kaye, Smith 240; **4** Irvine 152; **5** Gravett 114; **6** Cox 88

AUTO TRADER RAC

BTCC ROUND-BY

AUTO TRADER RAC BRITISH TOURING CAR CHAMPIONSHIP • ROUNDS 20 & 21

Snetterton, 28 August, 18 & 20 laps, 35.14 & 39.04 miles/56.54 & 62.81 km

RACE 1

Pos.	Name (Nat.)	No.	Entrant	Car	Tyres	Q Time	Q Pos.	Time/Status	Fastest lap
1	**Kelvin Burt (GB)**	33	**Valvoline Team Mondeo**	**Ford Mondeo Ghia**	M	**1m12.920s**	9	**23m57.61s** 87.98 mph/ 141.59 km/h	**1m15.98s**
2	**Patrick Watts (GB)**	8	**Total Team Peugeot**	**Peugeot 405**	M	**1m13.227s**	18	**24m18.29s**	**1m16.16s**
3	**Robb Gravett (GB)**	27	**Foesport**	**Ford Mondeo Ghia**	M	**1m12.835s**	8	**24m19.87s**	**1m15.77s**
4	**Gabriele Tarquini (I)**	1	**Alfa Romeo Old Spice Racing**	**Alfa Romeo 155TS**	M	**1m13.844s**	20	**24m22.50s**	**1m16.92s**
5	**Richard Kaye (GB)**	23	**Mint Motorsport**	**Ford Mondeo Ghia**	D	**1m13.457s**	19	**24m22.63s**	**1m15.23s**
6	**Tim Sugden (GB)**	12	**Team Toyota GB**	**Toyota Carina E**	M	**1m13.051s**	14	**24m23.78s**	**1m16.73s**
7	**Mike Briggs (ZA)**	24	**Vauxhall Sport**	**Vauxhall Cavalier 16V**	M	**1m13.209s**	17	**24m25.89s**	**1m17.14s**
8	**David Leslie (GB)**	20	**Honda Team MSD**	**Honda Accord**	Y	**1m13.083s**	15	**24m27.78s**	**1m16.00s**
9	**Paul Radisich (NZ)**	3	**Valvoline Team Mondeo**	**Ford Mondeo Ghia**	M	**1m12.827s**	7	**24m35.20s**	**1m20.34s**
10	**Johnny Cecotto (YV)**	16	**BMW Team Motorsport**	**BMW 318iS**	M	**1m12.938s**	10	**24m46.61s**	**1m14.95s**
11	Julian Bailey (GB)	11	Team Toyota GB	Toyota Carina E	M	1m12.799s	5	24m46.88s	1m20.56s
12	Will Hoy (GB)	22	Williams Renault Dealer Racing	Renault Laguna	M	1m13.016s	12	24m48.09s	1m19.88s
13	John Cleland (GB)	4	Vauxhall Sport	Vauxhall Cavalier 16V	M	1m12.507s	3	24m53.84s	1m21.60s
14	Rickard Rydell (S)	15	Volvo 850 Racing	Volvo 850 20v	D	1m12.369s	1	24m54.04s	1m21.31s
15	Matt Neal (GB)	77	Team Dynamics	Ford Mondeo Ghia	D	1m12.951s	11	25m00.10s	1m20.68s
16	David Brabham (AUS)	17	BMW Team Motorsport	BMW 318iS	M	1m13.187s	16	@ 1 lap	1m15.04s
17	Nigel Smith (GB)	25	Team HMSO	Vauxhall Cavalier 16V	M	1m14.859s	23	@ 1 lap	1m22.06s
18	James Kaye (GB)	21	Honda Team MSD	Honda Accord	Y	1m12.800s	6	@ 1 lap	1m21.14s
19	Simon Harrison (GB)	18	Total Team Peugeot	Peugeot 405	M	1m13.032s	13	@ 1 lap	1m15.10s
20	Charlie Cox (AUS)	19	Thames Ford Dealer Team	Ford Mondeo Ghia	D	1m13.947s	21	13 laps-radiator	1m27.21s
21	Hamish Irvine (GB)	26	SCB Motorsport	Peugeot 405	M	1m15.566s	24	11 laps-accident	1m20.68s
22	Alain Menu (CH)	2	Williams Renault Dealer Racing	Renault Laguna	M	1m12.386s	2	2 laps-accident	1m23.18s
23	Tim Harvey (GB)	9	Volvo 850 Racing	Volvo 850 20v	D	1m12.559s	4	2 laps-accident	1m23.81s
24	Derek Warwick (GB)	55	Alfa Romeo Old Spice Racing	Alfa Romeo 155TS	M	1m14.303s	22	1 lap-engine	1m37.96s

Fastest lap: Cecotto 1m14.95s, 93.75 mph/150.88 km/h

RACE 2

Pos.	Name	Q Time	Q Pos.	Time/Status	Fastest lap
1	**Hoy**	**1m12.695s**	4	**24m42.79s** 94.78mph/ 152.53 km/h	**1m13.16s**
2	**Harvey**	**1m12.686s**	3	**24m43.29s**	**1m13.21s**
3	**Cleland**	**1m12.821s**	6	**24m44.36s**	**1m13.20s**
4	**Neal**	**1m12.736s**	5	**24m53.82s**	**1m13.77s**
5	**Briggs**	**1m12.916s**	8	**25m05.79s**	**1m14.02s**
6	**Bailey**	**1m13.035s**	12	**25m05.99s**	**1m13.97s**
7	**Sugden**	**1m12.857s**	7	**25m06.60s**	**1m13.93s**
8	**Leslie**	**1m31.154s**	14	**25m09.86s**	**1m13.90s**
9	**J.Kaye**	**1m13.030s**	11	**25m10.24s**	**1m13.75s**
10	**Menu**	**1m12.603s**	2	**25m11.36s**	**1m13.74s**
11	Harrison	1m12.970s	10	25m13.98s	1m14.18s
12	Burt	1m13.265s	16	25m15.83s	1m14.20s
13	Warwick	1m14.342s	22	25m16.86s	1m14.52s
14	R.Kaye	1m13.779s	19	25m17.94s	1m14.48s
15	Smith	1m14.473s	23	25m31.11s	1m15.13s
16	Cox	1m14.135s	20	25m43.28s	1m15.33s
17	Brabham	1m13.113s	13	@ 1 lap	1m14.65s
18	Cecotto	1m13.180s	15	18 laps-accident	1m13.57s
19	Rydell	1m12.137s	1	14 laps-accident	1m13.13s
20	Radisich	1m12.931s	9	14 laps-tyres	1m14.18s
21	Tarquini	1m13.676s	18	2 laps-tracking	1m15.99s
22	Watts	1m14.298s	21	0 laps-fuel rail	
23	Gravett	1m13.437s	17	0 laps-accident	
24	Irvine	1m15.049s	24	DNS	

Fastest lap: Rydell 1m13.13s, 96.09 mph/154.64 km/h

Championship positions: 1 Cleland 294; **2** Rydell 242; **3** Menu 215; **4** Harvey 163; **5** Hoy 135; **6** Radisich 130; **7** Thompson 124; **8** Burt 102; **9** Bailey 76; **10** Watts 58 etc.

Total Cup: **1** Neal 348; **2** R.Kaye 276; **3** Smith 262; **4** Irvine 152; **5** Gravett 138; **6** Cox 98

AUTO TRADER RAC BRITISH TOURING CAR CHAMPIONSHIP • ROUNDS 22 & 23

Oulton Park Fosters, 10 September, 22 & 24 laps, 36.30 & 39.60 miles/57.92 & 63.72 km

RACE 1

Pos.	Name (Nat.)	No.	Entrant	Car	Tyres	Q Time	Q Pos.	Time/Status	Fastest lap
1	**Alain Menu (CH)**	2	**Williams Renault Dealer Racing**	**Renault Laguna**	M	**1m100.915s**	1	**22m48.71s** 95.70 mph/ 154.02 km/h	**1m01.44s**
2	**Will Hoy (GB)**	22	**Williams Renault Dealer Racing**	**Renault Laguna**	M	**1m01.206s**	4	**22m54.21s**	**1m01.80s**
3	**John Cleland (GB)**	4	**Vauxhall Sport**	**Vauxhall Cavalier 16V**	M	**1m00.919s**	2	**22m54.92s**	**1m01.73s**
4	**Gabriele Tarquini (I)**	1	**Alfa Romeo Old Spice Racing**	**Alfa Romeo 155TS**	M	**1m01.535s**	8	**22m59.81s**	**1m01.71s**
5	**Rickard Rydell (S)**	15	**Volvo 850 Racing**	**Volvo 850 20v**	D	**1m01.288s**	6	**23m00.37s**	**1m01.98s**
6	**David Leslie (GB)**	20	**Honda Team MSD**	**Honda Accord**	Y	**1m01.249s**	5	**23m02.06s**	**1m01.92s**
7	**James Kaye (GB)**	21	**Honda Team MSD**	**Honda Accord**	Y	**1m01.520s**	7	**23m06.79s**	**1m02.17s**
8	**Derek Warwick (GB)**	55	**Alfa Romeo Old Spice Racing**	**Alfa Romeo 155TS**	M	**1m01.784s**	15	**23m13.35s**	**1m02.12s**
9	**Simon Harrison (GB)**	18	**Total Team Peugeot**	**Peugeot 405**	M	**1m01.688s**	11	**23m14.37s**	**1m02.08s**
10	**Kelvin Burt (GB)**	33	**Valvoline Team Mondeo**	**Ford Mondeo Ghia**	M	**1m01.945s**	16	**23m16.92s**	**1m02.32s**
11	David Brabham (AUS)	17	BMW Team Motorsport	BMW 318iS	M	1m02.159s	19	23m17.19s	1m02.28s
12	Mike Briggs (ZA)	24	Vauxhall Sport	Vauxhall Cavalier 16V	M	1m01.721s	13	23m17.51s	1m02.33s
13	Matt Neal (GB)	77	Team Dynamics	Ford Mondeo Ghia	D	1m02.081s	18	23m22.03s	1m02.18s
14	Nigel Smith (GB)	25	Team HMSO	Vauxhall Cavalier 16V	M	1m02.678s	23	23m26.81s	1m02.63s
15	Richard Kaye (GB)	23	Mint Motorsport	Ford Mondeo Ghia	D	1m02.308s	20	23m27.60s	1m02.37s
16	Robb Gravett (GB)	27	Foesport	Ford Mondeo Ghia	M	1m02.606s	22	23m35.32s	1m02.80s
17	Hamish Irvine (GB)	26	SCB Motorsport	Peugeot 405	M	1m04.463s	24	@ 1 lap	1m04.84s
18	Tim Harvey (GB)	9	Volvo 850 Racing	Volvo 850 20v	D	1m01.603s	9	15 laps-engine	1m01.90s
19	Patrick Watts (GB)	8	Total Team Peugeot	Peugeot 405	M	1m01.730s	14	13 laps-engine	1m02.18s
20	Julian Bailey (GB)	11	Team Toyota GB	Toyota Carina E	M	1m01.170s	3	13 laps-steering	1m01.88s
21	Johnny Cecotto (YV)	16	BMW Team Motorsport	BMW 318iS	M	1m01.645s	10	12 laps-damage	1m02.36s
22	Charlie Cox (AUS)	19	Thames Ford Dealer Team	Ford Mondeo Ghia	D	1m02.556s	21	6 laps-accident	1m03.39s
23	Paul Radisich (NZ)	3	Valvoline Team Mondeo	Ford Mondeo Ghia	M	1m01.699s	12	3 laps-fire	1m04.88s
24	Tim Sugden (GB)	12	Team Toyota GB	Toyota Carina E	M	1m01.075s	17	0 laps-accident	

Fastest lap: Menu 1m01.44s, 96.91 mph/155.96 km/h

RACE 2

Pos.	Name	Q Time	Q Pos.	Time/Status	Fastest lap
1	**Menu**	**1m00.344s**	1	**26m38.58s** 89.39mph/ 143.86km/h	**1m01.30s**
2	**Cleland**	**1m00.455s**	2	**26m44.25s**	**1m01.37s**
3	**Leslie**	**1m00.506s**	3	**26m44.45s**	**1m01.57s**
4	**Bailey**	**1m00.680s**	5	**26m45.29s**	**1m01.77s**
5	**Harvey**	**1m00.669s**	4	**26m51.23s**	**1m01.79s**
6	**Cecotto**	**1m00.805s**	8	**26m52.54s**	**1m01.93s**
7	**Burt**	**1m00.925s**	9	**26m53.54s**	**1m01.88s**
8	**Briggs**	**1m01.039s**	12	**25m55.65s**	**1m01.88s**
9	**J.Kaye**	**1m00.773s**	7	**26m57.59s**	**1m02.04s**
10	**Rydell**	**1m01.399s**	18	**26m57.94s**	**1m01.99s**
11	Neal	1m01.209s	14	26m59.82s	1m02.16s
12	Radisich	1m01.443s	19	27m01.16s	1m02.21s
13	Tarquini	1m00.992s	11	27m34.42s	1m02.04s
14	Smith	1m01.536s	20	27m38.62s	1m03.01s
15	R.Kaye	DQ	24	27m43.56s	1m03.02s
16	Irvine	1m02.951s	23	@ 1 lap	1m03.66s
17	Brabham	1m01.315s	17	23 laps-suspen.	1m01.99s
18	Harrison	1m01.081s	13	21 laps-engine	1m02.08s
19	Warwick	1m01.235s	15	11 laps-accident	1m02.07s
20	Watts	1m00.958s	10	2 laps-accident	1m11.72s
21	Hoy	1m00.754s	6	1 lap-accident	
22	Sugden	1m01.263s	16	0 laps-accident	
23	Gravett	1m02.376s	21	DNS	
24	Cox	1m02.488s	22	DNS	

Fastest lap: Menu 1m01.30s, 97.13 mph/156.32 km/h

Championship positions: 1 Cleland 324; **2** Menu 263; **3** Rydell 251; **4** Harvey 171; **5** Hoy 153; **6** Radisich 130; **7** Thompson 124; **8** Burt 107; **9** Bailey 86; **10** Watts 58 etc.

Total Cup: **1** Neal 396; **2** R.Kaye 300; **3** Smith 298; **4** Irvine 170; **5** Gravett 148; **6** Cox 98

ROUND RESULTS

AUTO TRADER RAC BRITISH TOURING CAR CHAMPIONSHIP • ROUNDS 24 & 25

Silverstone National, 24 September, 28 & 29 laps, 47.20 & 48.88 miles/75.95 & 78.65 km

RACE 1

Pos.	Name (Nat.)	No.	Entrant	Car	Tyres	Q Time	Q Pos.	Time/Status	Fastest lap
1	**Alain Menu (CH)**	**2**	**Williams Renault Dealer Racing**	**Renault Laguna**	**M**	**1m00.689s**	**2**	**32m34.72s** 87.69 mph/ 141.13 km/h	**1m01.43s**
2	**Will Hoy (GB)**	**22**	**Williams Renault Dealer Racing**	**Renault Laguna**	**M**	**1m00.781s**	**4**	**32m35.83s**	**1m01.63s**
3	**John Cleland (GB)**	**4**	**Vauxhall Sport**	**Vauxhall Cavalier 16V**	**M**	**1m00.677s**	**1**	**32m40.47s**	**1m01.52s**
4	**Kelvin Burt (GB)**	**33**	**Valvoline Team Mondeo**	**Ford Mondeo Ghia**	**M**	**1m01.051s**	**7**	**32m41.44s**	**1m01.62s**
5	**David Leslie (GB)**	**20**	**Honda Team MSD**	**Honda Accord**	**Y**	**1m00.872s**	**5**	**32m50.11s**	**1m01.96s**
6	**Mike Briggs (ZA)**	**24**	**Vauxhall Sport**	**Vauxhall Cavalier 16V**	**M**	**1m01.088s**	**8**	**32m51.37s**	**1m02.10s**
7	**Rickard Rydell (S)**	**15**	**Volvo 850 Racing**	**Volvo 850 20v**	**D**	**1m01.095s**	**9**	**32m54.44s**	**1m02.20s**
8	**Derek Warwick (GB)**	**55**	**Alfa Romeo Old Spice Racing**	**Alfa Romeo 155TS**	**M**	**1m01.274s**	**11**	**32m56.15s**	**1m02.43s**
9	**David Brabham (AUS)**	**17**	**BMW Team Motorsport**	**BMW 318iS**	**M**	**1m01.371s**	**17**	**32m59.20s**	**1m02.31s**
10	**Tim Harvey (GB)**	**9**	**Volvo 850 Racing**	**Volvo 850 20v**	**D**	**1m01.484s**	**18**	**33m00.77s**	**1m02.45s**
11	Patrick Watts (GB)	8	Total Team Peugeot	Peugeot 405	M	2m51.270s	24	33m02.57s	1m02.31s
12	Richard Kaye (GB)	23	Mint Motorsport	Ford Mondeo Ghia	D	1m02.609s	23	33m23.67s	1m03.24s
13	Tim Sugden (GB)	12	Team Toyota GB	Toyota Carina E	M	1m01.282s	14	33m25.95s	1m02.32s
14	Hamish Irvine (GB)	26	SCB Motorsport	Peugeot 405	M	1m02.491s	21	33m32.73s	1m03.54s
15	Robb Gravett (GB)	27	Foesport	Ford Mondeo Ghia	M	1m01.914s	19	33m33.95s	1m03.13s
16	James Kaye (GB)	21	Honda Team MSD	Honda Accord	Y	1m01.232s	10	@ 11 laps	1m02.27s
17	Matt Neal (GB)	77	Team Dynamics	Ford Mondeo Ghia	D	1m01.295s	15	@ 12 laps	1m02.50s
18	Paul Radisich (NZ)	3	Valvoline Team Mondeo	Ford Mondeo Ghia	M	1m00.718s	3	@ 13 laps	1m02.10s
19	Charlie Cox (AUS)	19	Thames Ford Dealer Team	Ford Mondeo Ghia	D	1m02.492s	22	24 laps-accident	1m03.24s
20	Gabriele Tarquini (I)	1	Alfa Romeo Old Spice Racing	Alfa Romeo 155TS	M	1m01.275s	12	24 laps-accident	1m02.32s
21	Johnny Cecotto (YV)	16	BMW Team Motorsport	BMW 318iS	M	1m01.337s	16	22 laps-tyres	1m02.55s
22	Julian Bailey (GB)	11	Team Toyota GB	Toyota Carina E	M	1m00.968s	6	16 laps-body	1m01.86s
23	Nigel Smith (GB)	25	Team HMSO	Vauxhall Cavalier 16V	M	1m02.031s	20	1 lap-accident	1m15.65s
24	Simon Harrison (GB)	18	Total Team Peugeot	Peugeot 405	M	1m01.280s	13	0 laps-accident	

Fastest lap: Menu 1m01.43s, 96.22 mph/154.86 km/h

RACE 2

Pos.	Name	Q Time	Q Pos.	Time/Status	Fastest lap
1	**Hoy**	**1m00.851s**	**2**	**31m55.43s** 86.41mph/ 139.06 km/h	**1m01.34s**
2	**Menu**	**1m00.713s**	**1**	**31m55.97s**	**1m01.26s**
3	**Cleland**	**1m01.126s**	**6**	**31m58.62s**	**1m01.62s**
4	**Leslie**	**1m00.919s**	**3**	**32m01.23s**	**1m01.71s**
5	**Bailey**	**1m01.275s**	**7**	**32m02.99s**	**1m01.46s**
6	**Sugden**	**1m01.456s**	**10**	**32m13.48s**	**1m01.87s**
7	**Harvey**	**1m01.782s**	**17**	**32m15.02s**	**1m02.13s**
8	**Watts**	**1m01.837s**	**18**	**32m15.64s**	**1m02.47s**
9	**J.Kaye**	**1m01.291s**	**8**	**32m16.28s**	**1m02.04s**
10	**Warwick**	**1m01.877s**	**19**	**32m17.69s**	**1m02.21s**
11	Neal	1m01.450s	9	32m17.83s	1m01.94s
12	Radisich	1m01.069s	4	32m30.11s	1m01.55s
13	R.Kaye	1m02.236s	23	32m30.32s	1m03.32s
14	Cox	1m02.370s	21	32m51.04s	1m02.97s
15	Tarquini	1m01.493s	12	@ 2 laps	1m01.92s
16	Gravett	1m02.581s	22	11 laps-accident	1m03.15s
17	Briggs	1m01.459s	11	10 laps-accident	1m01.86s
18	Cecotto	1m01.563s	13	8 laps-accident	1m02.31s
19	Brabham	1m01.777s	16	3 laps-accident	1m02.39s
20	Irvine	1m03.745s	24	3 laps-engine	1m06.16s
21	Rydell	1m01.570s	14	2 laps-accident	1m02.86s
22	Burt	1m01.092s	5	2 laps-accident	1m19.47s
23	Smith	1m02.267s	20	DNS	
24	Harrison	1m01.758s	15	DNS	

Fastest lap: Menu 1m01.26s, 96.361 mph/155.08 km/h

Championship positions: **1** Cleland 348; **2** Menu 305; **3** Rydell 205; **4** Hoy 195; **5** Harvey 176; **6** Radisich 130; **7** Thompson 124; **8** Burt 117; **9** Bailey 94; **10** Watts 61 etc.

Total Cup: **1** Neal 430; **2** R.Kaye 342; **3** Smith 298; **4** Irvine 188; **5** Gravett 160; **6** Cox 110

AUTO TRADER RAC BRITISH TOURING CAR CHAMPIONSHIP

FINAL POINTS TABLES

DRIVERS' CHAMPIONSHIP

Pos.	Name (Nat.)	No.	Entrant	Car	Points
1	John Cleland (GB)	4	Vauxhall Sport	Vauxhall Cavalier 16V	348
2	Alain Menu (CH)	2	Williams Renault Dealer Racing	Renault Laguna	305
3	Rickard Rydell (S)	15	Volvo 850 Racing	Volvo 850 20v	255
4	Will Hoy (GB)	22	Williams Renault Dealer Racing	Renault Laguna	195
5	Tim Harvey (GB)	9	Volvo 850 Racing	Volvo 850 20v	176
6	Paul Radisich (NZ)	3	Valvoline Team Mondeo	Ford Mondeo Ghia	130
7	James Thompson (GB)	14	Vauxhall Sport	Vauxhall Cavalier 16V	124
8	Kelvin Burt (GB)	33	Valvoline Team Mondeo	Ford Mondeo Ghia	117
9	Julian Bailey (GB)	11	Team Toyota GB	Toyota Carina E	94
10	Patrick Watts (GB)	8	Total Team Peugeot	Peugeot 405	61
11	David Leslie (GB)	20	Honda Team MSD	Honda Accord	61
12	Johnny Cecotto (YV)	16	BMW Team Motorsport	BMW 318iS	49
13	David Brabham (AUS)	17	BMW Team Motorsport	BMW 318iS	48
14	Tim Sugden (GB)	12	Team Toyota GB	Toyota Carina E	48
15	Mike Briggs (ZA)	24	Vauxhall Sport	Vauxhall Cavalier 16V	35
16	Gabriele Tarquini (I)	1	Alfa Romeo Old Spice Racing	Alfa Romeo 155TS	33
17	Giampiero Simoni (I)	5	Alfa Romeo Old Spice Racing	Alfa Romeo 155TS	27
18	James Kaye (GB)	21	Honda Team MSD	Honda Accord	26
19	Derek Warwick (GB)	55	Alfa Romeo Old Spice Racing	Alfa Romeo 155TS	15
20	Robb Gravett (GB)*	27	Foesport	Ford Mondeo Ghia	13
21	Matt Neal (GB)	77	Team Dynamics	Ford Mondeo Ghia	12
22	Simon Harrison (GB)	18	Total Team Peugeot	Peugeot 405	9
23	Charlie Cox (AUS)	19	Thames Ford Dealer Team	Ford Mondeo Ghia	8
24	Richard Kaye (GB)	23	Mint Motorsport	Ford Mondeo Ghia	8
25	Jeff Allam (GB)	10	Vauxhall Sport	Vauxhall Cavalier 16V	3

** Also drove Vauxhall Cavalier 16V no. 30*

TOTAL CUP

Pos.	Name (Nat.)	No.	Entrant	Car	Points
1	Matt Neal (GB)	77	Team Dynamics	Ford Mondeo Ghia	430
2	Richard Kaye (GB)	23	Mint Motorsport	Ford Mondeo Ghia	342
3	Nigel Smith (GB)	25	Team HMSO	Vauxhall Cavalier 16V	298
4	Hamish Irvine (GB)	26	SCB Motorsport	Peugeot 405	188
5	Robb Gravett (GB)*	27	Foesport	Ford Mondeo Ghia	160
6	Charlie Cox (AUS)	19	Thames Ford Dealer Team	Ford Mondeo Ghia	110

MANUFACTURERS' CHAMPIONSHIP

Pos.	Manufacturer	Car	Points
1	Renault UK Ltd	Renault Laguna	419
2	Vauxhall Motors Ltd	Vauxhall Cavalier 16V	414
3	Volvo Car Corporation	Volvo 850 20v	359
4	Ford Motor Company Ltd	Ford Mondeo Ghia	236
5	Toyota (GB) Ltd	Toyota Carina E	172
6	BMW	BMW 318iS	144
7	Honda UK Ltd	Honda Accord	136
8	Alfa Romeo	Alfa Romeo 155TS	132
9	Peugeot Sport	Peugeot 405	127

TEAMS' CHAMPIONSHIP

Pos.	Team	Car	Points
1	Vauxhall Sport	Vauxhall Cavalier 16V	510
2	Williams Renault Dealer Racing	Renault Laguna	500
3	Volvo 850 Racing	Volvo 850 20v	431
4	Valvoline Team Mondeo	Ford Mondeo Ghia	247
5	Team Toyota GB	Toyota Carina E	142
6	BMW Team Motorsport	BMW 318iS	97
7	Honda Team MSD	Honda Accord	87
8	Alfa Romeo Old Spice Racing	Alfa Romeo 155TS	75
9	Total Team Peugeot	Peugeot 405	70
10	Team Dynamics	Ford Mondeo Ghia	12

Honda -the race is on

The Honda Accord may turn heads in the street, but in its first year in the fiercely competitive world of Super Tourer racing, the Accord is already making people sit up and take notice.

HONDA has spent 1995 proving its wares in the white heat of the world's most competitive touring car racing series, the British Touring Car Championship. And it has been an exceptionally successful year, moving from a clean sheet of paper in September 1994 to podium finishes in just one year.

The BTCC and other Super Touring championships run to the same technical rules around the world, are now seen as important arenas in which car manufactures can gain publicity for their products both in front of large crowds and, more importantly, on television.At the same time these championships can imbue a car and range with a sharper image.Honda is well aware of the benefits that can come from motor racing from the excellent results it achieved with its dominant Formula 1 engines. Now Honda is using the great popularity of Super Touring races for similar ends.

Honda UK's Paul Ormond is the man responsible for the BTCC team and he is absolutely clear about the commercial benefits: 'We are racing to get exposure and more recognition for the Accord as well as to promote a European image for Honda", he says. He is also happy that the first year results have exceeded all expectations. For example the third place gained at Oulton Park in September and the final round battle with the Renaults at Silverstone gained excellent TV

ACCORD FROM ROAD TO TRACK...

The Accord range runs from 2-litre saloons, through the five-door Aerodeck to the sporting Coupes. The sleek Coupe might seem the obvious basis for the race car, but the Super Touring rules demand a four–door saloon, so the Honda Accord 2.0i LS Saloon was chosen. And it is an excellent starting point for a Super Touring racer.

The rules give considerable freedom within certain rigid limits, but that does not mean that the quality of the base car is irrelevant to its effectiveness as a racer. The Accord has a number of advantages over most of its rivals. First of all there is the standard body shape - the Accord's is low in drag and the coupe-like rear window also feeds very 'clean' air to the aerodynamic rear wing which was allowed for the first time in 1995. Suspension has to be of the same basic type and configuration as that of the road car and the Accord's sophisticated double wishbone front suspension layout is inherently better than the MacPherson struts used by most others.

The base car's size is also highly relevant. Essentially the longer a car's wheelbase and the wider its track, the more stable it will be in a racing environment, particularly when the car is mercilessly slammed across high kerbs as any BTCC car will be on a regular basis. The Accord's wheelbase is the longest in the current BTCC field and its track is suitably wide. It may seem strange, but the size of the engine bay can also be crucial. This is because the engine may be moved back in the car, but not behind the front bulkhead. There are significant advantages to be gained if you can, as in the Accord and certain other 'new generation' Super Touring cars, move the engine behind the line of the front axle. Indeed Pilbeam's Accord racer has almost all its weight between the two axles and also kept very low to ensure an advantageously low centre of gravity.

The 2-litre engine which powers the car is also highly modified. The main restriction the engine builder (Neil Brown Engineering in this case) has to deal with is a mandatory 8500rpm rev-limiter. To some extent this equalises power-outputs to ensure that a large number of car manufacturers can race competitively in the category, but you do still need a good modern base engine. The Accord unit is based on the 2.2-litre unit used in the Prelude and it's rapidly being developed into one of the very best in the category – engines may be based on those from any model in a manufacturer's range.

DAVID LESLIE

A 41-year-old Scot with a long and very successful racing history, Leslie also has a great reputation as a car developer, which made him the ideal man to lead the Honda driving force in the Accord's first season.

David started racing in karts as a junior almost 30 years ago and before switching to car racing in 1976, he'd notched up five Scottish championship titles. Once into single-seater car racing the wins and the championship titles kept coming until lack of finance slowed his progress when he was racing in Formula 3.

A switch to sportscar racing in 1984 gave David the chance to develop his career as a professional and he drove for both the factory Aston Martin and Jaguar teams.

A couple of one-off BTCC drives in BMWs in 1991 set him on his current successful career path as he became a full-time BTCC driver with the Ecurie Ecosse Vauxhall team in 1992. He's been one of the top contenders in the series ever since.

JAMES KAYE

Determined young Yorkshireman James Kaye began his career in karting but then, rather than following the herd into single-seater car racing, he chose saloons and he's been winning races and titles in tin-tops ever since.

Kaye, now 31, started out in production saloon racing in 1983 and was soon a regular class winner. In 1984 he took the class title in two separate championships and went on to win either class or overall titles each year until 1988, when he was second in the one-make Renault 5 Turbo series.

In 1992 James contested the BTCC as a privateer and won the TOCA Cup award as the top privateer. After a year as a semi-works driver in 1993, he was again the top privateer in1994, winning the Total Cup and earning his chance as a full works driver with Honda for 1995.

Far left: The heart of the matter: the Accord's 300 BHP 2–litre powerplant.
Left: The BTCC drivers are always accessible and always in demand – Honda's David Leslie will sign hundreds of autographs over the course of a race weekend.
Main picture: Many of the established touring car teams were often challenged by the Hondas in their first year. Here both team cars head a marauding bunch of Renaults, Alfas, Vauxhalls and Toyotas

and media coverage throughout Europe and even Japan! Excellent crowds at the circuits throughout the UK have brought further marketing gains.

The 1995 season has been great for Honda in the BTCC. A year ago the company had no involvement in the championship but now they've been dubbed the team making the biggest strides forward. Definitely the dark horse for the 1996 Championship. But how do you go from nothing at all, to a competitive car in just a few months?

The design and build of the Super Touring Accord was entrusted to Motor Sport Developments (MSD), a Milton Keynes-based company with a long history of success with manufacturer programmes in rallying and more recently, racing. MSD, under its managing director David Whitehead, took on a handful of new staff with touring car experience specifically for the new project, but the basic infrastructure of an effective team was already in place. Former BRM F1 designer Mike Pilbeam is a crucial part of the set-up. He's worked on a subcontract basis for MSD since 1986 and it was he who designed the Accord racer.

MSD not only designed and built the cars, it also runs the two Accords which contested the BTCC. It's been an excellent first year. Comparisons are inevitably being made between Honda and Volvo's 850 debut the season before. However, judged by any standards the Honda Accord has been ahead of the Volvo '94 progress throughout the year. Leslie qualified ninth for the first round

Above: David Leslie "hops" the kerb at Donington
Left: James Kaye at work in the "office"
Below: The Accords were also competitive in both the German and Belgian series.
Right: The view of the Accord that awaits the opposition in 1996...

and Kaye joined the points scorers on that first weekend of the season. So good was progress in the early races that the team was in the strange position of being disappointed when 'only' achieving some of the targets set out pre-season. By the end of the year the Accord was able to consistently challenge for top three places in the last three meetings of the year, with Leslie achieving the coveted first year podium position, missed by Volvo in '94, at Oulton Park in September.

In Europe cars were run in both Belgium and Germany, with Armin Hahne and Klaus Niedzwiedz, showing excellent form in Germany and spearheading a superb showing in the biggest event in the Super Touring calendar, the FIA World Cup. Honda finished third in the points table ahead of seven other manufacturers all with far more Super Touring experience.

The highlight of the year for the Belgian car was that highly impressive third place in the Spa 24 Hours. MSD boss Whitehead also points out the Accord's excellent reliability record. In all, the cars started 97 races and finished 78. When you consider that several of the non-finishes were due to accidents, it's a record which any manufacturer would be proud of and to achieve that in the first year of competition is exceptional.

PHOTO BY BOTHWELL PHOTOGRAPHIC

Next year the aim is to start winning races in the UK, Belgium and Germany. A new car will be built, based on the new Accord range which will go on sale in the UK in March 1996. The new racer will essentially be an evolution of the 1995 car and MSD intends to have its first '96-spec racer out testing before Christmas.

With the green light for the project only pressed on 1 September 1994, there was little time to test before the 1995 season, but that will not be a problem this time. Whitehead and his team will have time to attend to all the little details which are so important to racing success. He also promises a car which will be stiffer, carry even more weight low in the chassis, and have better aerodynamics.

There are plenty of people working for rival teams who fear the 1996 Honda Accord. With all the advantages it gains from its road car cousins and the excellent work of MSD enhanced by a year's experience, it will be a very hard car to beat.

Place your bets now.

***AUTO TRADER* RAC**

BRITISH TOURING CAR CHAMPIONSHIP
TEAM-BY-TEAM REVIEW

WILLIAMS RENAULT DEALER RACING

Team Director: Ian Harrison
Team Manager: Dick Goodman
Chief Engineer: John Russell
Race Engineers: Mark Ellis (Menu); Chris Gorne, then Greg Wheeler (Hoy)
Number One Mechanics: Greg Baker (Menu), Toby Brown (Hoy)
Number One Mechanic (T-car): Jerry Cave

One day Ian Harrison – for two seasons the Team Manager of Williams Grand Prix Engineering – was hugging Nigel Mansell after an emotional victory in the 1994 Australian Grand Prix, the next he was setting up a touring car team from scratch.

The first motor racing venture for Williams outside Formula One proved hectic, but ultimately successful. Considering that Alain Menu's race car did not run until the day before the opening round at Donington Park, his seven and the team's ten wins were remarkable achievements . . . achievements that were rewarded by the manufacturers' championship.

Williams had stepped into the shoes of GB Motorsport, which ran the Renault 19 16V in 1993 and Laguna in '94, and thus it was able to use the latter car as a template for its first BTCC challenger. As is usually the case with such projects, however, the build process took much longer than had been anticipated; from hopes of 'changing just 20 per cent' of last year's car, Williams ended up 'fiddling with about 80 per cent of it'. Even then, its cars (four in total) ran with items it considered to be fundamentally wrong, but which it had no time to change. Harrison admitted that, with time, the cars could have run with a greater comfort zone, and he reckoned that this was partly to blame for a number of failures.

The basis for the '95 Laguna was still a sound one, however, and it proved to be on the pace from the start – in Menu's hands, at least. Hoy was bedevilled by bad luck; while the Genevois was opening his '95 victory account at Thruxton, Will was losing his front row spot for the second race at the Hampshire track because of a leaking power steering pump. It wasn't until his meeting of minds with new race engineer Greg Wheeler, a South African with a background in rallying, that he turned his season around.

Menu, in contrast, was a title threat from the off. At the start of the season the Laguna continued to display its fast-corner oversteer characteristic, of which the Swiss is a master. The team had targeted the front suspension in an effort to reduce the slow-speed understeer that had been its 1994 bugbear, and the 'articulated beam' rear end remained virtually untouched this season. It will be outlawed by a change in the regulations for '96, but the team was planning to replace it in any case.

The chassis was improved as the season progressed, but it was not until the last two rounds of the year that the Laguna was comprehensively the best car in the field, scoring three 1-2s in four starts.

This coincided with the arrival of the latest-spec engine from Sodemo. Power has always been a Laguna strong-point, and the other teams noted with awe the amount of rear wing it was running. Initially, however, Menu stated that this item had cost the blue-and-yellow machine its straightline edge. But this was restored by the season's end, so that Menu and Hoy could stretch away from the rest with some ease.

The team itself was learning all the time, building up a database, and Knockhill was its lowest point: both cars retired from the first race, and then Hoy suffered the same gearbox problem that had cost his teammate a victory earlier in the day.

It made mistakes, too: it gambled on the wrong tyres at the first Brands Hatch meeting; a misted-up windscreen cost Menu a strong finish in the British GP support race; it made too conservative a tyre choice for the first Snetterton race. At the end of the year, however, it looked incredibly strong.

Part of the reason for this was a set-up Hoy used at Brands Hatch to score his first win. In desperation he had ditched his race car for the 'spare', and immediately finished second in the British GP support race. After more problems at Knockhill, he then dumped his 'helper' springs at the Kent circuit – this was a set-up Menu and his engineer, Mark Ellis, had tested but not yet raced. It transformed Will's performance. Alain followed his lead and, although the gap to John Cleland was too great, he overhauled Rydell to repeat his championship second place of last year. Hoy meanwhile, his confidence sky-high, scored three wins in the second part of the season.

It is clear that a big budget was involved here, while the arrival of Williams was likened to the sledgehammer/walnut scenario. Of course money is a factor, but this was a season where it could have been so easily channelled in the wrong direction. This was a year of man-management, of creating an *ésprit de corps*, and the efforts of Harrison and his right-hand man, Dick Goodman (a long-time Prodrive employee) deserve to be widely recognised. The team's name is undoubtedly a motorsport rallying call, but this success was the result of sheer hard work. Only the adrenalin provided by success kept its personnel going towards the end of an incredible year.

Williams starts with a clean sheet of paper for next season. There will be no compromises: seven full-time engineers, three draughtsmen and the facilities made available to it by its Formula One cousin will undoubtedly ensure its continued status as the BTCC team to beat.

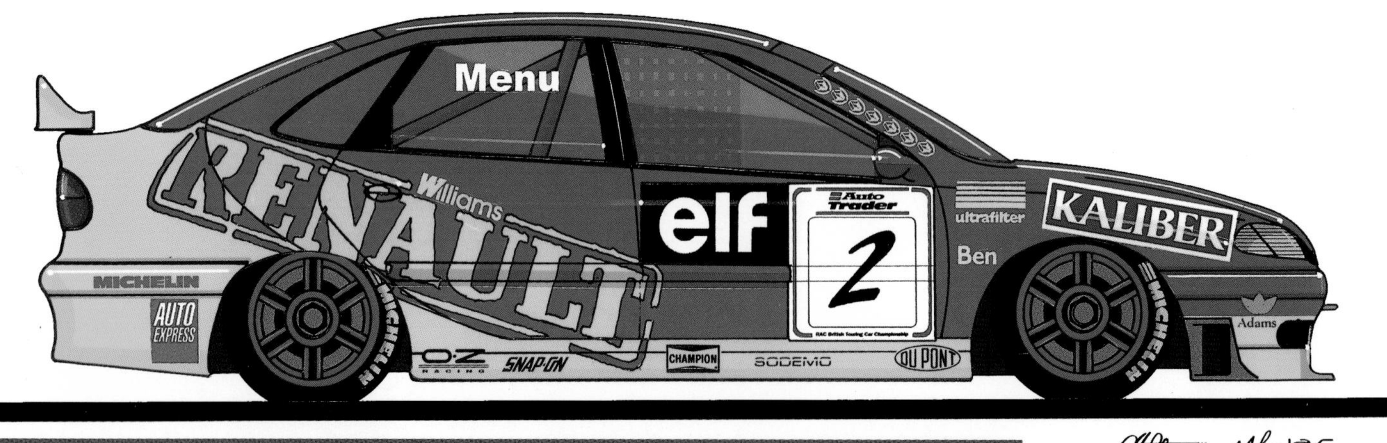

RENAULT LAGUNA 2.0RT

Type: Four-door saloon

ENGINE **Type:** Water-cooled, in-line, four-cylinder, DOHC, 16-valve (iron block/alloy head) **Mounting:** Transverse **Capacity:** 1998 cc **Management system:** Magneti Marelli **Spark plugs:** Champion **Oil:** Elf

BODY AND CHASSIS **Dimensions: Height:** 1433 mm **Length:** 4508 mm **Width:** 1752 mm **Wheelbase:** 2670 mm **Track:** 1525 mm (front)/1490 mm (rear) **Kerb weight:** 975 kg **Fuel capacity:** 45 litres

TRANSMISSION Front-wheel drive **Gearbox:** Hewland, six-speed sequential **Clutch:** AP Racing, 5.5 in. twin-plate carbon **Differential:** Plate-type or viscous coupling

SUSPENSION **Front:** MacPherson strut **Rear:** Trailing arm, torsion bars **Shock absorbers:** Penske **Springs:** Eibach Driver-adjustable front and rear anti-roll bars

BRAKES AP Racing **Front:** Twin four-piston calipers, water-cooled **Rear:** Single two-piston calipers **Discs:** 378 mm ventilated (front)/280 mm drilled (rear)

Steering: Renault, rack-and-pinion, power assistance **Tyres:** Michelin **Wheels:** O.Z. Racing **Instrumentation and data-logging:** Magneti Marelli/Williams **Driver's seat:** Sparco

Drivers: JOHN CLELAND, JAMES THOMPSON, JEFF ALLAM & MIKE BRIGGS

VAUXHALL SPORT

Team Manager: Ray Mallock
Competitions Manager: John Nixey
Operations Manager: Daryl Cozens
Data Engineer: Jakob Andreasen
Race Engineers: Phil Barker (Cleland), Keith Knott (Thompson/Allam/Briggs)
Number One Mechanics: Paul Hayden (Cleland), Paul Robson (Thompson/Allam/Briggs)
Engine Technician: Kevin Kuchta

At its sixth and final attempt the ever-present combination of John Cleland and the Vauxhall Cavalier finally took the spoils.

As Honda, Renault and Volvo ushered in the next generation of Super Touring cars, Ray Mallock's machine epitomised the very best of what is to be replaced. His work has breathed new life into the Cavalier's design: its semi-trailing rear end is potentially not the best, nor is its MacPherson strut front or weight distribution (a lack of engine bay space ensuring that the motor and gearbox would remain firmly over the axle line), but six years of development – begun by Dave Cook in 1990 – has honed this package to perfection. Only when Williams truly clicked in September was the Cavalier knocked off its perch, and even then Cleland was on pole for the penultimate round.

Since 1993, Mallock's car has been marked down as the best-handling front-wheel drive chassis: only a lack of budget with Ecurie Ecosse, and wings in his first year with Vauxhall Sport, had held it back. With wings and Michelins – the works Vauxhall's third tyre manufacturer in as many seasons, following on from Yokohama and Dunlop – the car was expected to be a major player. This was a view firmly held by Cleland himself after the revelation provided by the brief run he had at Brands Hatch in a car destined for the Conrero team in Spain. The Borders man had always been complimentary of the Mallock Cavalier's slow-corner traction, and now it had the fast-corner stability missing in 1994.

The Scot was surprised by the pace of Rickard Rydell's Volvo at Donington Park, and made a pig's ear of the following Brands Hatch meeting. But he kept his cool. He had laid down a lot of ground rules before the start of the season and got his way – he knew, therefore, that he couldn't afford to throw it away with any more rash mistakes.

He was adamant that everything was in place for him to win the championship: Swindon Racing Engines had found another seven bhp and a little more torque from its reversed-head engine (Cleland thought it had the best mid-range torque of all); in spite of tests with viscous couplings and locked diffs, Cleland stuck with the plate-type he has used since the car's racing inception. Here was a man at one with his machine; a man determined not to get lost in the set-up labyrinth that surrounds these vehicles. In this respect, he asked for Phil Barker to be his race engineer rather than Mallock. Naturally, this caused waves, but it was logical: the team's boss was supervising a move to new premises in Wellingborough, as well as overseeing development work on the new Vectra for 1996 – he had plenty on his plate. It was also obvious that Cleland had a better race weekend relationship with Barker.

It worked like a charm. Only at Knockhill, the team's bogey circuit, was the car anything but a front-runner. It was fantastically reliable – not once did Cleland retire because of a mechanical failure – and the Scot hit a rich vein of form mid-season that was to be the crux of his title bid.

The car's unparalleled ability to mollycoddle its tyres was a source of constant amazement to its rivals. So gentle was it, that failing to make a qualifying tyre work was the only thorn in Vauxhall Sport's side; Cleland used them twice with no effect, and even James Thompson's youthful brio was insufficient to make gains on them. This left the door open for Rydell to score a host of pole positions but, even on race rubber, as often as not it was a Vauxhall Cavalier that was alongside him. This was a niggle for Cleland, but he never let it cloud his focus.

Nor did Thompson's horrendous 125 mph accident during testing at Knockhill deflect the team from its chosen course. The York lad was the sensation of the opening stages of the season, becoming the youngest-ever winner in the BTCC when, at the age of 21, he was victorious at Thruxton.

He caused some damage, too, severely bending a car in a testing shunt at Oulton Park – he put it on pole two days later! – and rolling his replacement to destruction in that infamous shunt in Scotland.

His resultant eye injuries meant that Jeff Allam (Knockhill) and the recently crowned South African Touring Car Champion Mike Briggs (Brands Hatch/Snetterton/Oulton Park/Silverstone) were drafted into the second car. Neither man was able to match the qualifying pace of Thompson, but they both raced well enough to ensure that the team prize would back up Cleland's drivers' title.

Any team that beats Williams and TWR, even with an advantage in terms of experience, is clearly very, very good. Only once did Vauxhall Sport let its grip slide, when Thompson lost his provisional pole position for the British GP support race because his car was discovered to be four millimetres too wide. Otherwise, it had the nous and bottle to address the problems it had suffered in '94, and the expertise and nerve to win in the most competitive year of the two-litre formula to date.

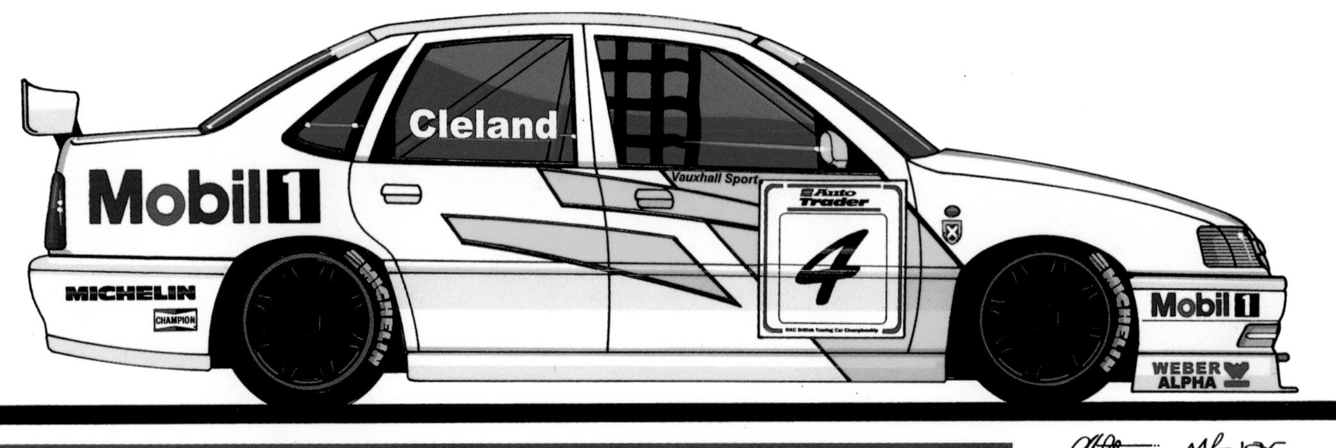

VAUXHALL CAVALIER 16V

Type: Four-door saloon

ENGINE **Type:** Water-cooled, in-line, four-cylinder, DOHC, 16-valve (iron block/reversed alloy head) **Mounting:** Transverse **Capacity:** 1998 cc **Bore and stroke:** 86 mm x 86 mm **Compression ratio:** 12:1 **Management system:** Weber Alpha **Power output:** 295 bhp @ 8400 rpm **Maximum torque:** 260 Nm @ 6250 rpm **Spark plugs:** Champion **Oil:** Mobil

BODY AND CHASSIS **Dimensions: Height:** 1400 mm **Length:** 4430 mm **Width:** 1700 mm **Wheelbase:** 2600 mm **Track:** 1460 mm (front)/1468 mm (rear) **Kerb weight:** 975 kg **Fuel capacity:** 60 litres

TRANSMISSION Front-wheel drive **Gearbox:** Xtrac, six-speed sequential **Clutch:** AP Racing, 5.5 in. triple-plate, carbon **Differential:** Plate-type or viscous coupling

SUSPENSION **Front:** MacPherson strut, lower wishbones **Rear:** Semi-trailing arms **Shock absorbers:** Dynamics **Springs:** Eibach Driver-adjustable front and rear anti-roll bars

BRAKES AP Racing (front)/Brembo (rear) **Front:** Single six-piston calipers, or twin four-piston calipers **Rear:** Single two-piston calipers **Discs:** 385 mm ventilated (front)/295 mm cross-drilled (rear)

Steering: Vauxhall, rack-and-pinion, power assistance **Tyres:** Michelin **Wheels:** Dymag **Instrumentation and data-logging:** PI Research **Driver's seat:** Sparco

Drivers: RICKARD RYDELL & TIM HARVEY

VOLVO 850 RACING

Team Director: Roger Silman
Operations Manager: Ken Page
Chief Engineer: John Gentry
Chief Engine Development Engineer: Charlie Bamber
Race Engineers: Gentry (Rydell), Dave Kelly (Harvey)
Chief Mechanic: Jeff Wilson
Number One Mechanics: Alva Claxton (Rydell), Viv Cowley (Harvey)

In its second year with Volvo, TWR came perilously close to achieving its stated objective a season early. As anticipated, its 850 saloon pushed the Super Touring regulations to their outer limits, as a logical development of the advanced, but flawed, estates it had run in 1994. And, for a brief time, the Dunlop-shod machines looked set to run away with the championship.

However, a mixture of surprising errors, a lack of experience of these cars in wet conditions, a handful of mechanical failures, some poor starts and the gradual tightening of Michelin's championship stranglehold in the latter stages of the season ensured that Rickard Rydell and Volvo would finish third in their respective championships.

This is about what both parties had anticipated: the second phase of this three-year programme was for winning races; it's the third that is supposed to witness the big push for the title. However, the team came too close to achieving the latter this year not to be disappointed with its lacklustre conclusion to the season.

With more winter testing miles behind them than any of their rivals, the Volvos made the early running. Had the first race been anywhere other than Donington Park, it is unlikely that John Cleland would have posed such a threat, while the 850s' April dominance at Brands Hatch, wet or dry, was awesome. But it was here that the first slip occurred, Rydell losing the lead of the first race because of a misted-up windscreen.

Another flaw reared its head at Thruxton, the square-edged 850 proving itself to be a little down on straightline speed. Its five-cylinder engine was not the strongest in the pack, and this allowed Paul Radisich's Ford to beat Rydell in one of the May races at the Silverstone National circuit. But at the more twisty, mid-speed tracks – Oulton Park, Brands Hatch GP and Knockhill – the balance it demonstrated was perhaps the best of the year. It had retained its predecessor's fast-corner prowess and ability to brake later than the rest, while dialling out its hatred of slow corners.

Couple Rydell's uncanny feel for a qualifying lap to an exclusive deal with the highly rated Ohlins shock absorbers, a massive front undertray provided by its long frontal overhang and the 850's centralised weight distribution, and you had the fastest one-lap combination of the year, with a remarkable 13 pole positions to its credit.

It was a different story in the races: bad starts became a feature of Rydell's year, and the Volvo often lacked the straightline speed to be the aggressor in a dice situation and recover the lost advantage. The team played the 'start' factor down, yet organised tests purely for this purpose. By the end of the year the Swede had it cracked – but it was too late.

In contrast, Tim Harvey raced better than he qualified. Having matched Rydell in the bulk of the pre-season tests, he was rarely able to find a balance he was happy with, in spite of swapping to the T-car. If ever a man should be disappointed with fifth place in a championship, it is he. At times, this combo's slumps in qualifying beggared belief. Rydell managed to avoid such pitfalls until the final two races of the season.

A crash caused by brake failure at Brands Hatch in June and another misted windscreen, this time at the British GP support race, cost Rickard dear in terms of points. He was still in with a chance of the title, however, until the weather and yet another brake failure – caused by a loose wheel – conspired against him at Snetterton.

The cracks were starting to show.

At Oulton Park, the team fitted two fifth gears to the Swede's car before second practice. And at Silverstone, the partnership with his race engineer, John Gentry – the car's designer – made its first set-up mistake of the season, a second-session gamble going well awry. That Matt Neal's privateer Ford should be the leading Dunlop runner (ninth) on this occasion was particularly galling . . . clearly, the slump was not purely down to the tyres.

As is regularly the case with TWR, the uncharitable spread a variety of rumours regarding this downturn in speed, but truly the team seemed to have lost its way. For an outfit that had gone to the trouble of creating a saloon from an estate in order to start testing as early as possible – a team with such a proven record – this was extremely unexpected. It *was* indicative of the high level that this saloon car series now operates at, but that problems should repeat themselves is always inexcusable at this said level. The team will be kicking itself.

Meanwhile, the 'uncharitable' were given further ammunition when Volvo 850 Racing was on the receiving end of a record £10,000 fine from TOCA, for a breach of its Sporting Regulations at Snetterton. It was emphasised that this was not a performance-related transgression, but it cast another cloud over this oft-controversial team. In a series where a manufacturer's image is paramount, it must learn that there is more to it than success on the track.

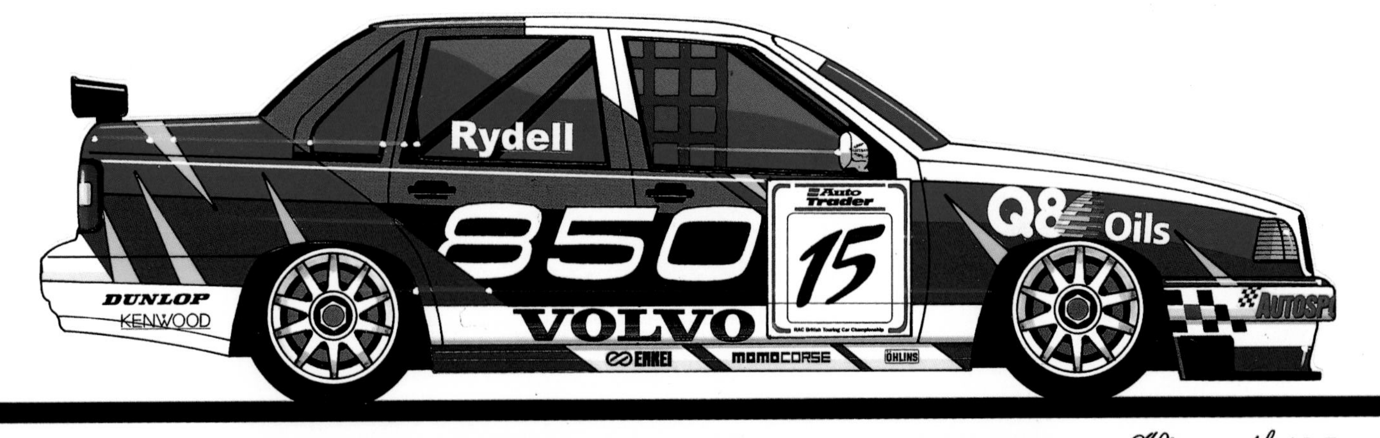

VOLVO 850 20v

Type: Four-door saloon

ENGINE **Type:** Water-cooled, in-line, five-cylinder, DOHC, 20-valve (all-alloy) **Mounting:** Transverse **Capacity:** 1999 cc **Bore and stroke:** 83 mm x 73.9 mm **Management system:** Zytek **Power output:** 280+ bhp @ 8500 rpm **Spark plugs:** Champion **Oil:** Q8

BODY AND CHASSIS **Dimensions: Height:** n/a **Length:** n/a **Width:** n/a **Wheelbase:** n/a **Track:** n/a **Kerb weight:** 975 kg **Fuel capacity:** 40 litres

TRANSMISSION Front-wheel drive **Gearbox:** TWR/Xtrac, six-speed sequential **Clutch:** AP Racing, 5.5 in. triple-plate, carbon **Differential:** Plate-type or viscous coupling

SUSPENSION **Front:** MacPherson strut **Rear:** Volvo Delta link (semi-independent trailing arms) **Shock absorbers:** Ohlins **Springs:** TWR Adjustable front and rear anti-roll bars (only the latter is driver-adjustable)

BRAKES Brembo **Front:** Single six-piston calipers **Rear:** Single two-piston calipers

Steering: Volvo rack-and-pinion, power assistance **Tyres:** Dunlop **Wheels:** ENKEI Sport **Instrumentation and data-logging:** TWR/CIC **Driver's seat:** Momo

VALVOLINE TEAM MONDEO

Team Principal: Andy Rouse
Team Manager: Vic Drake
Designer: Roger King
Workshop Manager: John Dorrans
Race Engineers: Drake (Radisich), Dorrans (Burt)

The simplicity of Andy Rouse's design was in stark contrast to those of Honda, Renault, Vauxhall and Volvo: the Ford's rollcage was far less complex than that of its rivals; its driver had not been pushed back level with the B-post; there was no electrical spaghetti cluttering up the passenger footwell . . .

Yet his past record ensured that those who discounted Rouse did so at their own peril. There can be no doubt now, however, that Ford's disappointing season has increased the belief that the four-times champion has been left behind in the technology race.

When the Mondeo finally appeared, in the second half of 1993, its long, wide platform enabled newcomer, Paul Radisich, to climb all over the kerbs on his way to a string of victories and podium finishes. He's been climbing over them ever since but has just three more BTCC victories – and, admittedly, two World Cups – to show for it.

In comparison to this season's pace-setters, the Ford resembled a pantechnicon. Both Radisich and Kelvin Burt complained of its unwillingness to change direction, while it chewed through its front tyres at an alarming rate. The latter was convinced that it was running way too soft at the start of the year, and both he and Radisich were a little happier when a stiffer approach was adopted for the May Silverstone meeting – the Aucklander scoring a first and second on this very occasion.

But the only factor that kept this car vaguely competitive was the strength of its Cosworth-developed V6. Ironically, this also lay at the crux of the problem: under-bonnet packaging is becoming more and more important in the BTCC, and it would be difficult to site this wider unit lower and further back in order to shift weight off the front axle and push the diff for'ard *à la* Volvo and Honda.

The Binley-based concern chipped away at the problem, mounting the V6 solid in the frame to lower it slightly, and moving some of its ancillaries into the boot. It even went to the extent of building a couple of 'dragsters' – falling into line with the Vauxhall/Volvo/Renault approach by moving its driver lower and further back. Burt won with one of these at Snetterton, but this was due more to an inspired tyre choice than anything else. And after several all-nighters spent altering the cars, one can imagine the mechanics' feelings when Radisich asked them to put his car back to how it was, while Burt switched to the spare!

In the dry, the car was competitive only at the Silverstone National circuit – a series of three drag strips where the V6 could stretch its legs.The weight over the front axle, meanwhile, usually ensured the sort of traction that made it a major player in the wet. It also allowed Radisich (regularly) and Burt (sometimes) to screw a time out of the car on Michelin's qualifiers, while the better chassis were not always able to give them enough grief to make the ploy effective. This ensured that Radisich would often form a mobile chicane before dropping inexorably down the field with terminal understeer.

The New Zealander even ran without power steering, and stuck to the single-caliper arrangement, in an effort to keep the weight down – a major problem for these cars this season – especially at the front.

However, a proposal from Rouse concerning the future use of a four-cylinder engine was apparently rejected by Ford, on the grounds of cost. It had gone through this selection process in '93, when the V6 was deemed to be the only choice open to it . . .

So is this the end for Rouse? No. But it is probably the last time he will engineer, build and run works cars in the BTCC. He could play any of these roles, but this series is no longer the domain of the one-man band.

Clearly, his team did not stand still, developing three new rear ends in an effort to cure the dreaded understeer, while Rouse will point to the fact that he was only given the green light for the programme in January. Plus secret tests of the V6 on his dyno have apparently convinced him that Cosworth has been unable to squeeze any more power out of the engine.

Ford needs an injection of new blood, new ideas, but to hand over the building and running of its cars to two outfits new to touring cars is a big risk. Rouse is a stubborn man, however, and the thought of running somebody else's cars or building them to be then passed over to another team will not appeal. But he and his team must adapt if they are to survive. His workforce is a loyal and able one, but it needs to grow; the fact that Radisich was virtually engineering his own car this season is unacceptable at this level. Rouse himself, meanwhile, has yet to settle into his weekend role now that he has stepped out of the cockpit.

If Ford is to enjoy the sense of purpose that pervaded Vauxhall Sport this season, a careful weaving together of old and new is required. Whether the Blue Oval's internal politics will facilitate this is a moot point. Whatever, to dispense totally with the man who brought it two World Cups would be a huge step to take.

FORD MONDEO GHIA

Type: Four-door saloon

ENGINE **Type:** Water-cooled, 60-degree vee, six-cylinder, 24-valve (all-alloy) **Mounting:** Transverse **Capacity:** 2000 cc **Management system:** Bosch **Power output:** 295 bhp @ 8500 rpm **Spark plugs:** NGK **Oil:** Valvoline

BODY AND CHASSIS **Dimensions: Height:** 1425 mm **Length:** 4481 mm **Width:** 1749 mm **Wheelbase:** 2704 mm **Kerb weight:** 975 kg **Fuel capacity:** 60 litres

TRANSMISSION Front-wheel drive **Gearbox:** Xtrac, six-speed sequential **Clutch:** AP Racing, 5.25 in. twin-plate, carbon **Differential:** Plate-type or viscous coupling

SUSPENSION **Front:** MacPherson strut, two-piece lower wishbone **Rear:** Quadralink (MacPherson strut located by parallel arms/forward link **Shock absorbers:** Proflex **Springs:** Eibach

BRAKES AP Racing **Front:** Single six-piston calipers, or twin water-cooled four-pot calipers **Rear:** Single two-piston calipers **Discs:** 15 in. ventilated (front)/12 in. (rear)

Steering: Ford, rack-and-pinion, optional power assistance **Tyres:** Michelin **Wheels:** Dymag **Instrumentation and data-logging:** Bosch **Driver's seat:** Corbeau

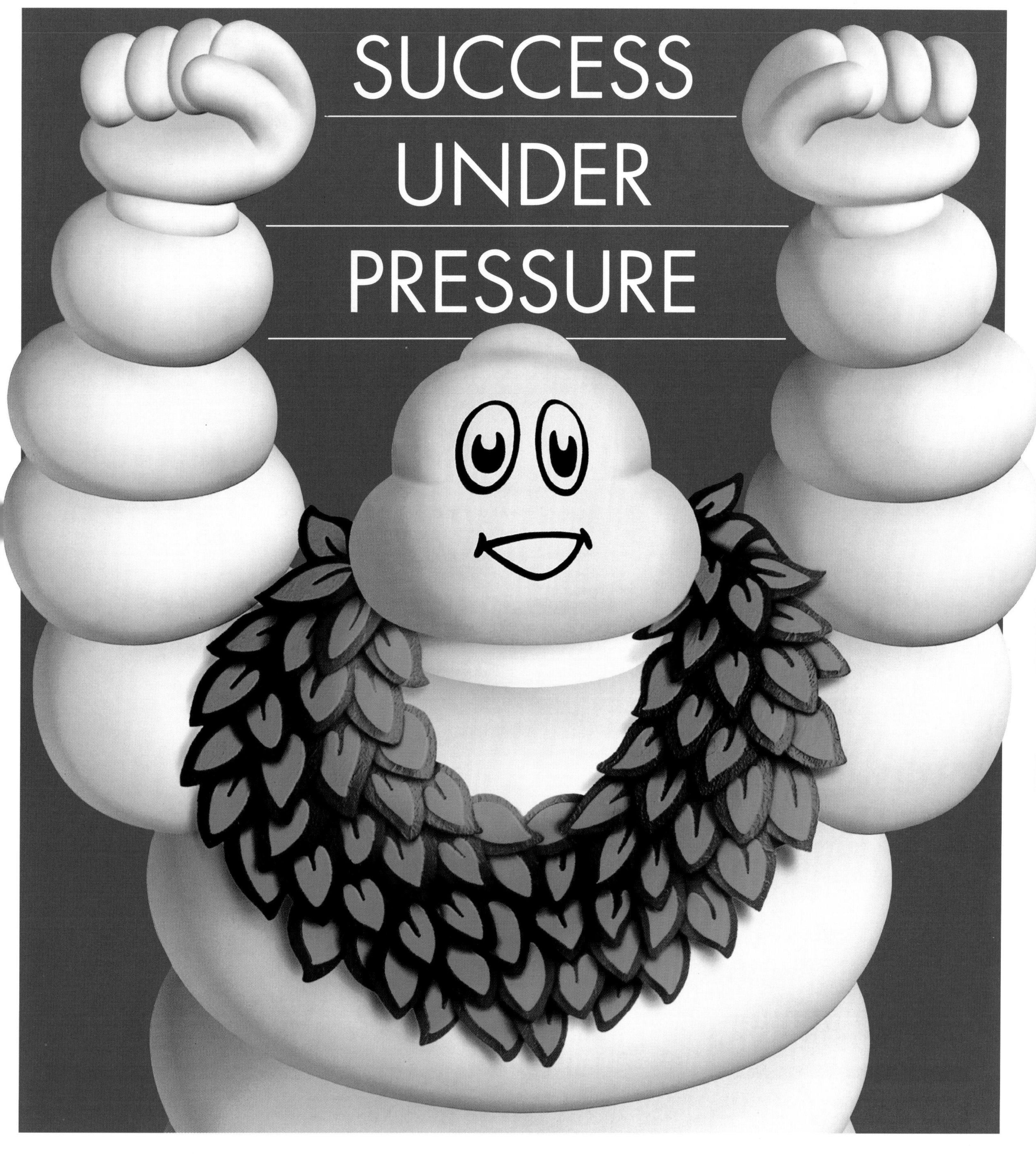

MICHELIN PILOTS FLY IN FIRST AGAIN.

For the second year running, Michelin Pilot tyres have taken top honours in the British Touring Car Championship. John Cleland in the Vauxhall Cavalier won the drivers' championship and Alain Menu and Will Hoy in the Renault Lagunas won the constructors' title on Pilots. Fit Pilots to your car and you'll benefit from the same investment in technology that led to this sporting achievement. For more information about Pilot tyres, contact your local dealer.

MICHELIN
Pilot

TEAM TOYOTA GB

Motorsport Manager: Paul Risbridger
Chief Engineer: Alastair MacQueen
Race Engineers: Stuart Ayling (Bailey), MacQueen (Sugden)
Chief Mechanic: John Woodward
Engine Shop Manager: Ewan Cameron

The Carina E's third BTCC season proved to be another awash with midfield frustration. Only at the culmination of the year did it break from the pack and show its true potential.

The programme set out with high hopes thanks to a bigger (although still modest) budget, Michelin tyres and the input of Team Toyota Europe. The resources of this Cologne-based company – better known for rallying success with the four-wheel drive Celica – were used to build two brand new left-hand Carinas for the start of the season, plus a further example which TTE intended to run in a concurrent test programme.

The idea was good, but it proved a failure. While there remained the opportunity for four-wheel drive, turbocharged machinery to be rallied at the highest level, this would clearly be TTE's priority. Touring cars were little more than a safety net while the FIA discussed the future of rallying – the gist of which had been that it would be inextricably linked with two-wheel drive kit-cars. But when 'total traction' was given its reprieve, the touring car project was put on TTE's back-burner.

Julian Bailey conducted a number of tests with TTE, while François Chatriot – a French rally star with little experience of a front-wheel drive touring car – attended some of the official TOCA tests. But little came of it; TTE lacked knowledge of the category and, without the spur of a racing deadline every fortnight, was unable to keep abreast of the fast pace of BTCC development.

Its Carina seemed blighted with the same problems its TOM'S predecessor had: a very small window of rear tyre temperature in which to work, a crippling power loss in the higher ambient temperatures, an aversion to kerbs and a lack of slow-speed traction.

Some of this was improved by a new suspension system introduced at Brands Hatch in June. It was far from being the ultimate solution, however. Bailey and Tim Sugden had both raced well, but the high-spots to date had been an inherited fourth place by the latter in a high-attrition Thruxton race, and a similar placing for Bailey at Oulton Park. It was only when TOM'S GB introduced its right-hand drive car that matters improved – greatly.

It seemed odd that a team with two years' experience of the BTCC should not be allowed to build the car in the first place. Admittedly, its previous efforts had been no great shakes, but it would appear that, eventually, it had the right ideas in place for '95 – if not the time, the budget or the green light from Toyota. More internal politics.

The pressures of the season ensured that the build time of this car was slow, and it was given its belated debut by Sugden at Snetterton in August, where it showed much promise. At last, we had a Toyota that appeared to be on the cutting edge of Super Touring: its driver pushed back and closer to the centreline, a much lower ride-height (this required the engine to be raised) and new motor from TOM'S with a Kevlar air intake in place of the easily over-heated aluminium affair. The upshot of all this was that it was comfortably quicker than its TTE cousin in the faster corners, and on a par with it in the nadgery stuff. It was little wonder that Sugden had a face like a wet weekend when the car was handed over to Bailey for the last four races.

Re-established as one of the more powerful four-cylinders, it was a revelation at the conclusion to the season, with Julian pushing Renault, Vauxhall and Honda hard for the podium finishes. He was to be denied this pleasure, but these were performances that might just have saved Toyota's BTCC bacon – if not Toyota GB's motorsport arm.

The decision not to take up the option of a guaranteed place at the FIA Touring Car World Cup emphasised that its budget hardly bordered on the flamboyant. And as Toyota continues to purchase chunks of Inchcape – the owners of Toyota GB – the British subsidiary was unwilling to fund a BTCC programme, and withdrew its support for 1996 in late October.

However, the recent shock news that TTE has been banned from the 1996 World Rally Championship – pending an appeal – has thrown everything into the melting pot. Toyota Motor Corporation has a commitment to a 1996 European Super Touring campaign, but as yet there is no outward sign of what form this will take.

Vitally, though, there is a clear lesson to be learned from '95: those teams given a clear mandate and a realistic budget were Renault, Vauxhall and Volvo . . .

TOYOTA CARINA E

Type: Four-door saloon

ENGINE **Type:** Water-cooled, in-line, four-cylinder, DOHC, 16-valve (iron block/reversed alloy head) **Mounting:** Transverse **Capacity:** 1998 cc **Bore and stroke:** 86 mm x 86 mm **Compression ratio:** 14:1 **Management system:** Zytek **Power output:** 300 bhp @ 8500 rpm **Maximum torque:** Approx. 180 lb/ft **Spark plugs:** NGK **Oil:** Mobil

BODY AND CHASSIS **Dimensions: Height:** 1410 mm **Length:** 4530 mm **Width:** 1695 mm **Wheelbase:** 2580 mm **Track:** 1455 mm **Kerb weight:** 975 kg **Fuel capacity:** 60 litres

TRANSMISSION Front-wheel drive **Gearbox:** Xtrac, six-speed sequential **Clutch:** AP Racing, 5.5 in. triple-plate, sintered **Differential:** Plate-type or viscous coupling

SUSPENSION **Front:** Toyota Super-strut **Rear:** MacPherson strut **Shock absorbers:** Dynamics **Springs:** Eibach Driver-adjustable front and rear anti-roll bars

BRAKES Brembo **Front:** Single six-piston calipers **Rear:** Single two-piston calipers **Discs:** 355 mm ventilated (front)/275 mm cross-drilled (rear)

Steering: Toyota, rack-and-pinion, power assistance **Tyres:** Michelin **Wheels:** O.Z. Racing **Instrumentation and data-logging:** PI Research **Driver's seat:** Corbeau

BMW TEAM MOTORSPORT

Team Principal: Günther Warthofer
Chief Engineer: Martin Moosleitner
Engineers/Mechanics: Jürgen Junklaus, Thomas Mattes, Jörg Faust, Frank Rohwer, Jörg Baldes, Dierk Weinbach, Klaus Brumme, Steve Bunkhall, Hans Huber, Rainer Weigert, Christof Matzke, Jeremy Griffiths, Stefan Wenner

The racing advantage of the rear-wheel drive lay-out is one that its artificially lighter front-wheel drive cousin has been reducing since the latter half of '93. The FIA responded to this attack by halving the former's 100-kilogramme weight penalty on 1 July 1994. It was halved again one year later, but this still wasn't enough. The advent of a wing regulation that favoured the front-wheel drive cars saw them demote the once dominant 318 to the role of also-ran, in the BTCC at least.

Yet at the start of the year the signs were good. Outgoing champion, Jo Winkelhock, had won four races in the second half of the 1994 BTCC season, albeit aided by a specially homologated wing package and reduced weight penalty. True, Schnitzer had gone, but it had been replaced by Günther Warthofer's Nürburgring-based team. Although this was a relatively inexperienced outfit, it was clearly well thought of by BMW, which had given it the job of developing its new S42 racing engine in '94, a task it completed by winning the ADAC Cup in Germany with Johnny Cecotto.

The latter was also expected to be a big plus in the team's first season outside Germany. Both had a lot to learn about the BTCC, but the ex-'bike World Champion's ability to get a unit behind him – and get what he wants from BMW – is legendary.

Even this was not enough, however.

In an effort to stem the front-wheel drive tide, BMW announced mid-season that it would run a parallel UK-based test team under the auspices of Ralph Bellamy. This smacked of panic. And according to sources in Warthofer's team, little, if anything, filtered down to it from the Aussie's outfit.

According to the former F1 designer, the new wing regulations allowed the front-wheel drive cars a huge advantage. By his calculations BMW's rivals had 35 per cent more downforce – downforce that came without the corresponding drag because it was derived from the ground effect of their front splitters.

Bellamy's detractors suggested that BMW had simply got its sums wrong, or had tailored its wings to suit the faster circuits of the ADAC Cup. This argument was given some credence when it homologated a new aerodynamic package for the second half of the German series – an option that was not open to it in the BTCC.

But a bigger rear wing would have simply meant more drag, and both Cecotto and David Brabham were struggling for straightline speed as it was. Theirs was a frustrating scenario: they rarely got close enough along the straights to consider a pass and, when they did, they were out-braked in any case, for even their stopping advantage – the result of a more even weight distribution – had been nullified by the new-found stability of the front-wheel drive cars.

The rear-wheel drive format still looks after its tyres better, but this is of little advantage in a 20-lapper if you begin your late-race charge from 12th or 13th place.

In the immediate aftermath of the weight reduction eyebrows were raised at the fourth places scored by each driver at Knockhill, and their stitching up of a third row at the following Brands Hatch Indy meeting. There is an understandable front-wheel drive paranoia that surrounds the BMW's weight – just two years ago 100 kg was insufficient to prevent them from winning – but this was to be a false dawn for the 25-kilogramme penalty. They were simply circuits that suited the car.

This was a new experience for BMW and its reaction was sluggish. In Japan, Italy and Britain its drivers complained of a lack of power from the new engine, yet this was never satisfactorily resolved.

Its engineers had advised all the works-supported teams to use Penske shock absorbers, but by the middle of the season the BTCC cars were back on Bilsteins. Yet still the car's tail bounced around. Perhaps it always had done. It was just that now its drivers were powerless to prevent their front-wheel drive rivals from disappearing into the distance.

The pace of development in the British series hardly seemed to strike a chord with the bosses back in Germany. Indeed, the programme reached such a parlous state that BMW GB, worried about the brand's image in this country, reportedly requested that the programme be terminated mid-season. Munich demanded that it be completed.

It remains to be seen if it will return, though. As the German series continues to expand this will naturally become its Super Touring focus, and whether it will wish to race in Britain against the 'big hitters' that concentrate on a single series remains to be seen. This is not a company noted for throwing in the towel, however, particularly in touring cars.

Outnumbered by the *traction avants,* this was always a process that BMW would have to pass through. It will be interesting to see what emerges. Without its support Super Touring might have faltered at the first hurdle, but as this formula evolves so the manufacturers' *modus operandi* has shifted. If BMW is to regain its superiority, it must streamline its involvement. It will.

BMW 318iS

Type: Four-door saloon

ENGINE **Type:** Water-cooled, in-line, four-cylinder, DOHC, 16-valve **Mounting:** Longitudinal **Capacity:** 1998 cc **Bore and stroke:** 86.5 mm x 85 mm **Management system:** BMW **Compression ratio:** 12.5:1 **Power output:** 285 bhp @ 8300 rpm **Maximum torque:** 184 lb/ft @ 7000 rpm **Oil:** Fina

BODY AND CHASSIS **Dimensions: Height:** 1270 mm **Length:** 4433 mm **Width:** 1698 mm **Wheelbase:** 2700 mm **Track:** 1470 mm (front)/1510 mm (rear) **Kerb weight:** 1000 kg **Fuel capacity:** 90 litres

TRANSMISSION Rear-wheel drive **Gearbox:** Hollinger, six-speed sequential

SUSPENSION **Front:** MacPherson strut **Rear:** Semi-trailing arm **Shock absorbers:** Penske, then Bilstein **Springs:** Eibach Driver-adjustable front and rear anti-roll bars

BRAKES Brembo **Front:** Single six-piston calipers **Rear:** Single two-piston calipers **Discs:** 342 mm ventilated (front)/283 mm ventilated (rear)

Steering: BMW rack-and-pinion **Tyres:** Michelin **Wheels:** BBS **Instrumentation and data-logging:** BMW M GmbH **Driver's seat:** Recaro

HONDA TEAM MSD

Team Principal: Dave Whitehead
Team Manager: Rod Benoist
Designer: Mike Pilbeam
Chief Engineer: Eddie Hinckley
Race Engineers: Hinckley (Leslie), Graeme Garvin (Kaye)
Engines: Neil Brown
Number One Mechanics: Graham Greene (Leslie), David Sheard (Kaye)

To read the Accord's specification sheet is to whet the racing appetite: long, wide and aerodynamic, with double-wishbones all round – the potential was there to see. And Milton Keynes' Motor Sport Developments made the most of it with an ambitious reworking of the base car for its first season in the BTCC.

A team better known for its rallying exploits, MSD's only previous connection with Super Touring was its building of the Vauxhall Astras that won titles in Portugal and South Africa in 1992 and 1993, respectively. Thus it faced a hectic schedule when it won the contract to build all the cars for Honda's 1995 European programme (the Accord also raced in Germany and Belgium) as well as to run the cars in the BTCC.

But it jumped in with both feet.

With the input of designer, Mike Pilbeam – of single-seater hillclimb fame – it produced a car with an eye to the future. It followed the lead of last year's Volvo by making the most of a large engine bay to centralise and lower the weight distribution as much as possible. The gearbox and diff were sited in front of an engine that was pushed hard against the bulkhead – a process that required the steering column to pass through the centre of the bellhousing. Combined with the unique (in BTCC terms) suspension system, the Accord was an instant success and one of the best handling cars in the series. Of course, there were niggling problems, but from the moment David Leslie set the fourth-fastest time during the morning warm-up at Donington in April, the car's race-winning potential was plainly evident.

The fact that it didn't win can be laid partly at Yokohama's door . . .

Honda benefited from an exclusive BTCC deal with the Japanese tyre manufacturer this season, but it didn't work as hoped . . .

Its wet we can forget about – it is truly terrible; its intermediate (a soft cut slick) is good, but for some reason the team often fought shy of using it; the slick went through several major changes and improved greatly during the season. Starting out as an 18-in. tyre – that grew from 640 mm diameter to 650 mm – the early part of the season was highlighted by a good qualifier, but hindered by a race tyre that was slow to heat up and tailed away markedly compared to the Michelin and Dunlop. The arrival of the 19-in. slick was the biggest step forward, Leslie using it to secure a podium place at Oulton Park, and battle with the Renaults at the Silverstone finals.

So progress was made in this department, but the partnership remained a fractious one. MSD was annoyed by the long delivery time and lack of examples, which regularly forced James Kaye to lag behind his team-mate in terms of tyre development. The team held 'secret' tests with both Michelin and Dunlop at Pembrey, much to the chagrin of Yokohama, and it was rumoured that it had threatened to use Dunlops should it rain at Oulton Park in September. It came as no surprise when it jumped ship – to Michelin – at the end of the season, although some felt it may have done so a fraction too soon.

At the start of the year, the car was superb through the fast corners, only to lose out through hairpins and the like. Its pace at Knockhill, where Kaye was fastest in the morning warm-up, proved that slow-corner progress had been made. However, it is fair to say that this performance came as a bit of surprise to the team.

The Neil Brown-prepared engine finished the season as one of the strongest in the field. For the last two meetings it featured a new exhaust system that improved its torque greatly. On the whole the unit was very reliable, while the V-Tec system is waiting in the wings for '96 . . .

The biggest mechanical concern in the first half of the season was an inconsistent brake pedal that troubled both drivers. This was linked to a worrying tendency for the front wheels to work loose – perhaps attributable to a flexing hub – which in turn caused pad knock-off. This was cured at Knockhill by double-locking the wheels.

The introduction of power steering also proved a big help, especially for Kaye, who tended to use a viscous coupling, whereas Leslie preferred a plate-type differential.

This was a very impressive first effort. But might it have been better?

MSD was almost agog at its car's performance, and sometimes gave the impression that it didn't dare win in its first year. Making the car work appeared to hold fewer fears for it than than making the team work.

Unsurprisingly, it made some errors – particularly the strange tyre decisions in the wet at Brands Hatch and Snetterton – and occasionally appeared to lack direction.

This can't have been helped by the unusual circumstance of having a separate test team run by Honda Motors Europe and not Honda UK, which funded the race programme. The idea sounds good, but it only came about via a web of internal politics that can only serve to weaken the programme. Next year MSD will face the pressure of expectation for the first time, and if it is to compete with Williams and TWR it must have no such distractions.

HONDA ACCORD 2.0iLS

Type: Four-door saloon

ENGINE **Type:** Water-cooled, in-line, four-cylinder, DOHC, 16-valve (all-alloy) **Mounting:** Transverse **Capacity:** 1998 cc **Bore and stroke:** 86 mm x 86 mm **Management system:** MBE **Power output:** Approx. 300 bhp **Spark plugs:** NGK **Oil:** Mobil

BODY AND CHASSIS **Dimensions: Height:** 1380 mm **Length:** 4675 mm **Width:** 1715 mm **Wheelbase:** 2720 mm **Track:** 1475 mm (front)/1480 mm (rear) **Kerb weight:** 975 kg **Fuel capacity:** 75 litres

TRANSMISSION Front-wheel drive **Gearbox:** Motor Sport Developments/Xtrac, six-speed sequential **Clutch:** AP Racing, 5.5 in. twin-plate, carbon **Differential:** Plate-type or viscous coupling

SUSPENSION **Front:** Double-wishbone **Rear:** Double-wishbone **Shock absorbers:** Dynamics **Springs:** Eibach Driver-adjustable front and rear anti-roll bars

BRAKES AP Racing **Front:** Twin four-piston calipers, water-cooled **Rear:** Single two-piston calipers **Discs:** 355 mm ventilated (front)/270 mm cross-drilled (rear)

Steering: TRW, rack-and-pinion, power assistance **Tyres:** Yokohama **Wheels:** ENKEI Sport **Instrumentation and data-logging:** PI Research **Driver's seat:** Corbeau

HONDA
20
HONDA
clarion
CAR AUDIO
Enny
ACCORD
YOKOHAMA
YOKOHAMA
Enny
SIMPSON
Enny

HONDA
Kaye
ACCORD
Auto Trader
21
HONDA
clarion
CAR AUDIO
Enny
Enny
YOKOHAMA
ACCORD
YOKOHAMA
Enny
SIMPSON
Enny
YOKOHAMA

Drivers: DEREK WARWICK, GIAMPIERO SIMONI & GABRIELE TARQUINI

ALFA ROMEO OLD SPICE RACING

Team Manager: Steve Farrell, then Dave Benbow
Race Engineers: Benbow, then Peter Harrison (Warwick), Harrison (Simoni), Maurizio Nardon (Tarquini)
Chief Mechanic: Jim Adamson
Number One Mechanics: Dave Wilcock (Warwick), John Barmby (Simoni), Roy Hingston (Tarquini)
Engine Technician: Alex Livadeas
Administrator: Peter Ford

In spite of Prodrive's sterling efforts, this programme failed to bloom in the shadow cast by Alfa Romeo's all-consuming Class 1 commitment to the German Touring Car Championship and International Touring Car series. Last year's clean sweep of the BTCC titles was always going to be a tough act to follow, but the truth is that Alfa Corse – the team that out-thought and out-fought its Super Touring rivals in 1994 – made only a half-hearted attempt to do so.

Derek Warwick was the BTCC's biggest signing during the off-season, and at the turn of the year the ex-Formula One star held high hopes after matching the times of reigning champion, Gabriele Tarquini, in a familiarisation test at Mugello. They were hopes soon to be dashed.

All the pre-season development work on the 155TS was done on the continent; this work ran late, so Warwick and Giampiero Simoni did not drive a '95 car until the end of March at Snetterton, where it proved to be disappointingly unbalanced. At the time, this was put down to its newness . . .

The biggest change had been the addition of roughly an inch to its front track. This was just one of the perceived shortfalls of the '94 car, the controversial wings of which had allowed it to win all the same. The 155, some of its rivals said, was not a good basis for a touring car, being narrow and possessing a high centre of gravity . . .

Other changes for 1995 included a switch from Magneti Marelli to a TAG engine management system and from Bilstein shock absorbers to Penske. These were understood to be sweetener deals, put together after the input of these two companies in the development of an active suspension system for Class 1 had been wiped out at the eleventh hour by the rule-makers. Not the best of reasons for change.

From the outset the Alfa Romeo was off the pace, both drivers complaining of its extremely nervous tail. It is ironic that the team which caused the fuss about wings in the first place had got its aerodynamic sums wrong this time; testing at Monza and Mugello had endowed the resultant rear wing with insufficient downforce for the long-straight-free British circuits.

Progress was slow until June. But the programme eventually began to gather pace when Tarquini's Italian Superturismo campaign was axed. He replaced Simoni from Knockhill onwards, and Prodrive was given *carte blanche* to develop the car in readiness for October's FIA Touring Car World Cup.

Tarquini had already made a BTCC appearance before his full-time arrival, contesting the May Oulton Park meeting in his Italian-spec car. On that occasion he was out-performed by both Warwick and Simoni. Prodrive was clearly making headway.

The development was stepped up, with the team paying close attention to the rear suspension. The potentially excellent but apparently difficult-to-dial-in Penskes were replaced as efforts were made to lower the car substantially and prevent it from picking up its inside rear wheel – a legacy of the 'no-droop' set-up of '94. Bit by bit this work was introduced and, along with a new front suspension geometry, the competitiveness of Tarquini (as evinced by a string of fourth places) and Warwick increased. At the September Oulton Park rounds the 155s finally looked balanced, while for the Silverstone final Warwick ran the car 15 mm lower than ever before

This development continued in the immediate post-season, and Warwick suffered the frustration of finding over half a second in testing at Silverstone, in what was probably his last drive in the car!

Prodrive also made improvements on the engine front, but this remained a weak point. A twin-spark unit was predicted at the start of the season but, although it was supposed to have run on the dyno, it never appeared.

The Banbury outfit used its rallying experience to develop a new diff, too. Warwick persevered with this for the last eight races as he felt it had more potential, but it was still proving troublesome by the end of the BTCC season.

In all other respects, Tarquini used a Prodrive car. His discarded Superturismo machine, meanwhile, had its shell and rollcage stiffened in preparation for the World Cup, and this was the car which Warwick tested so promisingly in late September.

On the team front, it was a surprise when Steve Farrell, who had learned the ropes with Alfa Corse as Simoni's race engineer in 1994, was taken off the project. His shoes were filled by Dave Benbow, a man fresh from Indy cars, who was now left with the task of husbanding the team and engineering Warwick's car. It was too much. His dilemma was eased when Tarquini brought with him his own engineer, Maurizio Nardon, allowing Peter Harrison to switch from Simoni to Warwick.

Prodrive did a remarkable job all things considered, but the base car was simply not good enough to win without its aerodynamic advantage.

ALFA ROMEO 155TS

Type: Four-door saloon

ENGINE **Type:** Water-cooled, in-line, four-cylinder, DOHC, 16-valve (iron block/alloy head) **Mounting:** Transverse **Capacity:** 1998 cc **Bore and stroke:** 86 mm x 86 mm **Compression ratio:** 12.5:1 **Management system:** TAG **Power output:** 275 bhp **Maximum torque:** 180 lb/ft **Spark plugs:** Champion **Oil:** Selenia

BODY AND CHASSIS **Dimensions: Height:** 1425 mm **Length:** 4443 mm **Width:** 1730 mm **Wheelbase:** 2540 mm **Track:** 1495 mm (front)/1437 mm (rear) **Kerb weight:** 975 kg **Fuel capacity:** 60 litres

TRANSMISSION Front-wheel drive **Gearbox:** Hewland, six-speed sequential **Clutch:** AP Racing, 5.5 in. twin-plate, carbon **Differential:** Plate-type or viscous coupling

SUSPENSION **Front:** MacPherson strut **Rear:** Trailing link **Shock absorbers:** Penske **Springs:** Eibach Driver-adjustable front and rear anti-roll bars

BRAKES Brembo **Front:** Single six-piston calipers **Rear:** Single four-piston calipers **Discs:** 15 in. ventilated (front)/10 in. ventilated (rear)

Steering: Alfa Romeo, rack-and-pinion, power assistance **Tyres:** Michelin **Wheels:** Speedline **Instrumentation and data-logging:** TAG/PI Research **Driver's seat:** Sparco

TOTAL TEAM PEUGEOT

Motorsport Manager: Mick Linford
Race Engineers: Andy Thorburn (Watts), Steve Ridgers (Harrison)
Chief Mechanic: Gary Timms
Engine & Gearbox Technician: Richard Jones

Do not be fooled by this team's status as the only true works team in the BTCC. It may be run from within Peugeot's UK base at Ryton, but it is the smallest works outfit in terms of workforce and budget, while Mick Linford is the only team boss faced with working to union rules!

For a brief time last season the 405 of Patrick Watts was the closest rival to the all-conquering Alfa Romeos. This year, however, not even the Kentishman's renowned seat-of-the-pants skill could overcome the shortcomings of his car's suspension – MacPherson strut front and trailing-arm rear.

The team was well aware of these problems, and spent much of the winter developing a 'double-pivot' front end, which the French-built 405s had used to win the '94 Supertourisme title. The idea behind this is for the steering to work on a different axis than that of the strut. This allows the kingpin to remain as upright as possible, thus maintaining a flatter 'footprint'. It worked in testing – vastly reducing the understeer that had plagued the car in its late-'94 outings and thus improving tyre life.

Then it was banned.

Much to Linford's annoyance, the FIA left the determination of this system's BTCC legality in the hands of TOCA, which deemed it unacceptable. But why had the FIA given Peugeot France dispensation to run it in the first place? The UK team's anger was understandable, feeling as it did that the Toyota Super-strut arrangement and Renault's rear suspension interpretation constituted 'double pivot' systems. This was a blow from which it was never to recover.

With money and time very short, it set about making a silk purse out of a sow's ear, and spent the bulk of the early-season working on a front suspension evolution. And by the time it had gone as far as it could with this, any thoughts of fitting an 'articulated beam' rear end akin to that of the Laguna – the brainchild of Steve Ridgers, now at Peugeot – had to be shelved.

Thus the 405 was rarely a balanced car: its trailing-arm rear end causes the tyres' inside edges to lift when under load, and as the back was softened and camber was added in the search for more rear grip, so the understeer increased. None of which made it suited to the lower profile Michelin slicks that were being developed for cars with more sophisticated suspensions. Andy Thorburn engineered a form of rear-wheel steer in an effort to compensate, but this was only a stop-gap measure.

The car had its moments: a third for Watts at Thruxton, a track it has always suited; Patrick's storming drive to second from the back of the grid in that memorable wet-dry race at Snetterton. But this model had missed its chance to win in the BTCC as far back as 1993. It looked positively old hat this season.

Once in possession of one of the stronger four-pots in the series, the lack of budget meant that there was little engine development during the season – even over the winter! – and the car was no more than run-of-the-mill in this department by the end of the year. Zytek developed a new management system which showed gains in every facet of performance when run on the dyno, yet neither driver reported a major improvement when it was used on the track.

The upshot of the above was that Peugeot finished last of the manufacturers, providing an object lesson in how not to go about it: no spare car, little testing and limited development. The stakes have been raised massively, and yet Peugeot UK insists on doing it on the cheap. It must be getting some benefit from it otherwise it wouldn't be doing it; but it is hard to pinpoint exactly what this is.

The imminent arrival of the 406 must be its last chance. Without this 'new leaf' to turn over, there seemed little chance of 'The Lion' returning to the BTCC next season. Wider and longer than the 405, and blessed with a much more sophisticated suspension system, the 406's racing potential is evident from the rave reviews its road cousin has received. If it is to succeed, however, the UK subsidiary must stop playing at it – give the project a decent budget or get out.

A little more help from Peugeot Sport France wouldn't go amiss either. Car companies' internecine rivalries never cease to amaze, and the mother company's refusal to build a couple of Super Touring 406s for its UK arm was typical of this. There would appear to be little love lost here.

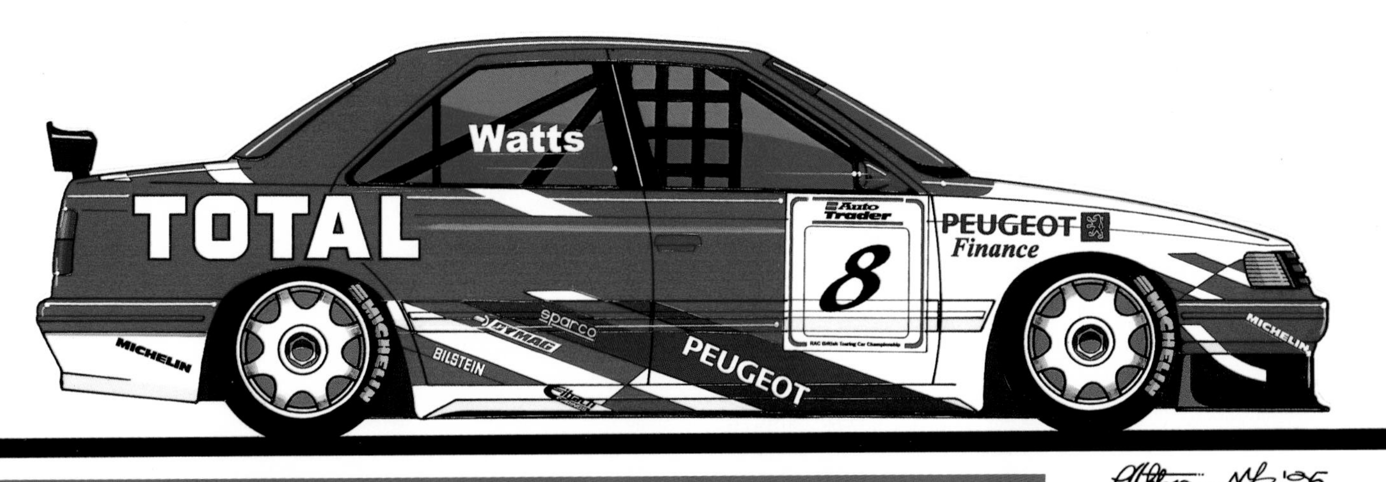

PEUGEOT 405

Type: Four-door saloon

ENGINE **Type:** Water-cooled, in-line, four-cylinder, DOHC, 16-valve (all-alloy) **Mounting:** Transverse **Capacity:** 1998 cc **Bore and stroke:** 86 mm x 86 mm **Management system:** Zytek **Power output:** 286 bhp **Maximum torque:** 180 lb/ft **Spark plugs:** Champion **Oil:** Total

BODY AND CHASSIS **Dimensions: Height:** 1250 mm **Length:** 4408 mm **Width:** 1704 mm **Wheelbase:** 2669 mm **Kerb weight:** 975 kg **Fuel capacity:** 50 litres

TRANSMISSION Front-wheel drive **Gearbox:** Hewland, six-speed sequential **Clutch:** AP Racing, 5.5 in. twin-plate, carbon or sintered **Differential:** Plate-type or viscous coupling

SUSPENSION **Front:** MacPherson strut **Rear:** Trailing arm, transverse torsion bar **Shock absorbers:** Bilstein **Springs:** Eibach Driver-adjustable front and rear anti-roll bars

BRAKES Brembo (front)/AP Racing (rear) **Front:** Single six-piston calipers **Rear:** Single two-piston calipers **Discs:** AP Racing, 355 mm ventilated (front)/264 mm (rear)

Steering: Peugeot rack-and-pinion, power assistance **Tyres:** Michelin **Wheels:** Dymag **Instrumentation and data-logging:** PI Research **Driver's seat:** Sparco

by Paul Fearnley

WALKING TALL

LAT Photographic

Matt Neal is tall. Very tall. Too tall to contemplate a career in single-seaters. Almost too tall to be a touring car driver. When Colin McRae came to play with the BTCC 'sissies' in a one-off outing at Knockhill three-and-a-half seasons ago, imagine his surprise when six foot six of seriously upset Midlander came stomping through the paddock in search of him. The Scot had spun Matt's BMW out of the race, and the world's fastest gravel driver reportedly hid in Prodrive's motorhome – locked motorhome – until the not-so-jolly giant had gone.

Matt had no intention of being gentle on that particular occasion, but the man who once held ambitions for a rugby career usually exhibits that clichéd giant characteristic. In fact, so gentle is he, the works bully boys regularly push him around. The races at Thruxton in May were indicative of this: the red Team Dynamics Ford Mondeo had qualified in the top ten for both races at this super-fast track, only to come off worst in a couple of early-laps tangles and score zero points. There are always two sides to such stories but, reading between the lines, it would appear that a works driver had taken a liberty with a privateer, whom he felt had invited the lunge by a moment's hesitation.

This had all changed by the end of the season. When Matt outbraked the works Ford of twice World Champion Paul Radisich, and rushed off to a fair-and-square fourth position at Snetterton, the BTCC *cognoscenti* nodded sagely in acknowledgement. Respect. And Matt knew it. A hard battle had been won.

'It's been a roller-coaster year for me mentally,' admitted the recently married alloy wheels entrepreneur. 'I'd have a couple of consistent finishes and take maximum points in the Total Cup. Then I'd think, "Right, I can have a real go at the works boys now." But then I'd have a couple of non-finishes and I would revert back to my cautious approach.'

With hindsight, he got the balance about right, securing the £25,000 first prize in the Total Cup, plus a £5,000 bonus for the most privateer pole positions – both of which he won with some comfort. In the process, he shook up the establishment sufficiently for the snorts of derision which accompanied suggestions that Team Dynamics was in line for the works Ford deal to subside to a sniff.

'A couple of the works guys have come up to us towards the end of the season and said that we can't be ignored any more, that we have to be considered a threat,' reveals Matt.

There is no question that Steve Neal, Matt's father, a former Mini racer of repute and the owner of Team Dynamics, has big plans for the outfit. So much so, that when he considered the Michelins on offer to be lagging too far behind those given to the works cars, he switched to Dunlop in an instant.

He has big plans for his son, too. But only if he can cut the mustard . . .

'I can't argue that I'm in the position I'm in because of my father, but he's the first person to criticise me, to put me down,' pleads Matt. 'He's a businessman. He's been successful in everything he's done, he loves motor racing, and if he thought I was holding the team back he wouldn't hesitate to drop me.'

In this respect, the 28-year-old suffers from the same 'spoiled by dad' jibes that the late Kieth O'dor did. And in the same way as Kieth, Matt is underrated. He is not the most outstanding touring car driver the world has ever seen – he perhaps needs to show a little more aggression behind the wheel – but he is far from being the bumbler that some rivals hold him up to be. If he passes them it's purely down to the car, they say.

There can be no denying that he has made the switch to front-wheel drive with relative comfort. His half-season with the Mazda Xedos 6 in 1994 surprised many, his proximity of speed to the well-respected David Leslie providing a worthy benchmark. And in a far happier frame of mind, back in the bosom of Team Dynamics, this process has continued with the Mondeo.

'I dropped into driving front-wheel drive quite easily. I don't know how or why, but I just settled into a groove. The Xedos was not an easy car to drive. The [Mazda] 323F was better, and the Mondeo with wings is another step up, especially how we've got it now.'

This is where the programme gets very impressive. Matt rises to the bait when it is suggested that his team is not strictly privateer. It is, but there's no doubting that it was the 'fat cat' of this year's Total Cup: it did more testing than the others; employed more – and more experienced – staff than the rest; it rarely went short of first-hand rubber. But if you want to follow in the wheel-tracks of Ray Mallock, whose success with the Ecurie Ecosse Vauxhalls led him to the door of Vauxhall Sport and the works Cavalier deal, you must speculate to accumulate. And with the experience of Roy Baker, Barry Plowman and highly-rated engineer, Nick Wasyliw, on board, this team is ready to step up.

'We've got some very good people with us, people who know the ropes, and this just allows me to turn up, get in the car and drive. You have to be like that if you want to make a success of it.

'There's no question that I want to be a works driver. My dad knows that if I get an opportunity with another team I would definitely take it. Of course, I would love to move up with Team Dynamics. We've worked very hard this year. We've gone our own way with a lot of things on the car – diffs and dampers, stiffened it up a lot – and I think it's comparable with the works Fords now.' Certainly, Paul Radisich was sufficiently intrigued to test it at Snetterton. 'You have to remember that Andy Rouse has had the Mondeo for three years to get to know it,' Matt emphasises.

And I've had three years to get to know Matt. At the start of the season he had plenty to convince me of. At times, I haven't even been sure that he wanted to be a racing driver. I am now. Not the best. But a very good one. One who's about to throw his weight around a bit more.

by Paul Fearnley

BTCC: TOTALITARIAN STATE?

The weight of manufacturer support within the British Touring Car Championship ensures that its privateers are generally forced to survive on its periphery.

Conversely, for the more ambitious – and better-funded – teams, its high profile offers them a slim chance of grabbing a piece of the works pie, while James Kaye and James Thompson have shown that privateer success can set one upon the path towards a works drive.

The third year of the Total Cup was perhaps the best to date, the single highlight of which was Robb Gravett's third place at Snetterton – the first time a privateer has stood on the podium during the two-litre era.

The ex-champion drove a Ford Mondeo Ghia on that occasion, and the promise of some privateer support from Ford Motorsport, plus the ready-ish availability of one- and two-year old Mondeos, ensured that the Blue Oval was well represented in this category.

The most successful of these was Matt Neal's Team Dynamics car, which made the biggest non-works impact on the grids since Ray Mallock's spell with the Ecurie Ecosse Vauxhalls in 1992 and '93 (the latter, however, were not classed as privateer entries).

Neal had his fair share of early disappointments, and for a while Richard Kaye (Ford Mondeo) and Nigel Smith (Vauxhall Cavalier) sat squarely on his exhaust pipes in the title race. This was a threat Matt extinguished with a switch from Michelins to Dunlops and a succession of confident victories in the latter half of the season.

The battle for the £15,000 runner-up spot went down to the penultimate round at Silverstone, and passed the way of the Brighton-based Kaye when Smith endured the damp squib of being nerfed into the gravel on the second lap.

A few years ago, the younger brother of James returned from Spain with only a credit card to his name. Consequently, last season's attack on the Ford Credit Fiesta Challenge was his first racing for a long while; he wasn't crowned champion, but exhibited race-winning form, and then engaged in a headlong, ambitious, underfunded flight into the BTCC. Thus was Mint Motorsport created.

Whereas Neal's car was in '94 specification, Kaye's was the example that Paul Radisich had used to win the FIA Touring Car Challenge at Monza the year before. In the early part of the season, therefore, he was down on power compared to some of his rivals. He eventually got his hands on a '94-spec engine for the second half of the year, but even this never appeared to be a match for Neal's sweet-sounding unit.

Kaye's year was further complicated when he broke his right leg in a cycling accident in June. Against doctor's advice he continued to race, learned how to left-foot brake and immediately took maximum points at Donington Park. His biggest handicap, however, was the lack of experience within his team. The car looked to be running far too soft for much of the season, and only when he stumbled across a set-up (it had had the wrong rear anti-roll bar fitted), and moved away from the Rouse-supplied shock absorbers, did he have the green Ford handling to his liking.

It was clear that the car wasn't good, but the dozen or so wrecked splitters can't all have been down to understeer. Richard tried too hard on occasions and sometimes shoved his bonnet in places where he shouldn't, but there should be no doubting his speed or potential.

In my book a Vauxhall Cavalier is potentially the best privateer machine. But Nigel Smith's version – a '93 Ecosse car – was maybe a little long in the tooth to cope with the Fords' power advantage.

The irrepressible Chippenham businessman was in his second year of the Total Cup, and again proved himself to be a very competent driver. When his smooth style was allied to a track he likes – Brands Hatch Indy, in particular – he was a real threat to Neal, sometimes his leader and conqueror.

His sourcing of sponsorship from HMSO Books, and the presentation of his team and car on what was still a marginal budget – one big accident would have ended his season – also did him much credit. A great talker, the paddock would be a duller place without him.

A journalist, like a lady, should be allowed the odd change of mind. In a review of the 1994 season printed in a weekly magazine, I stated that the BTCC was not in need 'of this kind of support'. I was referring to Hamish Irvine and his BMW. I was not singling out the driver, or the car, for criticism, only the combination of the two.

The Scot is a determined man, however, and decided to go the front-wheel drive route this season, purchasing the ex-Ian Flux/James Thompson Peugeot 405. The oldest car in the series looked as out of place as his BMW had, but the bearded former Triumph Dolomite Sprint racer grabbed it by the scruff and became the darling of the crowds.

In such circumstances, all an individual can do is improve on his own performance. And that's exactly what he did. Selling farm equipment as and when he desired new rubber, and sporting fibreglass wings and splitters moulded from those on the works car, he gradually reduced the gap between himself and the rest. He won, too, starring in the rain at Brands Hatch in June. Indeed, he was only denied a double success there when Kaye dived past him right on the line.

A succession of engine failures continually threatened his season, but he soldiered on. Hamish, I will never understand why you do it, but I'm glad you do. I was wrong.

The silence that surrounded the Press viewing area at Thruxton was chilling. The sight of a Ford Mondeo barrel-rolling out of view was a sickening one. Affable Aussie Charlie Cox suffered a cracked skull, haemorrhaging of the eyes and severe bruising in an accident caused by locking rear brakes at 145 mph. These were injuries that forced him to sit out the next three months.

That he returned was a miracle. To do so having built a brand-new car was a 'bloody miracle'. The National Saloon Car Cup star had amazed us all with a fifth place in the wet at Brands Hatch in April, only for the 1994 World Cup-winning car to be consigned to history three weeks later. But, as he recuperated, he worked with his small but enthusiastic team to re-shell the wreck into a hatchback Mondeo. This was done with the help of Matter in Germany, and with a view to keeping his four-wheel drive options open, as only the five-door version is homologated for this format.

Incredibly, it almost went up in smoke after just one lap of his August Brands Hatch return – 'I think somebody's trying to tell me something' – but survived to lead the penultimate round of the Total Cup before clashing with Gravett. Sponsor-conscious, very quotable, and more than handy at the controls, he could be a threat for the privateer honours next season.

Robb also missed the middle of the season. This was the consequence of an acrimonious split with Roy Kennedy Racing after just two races in its Vauxhall Cavalier.

Undeterred, the Maidenhead driver created Foesport and, with the aid of Jerry Mahony and Kevin Maxted, ran a Mondeo from the GP support race onwards.

His experience of Snetterton saw him gamble on slicks for the first race there, and this led to his memorable return to the podium. But the startline shunt he suffered in the second Norfolk encounter appeared to affect the car for the remainder of the year.

For the 1990 champion this was just a means to an end. It strikes me that being a privateer is not something he relishes. If his talks with manufacturers do not bear fruit in the off-season, it will be a bitter pill for him to swallow. However, he is not easily deflected from his purpose, on or off the track.

The Total Cup will be there for him if he wants it, for the deal is already in place. This is vital. These are halcyon days for the BTCC, but a cull of the manufacturers appears to be in the offing. If this happens, a strong privateer support will be crucial if grids are not to dwindle to worrying proportions.

TOCA has always stated that it cannot fund the privateers to go racing. A slightly more paternalistic approach would not go amiss, however.

Photos: LAT Photographic

Top to bottom: **The efforts of Charlie Cox, Richard Kaye, Nigel Smith and Robb Gravett served to make this the most competitive season of the Total Cup yet. Matt Neal *(opposite)* outpaced them all.**

SPLITTER CLOUT

by Paul Fearnley

On April Fool's Day 1994, mouths were agape when a swarm of blue-overalled mechanics wheeled out Alfa Romeo's BTCC challenger. Its appearance was accompanied by some nervous laughter. But this was no joke.

When the Milanese manufacturer confirmed its intention to contest the world's most competitive Super Touring (or Class 2 as it was then called) championship, it stunned the journalists assembled at its annual winter motorsport press conference with the revelation that it would build an 'homologation special' to do so. This latter news clashed vividly with the BTCC's *modus operandi;* its original regulations had been carefully couched to militate against such cars. Andy Rouse, one of the masterminds behind the two-litre formula, considered these 'specials' to be a destructive element, a deterrent to manufacturers without a long sporting history from entering the category. He, for one, was angry that this stance had not been protected sufficiently by the FIA when it took the formula on board for 1993.

In its defence, Alfa Romeo was simply following innumerable precedents, its own traditions and the rules in developing a limited-edition road car with distinct built-in advantages from which its motorsport arm could profit. The homologation figure now stands at a prohibitive 25,000, but was less by a 'very inviting' factor of ten in 1994 – so the 155TS Silverstone was born. And at first sight it did not look so outrageous, sporting the type of front airdam and rear wing regularly seen on the open road.

This all changed on that rainy morning at Thruxton. Just three days before the start of the season, Alfa Romeo homologated three packing pieces that served to raise the 155's rear wing into 'cleaner' air, and a front splitter that could be extended forwards. Downforce suddenly became an issue in the BTCC.

In stark contrast, most road cars generate lift at speed. Their slick, multi-million pound advertising campaigns boast of 'slippery shapes', low cd figures and the like – downforce simply doesn't feature in the car market war. In racing, however, it is the pot of gold at the end of the rainbow. And Alfa Romeo found it first.

As the various parties argued about the whys and wherefores, Gabriele Tarquini won the first five races of the season, eight in total, and the red machines took a clean sweep of the titles. Now we know why . . .

For this season all the cars sprouted a rear wing and front splitter; the FIA had decided that the only way to circumvent a repeat of last year's wing ding-dong was to allow every manufacturer to run the said items without having to go through the rigmarole of homologating thousands of examples to do so. Instead, the manufacturers were given very specific dimensions within which to work, and had until mid-February to lodge templates with the governing body.

Most parties agree that this action levelled the BTCC's playing field, and narrowed the performance advantages this season. But should wings and things be allowed at all? Is this the thin end of the wedge?

Vauxhall's engineering guru Ray Mallock thinks not: 'There's no doubt that last year we were losing out to the Alfa, the BMW and the Renault [the latter pair homologated wing packages for the second half of the season] because of our lack of wings. That changed with the new FIA rules; we were confident that when they were announced we were going to be able to make this a competitive package, and that's exactly what happened.

'We realised that it [downforce versus drag] was going to be the single most important factor in getting the car to work and be competitive.'

Twelve months previously his Cavalier undoubtedly had a better racing chassis than did the Alfa Romeo, which rocked and rolled and yet possessed superior grip and traction. And with the unseen 'boot' of downforce now planted firmly on his roof, John Cleland only saw the Alfas in his rear-view mirror as he raced to this year's title. So just how big a change did the new aerodynamic rules make to the Vauxhall?

Mallock was typically cagey, refusing to give specific figures – as did everybody else, in fairness – but he revealed that the weight of downforce enjoyed in 1995 was about equal to the lift suffered in '94. A net gain of 100 per cent, far greater than the FIA had bargained for . . .

'It's about what *we* expected,' counters Mallock. 'It gives the tyres a much easier time. It just makes it much more like a racing car. It makes the job of engineering the whole thing much simpler. When the front end of a front-wheel drive car starts lifting, it's a big, big problem.'

Clearly, the effect of the touring car wings falls well short of those used in the single-seater world, where downforce is king. But on a grid that is regularly covered by just over a second, the part played by this factor is no less significant in the BTCC. In many respects, there was a more subtle, complex balance to be struck . . .

'In Formula One and Group C the amount of downforce is such that suspension geometry plays a very minor role,' ventures one BTCC team manager. 'In F1 you can have quite a big change in spring rates without making much difference, yet an extra half-degree of rear wing can make a huge difference. We had to combine our new parameter of downforce with the suspension movement a touring car requires.

'Clearly, most of our gains were in the faster corners: we would find huge advantages at places like Redgate, the Craners, McLeans and Coppice at Donington Park, but indirectly we gained in the slower corners, too. The downforce in the faster corners allowed us to run our car softer – 20 to 30 per cent softer – than last season without compromising its poise in the quick stuff, and this gave us more traction in the slow, second-gear corners. We would also gain in these sort of corners because the wings made the car more stable under braking, and so the driver could brake later and carry more speed into the corner.

'As a general rule, I would say that we have been a second a lap faster everywhere with the new aerodynamics.'

But does 'faster' equate to better racing?

It can be argued that the early-season criticisms of the BTCC's 'new look' were premature. As the drivers got a feel for their new working environs, the number of passing manoeuvres increased substantially. But have the new aerodynamics reduced the gap between the good and not-so-good driver by making the cars easier to drive?

Ask a BTCC pilot to name his best seat-of-the-pants colleague, and Patrick Watts will be mentioned regularly. So does Peugeot's acrobatic ace believe that the need for such saloon car skills has been done away with?

'They are different to drive, certainly,' reveals the Tonbridge man of the bewinged cars. 'When I first tried the wings, at Silverstone, I couldn't believe the difference they made. In some respects, it has made them *more* difficult to drive: it's now much more critical when you brake because the braking distances are much shorter; often you are beginning to brake just as you turn in, whereas previously you would brake, then regulate it through the corner before getting back on the power.

'One particular gain that we made was that the rear wing acted like the feathers on a dart; on the old car I could get very sideways under braking if I didn't have the bias exactly right, but with the wing this was much less of a problem.

'As for all the talk about less overtaking, I think that has more to do with a fear of a big fine if you make a botch of it, rather than the wings. I don't think the cars are any less sideways, either.

'I like the fact that it equalised the cars' performances. And we all like to look at our faster lap times – to lap at 100 mph and not 99 mph, to be faster than the TVR Tuscans and the Vauxhall Caterhams – but if there was some way to equalise the cars without the wings, I would prefer it, because they probably have made the cars easier to drive – just.'

The likes of Cleland and Alain Menu would concur. Rickard Rydell prefers to differ. It's horses for courses.

Not for BMW it's not. This marque would absolutely prefer some other way of 'equalising' performance. The Bavarian manufacturer usually keeps quiet counsel, a stance no doubt encouraged by the vast array of trophies its commitment to Super Touring has brought it since 1993. At the outset of the category, its rear-wheel drive format clearly held dynamic advantages over its front-wheel drive rivals, to the extent that a 100-kilogramme weight limit could not prevent Joachim Winkelhock and Steve Soper from dominating the 1993 BTCC. Towards the latter stages of that season, however, it became apparent that the performance gap was shrinking. As has the BMW's penalty; it currently stands

Opposite page and left: **They may not look much, but the extended front splitter and raised rear wing were the keys to Alfa Romeo's success in 1994, and the catalyst to this year's regulations change.**

Above: **The Renault Laguna's 'barn door' rear wing raised a few eyebrows. In spite of the strict dimensions, interpretations varied widely.**

Left: **Ford's Andy Rouse, one of the creators of this formula, was strongly opposed to the introduction of the aerodynamic aids. In spite of his pose, this year's wings were not adjustable.**

Below: **Patrick Watts takes this wing thing too seriously and attempts to take off at Brands Hatch. Clearly, the new regulations did not glue the cars to the track.**

Photos: LAT Photographic

BMW feels that the aerodynamic regulations militate against its rear-wheel drive format. Especially in the BTCC, where the competition is fierce and the tracks are high-downforce.

LAT Photographic

at just 25 kg, yet it was little more than a make-weight this season.

BMW set up a test team mid-season under the auspices of ex-Formula One designer, Ralph Bellamy. The laconic Australian is very critical of the new rules . . .

'Instead of allowing you to homologate rear wings of different sizes and shapes, like they did last year [NB. the wing package BMW introduced for the second half of 1994 was probably more effective than that provided by the new guidelines], the FIA decided that they would make a standard rear wing. So they came up with a rear wing package that would have to fit inside a 150 mm square box, and they obviously thought that if everybody had the same rear wing that it would be equal for everybody . . .

'Of course, it's not,' he argues. 'Everybody finishes up with the same rear downforce because everybody did an equally good job with their rear wings. The trouble is, with a front-wheel drive car you've got a lot more weight over the front axle, so you can put a lot more downforce on the front and still have inherent stability within the car.

'If you make the calculation based on weight distribution, a front-wheel drive car will have at least 35 per cent more overall downforce than we will have. That's a huge amount, and that's built into the rules. When you add that to our weight penalty . . .'

The BMW is also handicapped by its small frontal overhang – a shape that cannot be changed, of course. In comparison, the well-endowed Volvo may fit a far larger and more effective front splitter, as the regulations allow this item to reach back as far as the centreline of the front wheels. The rear wings may catch the eye, but it is at the front where the true gains are made for the bulk of the BTCC field.

'If you gave us a bigger rear wing it wouldn't help, because that brings with it more drag,' continues Bellamy. 'Frontal downforce comes drag-free because it's ground-effect, it's underneath.'

Outnumbered eight to one by the *traction avants,* it is little wonder that Bellamy's voice echoed around a garage at a distant end of the Silverstone pits. The rest are happy with the *status quo* and requested that the FIA gave its mandate to a further year of stability in the regulations. It did.

'Ask yourself why all of the other manufacturers, most of which have a rear-wheel drive variant, choose to race a front-wheel drive car. It's because they are better under these regulations,' concludes Bellamy.

Mallock: 'I think what he [Bellamy] is saying is that your aerodynamic balance should roughly equate to the weight distribution, so on a front-wheel drive car you want relatively more on the front than you would on a rear-wheel drive car. With the regulations that we've got, most of the teams have been able to use them to give us the downforce that we want at the front, whereas the BMW can't use all that downforce. They need relatively more at the back. Having said that, looking at the BMW's rear wing, they are not using as much rear wing as some of the front-wheel drive cars . . .' The implication is that the 318iS was not designed with the short straights of the British circuits in mind.

Bellamy's suggestion that there should be a return to standard front bodywork also finds little support elsewhere in the paddock.

'Some road cars are fundamentally aerodynamically better than others from a racing point of view, and it must make sense to do it this way; the one thing that has a big effect relative to the various suspension pick-up points is aerodynamics,' argues Toyota GB's Motorsports Manager, Paul Risbridger.

'I don't think you can do that really,' adds Mallock, 'you'd have very odd-looking cars if you stripped away the lower edge of some of the bumpers. I think the aerodynamic rules have made the cars a lot more competitive. Some people have said that the racing's not as good, but part of that is the fact that the cars are actually closer in performance this year.'

FIA President Max Mosley is believed to be keen to see a return to the road-car look. And a regularly referred to strength of this category is the instantly recognisable shapes on the tracks. It was feared that the aerodynamic aids would compromise this, yet only one marketing department has so far questioned the more aggressive stance the wings and splitters have endowed the cars with.

The tyre companies have no complaints either.

But it was only a learning year . . .

'I'm sure all of us will homologate something a little bit different,' explains Risbridger. 'Personally, I would like to see the rear wings stay the same size, but be made to look a touch more like those on the road car.'

The idea is not bullet-proof, but the new wings solved more problems than they caused.

Ironically, the only driver of a front-wheel drive car to suggest that his aerodynamics had been a serious hindrance had a swarm of blue-overalled mechanics around him!

LAT Photographic

CONSIDER YOURSELF AT HOME

by Stewart Williams

After three relatively straightforward titles for Paul Stewart Racing, the British F3 Championship sprung a few surprises in 1995: seven different winners, a conclusion to the season that was sprinkled with controversy, and a title battle that veered this way and that and went down to the wire. The eventual upshot was that Oliver Gavin finally broke the PSR stranglehold – but it was touch and go for the lanky Bedford man.

Edenbridge Racing entered F3 back in 1991 and since then has been the second most successful team in terms of race wins, naturally to PSR. All it needed, as team owner Peter Briggs had decided to move up to F3000 for '96, was a title to exit the formula on a high note. In Gavin, a winner of five races for him back in '93, Briggs knew he had the man to do the job. And he duly brought home the bacon. But only just.

With Italian chassis manufacturer, Dallara, still ruling the roost, and no outstandingly dominant engine of the five different units – Mugen, HKS Mitsubishi, Vauxhall, Toyota and Fiat – the onus was squarely on the drivers. And three names were on everybody's lips pre-season: Gavin, Warren Hughes and Cristiano da Matta. Sure, Paul Stewart Racing's two new boys, Ralph Firman and Helio Castro Neves, had to be considered, especially when you took into account the team's three consecutive titles, but they would have to up their games somewhat to be title contenders.

How wrong can you be?

From the Silverstone season-opener in March to Thruxton in October, the two PSR pilots were in the hunt. Firman blew all predictions into the wind with a brace of wins in the first of the year's double-headers, and the chase was on.

Castro Neves had been his closest rival at Silverstone until he got a little bit too friendly at Becketts on the first lap and spun off. Da Matta (second and fourth) and Hughes (fourth and third) both made good, solid starts, too.

Gavin didn't. He wasn't even the best Edenbridge Dallara-Vauxhall driver. His team-mate, Steve Arnold, left the Northamptonshire circuit second in the championship thanks to a second and third, as Olly languished well down the order with two ninths.

And that was the story of the season: on top one week, down the next. Castro Neves apart, there weren't any consistent high scorers, and this made for a fascinating battle.

Olly fought back immediately after Silverstone with his own pair of victories at Thruxton, although he will be the first to admit that they were both a little fortuitous.

In the first race, round three, the Alan Docking-run Dallara F395-HKS Mitsubishi of Hughes – always a star at this track and a double pole-sitter on this occasion – was scrapping with the '94 star of Formula Renault, James Matthews. After an outstanding manoeuvre round the outside of the David Sears Motorsport Mugen-powered car at the chicane on the penultimate lap, Hughes found himself needing to repeat the move as a result of a mistake at the Complex. This time he made a mess of it and the leading pair exited stage left. Gavin, who had been waiting in the wings, came through to win. 'I could see that one of them was going to fall off – I had a feeling,' he said afterwards.

Two hours later, in appallingly wet conditions, he sped past a stalled Hughes, only to slide off at the Complex and then inherit the lead when first Matthews and then Firman found the excess water too much to handle.

For Matthews, this was easily his most competitive meeting. An early victory might have made all the difference to his year, but third in round four was the closest he would get to the winner's circle until the penultimate meeting at Silverstone. A driver new to F3, in a team new to F3, was a combination that didn't work on enough occasions to reinforce the talent that Matthews obviously has. Too often he would struggle simply to get into the top ten, and only after some personnel changes in late August did the smile begin to return to his face.

His DSM team-mate, Luiz Garcia Jnr, managed a fourth on the team's home track – Snetterton – but never figured elsewhere.

Left: **A jumped start at Oulton was one of the slips that cost Ralph Firman (1).**

Jérémie Dufour *(below)* was a brief leader of the championship.

The unthinkable happened at Donington Park, round five. No, not that the Mugen-powered Firman slid off after tangling with Jamie Spence and thus failed to score for the second time in three races. Or that Castro Neves notched up his first British F3 victory . . .

The big news?

For the first time since early 1992, a PSR driver wasn't leading the championship!

Castro Neves thoroughly deserved his win, especially after forcing his way back past Uruguayan, Gonzalo Rodriguez – in the second HKS/ADR car – following a poor start. But it was Gavin who was now top of the pile – the first time an Edenbridge driver had been in such an exalted position.

Castro Neves was by now a relaxed and confident driver, fully ensconced in the Milton Keynes team. Further back, however, things were not so hot for Arnold. The experienced F3 pilot had started the year well and looked comfortable with his new team, but already he was down to fourth in the championship and, after a good showing in the Grand Prix support race, the Stroud man's season rather fizzled out.

Vincini Motorsport's best result came here (although Jason Elliott finished second in October's non-championship Donington race), yet eighth for Mark Shaw wasn't a lot to show for the only Dallara-Fiat in the field. Similarly, Garth Waberski could do no better than two hauls of three points for DAW Racing (at Thruxton and Donington) before he ran out of money.

PSR and Firman wasted no time in restoring the *status quo*. Silverstone at the end of May – the last race before the GP support in July – belonged to Frenchman Jérémie Dufour. But Ralph followed him home as Edenbridge lost the plot completely, failing to get either Gavin or Arnold into the top ten.

Jamie Spence's third, in only his second race for Fortec following Roberto Xavier's retirement, was impressive but, with Jamie Davies soon to move to the team having left TOM'S GB, the Essex man's year was to be a brief one. After a couple of outings for the team that Davies had just departed, that was it for the underrated 1993 Class B champion.

By now, the title contenders were beginning to mass behind Firman.

Silverstone had marked Dufour's emergence as a serious challenger. For his third year of British F3, the ginger-haired man from Roanne had joined forces with Ligier and TWR, no mean combination. The formation of a junior team by an F1 outfit may prove to be a trendsetting move. Run by TWR, and with a Mugen engine, it was no surprise to see Jérémie claim his first championship victory, even if it came a little earlier than anticipated. 'It's been a steady climb, racing against teams that

Never the twain shall meet

The British Touring Car Championship and British Formula Three Championship once co-existed in harmony. Shared meetings – with TV coverage of both formulae gracing the screens via *Grandstand* – were, if not the norm, a reasonably regular occurrence.

Yet they are now firmly ensconced in rival camps.

If TOCA boss, Alan Gow, is to be believed, F3 is a series bereft of personality and excitement. He has no intention of stepping back into the ring with the UK's premier single-seater series. It's a mismatch, according to the Aussie.

Yet the ebullient Formula Three Association Chairman, Dave Price *(above)*, comes out fighting. 'You can suffer from severe tunnel vision,' he argues. 'If you're involved in Formula One you think the world doesn't exist outside F1. I'm sure there are people in F1 who have the same opinion about Alan Gow. Because Alan now deals with touring cars in England, Australia and America, he doesn't get the chance to see anything else.'

Price isn't blind to F3's failings, but he feels that TOCA should look to its own house first. 'To be honest, there is a certain degree of truth in what he says,' he admits, 'but his package, after the touring cars, isn't *that* good.'

In an ideal world the two warring parties should have been together from the word go, a concept that Price argues he was, and still is, in favour of.

'I'd have loved it,' says the former F3 team owner. 'I've always said that the only way for motor racing in this country to go forward would be for F3 and touring cars to get together to make ten major meetings. And I still think that. There's too much crap around; we have too many race meetings with too much dross.'

So why didn't it happen back in 1993? Did F3 turn TOCA down? Not according to Price: 'He [Gow] didn't want us to join,' he says. 'He didn't ask us, and there's a big misconception that he did. Alan Gow, at no stage, was bold enough or brave enough to take F3 on. No one actually spoke to me directly. They went through the back door to a lot of the teams, but an official approach for us to join up was never made.

'It would still work, but for sure now you wouldn't be able to do it because there's too many egos involved, and it's too much money for F3.'

I was wondering when it would come to that. 'The reason Alan wouldn't take F3 is that we won't pay,' maintains Price. 'Everyone he's got now pays, so he surely won't take someone that won't pay.'

So it would seem that the series are destined to remain forever in competition. And on that score the BTCC appears to be winning hands down, with a circus of 'names' to sell to the public. Price acknowledges, with a grin, that F3 can't compete in this respect.

'It's easy to build up personalities in touring cars. The same guys are there year after year because they've got nowhere else to go – they're at the end of their careers,' he says bullishly. 'Because F3 is so transient, you can't build up the personalities because they're not there the next year. The only thing you can build up is the teams. This is why our television coverage next year will feature more on the teams, F3 and what it does. I haven't got anything else to sell. I can only work with what the FIA says F3 should be.'

There may, however, be a new angle for the British series in 1996, in response to what Price feels the BTCC represents: 'Going to watch John Cleland and all the other old boys is like having a day out with your dad, watching your dad drive,' he says audaciously. 'If you go and watch an F3 race when you're just old enough to have a driving licence, then at least the bloke racing is the same age as you. We're trying to give F3 a new, major shift in image – we want to aim it at the younger market.'

He concludes: 'F3 will only ever be what it is – the breeding ground for young drivers for F1.'

And that's no bad thing.

LAT Photographic

LAT Photographic

LAT Photographic

LAT Photographic

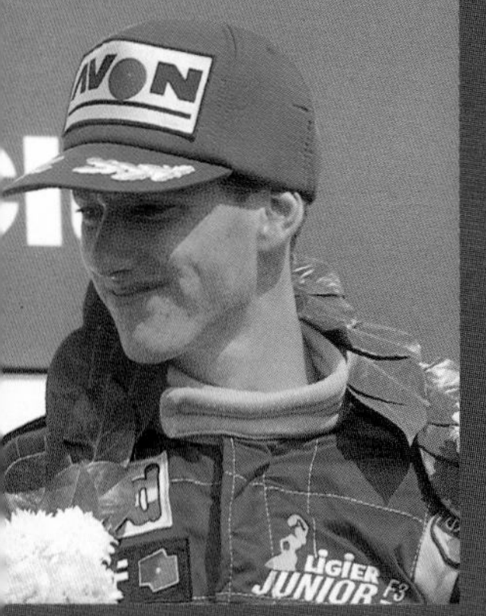

LAT Photographic

One-off winners: Gonzalo Rodriguez *(top)*, Cristiano da Matta *(middle)* and Dufour *(bottom)*. Gonzo's moment of glory was briefer than most: he was thrown out of the Silverstone results soon after this celebration because of a cracked airbox.

Clockwise from right: **Firman ponders his predicament. Da Matta was a tad disappointing – Luiz Garcia Jnr very. Warren Hughes *(right)* and Alan Docking gave the Mitsubishi engine its inaugural F3 win. Helio Castro Neves (2) proved more controlled performer than many had anticipated.**

LAT Photographic

Oliver Gavin wasn't smiling when Gualter Salles *(left)* pressured him into a silly mistake in the biggest race of the season. But he was at the end of the year *(below)*.

have established in years what we have in months,' said team boss Andy Morrison. 'I was hoping for a win at some point, but it's nice to savour one this early.'

Unfortunately, Dufour was not in with a realistic shout of the title when it mattered, interspersing podium slots from disappointing qualifying positions with races when he never seemed on the boil at all.

But when Gavin made his worst mistake of the year, sliding off and out of the lead at Club on the first lap of the Grand Prix support race, Dufour moved ahead of the Bedford driver to became Firman's nearest challenger, while the PSR man consolidated his position with third behind Gualter Salles and Jérémie.

This was a year of firsts: Salles took his maiden win, also after three years in the formula. This marked a return to glory for the Brazilian's team, too. Fortec Motorsport, owned by David Balfe and now with former Jordan and Lotus F1 man, Trevor Foster, as its team manager, had not won since Kelvin Burt triumphed twice back in 1992.

The happy Brazilian had to be content with a delayed victory, however, for Rodriguez had crossed the line first, only to be excluded for a cracked airbox. Apart from Oulton Park, Gualter's season never hit such peaks again. Meanwhile, his Alan Docking Racing team-mate, Geoffroy Horion, struggled all year, rarely venturing into the top ten.

Castro Neves, who was already stringing together an impressive run of results, Arnold, Hughes and Salles were all snapping at the heels of the leading championship trio. And the tempo was about to increase, with the last seven meetings – 11 races – being squashed into just ten weeks.

Firman and Gavin scored a win apiece at Donington Park in July, as Davies proved his worth with a second place in round nine. Marc Gene, meanwhile, gave West Surrey Racing its first podium finish since the opening race, while Dufour briefly headed the championship after round eight.

Then, just when it seemed that Firman, Gavin and Dufour were about to pull away from the rest, all three failed to score heavily at Oulton Park, where da Matta ended his run of seven no-scores with a debut win. This only came after the leading, and pulling away, Firman was penalised ten seconds for jumping the start.

This was a strange race: Gavin stalled at the lights and Dufour was also penalised ten seconds – for dangerous driving – both of which dropped them out of the points.

This allowed Hughes to gain ground with one of the drives of the year. The Geordie was suffering with a gastric virus, yet tigered his way up from 12th to third, behind the Brazilian duo of da Matta and Salles.

Top to bottom: **Brazilians all – da Matta (3) leads Castro Neves at Pembrey. Hughes makes a rare mistake, sliding off at Brands Hatch's Druids. Martin Byford was this year's Class B Champion.**

Clive Challinor

Gary Hawkins Photography

This win was to prove the highlight of Cristiano and WSR's season. 'I knew it would come,' said team boss Dick Bennetts, but unfortunately it didn't come again. The Brazilian F3 Champion was a disappointment, although Bennetts will probably admit that 1995 wasn't one of his team's best years. And it may be its last in the formula for a while, a '96 BTCC programme with Ford being in the offing. Of Bennetts's other '95 charges, Gene showed promise and Brian Cunningham continued to improve, but more often than not, all three were involved in minor skirmishes – often with each other!

The season's only visit to Brands Hatch proved fruitful for Firman. He was inspired as he took maximum points. Nobody looked remotely like matching his speed all weekend, as he set lap record after lap record, including the first 42-second F3 tour around the Indy circuit. He was supreme. This was, without doubt, the highlight of his season.

But it wasn't to be his springboard to the championship . . .

Unable to match his team-mate, Castro Neves had at least moved ahead of Gavin, who now trailed the Brazilian by two points and the Briton by 48. Situation normal: PSR first and second in the points. It seemed to be all over . . .

That was without reckoning on Firman falling over his own feet, almost literally, at Snetterton. A fine win for Gavin in round 13 was made extra sweet when Firman took himself and second-placed Hughes off at Sear. The problem was his right foot: 'I just couldn't get it back off the throttle and onto the brake because I got it caught on the side of the brake,' admitted a disbelieving Ralph. 'I wasn't even trying – I'd settled for third.'

If that was the case, the error was to stick so close to the rear of Hughes's car when there was no real need to . . .

So with five races left – double-headers at Pembrey and Silverstone plus a single race at Thruxton – the tension was starting to mount. And it showed.

Gavin was penalised for a jumped start in round 14, and was more than a mite disgruntled until his main rival, who had won the race from Castro Neves, was also handed a ten-second penalty, for hanging too far back behind the Safety Car and controlling the pace to his liking. Firman reckoned that he had done nothing wrong, especially as he had been praised by another Clerk of the Course for a similar action earlier in the year. PSR appealed and the initial decision was overturned by the Stewards. This was to be Firman's sixth – and last – win.

A fifth victory for Gavin, in round 15, kept him within sight of Firman, although the situation then became even more unclear: Edenbridge appealed the Pembrey Stewards' decision. This was never likely to be heard before the end of the season, and the worst possible scenario of the title being settled by lawyers reared its ugly head.

As usual, Pembrey provided the best result for Christian Horner – sixth. He had taken over the Toyota-engined Dallara of TOM'S GB from Spence, the soon-to-be Japanese F3 Champion Pedro de la Rosa and Davies. The team and engine both showed promise, but could have done with the continuity of one driver throughout the season. For 1996, it will attempt the F3 equivalent of climbing the north face of the Eiger by producing a new chassis in an effort to break Dallara's monopoly.

The domination of the Italian marque has even spread to Class B, which is run for year-old cars without the latest engine management systems. This championship was settled in Wales: Martin Byford's ten victories in the Z-Speed Dallara F394-Vauxhall being more than enough to give the former Formula Fordster a well-deserved title. He mixed some dominant performances with wins conjured out of thin air.

He was challenged initally by Johnny Mowlem (Mark Bailey Racing), the winner of four races spread over the season. But he was beset by sponsorship problems, so Byford's biggest threats were then Werner Lupberger (DAW) and Takashi Yokoyama (TOM'S GB). The latter rightfully got the nod for the runner-

LAT Photographic

up slot thanks to his four victories, the Japanese driver much improved and almost unrecognisable from his days in Formula Vauxhall.

The crunch, literally, for Firman came at Silverstone, venue for the final double-header. Drizzle brought about some unusual grid slots: Firman sixth and tenth, Gavin ninth and pole, Castro Neves third and ninth . . .

And Hughes strolled to a comfortable first F3 victory for the HKS Mitsubishi engine. This was only the Sunderland driver's second career F3 triumph, the first coming back in 1992's GP support race.

Even in terms of this season, it had been a long time coming for Warren, who should have won at least once at Thruxton in April. 'I'd started to forget what winning was like,' he said, very relieved. ADR hadn't won since 1992 either, and the strain of running a four-car team suddenly seemed worth it.

Rodriguez showed himself to be a battler much like Hughes, while one of ADR's Mugen-powered drivers, Belgian Kurt Mollekens, was a consistent top-ten runner in the second half of the year. And when Christian Horner left to go to TOM'S GB, his Dallara-Mugen became a third Dallara-Mitsubishi, for Owen McAuley. The highlight of the Ulsterman's year was his victory in the non-championship race at Donington, the weekend after the Thruxton finale.

Meanwhile, as Castro Neves threw his hat most definitely into the championship ring by claiming his fourth second place in six races, Firman was doing his best to throw his chances away. The Norfolk youngster had recovered well from his lowly grid position to lie fourth, behind Davies, only to once again get too close to the car in front. This time he managed to keep it going, albeit minus part of his front wing. By lap six he had dropped to seventh, with Gavin, Cunningham and several other cars gathering impatiently behind him . . .

Lap after lap Olly's advances were repelled, including the Edenbridge driver being forced onto the grass on the inside at Copse. Cunningham managed to sneak through on lap 11, but Gavin's final attempt, at Brooklands on the last lap, ended in tears. Ralph rejoined to finish eighth, only for the Stewards to exclude him, fine him and endorse his licence. Thus Gavin was 19th.

Matters worsened for Firman when he made contact with Cunningham in the second race. This time he slid down to 12th before having his licence endorsed yet again. If that wasn't enough, Gavin won the race to set up a nail-biting finale: Olly and Ralph were level on points going into Thruxton, with Helio (who, unfortunately, had retired from the second race at Silverstone) only nine behind.

Nail-biting that is, if Firman would be allowed to race. Three

Please sir, can I have some more?'

LAT Photographic

It was a brave decision to return after a year away. It was a move that could have backfired on the tall, gregarious 23-year-old and effectively ended his career. It didn't. He came away with the championship and has high hopes for the future.

It's no mean feat finishing runner-up in the British Formula Three Championship: just ask Martin Brundle, Mika Salo and David Coulthard. But to do so twice . . .

For the bulk of this season, Oliver Gavin looked odds-on to do just that. He finished second behind Kelvin Burt in 1993 and, after a disastrous F1 testing deal with Pacific, plus a handful of disappointing Formula 3000 races with Omegaland in 1994, the Bedford-born driver was in grave danger of becoming a 'nearly man' as Ralph Firman strode into an early, and sometimes convincing, championship lead. Second would be perceived as a failure. Only the title would do.

The tension of seven months of tough, and occasionally bitter, competition has now been released. Yet he's still acutely aware that he's been looking down the barrel.

'Yes, it was quite a risk,' Olly admits freely, 'but one that Peter [Briggs, owner of Edenbridge Racing] thought was worthwhile. At the time, I definitely thought it was worthwhile – it wasn't looking like I could raise the budget to do F3000. It certainly paid off.'

A return to Edenbridge, whom he drove for in 1993, was a natural one, despite some interest from Paul Stewart Racing. 'It's not necessarily that I wouldn't have fitted in at PSR,' he says. 'It was the fact that I fitted in so well here at Edenbridge that I possibly didn't think of going anywhere else.'

The season started badly for the 1991 National Formula First Champion, with two disastrous results from the opening double-header at Silverstone. While he shrugs those blips aside as being car related, it wasn't all plain sailing on the driver front.

'I approached the year thinking I had to win the championship,' he explains, 'and that was why there were a few errors. There was pressure on me from sponsors and the like, and I was inflicting quite a lot on myself by thinking "I've got to be the quickest driver all the time. I've got to be winning all the races." '

Nowhere was this pressure more apparent than at the British Grand Prix meeting in July. The showpiece race should have been the start of a sustained title push as the championship swung back into gear after a five-week break. And pole position was duly converted into an early lead – only for the Vauxhall-powered Dallara to slide off at Club on the first lap, as Gualter Salles harried Olly into an error.

'We were very strong there. If I'd only kept my head for that first lap, I think that could have been the easiest 20 points I'd scored all year long,' he says honestly.

However, team and driver quickly recovered from that disappointment, which was the strongest single element of his challenge, Gavin feels. 'When we had a bad weekend we'd pull together and not sit there dwelling on it,' he says proudly. 'We'd try and work out what the problem was and, every time we came to the circuit for a race, we approached it in a fresh frame of mind. That is, I think, the main reason why we managed to keep it going throughout the season.'

Even so, it was looking bleak by the end of August, especially after Olly's major weakness this year, his starts, had seen him waste a front-row spot at Oulton Park. 'I had two bad starts at Silverstone and then, after Oulton, I did get a bit of a complex about it.' The worst thing about it was that he had no idea what was going wrong: 'I had a procedure and I just carried that out. It had worked so easily in '93 and then all of a sudden it stopped working. I couldn't put my finger on what had changed. I still can't.'

Following the Brands Hatch Bank Holiday meeting, he was fully 38 points adrift of a confident Firman. 'It was a bloody big gap and we only had six races left,' he remembers with some amazement. 'Mathematically, if I won all the races and Ralph finished second, he'd still have won the championship. But the main thing was that we never became disillusioned or disheartened.'

There followed a visit to Sir John Whitmore, a former European Touring Car Champion, and now a sports psychologist. 'He was very good,' admits Gavin. 'He just made me look at things a bit differently, to make sure that I was in control of the situation. He played a major part in turning my season around and getting me back on track. From then on we were strong.'

The tide started to turn after Brands. A victory at Snetterton, when Firman failed to finish after lying third for most of the race, was followed by a tempestuous Pembrey, and an even more controversial Silverstone when the title challengers clashed – the PSR driver landing two licence endorsements for his actions. There is a tinge of regret over the bitterness that emerged during the season, but Gavin is adamant that Firman was the provoker.

Entering the last race equal with Ralph, Gavin needed to finish in the points ahead of Firman and less than nine points behind Castro Neves to become the champion. And he felt strong at that crucial moment . . .

'I knew from the way Ralph had driven at Silverstone, and the pressure he had put on himself and that people had put onto him, that he wasn't dealing with it particularly well. If I kept a cool, clear head, I knew I could come away with the championship.'

Third at Thruxton was enough to secure the title, with Firman and Castro Neves unable to present a challenge: 'It was quite intense with Kelvin back in '93, but nowhere near as intense as Thruxton. I think it was just that I dealt with things a little bit better than Ralph did on the day.'

But surely Firman handed him the spoils on a plate? 'No, it wasn't that Ralph lost it,' refutes Gavin. 'I think we took it away from him. We just had a far stronger finish and he just couldn't respond.

'There was a great deal of effort behind me: Peter Briggs did an awful lot to make sure we got the right bits of kit and the right people. He went out of his way to make sure I was comfortable. It was always going to be hard, and the pressure was always on us from the word go, but I think we coped with it. Not so well at the start of the season, but very well towards the end.'

With a Superlicence supposedly in his pocket, F1 beckoned and Olly hoped to make his GP debut in Adelaide with Pacific . . . He's been down that road before, and as Edenbridge is graduating to F3000 in '96, the preferred option is to stick with the devil he knows, money permitting. 'It's not that I wasn't ready last time round,' he argues. 'I think I just got involved with the wrong people. That was something I paid a very big price for. It could well have ruined my career – if I hadn't won the championship.'

But he did and his career is back on track.

F3 Top Five

chosen by Stewart Williams

1 Oliver Gavin

Determination kept his season going after an inconsistent first half. Calm and cool under pressure, he used his experience to good effect in the closing stages of the title battle. Very articulate, even at his lowest moments and, crucially, never too despondent when it seemed to be slipping away from him. Of his six wins, Snetterton was the most conclusive. Overcame starting problem that threatened to ruin his season. Never outstanding in qualifying or race, but got on with the job quietly and efficiently. Fitted in with the team superbly.

2 Ralph Firman

Blindingly quick but erratic. Exploded out of the blocks in the first race, only to run out of steam in the final straight. Lost the title at Silverstone when he allowed Gavin to equal the scores, rather than at Thruxton. Unpopular following his Silverstone antics, but that shouldn't overshadow his six victories – an outstanding performance for a rookie in such a competitive year. A superb qualifier with nine pole positions. Won well from the front, but didn't pick up the crucial lower scores. Tended to get over-excited on occasion.

3 Warren Hughes

A talent that showed only in spurts until the last two meetings, when the Geordie was the pick of the crop and easily outscored the championship contenders. The best racer in the championship, his qualifying let him down badly – the car was to blame sometimes, but not always. Forced to make blinding starts and scythe his way through the field from appalling grid positions in the opening laps on too many occasions, and let that get the better of him sometimes. Proved that you can overtake in F3, but really should have done better than fourth in the points.

4 Helio Castro Neves

The surprise of the year. Expected to be quick and erratic – the mantle that Firman eventually took on – but was just the opposite: a bubbly, excitable character out of the car, over-exuberance got the better of him only once, at the first race. Fourteen consecutive top-six positions followed, and this kept him in with an outside chance of the title right up to the Thruxton finale. His early-season win at Donington Park had in it the promise of more, but that never came. Just one would have put him in the driving seat.

5 Jamie Davies

Didn't win a race, but came mighty close in the second half of the year. The Yeovil-born man blossomed once he left TOM'S for Fortec. One of the most consistent qualifiers thereafter, with an ability to set a time early in a session. He occasionally wasted these good grid positions, but his promise for next year lifted him above the other race winners.

Bubbling under

Jérémie Dufour
The experienced Frenchman led the championship briefly and, following his win at Silverstone, looked set to make a sustained challenge. It never materialised. Still one of the quickest racers, but qualifying was not his forte.

Gualter Salles
The amiable Brazilian deserved a victory and got one – in impressive style at the GP meeting. That aside, he was infuriatingly inconsistent, although he curbed a previous tendency to damage his front wings.

Cristiano da Matta
Started the season superbly and then went seven races without a point. He and team failed to convert pre-season testing form into race successes. After his Oulton win, he seemed to be surgically attached to team-mate, Brian Cunningham, which resulted in more than the odd accident.

Photos: LAT Photographic

endorsements usually mean a ban but, luckily, the one emanating from Pembrey was under appeal – an Edenbridge appeal!

So we were to have the climax everybody had hoped for at the outset of the season. Almost.

Picture the scenario: the last lap, Firman and Gavin diving into the chicane, the final corner of the season, side by side, with the title at stake . . .

Sadly not.

The three-way showdown was nothing more than a damp squib. Victory again went to Hughes, with Davies scoring another useful second. More importantly, Gavin had qualified and finished third. And that was enough, for the PSR boys had never got their – either qualifying or racing – acts together all day. Firman finished seventh, Castro Neves sixth and the title, regardless of appeals, was Gavin's.

With six wins apiece for both the leading protagonists (seven in all for Firman including the non-championship International Challenge at Donington in July), it all boiled down to who had claimed the more minor placings: that was where Gavin succeeded and Firman failed. However, there were definitely more errors from the pair of them than one would normally expect of title challengers.

Firman warranted second, ahead of the consistent Castro Neves, but should Edenbridge succeed in its Pembrey appeal, which was due to be heard on 5 December (after this book had gone to press), then he would slip down to an undeserved fourth.

At the end of the season, Hughes showed what might have been, and will be kicking himself that he did no better than fourth in the overall standings.

Another man purchasing shinpads will be Dufour, for fifth was a major disappointment for the Frenchman.

Davies just pipped Salles for sixth in the final analysis, although both can look back on a job well done, albeit for different reasons: Davies after a tricky start with TOM'S, Salles for finally calming down and claiming his first win.

Both PSR and Edenbridge were evenly-matched – even at Zandvoort for the Marlboro Masters of F3 where Castro Neves was third and Gavin fourth – while Alan Docking Racing made a welcome return to the winner's circle. Even if the formula loses WSR to the BTCC and Edenbridge to F3000, Fortec and Ligier/TWR will ensure that the competition will be just as fierce next year.

Ultimately, the British F3 Championship emerged from '95 smelling of roses. 'It's been excellent,' said Gavin upon lifting the title, 'and for everybody who has been watching, it's been brilliant to see. It has done the championship the world of good that it's gone down to the last round, and I'm delighted it swung my way.'

BRITISH FORMULA THREE CHAMPIONSHIP

	Driver (Nat.)	Entrant	Car	1	2	3	4	5	6	7	8	9	10	11	12	13	14	15	16	17	18	Points
1	Oliver Gavin (GB)	Edenbridge Racing	Dallara F395-Vauxhall	2	2	21*	21*	11*	0	3	20	8	0	10	12	21*	0	21*	E	20	12	184
2	Ralph Firman (GB)	Paul Stewart Racing	Dallara F395-Mugen Honda	20	20	0	15	0	15	12	0	21*	3*	21*	21*	0	20	4	0	0	4	176
3	Helio Castro Neves (BR)	Paul Stewart Racing	Dallara F395-Mugen Honda	0	–	15	6	20	10	6	10	10	10	15	10	15	15	6	15	0	6	169
4	Warren Hughes (GB)	HKS/Alan Docking Racing	Dallara F395-HKS Mitsubishi	10	12	8	0	15	8	0	6	12	12	0	0	0	12	10	20	12	21*	158
5	Jérémie Dufour (F)	Ligier/TWR Junior Team	Dallara F395-Mugen Honda	6	4	10	10	4	21*	15	16*	4	0	6	4	12	4*	15	1*	1*	8	141
6	Jamie Davies (GB)	TOM'S GB	Dallara F395-TOM'S Toyota	8	0	1	0	0	–	–	–	–	–	–	–	–	–	–	–	–	–	107
		Fortec Motorsport	Dallara F395-Mugen Honda	–	–	–	–	–	–	0	4	15	6	8	15	1	0	12	12	10	15	
7	Gualter Salles (BR)	Fortec Motorsport	Dallara F395-Mugen Honda	4	6	12	3	0	4	20	8	6	15	0	1	6	8	3	–	–	10	106
8	Cristiano da Matta (BR)	West Surrey Racing	Dallara F395-Mugen Honda	15	11*	0	0	0	DQ	0	0	0	20	12	6	0	0	8	3	6	0	81
9	Steve Arnold (GB)	Edenbridge Racing	Dallara F395-Vauxhall	13*	15	0	8	8	0	10	0	0	4	0	8	4	0	0	0	2	0	72
10	James Matthews (GB)	David Sears Motorsport	Dallara F395-Mugen Honda	0	8	0	12	2	0	2	0	0	0	1	0	8	1	0	10	15	1	60
11	Marc Gene (E)	West Surrey Racing	Dallara F395-Mugen Honda	0	1	6	4	0	3	1*	12	2	8	4	2	0	10	0	6	0	0	59
12	Gonzalo Rodriguez (URG)	HKS/Alan Docking Racing	Dallara F395-HKS Mitsubishi	3	0	0	2	12	6	DQ	1	0	0	0	0	2	2	0	8	4	2	42
13	Jamie Spence (GB)	Fortec Motorsport	Dallara F395-Mugen Honda	–	–	–	–	6	12	–	–	–	–	–	–	–	–	–	–	–	–	29
		TOM'S GB	Dallara F395-TOM'S Toyota	–	–	–	–	–	–	8	0	3	–	–	–	–	–	–	–	–	–	
14	Kurt Mollekens (B)	Alan Docking Racing	Dallara F395-Mugen Honda	0	0	0	0	0	0	0	2	0	0	3	3	3	4	2	–	3	0	20
15	Luiz Garcia Jnr (BR)	David Sears Motorsport	Dallara F395-Mugen Honda	0	0	0	0	0	1	1	0	1	0	0	0	10	0	0	0	0	3	16
16	Christian Horner (GB)	Alan Docking Racing	Dallara F395-Mugen Honda	0	0	2	0	0	0	0	–	–	–	–	–	–	–	–	–	–	–	14
		TOM'S GB	Dallara F395-TOM'S Toyota	–	–	–	–	–	–	–	–	–	3	0	0	0	6	1	1	1	0	
17	Brian Cunningham (USA)	West Surrey Racing	Dallara F395-Mugen Honda	1	3	4	0	0	0	0	0	0	0	0	0	0	0	0	4	0	0	12
18	Owen McAuley (GB)	HKS/Alan Docking Racing	Dallara F395-HKS Mitsubishi	–	–	–	–	–	–	–	–	–	–	–	–	0	0	0	2	8	0	10
19	Mark Shaw (GB)	Vincini Motorsport	Dallara F395-Fiat	0	0	0	1	3	0	–	–	–	1	2	0	0	0	0	–	–	–	7
20	Garth Waberski (ZA)	DAW Racing	Dallara F395-Mugen Honda	0	0	3	0	0	0	0	3	0	–	0	–	–	–	–	–	–	–	6
21	Alexander Wurz (A)	G+M Escom	Dallara F395-Opel	–	–	–	–	–	–	4	–	–	–	–	–	–	–	–	–	–	–	4
22	Geoffroy Horion (B)	Fortec Motorsport	Dallara F395-Mugen Honda	0	0	0	0	1	2	0	0	0	0	0	0	0	0	0	0	0	0	3
23	Pedro de la Rosa (E)	TOM'S GB	Dallara F395-TOM'S Toyota	–	–	–	–	–	0	–	–	–	–	–	–	–	–	–	–	–	–	0
24	Roberto Xavier (BR)	Fortec Motorsport	Dallara F395-Mugen Honda	0	0	0	0	–	–	–	–	–	–	–	–	–	–	–	–	–	–	0
	Class B																					
1	Martin Byford (GB)	Z-Speed	Dallara F394-Vauxhall	10	20	20	12	21*	0	20	21*	21*	20	10	16*	20	21*	16*	16*	20	–	284
2	Takashi Yokoyama (J)	TOM'S GB	Dallara F394-TOM'S Toyota	15	12	12	0	15	21*	0	0	0	0	8	8	8	15	20	20	16*	20	190
3	Werner Lupberger (ZA)	DAW Racing	Dallara F393-Vauxhall	12	10	0	16*	0	15	15	0	15	15	15	12	0	–	–	12	12	1*	150
4	Johnny Mowlem (GB)	Mark Bailey Racing	Dallara F393-Mugen Honda	21*	16*	16*	20	4	0	0	–	–	–	21*	20	–	–	–	–	–	–	118
5	Philip Hopkins (GB)	PHR/Prowess	Dallara F393-Fiat	4	–	10	0	12	10	12	12	0	–	0	6	10	8	–	8	8	15	115
6	Jim Carney (USA)	DAW	Dallara F393-Vauxhall	8	0	8	0	6	12	11*	15	0	0	4	0	–	10	12	6	0	10	102
7	Tavo Hellmund (USA)	Mark Bailey Racing	Dallara F393-Mugen Honda	–	–	–	–	–	–	–	0	10	10	6	0	12	12	8	3	3	–	64
8	Tony Renna (USA)	West Surrey Racing	Dallara F394-Mugen Honda	–	–	–	–	–	–	–	0	12	13*	12	10	16*	–	–	–	–	–	63
9	Alan Berkov (URS)	Z-Speed	Dallara F394-Vauxhall	–	–	–	–	–	–	6	10	8	8	3	4	6	0	10	2	4	–	61
10	Paula Cook (GB)	West Surrey Racing	Dallara F394-Mugen Honda	–	–	–	–	–	–	–	–	–	–	–	–	–	–	–	10	10	12	32
11	Daoud Abou Daye (SA)	West Surrey Racing	Dallara F394-Mugen Honda	–	–	4	10	10	–	–	–	–	–	–	–	–	–	–	–	–	–	24
12	Steve Allen (GB)	Mark Bailey Racing	Dallara F393-Mugen Honda	0	–	6	0	8	–	–	–	–	–	–	–	–	–	–	4	6	–	24
13	Zak Brown (USA)	Mark Bailey Racing	Dallara F393-Mugen Honda	–	–	–	–	–	8	8	–	–	–	–	–	–	–	–	–	–	–	16
14	Jason Rolf (GB)	Driver	Dallara F393-Mugen Honda	6	8	–	–	–	–	–	–	–	–	–	–	–	–	–	–	–	–	14

Subject to outcome of appeal by Edenbridge Racing

KEY

* *one point for fastest lap*

Key to rounds: 1 Silverstone National, 26 March; 2 Silverstone National, 26 March; 3 Thruxton, 17 April; 4 Thruxton, 17 April; 5 Donington Park (Short), 23 April; 6 Silverstone National, 29 May; 7 Silverstone Grand Prix, 15 July; 8 Donington Park Grand Prix, 30 July; 9 Donington Park Grand Prix, 30 July; 10 Oulton Park, 19 August; 11 Brands Hatch Indy, 27 August; 12 Brands Hatch Indy, 28 August; 13 Snetterton, 10 September; 14 Pembrey, 24 September; 15 Pembrey, 24 September; 16 Silverstone National, 8 October; 17 Silverstone National, 8 October; 18 Thruxton, 15 October.

Gary Hawkins Photography

Sporting Rover

Dunlop Rover Turbo Cup

ROVER SPORT

For further information on Rover Sport activities contact: Rover Sport, PO Box 400, Wallington, Surrey SM6 9SQ

Dave Loudoun leads 'new boy' Richard Dean. The wily Pershore driver was happy to see such 'interlopers' take points away from his title rivals.

LOUDOUN CLEAR

by Paul Lawrence

LAT Photographic

Dave Loudoun and Rover. The names are synonymous. In the last five seasons the Pershore driver has won Rover's headlining race championship four times. Only Ray Armes – the 1992 GTi champion – has spoilt this run.

In 1995, Loudoun completed back-to-back Dunlop Rover Cup titles, despite season-long pressure from Alastair Lyall. After a nail-biting climax just three points (from a total of almost 600) separated them. It was a time for cool nerves.

For the second season with its 220 Turbo Coupe, Rover worked hard to improve the package, based on the experiences of 1994. Notable among the changes were a revised engine and cooling system.

Impressively, from a list of 35 registrations, 20 were former race champions, and so a season of fierce competition was assured.

Having won the title in '94, Loudoun returned to defend his crown. But both Lyall and Piers Johnson were planning to, and capable of, beating him. And when the latter won both races in the first meeting of the year, at Silverstone, the pundits were quick to predict that this was going to be his season. However, a determined Lyall had just taken the lead of the first race when it was red-flagged . . .

Having finished third in '94, Lyall returned with Techspeed and backing from Loughborough Rover, and demonstrated at that first meeting that he was out to secure the title by winning races.

Loudoun, too, was fed up with people reminding him that he had won the 1994 title without a single victory to his credit. This year he was going to win races. If the title followed, so be it.

But it was Lyall, a master of the fast tracks, who proved unstoppable at Thruxton. Two red flags had his nerves jangling, but from each start he took control to win from the front. Johnson and Loudoun stacked up more points, but the advantage was firmly with Alastair.

It stayed that way for just six days. A season that had started so well went disastrously wrong at Donington Park. Driving tactics had been, shall we say, robust in the opening meetings, but now matters came to a head. Lyall was furious when punted from behind in a first-lap incident on the exit of Redgate. Left sitting helpless, facing the hard-charging pack at the top of the Craner Curves, he was out of the race. Both his car and title hopes had sustained a serious dent.

This was a weekend peppered with accidents, and there was plenty of tough talking after the race: Rob Schirle was fined and had his licence endorsed for his part in the accident, but this was cold comfort to Lyall. He had lost significant ground to Johnson and Loudoun, who had finished first and second. Every race bar the UK double-headers – where drivers took their better score – counted towards the championship, and Lyall could ill-afford to leave Leicestershire with nothing added to his points tally.

Loudoun is adept at staying out of trouble and scoring consistently, but it was at Silverstone in May that he finally laid to rest a personal ghost. On a warm day he won from the front as Johnson headed the chase. Enterprise Racing had gone radical on set-up and the car responded perfectly, eking out its tyre-life in the heat. Dave did the rest.

Lyall could only wish for the same as his tyres went away and left him to understeer into fifth. He was now trailing Johnson and Loudoun by 50 points.

Silverstone had been a calmer affair than Donington Park, but the combination of 27 evenly-matched Rovers and the Brands Hatch Indy circuit proved to be an explosive mix at the end of May. Especially for Johnson, whose series lead and car were destroyed when he plunged into, and over, the barriers at the foot of Paddock Hill Bend.

Once again Loudoun stayed clear of the action to win the second race. Lyall, meanwhile, got tangled up in a race-stopping shunt at Clearways in the first encounter, just as spots of rain started to fall. He survived that, and a damage-limitation exercise in the later race brought him second place behind Loudoun.

Category newcomer, Stephen Day, had been running strongly right from the start of the season, and won the other Brands Hatch race. His pace was such that he would be the only driver still with an outside chance of taking the title from Loudoun or Lyall at the year's end.

So both Lyall and Johnson had suffered their disaster days. When would it be Loudoun's turn, they wondered? Certainly not at Spa in June. A brace of fourth places was not outstanding, but they ensured that the title advantage remained with the defending champion.

But the championship *status quo* had been firmly shaken up in Belgium with the arrival of Jeremy Cotterill. With his single-seater career seemingly terminally stalled by a lack of funds, he had looked to saloon cars. And he certainly entered the Rover Cup in a blaze of glory, winning both races in the Ardennes for Rob Schirle's Cirtek team. Of course, it was too late to mount a title bid, but Jeremy was out to promote his name as much as possible in saloon cars – graduation to the BTCC his long-term ambition.

Lyall gave Jeremy a tough time at Spa, and was second on both occasions. But Johnson saw his title hopes slip ever further, struggling with a car hastily rebuilt around his old, and less effective, bodyshell.

The championship's annual showcase was next, the British Grand Prix support race at Silverstone. Even on Saturday afternoon it

Above: **Loudoun had some worrying moments in the final round, but survived to win his third Rover title in as many years.**

Right: **In contrast, his Enterprise Racing team-mate, Nick Carr, suffered a very inconsistent year.**

Alastair Lyall pushed Loudoun all the way, and lost out by just three points.

Mick Walker

played to a 45,000-strong crowd, which saw an unbeatable Lyall fend off Cotterill and an unwell Johnson. After the race – for the first time in three months – Alastair spoke of winning the championship. But fourth place for Loudoun meant that, after 10 of the 18 races, he led by 32 points.

The second overseas trip came early in August, with two races at the Dutch seaside track of Zandvoort. Rob Mears was a popular winner of the first race, as Loudoun pulled off an attacking drive to salvage second from eighth on the grid. Lyall was also well in the points, while Johnson came back strongly to win the second race.

The next 'interloper' arrived in time for round 13 at Oulton Park. The widely experienced Richard Dean took up the offer of a run in Ian Barnwell's car, and stamped his authority on the day by winning easily from pole.

Lyall was gutted. He loves the fast, demanding sweeps of the Cheshire track, and had started the day brimful of confidence. But when his best qualifying laps were wrecked by slower cars, it suddenly started to look less rosy. Ninth on the grid was nothing short of a disaster – as was his eventual fifth in the race.

Typically, Loudoun collected a healthy haul of points to boost his championship lead to 37. He also had a stroke of the sort of good fortune that helps win championships – his fuel pump failed . . . on the slowing-down lap!

It was back to Brands Hatch Indy for rounds 14 and 15. Loudoun was determined to keep out of trouble, while Lyall, although not particularly at home on this twisty track, badly needed to reduce the points deficit. The weekend brought them sharply contrasting fortunes.

Russell Grady became the eighth victor of the season by winning the first race from pole position, while Lyall shadowed him home for a 'banker' result. He then planned to throw caution to the wind in the second race. With excellent anticipation, he beat Grady away from the rolling start and stroked to a win.

In contrast, this was Loudoun's disaster day. Having qualified seventh, he was up to fifth when touched into a spin by Cotterill coming onto the pit straight. As his car rotated wildly, the pack went every which way to avoid Dave, who was remarkably fortunate to emerge unscathed from such a frightening moment. He rejoined to finish 19th.

However, rather than throw a tantrum, he took this major setback with commendable calm; he was simply relieved to have escaped from what could have become a massive shunt. In the second race he had to attack and passed ten cars on a track where overtaking is no easy matter. But this hard-worked-for ninth place still saw his lead shrink to 17 points.

The races at Castle Combe in mid-September provided two of the best scraps of the year, the fast, flowing Wiltshire track proving an ideal venue for the cars. It had been expected to suit Lyall. And Loudoun, too; he revels in its fast bumps, having scored his first-ever race win at the circuit some 17 years earlier. But qualifying was held on a drying track . . . Lyall left his run on new rubber until late in the session and, just as at Oulton Park a month earlier, slower cars ruined his shot. He qualified seventh. Loudoun could only manage ninth. And Johnson split them! This allowed Dean to win both races after hard battles with Cotterill, Johnson and Stephen Warburton.

In the thrilling first race, Loudoun managed to get ahead of Lyall in the early laps, and they finished sixth and ninth; by this stage of the season, Loudoun was only concerned with his position relative to Lyall's. Alastair got ahead in the second race, but only by one place, and so he trailed to the tune of 15 points going into the Silverstone final.

Qualifying at this meeting was a grim and drizzly affair, but Lyall was happy. He had made very careful use of his wet tyres to set pole position. Loudoun, like many others, was quick initially, but had his tyres go off later in the session, and was eventually bumped down to seventh. Should this state of affairs be replicated in the race, Lyall was set to win the championship by a single point.

And he certainly put his mark on the race, out-foxing fellow front-row man Warburton, even before the rolling pack reached the green light. And although Steve, Cotterill and Martin Jobling all harried, Lyall's lead was never in serious doubt.

With his rival in command of the race, the ball was in Loudoun's court. He had to finish in the top six. He had a rough time of it in the opening laps, though, losing his rear bumper after one attack from the snarling pack. However, by the fifth lap he was clear in a secure fifth place . . .

Loudoun has been one of the top one-make racers in the country for almost ten years and, at 43 (the same age as John Cleland), is racing at the top of his form. He acknowledges that his chance of securing a BTCC drive is slim, but his blend of speed and consistency, plus an uncanny survival instinct, is just what was needed to win this year's Dunlop Rover Cup.

And it was not just a triumph for the driver. Mike Southall's Enterprise Racing team had made it all possible, and again proved to be the team to beat.

For Lyall, anything other than winning the title was bound to be a disappointment. His frustration was understandable – even had he finished last on that fateful day at Donington he'd have been the champion.

Main photo: **David Cole goes grass-tracking at Donington Park.**

Below left: **A shell-destroying shunt at Brands Hatch severely hampered Piers Johnson's title challenge.**

The battle for third went right down to the wire, too. Day was a newcomer to the class, but brought with him vital knowledge of front-wheel drive racing gained while winning the VW Polo G40 Cup in 1993. And he quickly showed that he was far from overawed by the Rover 'establishment'. His team, Mardi Gras Motorsport, was also new to the championship, but this combination proved itself to be a competitive package throughout the year.

Aside from struggling at Thruxton, where experience is irreplaceable, Day was always a contender and headlined his season by winning at Brands Hatch. He went into the final round with a slim chance of winning the series, but it all went wrong when he was assisted into the gravel at Luffield. This also cost him third place in the series . . .

Johnson beat Day by just two points after a curate's egg of a season. His huge shunt at Brands Hatch effectively ended the title ambitions that had initially looked so strong. The small team, headed by Piers's father Mel, somehow got a car rebuilt for Spa just two weeks later, but the momentum was lost.

Piers was back on the podium at Silverstone (twice) and Castle Combe, took his fourth win of the season at Zandvoort, but struggled home a dejected 12th at Oulton Park. He is likely to stay on for '96, when he will again start the season as one of the favourites.

If Johnson's year can be described as inconsistent, Nick Carr had an absolute yo-yo of a season. Running alongside Loudoun at Enterprise, he began the year battling for a place on the podium and ended it struggling to get into the top ten. Second at Thruxton and third at Zandvoort – which netted the points for second as a guesting Cor Euser was ineligible for them – were proof enough of his pace. But on other days he was stuck in the midfield maul.

Photos: John Colley Photography

Seemingly every round of the championship from mid-season onwards was to be the last appearance of Warburton. The Malvern student, who celebrated his 21st birthday at the August Brands Hatch meeting, joined Mike Haines Racing with a budget for the first few races. Somehow, the irrepressible Haines stretched this shoestring to breaking point and beyond so that the youngster could complete a season that marked him out as a blossoming talent.

By September he was on pole at Castle Combe, and though 'mugged' by the experience of Dean and Cotterill on that occasion, ended the year on a high by running Lyall close in the final round. He will be a title contender next season and, if he can use his new tyres better in qualifying, should win races. At least.

The next three in the top ten were evenly-matched: Belgian Philippe Verellen, Troy Dunlop and Philip Burgess were all regular top ten finishers.

Verellen, who missed a couple of races due to clashing touring car commitments back home, spent another season with Enterprise Racing and topped his year with a fifth place at Spa.

Dunlop stepped up to Turbos as the Honda CRX champion, and had a strong learning year with GR Motorsport. In spite of less experience than most of his rivals at this level, he showed himself capable of mixing it with the best of them, and claimed a fourth place amid the shunts at Brands Hatch in May.

With barely two seasons of racing behind him, Burgess made a bold step forward into this category. The power of the cars and the level of competition were in a different league to anything he had known before, but he made remarkable progress and scored some truly impressive results for the Tracksport team.

Phil and his business partner, Ian Summerfield, both moved up. The former did the bulk of the testing, and ruffled a few feathers by taking a front-row slot at Zandvoort. Three podium finishes in the space of a week followed at Oulton Park and Brands Hatch.

Summerfield fared less well and paid heavily for his infrequent testing. However, he turned in the drive of the race at the final round, climbing from 27th to sixth.

Cotterill's half-season netted him enough points to grab the final spot in the top ten. His deal with Cirtek was on a financial wing and a prayer, but Jeremy and team boss Schirle wheeled and dealed to keep the car running. Having had his three-car Mirror Group squad stop racing in August for financial reasons, Schirle needed a front-runner to keep his team in action. Cotterill did just that.

Surprisingly, the wins of Spa were never repeated, while a minor technical infringement meant a no-score at Oulton Park. At Castle Combe he nearly eliminated half of the field with a monster spin, but otherwise Jeremy was a major player.

Nigel Edwards, Mark Hazell and John Llewellyn endured seasons littered with good and bad days: Ed-

wards started the year near the top of the pack, but a couple of shunts took the edge off his prowess; Hazell, often in the thick of the midfield squabbling, peaked with a fifth at Thruxton; the experienced Llewellyn had been touted as a potential champion, but his season never quite gelled, thanks in the main to a fair share of mechanical problems.

Both Grady and Mears won races and suffered massive early-season accidents. Tarporley Garage teammates, Alvin Heaton and Brian Heerey, brought good humour to the paddock and flashes of pace to the track. On a fast circuit, few are as brave as Alvin. Jobling was another impressive class debutant, topping his season with a third at Brands Hatch. Richard Hann bravely came back after a huge shunt at the same meeting, and scored a well-deserved fourth place and lap record at Castle Combe.

Finally, Dean, Schirle and Ian Flux would all have finished higher with full seasons.

Rover returns

With five one-make titles to his name, including three Rover crowns in the previous four seasons, Dave Loudoun could have been forgiven for loosening his grip on the Dunlop Rover Turbo Cup in 1995.

Not so. This vastly experienced driver came out fighting as hard as ever at the start of the year, as he set about defending the title.

Back with Enterprise Racing, he knew that he had a tough task ahead: 'I predicted that the championship would be between myself, Alastair Lyall, Piers Johnson and Ian Flux,' he recalls. Flux was to depart the series early on because of a budget shortfall but, that aside, Loudoun's assessment was spot on.

Johnson made the early pace when the championship opened at Silverstone, and Loudoun knew that Lyall would be unstoppable at Thruxton: 'He [Lyall] is very good at being on the absolute limit,' explains Loudoun.

However, it all changed at Donington Park when Lyall was knocked out of the race.

'My disaster wasn't as severe as his,' says Dave, referring to the moment at Brands Hatch in August when he was pitched into a spin by Jeremy Cotterill. While Lyall scored nothing at Donington, Dave was able to claw his way back up to ninth in the second Brands Hatch race to score 30 points. With just three points separating them at the end of the season, that was a significant recovery . . .

In between these two key moments, the reigning champion did something he had wanted to do for more than a year. At Silverstone, in early May, he won his first Turbo Cup race. He won again, over another destructive weekend at Brands Hatch, this time at the end of May.

That was the weekend when Johnson's title hopes took a major blow. Typically, Loudon steered clear of the carnage . . .

'I spend a lot of the time watching what is going on around me,' he offers. Twice that weekend he was close to becoming embroiled in someone else's accident. But a 'sixth sense' kept his car unmarked and ready to score points in the re-started races.

Throughout the second half of the year Lyall was clawing his way back into contention, in what effectively became a two-man race for the title. In this respect, Loudoun saw the arrival of single-seater hotshots, Cotterill and Richard Dean, as being to his advantage. 'I was happy for them to win races and take points off Alastair,' he admits.

Yet the coming-together with Cotterill at Brands Hatch almost cost him the title. It could have cost him a lot more, his car finishing broadside across the pit straight with its driver's door facing the oncoming traffic . . .

'That shook me up a little bit.' To his enormous credit, however, his first words to Cotterill after the race were: 'I think you owe me a beer!' And the next day he turned in his best drive of the year to finish ninth from 19th on the grid. 'I think that surprised a few people,' he grins.

Will he be back in pursuit of a hat-trick?

'It's very difficult. The Rovers have always been the best one-make championship – it would be very tough for me to replace it with anything. Before the season, I said that I wouldn't mind being beaten by Alastair . . .'

That just might happen in 1996.

DUNLOP ROVER TURBO CUP

	Driver (Nat.)	Entrant	1	2	3	4	5	6	7	8	9	10	11	12	13	14	15	16	17	18	Points
1	Dave Loudoun (GB)	Enterprise Racing	(40)	45	40	45	50	50	(38)	40	40	40	45	40	42	(10)	30	(36)	38	38	583
2	Alastair Lyall (GB)	Techspeed	45	(42)	50	0	38	45	(34)	45	45	50	42	42	38	(45)	50	(30)	40	50	580
3	Piers Johnson (GB)	Driver	50	(50)	38	50	45	–	0	26	32	42	38	50	24	(26)	32	(42)	45	28	500
4	Stephen Day (GB)	Mardi Gras Motorsport	(32)	40	16	40	40	–	50	42	42	38	30	38	40	(40)	40	(28)	42	0	498
5	Nick Carr (GB)	Enterprise Racing	36	(36)	45	30	0	38	(30)	12	16	34	34	45	32	(12)	28	(26)	28	22	400
6	Stephen Warburton (GB)	Mike Haines Racing	(16)	26	36	36	22	–	0	32	36	0	18	36	26	(32)	38	38	–	45	389
7	Philippe Verellen (B)	Enterprise Racing	34	(32)	28	–	–	36	(26)	38	34	18	26	28	22	(18)	24	(24)	34	26	348
8	Troy Dunlop (GB)	GR Motorsport	(24)	30	24	32	28	40	(28)	34	0	20	14	8	28	(36)	36	(32)	32	18	344
9	Philip Burgess (GB)	Tracksport	(14)	18	30	0	10	28	(10)	20	22	28	28	34	45	(42)	42	2	0	32	339
10	Jeremy Cotterill (GB)	Cirtek	–	–	–	–	–	–	–	50	50	45	36	32	–	38	0	45	(18)	42	338

KEY

() - Dropped scores for double header meetings in the UK (both scores count for Spa and Zandvoort)

Key to rounds: 1 Silverstone National, 26 March; 2 Silverstone National, 26 March; 3 Thruxton, 17 April; 4 Donington Park (Short), 23 April; 5 Silverstone National, 7 May; 6 Brands Hatch Indy, 29 May; 7 Brands Hatch Indy, 29 May; 8 Spa Francorchamps, 10 June; 9 Spa Francorchamps, 11 June; 10 Silverstone Grand Prix, 15 July; 11 Zandvoort, 5 August; 12 Zandvoort, 6 August; 13 Oulton Park Fosters, 19 August; 14 Brands Hatch Indy, 28 August; 15 Brands Hatch Indy, 28 August; 16 Castle Combe, 17 September; 17 Castle Combe, 17 September; 18 Silverstone National, 8 August.

PRECEDENT MARCOS?

by Paul Lawrence

Against a background of a worldwide expansion in GT racing, the British Racing Drivers' Club continued its bid to have a worthy home series. In terms of quality it succeeded, with more than ten different manufacturers involved at some point. What the series needed, though, was another ten cars.

The overall title went to Chris Hodgetts and the works Marcos team. The Westbury marque has come a very long way in the two seasons since the debut of its racing LM500 at the start of 1994. With participation at Le Mans for the first time since 1967 its major target, the Computacenter-backed outfit arrived at the start of the season with the latest evolution of the car, the LM600. This aggressive 6.1-litre, 520 bhp monster looked far more a purpose-built racer than had its predecessor, and Hodgetts was just the man to tame it.

Though he slipped down the order in the opening race at Silverstone when two cylinders went AWOL, Chris had shown race-winning pace in the GT2 class car. This victory went to John Greasley in his GT1 Porsche 993. The BRDC had aligned itself with the international classes and, on paper, the GT1 cars enjoyed an advantage in terms of tyres, wings and power. But that was of little concern to Hodgetts. The archetypal dicer, he was there to win races overall, and he did just that at Donington Park a month later.

The other winner at this double-header was the evergreen Thorkild Thyrring in the wonderful De Tomaso Pantera. Indeed, he might have won both races but for a spin on oil in the first. This ADA Engineering car had missed the opening round while away contesting international races in the hands of Thyrring and Andy Wallace. But now the Dane was back for the balance of the British championship, and he began a season-long battle with the Marcos team.

The next two major players, in terms of race-winning pace, arrived on the scene at Silverstone in May.

Klaas Zwart had been aiming to race his all-new Ascari FGT from the beginning of the season. It was late, but the prototype created by Lee Noble was a stunner. A dream debut netted it a win, but Thyrring won the second race after early leaders, Zwart and Win Percy, both had moments with back-markers.

Percy was making his championship debut, too, aboard the brand-new Harrier LR9C of former Rover racer, Richard Austin. The Evesham Mircos-backed car was beautifully presented by Dave Lampitt's Specfab team, and Win's ability more than did it justice.

There followed a six-week 'Le Mans' break.

Having achieved its aim of finishing at La Sarthe, Marcos arrived at Thruxton with Brazilian Thomas Erdos in its second car. Having raced up to, and including Le Mans, Chris Marsh had stepped down from racing to concentrate on the heavy workload back at the factory. Hodgetts meanwhile, had encouraged the team to give the perennially underrated Erdos a shot at Le Mans. It was a dramatic transformation for the single-seater racer, but he was straight onto the pace.

Though both cars faltered at Thruxton, Hodgetts was able to nurse his home to a fifth straight GT2 win. Zwart led overall until his tyres gave up the unequal struggle, and Percy side-stepped the spinning Ascari to score his first victory for Harrier.

The heat at Oulton Park two weeks later seemed to affect people as a bizarre race unfolded. Zwart was out before the race with major engine problems, while Austin had his first run in the Harrier as Percy headed to Australia for a touring car sortie. Thus the race came down to a Thyrring/Marcos battle. And it was Erdos who drove beautifully to carve out a healthy lead, while Hodgetts battled with the Pantera. As the race drew to its conclusion, Erdos slowed to allow his championship-bound team-mate by. Chris, however, refused to accept the gift and a bemused Thyrring motored through to win!

Thyrring won again on the Brands Hatch Indy circuit, but the following day was bettered by both Marcos, an inaugural win for Erdos heading the first 1-2 for the marque. With the Ascari and Harrier absent, Mark Hales forged the ever-improving TVR Cerbera into a brace of fourth places.

Two races at Snetterton in September were the low spot of the season, with just seven cars on the grid for the first race. Thyrring blitzed this meagre field, but a fine drive from Greasley netted him second ahead of Hodgetts. However, that was the latter's sixth GT2 class win of the season, which was sufficient to clinch the overall title for the former milkman from Redditch.

The second race in Norfolk was held on a very wet track and John Morrison – in the second Blue Coral Porsche entry alongside Greasley – played the ABS on his 911 to its maximum benefit. While he won the race, Thyrring and Hodgetts tangled on the pit straight and the freshly crowned champion ended his weekend with a precautionary trip to hospital!

Percy was back with the Harrier for the Silverstone finale and was in a class of his own, winning the race at a canter. Zwart also returned and headed a marvellous battle for second as Thyrring, Erdos and Greasley chased. The latter went into the race with an outside chance of beating Thyrring to the GT1 title, but Thorkild successfully backed up his '94 Lotus Esprit crown. Five overall

John Colley Photography

Mick Walker

Left: Hodgetts and Thyrring battle it out at Thruxton. *Above:* The same pair share a joke at Silverstone.

Top: Morrison was the closest title rival to Hodgetts, winning at a very wet Snetterton in his ABS-endowed 911. *Right:* One of Thyrring's five wins was scored at the same Norfolk track. *Below:* The fields weren't huge, but the cars are undeniably spectacular.

Gary Hawkins Photography

John Colley Photography

***Left:* The TVR Cerbera improved as the season progressed and should be a threat to Marcos in '96. *Below:* The striking Ascari FGT was on the pace, engine maladies permitting.**

wins made him the most successful driver in the championship, and he was quick to pay tribute to ADA. Missing the first race, and losing points due to the low number of starters in the class, meant that he could never really contest the overall title with Hodgetts, however.

For Greasley, second in GT1 was a commendable effort in his 993. The car was flying right from the start of the season and won the first race. Though the arrival of several quicker cars prevented him from winning again, he was a constant challenge to Thyrring. Only strife with the six-speed gearbox hindered his progress.

With just four starts from 12 races, Zwart did well to claim third in GT1. He never repeated his debut win, but the Ascari was a contender every time it raced. Major engine dramas kept it out of five races, and the car's appetite for tyres cost Klaas victory at Thruxton. Nevertheless, it was a fine start for this exciting road car project, which will undoubtedly benefit from this racing experience.

Other GT1 contenders were Porsche-mounted Mike Burtt, Gavin Mortimer and Steve O'Rourke, who later swapped his 935 for a brand-new, factory-built 911 GT2.

Finally, the two Harriers could not have enjoyed more differing fortunes. Percy took Austin's LR9C straight to the sharp end of the action and, despite lacking experience at this level, its owner drove commendably when he piloted it at Oulton – hardly the ideal place to make your debut in a 500 bhp sports car.

In stark contrast, Ian Jacobs had another character-building season with his LR9C. The car was debuted at Brands Hatch in August, but never ran long enough to show the potential it undoubtedly has.

The other marques to appear were Jaguar, Honda, Morgan and TVR: Peter Hardman ran a Chamberlain XJ220 at Silverstone, but sadly neither car nor driver were to reappear; Gary Ward borrowed the ex-Le Mans NSX for a couple of Silverstone races, and gave a glimpse of what might have been from a quality combination; although outclassed by more modern designs, Charles Morgan was a welcome contender in selected races with the works Plus 8 GTR.

In contrast, the TVR was a regular competitor. Hales started the year with the Techspeed Cerbera still short on development. This glorious-looking car suffered from cooling problems early in the season, and precious chassis tuning time was spent keeping the AJP engine, diff and gearbox temperatures down. However, the factory-blessed project made strong progress and, by August, Hales was able to chase the Marcos pair as chassis and aerodynamic work began to reap dividends.

The biggest GT2 challenge to Hodgetts, however, was Morrison's Porsche. This brand-new car was entrusted to the hugely experienced former single-seater exponent and he duly delivered. Had it not been for more than his fair share of punctures, he might have run Chris even closer.

In claiming his first championship since the 1990 TVR Tuscan crown, Hodgetts achieved just what Marcos set out to do when it announced its decision to go racing, at the 1993 Motor Show. And in Hodgetts and Erdos, it had a blend of speed, experience, youth and aggression.

Marcos aims to defend the title by dovetailing a domestic programme with more European forays. It would be well advised to sign up the same drivers for that campaign, too.

Barry Ambrose

TO THE MANOR BORN

by Marcus Simmons

Swift by sponsor, swift by nature: Guy Smith celebrates yet another victory.

LAT Photographic

Formula Renault may have metamorphosed into Formula Renault Sport over the winter of 1994. And the old 1700 cc, road-gearboxed category may have been swapped for the new two-litre, racing-'boxed 'mini Formula Three'. But the story of the ultrafilter international-backed championship remained the same.

Manor Motorsport and its lead driver dominated.

Guy Smith, at 21 already a veteran of almost every junior formula, stepped easily into the racing boots of reigning champion James Matthews to win nine of the 13 races and wrap up the title by Brands Hatch in mid-August.

But it hadn't been that way all season.

There were four different victors in the first five rounds, with Darren Turner, Russell Ingall and Duncan Vercoe winning once to Smith's twice. This quartet looked set to provide us with a year-long battle of Homeric proportions.

But this hope was scotched by Smith. An explosive mid-season run of form from the Yorkshireman gave him a considerable advantage and, by the time he erred at Snetterton and went out in a collision with Ingall, it no longer mattered. Had he avoided this incident, the amiable Hull driver could have entered the close-season claiming not to have been beaten since the end of May . . .

After the procrastination of Renault Sport in Paris – the category had originally been scheduled for introduction in 1994 – it was a relief when the cars eventually began to hit the tracks back in December. Their predecessors had been criticised for a lack of top speed and that notchy gearbox – but, disappointingly, it soon became apparent that the new cars were hardly any quicker. The eight-valve Laguna engine delivered its power smoothly, but there was still little performance at the top end. By March, however, the leading teams were beginning to make great strides with chassis development. And, courtesy of some strong engines from the continent (supplied in the main by Frenchman René Huger), progress was made on the motors. By the end of the season, the better powerplants were residing on the quick side of 160 bhp – in other words, within a few horses of Formula Vauxhall.

Radbourne Racing's John Millett – Renault UK's indefatigable technical man – had confidently predicted 20

MASTER
6
AUTOSPORT
VERCOE
aalco
E
HILTON
NATIONAL
BELOU
COMMUNICATIONS
AstraTech
RACING TECHNOLOGY
MOTUL
MOTOR OIL
AUTO GLYM
aalco
Philips Car Systems
PENSKE

Lloyds
Bowmaker
E
Panasonic
Batteries
ALKALINE
14
D.C.COOK
AA
Arai
MINTEX

Duncan Vercoe *(left)* was Smith's closest challenger once he had switched to the pretty Mygale chassis.

David Cook *(below left)* had everything in place to succeed, but was to be disappointed, and disappointing.

cars for the opening round at Donington. Well, Mystic Meg needn't worry, for that magic figure wasn't reached until the Silverstone finale. The smallest field of the year was at Thruxton, round three, which attracted just 14. This was to be expected, for a category's inaugural season always denies it the supply of year-old cars that tend to flesh out the grids. It was more a case of an overestimating Millett rather than disappointing support.

Apart from the regulars – numbering about 15 – the size of the field tended to depend on which one-off contestants could be coaxed out for each race. Two cars – the third and second Van Diemens of Manor Motorsport and Redgrave Racing – were occupied by six different pilots during the course of the 13 races, and it is only when the category is fully established that this state of affairs will change.

Certainly, those who flitted in and out of the series made little impact. As with any formula, preparedness was the key. Smith had been installed behind the wheel of his Van Diemen RF95 since January, and it came as little surprise when he hit the ground running as the championship rolled into action at Donington Park in April.

By this time he had already been cruelly denied a Formula Renault Eurocup win on the Bugatti circuit at Le Mans, when fuel-surge problems set in a few laps from home. Indeed, this particular problem was to prove a scourge of the formula, especially in qualifying, where cars necessarily run with as light a fuel load as possible.

Smith kept Ingall's Anglo European Motorsport Van Diemen at arm's length throughout the opening race, and the crucial psychological advantage was his. A cautious run at Brands Hatch, during which he shadowed Turner's Van Diemen, was followed by a second win at Thruxton. Then he made a botch of Silverstone; Guy switched off his overheating Mountune engine on the grid, and couldn't restart it when the two-minute board was held aloft . . .

A charging recovery to seventh was followed by a second at Oulton Park, behind an inspired Vercoe – and then began the purple patch.

John Booth's Manor Motorsport team undoubtedly benefited from the razor-sharp competition encountered on Smith's European forays, and the South Yorkshire outfit's driver became unbeatable on his home turf. Win after win was clocked up, including a couple of close calls at Knockhill in which he had to deal with the 'red mist' of Vercoe.

But, even with the close competition, Smith never fell into the trap that has claimed so many others during a hard-fought season. He's intelligent, a supremely nice bloke, and seems not to have an enemy in the world. Even when Vercoe became agitated at what he saw as 'rough house' tactics in the penultimate round at Oulton Park, Guy didn't mind. He understood his rival, gave him space and was chatting to him again within a matter of days. Besides, he reasoned, it doesn't do any harm if people think you're a hard case!

Formula Renault Sport suited Smith perfectly. He loves to carry speed into corners, and the Michelin-shod Van Diemen enabled him to do just that. Dave Baldwin's design was doubted by many for the first two months of its existence, but the development work of Manor Motorsport soon obliterated those question marks. Mountune's engines, while not quite on a par with the continental missiles, were reliable and powerful enough for the task.

It was a supremely professional job all round, and thoroughly deserving of the first British Formula Renault Sport title.

By contrast, Vercoe's entrant, the Martello Racing team run by Andy Chisholm, won't thank me for reminding one and all that its recalcitrant Swift was run out of the back of a van at Donington Park. Vercoe took a calculated risk in stepping down after dominating Class B of last year's British Formula Three Championship. And two frustrating runs to lowly points-scoring positions left him tearing his hair out. Then came salvation in the shape of Olympic Motorsport. Chris Creswell's team needed to farm out its Renault Sport operation, in order to concentrate on Formula Ford, and a deal to run works-supported Mygales and retrieve ex-Martello engineer Mike Langley was too much for Chisholm to resist. Olympic driver Kirsten Kolby came on board, while Vercoe was hastily provided with the second of the Jean-Claude Silani-penned French chassis.

Within six weeks of cancelling his plans to run an F3 team in 1995, Chisholm was then faced with a potential disaster when Kolby's Mygale caught fire in a testing shunt at Goodwood. Luckily, the Dane climbed out of the blaze with remarkably minor burns; but she vowed never to drive a Renault Sport again.

Undaunted, the team continued with Vercoe, and instantly found front-running form. He led at Thruxton, won at Oulton Park and never gave less than 100 per cent – more on occasions. Quite simply, the Warwickshire man doesn't know the meaning of the word caution. Absolutely breathtaking at a slippery Snetterton, he made all around him look distinctly third-rate on his way to win number two.

Martello deserves nothing but praise. After all, the Dorset team only started developing the Mygale in May, but was soon within striking distance of Manor's Van Diemen, which had had four months' head start. There is a lot of interest in the French firm's 1996 chassis . . .

Praiseworthy, too, were the efforts of Vector Power's Andy Kidby. He only stepped in to replace Martello's former engine supplier – Langford & Peck – at the British GP Eurocup round in July, but within six weeks his product was a winner.

Like Vercoe, Russell Ingall was another to step down from F3, this time from a Japanese campaign. Ken Stanford's Anglo European Motorsport was entrusted with the task of running what was basically the works Van Diemen. The ingredients were there: ace driver; good chassis; reliable engineer (in the form of Paul Leach). But there was one thing missing: power.

Being the works-supported Van Diemen driver is usually a good thing in motorsport, but when it ties you to using Mercury's Formula Renault Sport engine it begins to look less desirable. The firm's Formula Ford products were fine, but the way in which Ingall was blown off by David Cook's Huger-powered Swift on the straights at Knockhill led one to wonder whether someone hadn't slipped unnoticed an old 1700 cc motor in the back of his car!

The Australian's incredibly smooth driving style left many to question his commitment, and his longing looks at touring car machinery sometimes gave the game away. But Russell's a professional – he's grafted too long to ever give less than his best. Third place in the championship (with one win at Silverstone) will not go down as his greatest achievement, but it allowed him to stay race-sharp while he waited for that big saloon car chance. This was a wait that ended when he co-drove Holden Commodore ace Larry Perkins to victory in the Tooheys 1000 – his home country's most prestigious race – at Bathurst in October.

In stark contrast to Ingall, Darren Turner was extremely inexperienced going into the 1995 season. But this was easy to forget such was his pace during the early events with the lead Redgrave Racing Van Diemen.

The veteran of just two half-seasons in Formula First and Formula Vauxhall, Turner charged spectacularly from the back of the grid to be third at Donington Park in April, before holding off Smith to win an epic at Brands Hatch. There was a controversial incident with Vercoe at Thruxton as Darren went through into second place, but he was still very much in title contention. Then his season faltered a little. Testing feedback was never his strong point, and engineer Simon Finniss was left to rely on guesswork a lot of the time. The Camberley man's a tough racer, as he proved in his drive through to third in the wet final round at Silverstone, but he needs more experience.

With even less car mileage under his belt, Renault UK Kart Scholarship victor Jamie Hunter did a fantastic job to net fifth in the championship in his first season out of karts. Run by the family Frepau (Fred and Paula, his parents) Racing outfit, the amiable Yorkshireman – yes, another – was also comfortably the leading Swift driver in the standings.

Three splendid fourth places in the opening four rounds were a good start for the smooth-driving youngster, but it wasn't until Snetterton in August that he finally made the podium, in second place. That was the peak of a suitably encouraging debut season, which also saw him introduce Ron Tauranac's brand new Ronta chassis to the series at the Silverstone finale, under the wing of Anglo European Motorsport.

Other Swift drivers included David and Paula Cook, as well as Haywood Racing's pairing, Edward Horner and Marcin Filipowicz. It's a shame that Mark Bailey's chubby SC95R design didn't benefit from the yardstick of an established driver – none of its regular exponents had more than one year of car racing experience prior to 1995.

Beating all these drivers in just a half-season of activity, James Seccombe once again proved himself to

be one of British motorsport's most underrated talents. Once Christian Vann had defected to Martello Racing, GT Services was able to install its favourite Warwickshire – yes, another – redhead behind the wheel of a Martini MK71, and Seccombe duly finished all but one of the remaining races in the top five.

And James had only himself to blame for not scoring his first win in Britain (his only prior victory was the Zandvoort Eurocup round in 1994). He slithered straight on at Silverstone in the early stages of the final round, and ran out of time to catch race-winner Smith.

The other GT Martini seat was occupied most effectively by Damon Wellman, the chirpy Sussex short oval racer trying hard but stumbling through a lack of finance. Sadly, his season ended with a heavy shunt at Brands Hatch.

Finance certainly wasn't a problem at DC Cook Racing (né Lewis Motorsport). David and Paula Cook didn't want for anything: top team manager (Jonathan Lewis); star engineers (led by Paul Haigh); dynamite Huger engines; and the choice of five gleaming black Swifts. But, apart from monopolising the front of the grid at the final round, it just did not gel. Lewis left the team acrimoniously in July, hence the name change. By coincidence, David and Paula then got involved in numerous incidents, David in particular, which negated a largely trouble-free opening to the season.

Both Yorkshire siblings belied their lack of experience (one year of Vauxhall Junior each) with some occasionally fine showings: Paula's drive to second in May at Silverstone showed that she possessed a fair degree of skill, while David's qualifying at Knockhill highlighted the former downhill skiing expert's affinity with the more acrobatic circuits.

The first Briton ever to drive a Formula Renault Sport car (when he tried the Mygale at Magny-Cours in December 1994), Vann decided the Martini looked a better bet at GT Services, before reverting to Mygale with a mid-season switch to Martello Racing. For my money, his best showing was actually in the Martini at the Donington Park opener, where he stalked the leaders before mechanical problems intervened. Although 'Sherpa' attained a third place at Snetterton with Martello, this was gained as cars fell off left, right and centre in the slick conditions.

The first person to race a Mygale in a British championship was Kolby, but the Formula Vauxhall convert – run by Olympic Motorsport – failed to impress in the opening two rounds. She was then understandably scared off by that frightening fire at Goodwood. Olympic facilitated Martello's return to Renault Sport, before concentrating again on its favoured Formula Ford arena.

Thai driver Tor Sriachavanon made use of a Martini, the Fortec Motorsport man sneaking into the championship top ten at the end of the season. With just a couple of seasons in Formula First behind him, Sriachavanon was unsurprisingly not the most scientific of drivers. But some test sessions with former Fortec-run Renault champion Thomas Erdos provided a few solutions, so that Tor was able to place an impressive fifth in the last round.

Having proved himself a fairly rapid contender with Redgrave Racing in the final year of the old Formula Renault, Rollo McNally – running alongside Guy Smith at Manor Motorsport – was a major disappointment. He didn't get to grips with the Van Diemen RF95 anywhere near as effectively as he had the RF94, especially in the wet at Oulton Park, where he was black-flagged. There were a couple of reasonable showings on the short circuit at Brands Hatch, but by and large 1995 was a year for McNally to forget.

Brazil's Julius Carneiro drove a third Manor Motorsport Van Diemen early in the season, battling occasionally with McNally before returning home because of 'contractual difficulties'.

A promising debut season in Class B Formula Renault in 1994 suggested that Edward Horner would be capable of some respectable showings with a Haywood Racing Swift, but his form was anodyne throughout much of the season. Come the last round, however, he looked a different driver. Suspension changes, allied to no more pressure from 'A' levels, allowed the friendly Warwickshire – yes, yet another – teenager to finish sixth.

Team-mate Marcin Filipowicz proved that the British single-seater scene is a mite tougher than the Pol-

Left: **On the pace at the outset, Darren Turner's lack of experience saw his season tail off. It was still an impressive showing, however.**

ish karting arena. He just needs more time.

To design and build your own cars in the 1970s was fairly common. Sadly, in the 1990s, you might as well bang your head against a brick wall. Ross Tissington's two Stryx chassis hardly ever moved off the back of the grid, and Nick Dudfield's 'works' car didn't score a single point all year.

Fellow Vauxhall Junior graduate Michael Nippers drove the other car under the SLN Racing banner, and at least managed to notch up three top ten finishes.

The other chassis to show during 1995 was the Ray, which eventually appeared in the hands of Neil Riddiford at Silverstone in September. Run, as ever, by Tarry Racing, Riddiford qualified the car 14th with minimal testing, but lasted only as far as the Copse Corner gravel trap in the race.

And that was it. Numerous other drivers came out for one-off showings, the best placed of these being returning Formula Renault hero Jason Plato, who took fourth place in the ex Carneiro/Flynn/Erdos/Collins/Hanashiro Manor Motorsport Van Diemen RF95 at Silverstone. Ricky Flynn (Martello Mygale) and Derek Watts (Redgrave Van Diemen) both scored fifth positions.

A total of 38 drivers took part during the 1995 season, behind the wheel of seven different chassis. Of those that didn't race in the UK, French firm Alpa suffered through 1992/93 champion team Minister International's remarkable inability to find a paying driver for the season. Italian marques Tatuus and Ermolli made waves on the continent, and we can expect the former to be represented by a British team in 1996.

Therein lies the major appeal of Formula Renault Sport. Its variety of cars should be fantastic next season: the sharkfinned Tatuus; wide-track, low-slung Mygale; raised-nose Van Diemen; pointy Alpa; rounded Swift; and the oh-so-conventional Martini could all be there, as will the Ronta, an F3 car in disguise. And, with virtually all of Europe's slicks and wings racing categories being one make (except F1), that makes a refreshing change.

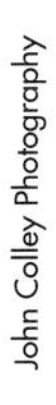

Zealous Guy

Guy Smith is a very fast racing driver. But he is also acutely aware that talent is not always enough. He's more prepared than most in this respect. At just 21, he seems to have been around for an age. A 'veteran' of just about every junior single-seater formula, he possesses an old head on his young shoulders – in and out of the cockpit.

But being known as an 'old hand' is just a side-effect of the master plan. With help from his manager Mark Smithson, Guy has accumulated 18 sponsors, which in a category like Formula Renault Sport means that he can make a profit and then plough it into his Formula Three activities at a later date. Clever, eh?

The flipside is that if you are to retain 18 backers, you need to be a winner. But the master plan is not likely to fail on this score. Smith has won in everything he's done: karting; the 1991 Formula First Winter Series; the 1992 Vauxhall Junior Championship; Formula Ford in '93; Formula Vauxhall in '94.

What he needed was a title . . .

Yes, surprisingly, his 1995 ultrafilter international Formula Renault Sport Championship – scored at the wheel of a Manor Motorsport Van Diemen – is the first car racing championship to bear his name.

'The last few years I've learned a hell of a lot,' he reveals. 'I've grown up and I've learned about the people in the sport. I've had some good years and some good, hard racing, but none of it quite worked out. This year it has.'

During those four-and-a-bit years in cars, Smith has raced against most of Europe's young talent at some stage or another. Calm, relaxed, chatty and with a natural friendliness, he is as confident in his own ability as he is in his dealings with the vital money men.

But there must have been a time when he thought that maybe he was destined to remain a runner-up: 'This year for me was going to be make-or-break year; if I didn't win in Formula Renault Sport it would have been really difficult to win in F3.

'Unlike Formula Vauxhall, the Renault suits my driving style. My style, which I developed from karting, is quite aggressive into the corners, carrying lots of speed, which the Renault allows me to do as it is quite a stiff car.'

And outside the car?

'Obviously, because I've won the championship, this year has been good, but in the last two years I've learned a lot about what makes me work, how to prepare myself for the race and how to control the atmosphere around me. It helps being with Manor Motorsport. [Team manager] John Booth is out there to win – he gets the best drivers he can and he works hard with them. It almost feels like a family – I enjoy spending time with the team, even away from the circuit. They're a good bunch of people, just like a group of friends. So I've really enjoyed my racing – I'm sure that's half the reason why we've been winning so much.'

And winning has been the story: 12 successes have been collected this season, nine in the British series and three in the Eurocup. The best of them, he reckons, was the Eurocup round that supported the British Grand Prix at Silverstone. Down on power compared to the leading continental runners, Guy took advantage of an electronics misfortune which befell Tommy Rustad, but then had to fight off Angel Burgueno when fuel-surge dramas set in within sight of the chequered flag.

It's all helped ready him for an arguably belated step up to F3: 'I think the Formula Renault Sports are miniature Formula Three cars. They need just a little bit more power but, apart from that, I think they're fantastic. You can be a second off the pace, but the slightest adjustment and you can find it – that really proves the car is working well.

'I think we'll definitely be doing F3 next year, unless something like the German Touring Car Championship comes up!'

You get the impression that he doesn't mind what he does in 1996. You also feel that, whatever it is, it won't be long before he's winning again.

ULTRAFILTER FORMULA RENAULT SPORT CHAMPIONSHIP

	Driver (Nat.)	*Entrant*	*Car*	*1*	*2*	*3*	*4*	*5*	*6*	*7*	*8*	*9*	*10*	*11*	*12*	*13*	*Points*
1	Guy Smith (GB)	Manor Motorsport	Van Diemen RF95	22	17	22	(4)	15	22	22	20	20	20	0	20	20	220
2	Duncan Vercoe (GB)	Martello Racing	Swift SC95R/Mygale FR95	8	(1)	10	6	22	14	12	17	17	10	20	12	0	148
3	Russell Ingall (AUS)	Anglo European Motorsport	Van Diemen RF95	15	8	12	22	12	10	15	12	12	15	0	–	–	133
4	Darren Turner (GB)	Redgrave Racing	Van Diemen RF95	12	20	15	12	8	15	8	0	8	10	(4)	10	12	130
5	Jamie Hunter (GB)	Frepau Racing/Anglo European Motorsport	Swift SC95R/Ronta RT96	10	10	0	10	3	0	4	10	4	3	15	10	3	82
6	James Seccombe (GB)	GT Services	Martini MK71	–	–	–	–	–	–	10	8	0	12	12	15	17	74
7	David Cook (GB)	DC Cook Racing	Swift SC95R	2	12	6	8	10	0	6	0	0	1	0	6	0	51
8	Paula Cook (GB)	DC Cook Racing	Swift SC95R	6	0	1	15	6	0	0	6	0	6	0	3	0	43
9	Christian Vann (GB)	GT Services/Martello Racing	Martini MK71/Mygale FR95	0	0	2	3	0	–	–	2	10	0	12	1	0	30
10	Tor Sriachavanon (TH)	Fortec Motorsport	Martini MK71	0	0	0	0	1	3	0	3	6	0	6	0	8	27

KEY

() Dropped Score

Key to rounds: 1 Donington Park, 2 April; 2 Brands Hatch Indy, 17 April; 3 Thruxton, 8 May; 4 Silverstone National, 14 May; 5 Oulton Park, 29 May; 6 Brands Hatch Grand Prix, 11 June; 7 Donington Park, 25 June; 8 Knockhill, 29 July; 9 Knockhill, 30 July; 10 Brands Hatch Indy, 13 August; 11 Snetterton, 28 August; 12 Oulton Park Fosters, 10 September; 13 Silverstone National, 24 September.

SLICK 50®

On the Track...

SLICK® 50 FORMULA FORD CHAMPIONSHIP

Star of tomorrow Mario Haberfeld, winner of the Slick 50 young driver award

Slick 50 plays a leading role in optimising performance and in supporting motorsport at all levels as part of a carefully planned motorsport support programme both in the UK and throughout the world.

Slick 50 is therefore an ideal partner for Ford as title sponsor for the most important championship in Formula Ford racing worldwide.

As the world's No 1 engine treatment it is most appropriate that Slick 50 should make the association with the world's leading motor racing category, a link-up which includes both the UK and Australia.

Although new to Formula Ford in 1995, Slick 50 is by no means a newcomer to the world of motorsport. The company supports motorsport in many countries, using it both as a promotional platform and as a means of technical development for its products.

British & European Formula Ford Champion Bas Leinders

American Indy Car racing, top level dragsters, the UK's largest saloon car racing series, the UK's two largest national kart racing series and one of Britain's brightest young motor cycle racers, are among many carrying the Slick 50 brand name.

In looking to expand its support programme Slick 50 chose Formula Ford as a natural progression in its plans. And by joining forces with Ford the two companies have been able to create a stepping stone to Grand Prix success for aspiring young drivers.

These days the majority of talented young drivers make their career start in karting. Now Slick 50 and Ford have combined to make the step from karting into cars all the easier.

Leading drivers in the Slick 50 Formula TKM National Championships (the largest UK karting category) including double winner Stuart Smith, and those in some other classes, were selected for the chance to test in Formula Ford cars at Silverstone in a unique new scholarship opportunity created by Ford and Slick 50. For some it will have been the next step towards a Grand Prix drive in the future.

Slick 50 has also linked with Honda in providing a dream come true for leading competitors in the Slick 50 Road Saloon Championship. To celebrate victory in the highly competitive series by Grant Elliott's Honda Civic, Honda has given three top drivers test drives in its Super Touring Accord.

Honda and Slick 50 have also worked together in promotion of the Honda Slick 50 Pro-Kart Challenge, the UK's most important series for four-stroke karts won in 1995 by Stuart Ferdinando.

Meanwhile Slick 50 is also helping drivers on the race track by improving the efficiency of their vehicles in the never ceasing quest for more power, performance and reliability.

The unique chemistry in Slick 50 incorporates PTFE, the world's most slippery man-made substance. Slick 50 Engine Formula bonds onto the critical surfaces within the engine to provide a low friction, low wear surface.

That reduced friction improves the efficiency of the engine, thereby optimising performance and reducing wear. It has been proven to be particularly beneficial under the conditions of boundary lubrication typically experienced during high stress racing operation.

Not surprising therefore that many motor sport competitors use Slick 50 engine, gear and other products to harness the maximum performance from their car, kart or motor cycle.

On the race track, where power is king, even the slightest improvement is important. On the road motorists enjoy the same benefits from Slick 50, though will probably be more grateful for the reduction in wear (up to 50 per cent over 50,000 miles from one treatment) and the potential for enhanced economy.

Whether for road or track you can be sure that extensive research and development has gone into products from Slick 50. And a part of that testing process comes from the Formula Ford competitors and hundreds of others around the world racing to success with Slick 50.

Further information on the Slick 50 championships from:-
The Slick 50 Motorsport Information Service,
1 Union Street, Bedford MK40 2SF

Grant Elliott on his way to victory

Class of '95. . . karting stars take their first tests in Formula Ford

-The Winning Formula

On the Road...

The unique chemistry in Slick 50 Engine Formula harnesses the latest polymer technology to improve the efficiency of all types of vehicle, reducing wear, optimising performance and helping cut running costs.

Every time you turn the key to start an engine you are instigating a process which will slowly but surely kill your engine. The friction of metal on metal contact as you first turn the key before the lubricating oil has been able to circulate and do its job accounts for around 80 per cent of all engine wear.

And friction while the engine is running is a limiting factor in the sheer efficiency of the power unit - efficiency also dictating the fuel economy and ultimate performance of the engine.

Any product which can reduce that wasteful friction is a winner...

Enter Slick 50, a product which has been developed through a multi-million pound budget over the past 16 years and which has gained world-wide market leadership and millions of satisfied users.

At first sight the claims made for Slick 50 Engine Formula can seem almost too good to be true. Engine wear reduced by up to 50 per cent for 50,000 miles with just one treatment.

But thanks to a massive investment in testing at some of the world's leading research centres, there is a mountain of carefully assessed data to back the claims the company makes.

Slick 50 Engine Formula is in fact a unique blend of products brought together with a secret formulation which has to overcome a tricky problem - how do you make the world's most slippery man-made substance adhere to the inside of an engine for 50,000 miles?

That's just what Slick 50's unique formulation achieves.

At the heart of the product is DuPont ®Teflon PTFE, a polymer which in various forms is used in applications as diverse as artificial limb joints and gun barrels. It is exceptionally strong and durable, chemically inert, and has the lowest coefficient of friction of any man-made substance. In other words it is super slippery - a little like rubbing two ice cubes together.

The PTFE in Slick 50 Engine Formula bonds to the engine surfaces in two ways thanks to specially developed advanced chemistry which includes the use of electron beams.

Once bonded onto the metal surfaces extensive testing has shown that Slick 50 Engine Formula stays in place throughout 50,000 miles and repeated oil changes. And because the Slick 50 Engine Formula protection is present at all times of course it plays that vital role of reducing wear at critical times such as start-up when the oil has not started being pumped around the engine.

Simply adding PTFE to engine oil will not have the same beneficial effects. The unique chemistry developed and refined by the Slick 50 research team is what enables the PTFE to bond itself to the metal surfaces, impervious to oil changes. Beware imitations!

Slick 50 is an engine treatment which bonds PTFE on the internal engine surfaces. It is, therefore, not to be confused with oil additives which alter the structure of the engine oil but of course still remain in the sump at start-up. Slick 50 chemistry has been proven to work with and complement top quality engine oils.

A measure of the success of Slick 50 in developing its PTFE chemistry can be gauged by a special joint technology agreement signed with the giant DuPont organisation. DuPont, owners of the Teflon PTFE brand, proposed the agreement for sharing technology in the development of improved lubricants and other products incorporating PTFE.

And that agreement with DuPont further underlines the desire of Slick 50 and its owners Quaker State Corporation, one of the world's leading oil companies, to be at the leading edge of lubrication technology for both automotive and other industrial and domestic purposes.

The Slick 50 range of products covers a wide variety of vehicle applications including two and four stroke petrol engines and diesels. Also included are products for transmission, through to light all-purpose lubrication.

Slick 50 Engine Formula comes in a variety of individual formulations to suit specific needs. Specialist products are made for high performance vehicles running with synthetic oils, while at the other end of the scale come packs of a suitable size and formulation to meet the needs of the heaviest of trucks.

Slick 50 offers two types of transmission treatment with differing specifications for manual and auto units. The manual transmission product can also be used in rear axles and transfer boxes and makes use of PTFE. However for auto units which need a certain amount of friction to operate, a totally different formulation is used which helps reduce wear while at the same time assisting seal life and fighting against corrosion and oxidation.

A fuel system treatment, high quality fully synthetic engine oil, power steering fluid, and high power all-purpose cleaner are recent additions to the Slick 50 range underlining the company's commitment to provide a complete service to the motorist.

On the road the extremes of lubrication achieved on the race track are never likely to be reached, but the same technology that gets to the chequered flag first can help win another very different contest - this time against all important running costs.

So the message very clearly is that Slick 50 is **NOT** just a gimmick. It is a proven product based on a scientific programme which has harnessed one of the world's most remarkable polymers.

Put another way, Slick 50 means real business ... and real business sense.

FURTHER DETAILS can be obtained from:-
Slick 50 at 140 Leicester Road, Wigston, Leicester. LE18 1DS. Tel 0116 2881522

IN THE MONEY LEINDERS

Bas Leinders *(inset)* was the surprise champion, defeating more experienced rivals, such as Justin Keen *(main picture)*.

by Charles Bradley

The Slick 50 Formula Ford Championship went down to the wire, with works Van Diemen and Swift drivers, Kevin McGarrity and Bas Leinders, contesting the title, which the latter unexpectedly won at the eleventh hour. This was indicative of the most unpredictable category on the TOCA package, which provided some superb racing in its first year of using slick tyres.

McGarrity entered the season's finale at Silverstone with a six-point advantage and a seemingly straightforward job of finishing in the top six to claim the crown, regardless of what Leinders did. Amazingly, in a quite calamitous race for him, McGarrity blew it by hitting Norman Simon's works Vector under braking for Brooklands and spinning away his championship-winning position.

Even then, the unscathed Van Diemen driver had only to make up three places in the remaining 15 laps to regain the result he needed. He passed team-mate Jiri de Veirman and First Division leader Austin Kinsella easily enough, to leave just Kristian Kolby between himself and the championship. But McGarrity slammed into the back of the Dane's Olympic Motorsport Vector, incurring irreparable suspension damage. Kevin blamed his rivals for driving like 'animals', but it appeared to most observers that the Northern Irishman had simply lost his head under intense pressure.

So Leinders was a worthy, if initially disbelieving, champion.

Perhaps the most telling statistics of his season are that he crashed out only once (at Brands, due to a non-existent clutch), spun once and was involved in a single serious collision (at Oulton Park, with Mario Haberfeld). In contrast, his rivals crashed into things, or each other, on a regular basis. And in this way Leinders redressed the balance for Swift, whose 1994 title was swiped from its grasp by engine misdemeanours.

The 20-year-old Belgian was much sought after by works teams over the winter, the former European karting champion plumping for the Chesterfield-based Swift equipe. This was a partnership that was not without its teething troubles; chassis production was late and little pre-season testing was achieved. But the opening round at Donington Park saw Leinders shoot to prominence, hassling McGarrity most impressively all the way to the chequered flag in both races, and then complaining about the Van Diemen pilot's defensive driving tactics.

The following round, at a wet Brands Hatch Indy circuit, saw Swifts to the fore, as McGarrity ploughed into the Paddock Hill Bend tyre-wall after making an error with his brake bias setting. This allowed Leinders to overcome a power-starved Michael Vergers (Andy Welch Racing Swift SC94Z) and team-mate 'Miku' Santavirta to head a Swift 1-2-3. This gave Bas a healthy championship lead.

A fallow period followed, as the SC95Z's suspension proved difficult to sort, a matter not helped by the inexperience of his team-mates Santavirta and Simon Wills. The following rounds at Thruxton and Silverstone were a disaster. Bas lost his fight with a wayward car at the former and was clipped, fortunately only slightly, by Kolby as he spun in the middle of the pack at the 130 mph Church Corner. If that wasn't bad enough, all three works Swifts stalled simultaneously on the startline at Silverstone a week later, and Leinders was smacked from behind by Vergers!

As the relationship between Leinders and Swift's engineering ace Mick Kouros blossomed, however, his season gradually began to pick up again, although three wins on the trot by Mario Haberfeld's Manor Motorsport Van Diemen RF95 had knocked him back to second in the championship after the May Silverstone meeting.

He was restricted to fifth place at Oulton Park due to an engine problem, but worse was to follow, a trip into the Druids gravel trap ending his hopes at Brands Hatch. The Belgian put this incident down to a recurring clutch problem, which the team struggled to rectify. At one point its driver thought he might have been resting his foot on the pedal accidently!

Despite an almighty qualifying shunt at Donington in June, Bas – now fourth in the points – increased his tally just as championship leader Haberfeld endured his nightmare phase of the season. Mario was used as a ramp by Simon at Donington Park, and then no-scored in both Knockhill races, due to an electrical failure and a shunt with de Veirman.

Bas prospered as the blond Brazilian faltered, winning the opening race at the twisty Scottish circuit and following that up with third place in race two. This effort lifted him to second in the series, three points shy of new leader McGarrity, and just one ahead of Vergers.

It might have been a different story had Vergers not spun into the gravel while attempting to wrest the

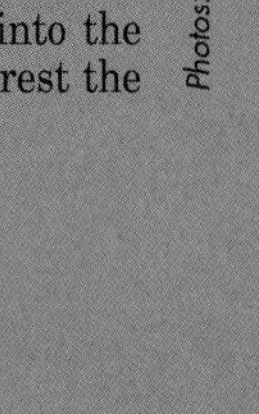

Photos: LAT Photographic

LAT Photographic

Left: **Michael Vergers, Keen and Mario Haberfeld all scored victories in one of the most competitive championships of the season.**

Below left: **Kevin McGarrity leads the pack at Brands Hatch; he should really have led the championship standings, too.**

lead from Leinders in race one. He made amends with victory in the next day's race – his second of the season, having also triumphed at Oulton Park.

A troubled Brands Indy meeting followed for Leinders, qualifying down in tenth and coming up against an obstinate McGarrity in the race. Their duel for fourth rekindled the feud that had begun at the start of the year. An incident on the slowing-down lap had McGarrity incensed, feeling that Leinders had brake-tested him, while Bas claimed that Kevin had threatened to 'kill him' after the race. The Belgian insisted that he was merely waving to the crowd when McGarrity had rammed him. It was all rather unnecessary.

The final double-header of the year was always going to be tense: McGarrity looked to have the upper hand until a clash with Vergers saw him limp home second to Leinders, in a car that was slowly disintegrating. The latter had carefully stayed out of trouble to take the win, which he followed up with third place in the second encounter. This was a typical 'no risks' run from the Belgian and, in spite of the fact that McGarrity had won the race to extend his slender championship lead, there appeared to be more of a structure to the former's title campaign.

McGarrity still looked strong, though, particularly at Oulton Park, where his Van Diemen was highly impressive through the fast Cascades sweep on the short Fosters circuit. Kevin even had the confidence to take the corner flat in fourth, while circuit instructor Vergers was using third!

But the works Vector of Justin Keen proved the wild card here, its driver at last finding race-winning form. McGarrity pushed him hard, though, and some of his attempts to take the lead looked more than a little risky given the finely balanced nature of the title race. His second place meant he held a six-point lead by the end of the penultimate round.

After such a hard-fought season, it is still hard to believe the way that McGarrity seemingly cast the title away. While it was unfortunate that third-on-the-road Leinders won the Silverstone finale – Keen and Haberfeld had jumped the start – McGarrity's job was not that difficult. A top six position should have been easily attainable . . .

McGarrity had taken a big risk by stepping back into Formula Ford, having proved himself a winner in Formula Vauxhall. Perhaps it was the pressure of knowing that he had to succeed in order to resurrect his career, or maybe it was that exerted on him as the number one driver in a works team. One thing that certainly didn't help his cause was the number of enemies he managed to accrue during the season. Not many sympathetic voices could be heard in the Silverstone paddock after the final race, a certain number actually taking pleasure in his misfortune. Having started the season so well at Donington, he came back brilliantly from three no-scores to record seven podium finishes in eight races – the sort of form that should have won him the championship . . .

Leinders and McGarrity were joined on four wins apiece by Haberfeld, who proved to be the sensation of the season. Three consecutive wins at Thruxton and Silverstone (twice) rocketed him to the head of the table after a disastrous start to the season. A first-corner shunt in the opening round at Donington Park was followed by a huge qualifying crash at Brands Hatch when a tail-ender spun in front of him. He bounced back at Thruxton with a virtuoso performance to win, taking full advantage of a squabble between Keen and McGarrity.

In spite of this victory at the fastest track of the season, Mario complained that the Van Diemen was down on straightline speed all year, questioning the car's aerodynamics rather than its excellent Mountune engine.

Haberfeld had contested a few races with Andy Welch in 1994, and chose John Booth's Manor Motorsport outfit over the works teams to avoid the politics and pressures involved with the latter. It was an inspired choice, the Brazilian looking to be a good championship bet until his season fell apart in the summer. Disasters at Donington and Knockhill were compounded by collisions in the Snetterton double-header, and Mario's title aspirations were extinguished, although he did win the Young Driver title.

As his team boss concurred, Haberfeld had made his mark and didn't really need to win the championship, having shown natural ability which can only get better with experience. His professionalism was without question, no doubt aided by knowing Nelson Piquet since he was eight and being a good pal of Rubens Barrichello.

The success of the privateer outfits in the championship was quite amazing. Booth's team had been the only Van Diemen team to win a race in last year's championship (with Geoffroy Horion), but Andy Welch Racing joined in on the act this season with its Dutch charger, Vergers.

The Lowlander's career has never quite taken off since his time with Van Diemen in 1990, which reaped him the British Formula Ford title. To come back and attempt the same feat with a small team such as AWR shows how determined he is to rekindle his single-seater ambitions. The ever-charming 26-year-old notched up three victories during the season, the best of them featuring a fantastic pass on McGarrity in the second race at Knockhill's daunting Duffus Dip. The day before, Michael had gone off while disputing the lead when, in hindsight, second place would have sufficed.

A huge shunt at Snetterton – which saw the car somersault a number of times – almost ended his underfunded season, but merely served to illustrate the resolve of this driver and his team in that they were ready to race the following day.

Welch's gamble to establish his team with the penniless but barnstorming Vergers came close to pulling off a title success that would have been the shock of the TOCA season . . . The offer to run the works Swift team in the '96 season was just reward for Andy, who left the works teams with red faces more than once in 1995. To be the top privateer team – Vergers snatching third in the title race from Haberfeld – proved his judgement to be sound.

The same might not be said of the works Vector team. The outfit suffered a huge blow in the close-season when proprietor Mick Goldney was remanded on drugs charges. It continued nonetheless, with Justin Keen leading its attack.

Keen, who incidentally won the first Zetec-engined Formula Ford race in Britain, in 1993 for Swift, proved to be the year's biggest disappointment. The Vector VF95 was an update of the previous season's championship-winning car, and proved to be just as effective in the speed department. Unfortunately, Justin's car also seemed to be the quickest to find a gravel trap or tyrewall . . .

The season-openers at Donington summed up his season: a first-corner shunt after clipping Haberfeld eliminated him from race one, then an out-of-control Vergers wiped him out in the second. Sometimes it was Justin's fault (although not as often as the paddock rumour-mongers would have you believe), other times the guy just seemed to be involved in every accident that was going.

The VF95 chassis was especially good under braking, an attribute acknowledged by rival works drivers, so it was a shame that Keen couldn't seem to turn it to his advantage. Instead, his early races appeared to revolve around a spat with McGarrity (the pair colliding with Schumacher/Hill-like regularity), which stemmed from a bout of 'road rage' between the two on the A303 after a Thruxton test! It culminated in a 130 mph spin for Justin at Woodham Hill at the same track, after Kevin allowed him the chilling option of 'go on the grass' or 'have a huge accident'.

Probably the most misunderstood driver in the paddock, the introverted Keen allowed himself to be dragged into a series of tit-for-tat episodes that did nothing but damage his reputation. There is no doubt that he is blindingly quick, and the manner in which he scored his victory at Oulton – plus a 'moral' win at Silverstone – was second to none. It is his attitude and approach that

LAT Photographic

Kevin Wallace was the 'First Division' champion in his Van Diemen.

appear suspect. Sixth place in the championship was a sad waste of obvious talent.

One place ahead of Keen, but equally dissatisfied with his season, was likeable Belgian Jiri de Veirman. A season with Manor Motorsport in 1994 saw him gain speed as the year went by, and he made the logical move into the second Duckhams Van Diemen seat for '95. A podium finish in the second race at Donington Park might have been the catalyst for a good season for the 22-year-old, especially when the momentum was sustained by solid results that left him third in the standings by Thruxton.

But, from then on, it went horribly wrong for Jiri. Only one more podium spot was attained (at Knockhill), and he became hugely disillusioned with the way the team focused on McGarrity's championship challenge. In much the same fashion as Vincent Vosse in '94, Jiri was unable to turn things around and he completed the season by going through the motions and picking up the odd top five placing when the leading runners dropped out.

Conversely, seventh-placed Simon Wills enjoyed a superb first season in Britain, the Kiwi absolutely beside himself after leading at Snetterton in his works Swift. Son of leading New Zealand Thundersaloon exponent Kieron, Wills concentrated on the Young Driver element of the championship and looked well placed to take it until he, like McGarrity, faltered at the final hurdle.

A superb pair of fourth places at the Donington double-header in April set his year off well and, despite a bout of homesickness mid-season, Wills appeared on the podium twice to cap an impressive season. One to watch next year . . .

His Swift team-mate, Mikael 'Miku' Santavirta, also impressed on occasion, although his year will probably be remembered for the loopiest of manoeuvres at Silverstone. The laconic 19-year-old Finn punted Kolby into a spin across the finishing line in a battle for seventh place, then incredibly blamed the Dane for 'overcorrecting the slide when I hit him'.

That incident notwithstanding, Miku drove a fine race at Brands Hatch in April and may have won the race had it not been red-flagged and had he had more than two gears to play with! A brilliant kartist, the quiet Scandinavian could certainly challenge for honours next year.

Norman Simon grabbed ninth in the championship at the final round, the 19-year-old German works Vector driver another man unhappy with his lot during the year. Third at Thruxton was the high point, but his steady scoring performances were offset by a tendency for big shunts, especially at Donington Park, where he seemed to spend most of the time flying over people!

He was another to suffer the 'number two at a works team' syndrome, but this time it was more to do with the budgetary constraints at Vector.

Rounding out the leading runners were Olympic Motorsport twins Giorgio Vinella and Kristian Kolby. Besides his Donington Park jinx – where he endured two separate fires – Giorgio proved his pace with a pole at Brands and a second-place finish at Silverstone in May. The hugely popular Italian was in his second year with Chris Creswell's team and, although his wet weather abilities are questionable, he showed a greatly improved turn of speed this season.

Sixteen-year-old Kolby proved one of the revelations of the year. The Dane is incredibly mature for his age and showed this by improving steadily throughout the season, standing him in good stead for 1996 – when he will remain with Creswell's happy team. The first 16-year-old to lead a National Formula Ford race in Britain, his high spot was at Brands Hatch in August when he qualified and finished second.

A 'First Division' class for year-old chassis was included for the first time in '95. The category was won by Kevin Wallace's Mick Gardner Racing Van Diemen RF94, after a year-long battle with the Swift SC94Z of John Loebell. Both drivers boasted an impressive 100 per cent finishing record – until the final round, that is, where they both crashed at the first corner!

Reigning FF1600 champion Austin Kinsella joined the series belatedly to take third in the title race in his luridly liveried ex-Martin Byford Van Diemen RF94. Scottish-domiciled Dane Mads Gisselbaek also featured strongly in his Van Diemen RF94, which was run by Rex Hart and, latterly, Anglo European Motorsport. Both he and Loebell took the occasional top five overall placing when the so-called 'Premier Division' contenders scored the odd own goal . . .

Swift took the Teams Championship to rub salt into Van Diemen's wounds – the Snetterton equipe having now won the championship only once in the last four years. Mountune won the newly instigated Engine Tuners Cup, thanks mainly to the Swift trio and Haberfeld.

Finally, the worry that the introduction of slicks might threaten the formula's excitement factor was quashed absolutely, and instead this long-lived form of racing enjoyed a rebirth that will stand it in good stead for years to come.

SLICK 50 FORMULA FORD CHAMPIONSHIP

Premier Division

	Driver (Nat.)	*Entrant*	*Car*	*1*	*2*	*3*	*4*	*5*	*6*	*7*	*8*	*9*	*10*	*11*	*12*	*13*	*14*	*15*	*16*	*Points*
1	Bas Leinders (B)	Swift Racing Cars	Swift SC95Z-Mountune	10	10	12	0	10	0	7	0	9	12	9	7	12	9	8	12	127
2	Kevin McGarrity (GB)	Duckhams Racing with Van Diemen	Van Diemen RF95-Mercury	12	12	0	5	0	0	10	12	10	10	10	8	10	12	10	0	121
3	Michael Vergers (NL)	Andy Welch Racing	Swift SC94Z-Langford & Peck	9	0	10	7	8	0	12	8	12	0	12	9	0	8	9	–	104
4	Mario Haberfeld (BR)	Manor Motorsport	Van Diemen RF95-Mountune	0	7	6	12	12	12	9	9	0	0	0	12	0	6	5	9	99
5	Justin Keen (GB)	Vector Racing Cars	Vector VF95-Vector Power	0	0	7	6	0	0	8	10	0	0	8	0	0	10	12	10	71
6	Jiri de Veirman (B)	Duckhams Racing with Van Diemen	Van Diemen RF95-Mercury	0	9	8	10	0	0	6	6	5	9	0	0	0	4	7	7	71
7	Simon Wills (NZ)	Swift Racing Cars	Swift SC95Z-Mountune	8	8	0	4	9	6	0	4	8	0	0	3	9	0	0	0	59
8	Miku Santavirta (SF)	Swift Racing Cars	Swift SC95Z-Mountune	6	6	9	0	0	0	3	0	7	6	4	4	0	5	6	0	56
9	Norman Simon (D)	Vector Racing Cars	Vector VF95-Vector Power	0	–	0	9	7	8	4	7	0	8	0	0	0	0	4	6	53
10	Giorgio Vinella (I)	Olympic Motorsport	Vector VF95-Vector Power	–	4	2	8	0	10	2	3	0	4	0	5	6	0	0	8	52

First Division

	Driver (Nat.)	*Entrant*	*Car*	1	2	3	4	5	6	7	8	9	10	11	12	13	14	15	16	Points
1	Kevin Wallace (GB)	Mick Gardner Racing	Van Diemen RF94-Scholar	10	12	9	12	12	10	12	9	10	(8)	(6)	9	9	10	9	0	133
2	John Loebell (GB)	Driver	Swift SC94Z-Minister	12	10	(8)	9	8	12	9	(7)	7	9	9	12	8	9	10	0	124
3	Austin Kinsella (GB)	Driver	Van Diemen RF94-Zagk	–	–	–	0	10	8	10	12	12	0	10	10	10	12	12	12	118
4	Thomas Guinchard (GB)	Driver	Swift SC94Z-Scholar	8	0	10	8	6	0	7	0	8	7	0	8	7	8	8	10	95
5	Mads Gisselbaek (DK)	Rex Hart Racing/Anglo European	Van Diemen RF94	9	0	12	10	0	0	8	10	6	12	12	0	12	0	–	–	91

KEY

() dropped scores

Key to rounds: 1 Donington Park, 1 April; 2 Donington Park, 2 April; 3 Brands Hatch Indy, 17 April; 4 Thruxton, 8 May; 5 Silverstone National, 13 May; 6 Silverstone National, 14 May; 7 Oulton Park, 29 May; 8 Brands Hatch Grand Prix, 11 June; 9 Donington Park, 25 June; 10 Knockhill, 29 July; 11 Knockhill, 30 July; 12 Brands Hatch Indy, 13 August; 13 Snetterton, 27 August; 14 Snetterton, 28 August; 15 Oulton Park Fosters, 10 September; 16 Silverstone National, 24 September.

LAT Photographic

At the double Bas

Bas Leinders found the events of the final round of the Slick 50 Formula Ford Championship at Silverstone hard to believe. Consequently, he has yet to come to terms with the concept of being the new champion.

'It's really strange,' reveals the 20-year-old Belgian. 'Because we didn't expect it at all. I just thought Kevin [McGarrity] would do enough to win it. But he didn't! I've just got to get used to the fact that I actually won!

'This year has been so different than when I won the Benelux Championship, because I've been up against McGarrity and Van Diemen, who are much more experienced. Of course, it's been more competitive and much harder to win as a result.'

Having dominated the Benelux Championship in 1994, Leinders was much in demand over the winter. He chose the works Swift team. 'A lot of teams wanted me to drive for them, including Van Diemen and Manor Motorsport, they knew I was capable of doing something in their cars,' he reckons.

Swift, of course, was determined to show that last year's dominant performances by Jonny Kane were not purely a result of the engine irregularities that cost him the title. And the year started brilliantly, with two second places at Donington and a win at Brands, despite the late production of the car.

'We only did five days of testing with the new car before the first race, so the first few races were very good results for us,' concedes Bas. 'I think I got stuck into it quicker than the other drivers. After Brands, then we saw the difference in speed, because of the problems we had with the car, so we had a lot of work to do.'

A feature of the 1995 championship were 'old hands' Michael Vergers and McGarrity, both of whom have achieved success in higher formulae. How did Bas cope with their levels of experience?

'When I signed for Swift I didn't know McGarrity was going to drive, nor Michael Vergers, nor [Justin] Keen. So it turned out to be one of the hardest years in Formula Ford, I think.'

He looks upon this as a good thing, an opportunity to learn from the wealth of experience he was up against. 'Although it is a junior formula, I think that it's fair that drivers like McGarrity and Vergers can compete, because it's good that people who have to learn, like Mario [Haberfeld] and myself, can learn even more. Maybe if they weren't there, then maybe Mario and me would finish first and second all the time and have good battles, but not extraordinary battles like this year!' he exclaims.

'I've been involved in very difficult and exciting battles with four or five cars for the win. I think it's just made it better. You could maybe see Vergers pass you with some good manoeuvre and you would say, "Wow, how is that possible?" Then after the race you can look at it and think, "Well, yeah, I made this small mistake so he could pass me." If you just had inexperienced drivers, they would never pass you unless you make a big mistake.

'Now I have a lot of racing experience thanks to Kevin and Michael, and if I do Formula Three next year, which I hope to do, if I didn't have that experience, then F3 would be even tougher.'

Leinders's season was no cakewalk, however. The late development of the car proved to be the catalyst for a number of niggling problems, which served to hinder his championship efforts. 'We had quite a few problems with the car mid-season, all sorts of things, so it feels even better now to know we got over all the bad stuff to win it – it's like a really good reward for hanging in there and trying to make the best of it,' surmises the Belgian.

If there was one point where he thought he'd turned his season around, it was the double-header at Knockhill. After a fraught qualifying, which saw the diff explode (a replacement had to be borrowed from Andy Welch Racing's spare car and changed between sessions), Bas bounced back to win the first race and place highly in the second. 'All of a sudden, we were going well again. We got the new alloy wheels and the telemetry – it made a big improvement, as that's where we were losing out in the early part of the season. Fom that point on, I knew we were back in the championship . . .'

His ability to avoid mistakes helped him stay there. While title rivals would often risk all in dubious overtaking moves, Bas would often sit back and take the points: 'I only went into the gravel once in a race [at Brands Hatch], because my clutch was gone, it was raining and I locked up. I think if you're driving, you always have to concentrate on what's in front, even if there's someone behind you. You shouldn't defend – like McGarrity always does – because that means you go slower. If you're stuck behind someone who's blocking you, you've got to think not about what's happening right now, but what he's going to do at the next corner and maybe avoid a crash,' he reasons.

'I think you can foresee accidents in most cases, and I think my karting experience at such a high level helps there. Apart from the technical bits in Formula Ford, it's still racing that really matters.'

A worthy sentiment, and typical of the eloquent Belgian – a thoroughly fitting champion after a superb season of racing.

Kevin McGarrity laughed when his rivals took themselves off, and laughed all the more when he snapped the cork in half.

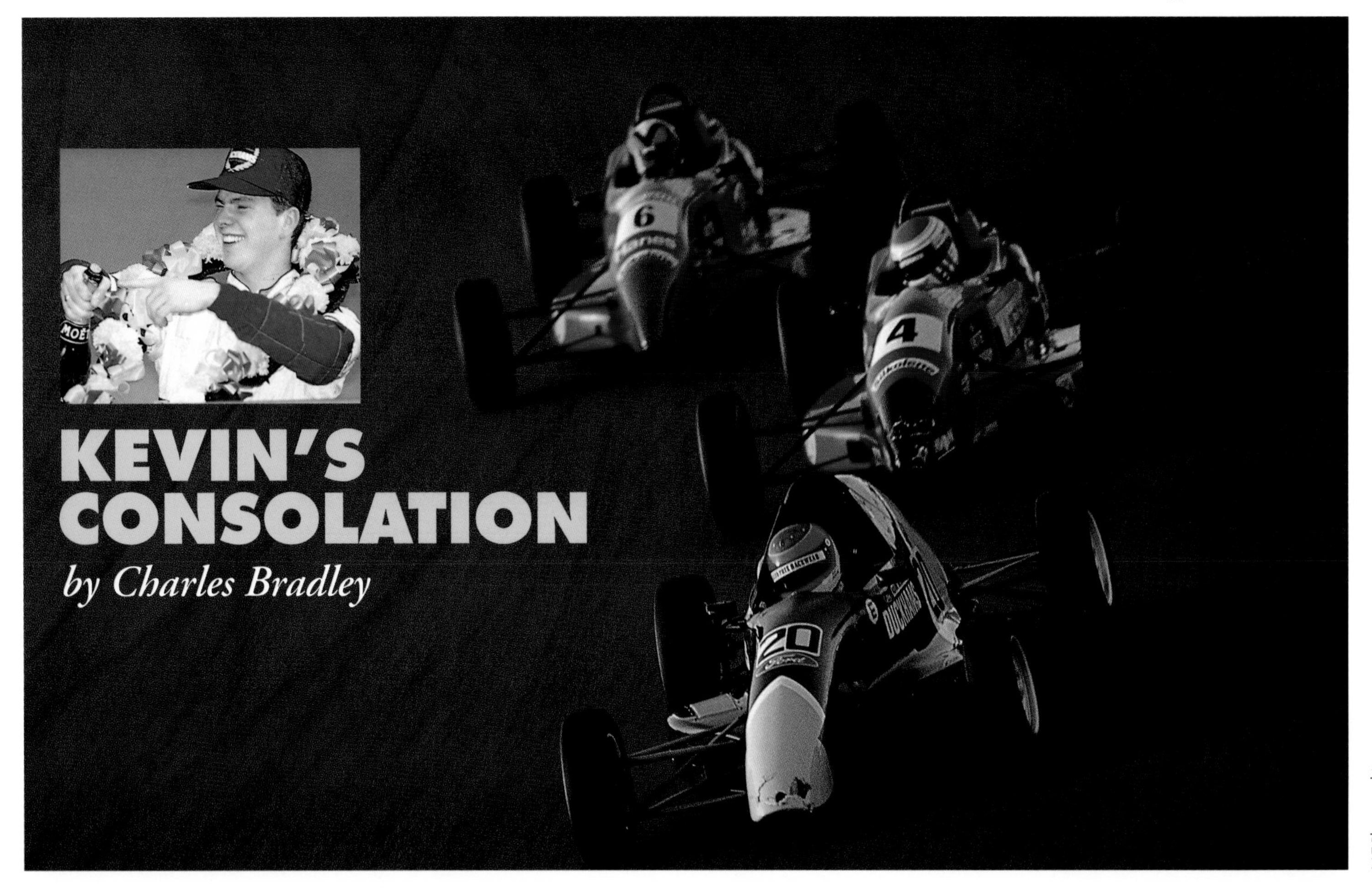

LAT Photographic

KEVIN'S CONSOLATION

by Charles Bradley

Kevin McGarrity was a man with a point to prove at the Formula Ford Festival. He knew that he'd lost the Slick 50 Formula Ford Championship, and the only way to atone for that failure was to win this prestigious meeting. That he did just that says a lot for the feisty Ulsterman's character, especially as he had to bounce back from a faulty airflow meter in qualifying and a blocked exhaust in his semi-final – both of which served to starve his engine of power.

Before the final, the title looked to be between front-row men, Kristian Kolby and Patrice Gay. The former had set the pace since testing on Tuesday, and the recently turned 17-year-old had scorched to victory in the first semi-final – beating McGarrity and new British Champion, Bas Leinders, in the process. He did so with a time good enough for pole position in the final. Gay's 'semi' victory was less emphatic, the French driver having to endure two stoppages in his race. Indeed, he was headed across the line in the last segment of this three-part race by Kolby's Olympic Motorsport teammate, Giorgio Vinella, and only took the victory on aggregate.

But if there is one fallibility in Kolby's arsenal it would be his starts. The young Dane had almost spun as he scrabbled frantically for traction on the tricky Brands starting slope in his semi-final, and Kristian had admitted to nerves before the final.

To further hamper him, the setting sun was reflecting off his mirror directly into his eyes, which meant that he couldn't see the lights. He thus had to watch Gay's start in his other mirror to know when to go! And again Kris allowed his Vector's engine to hit its limiter, causing him to wheelspin his advantage away.

In contrast, Gay made a fantastic getaway and was chased into Paddock Hill Bend by the equally fast-starting Vinella. Kolby was third. But McGarrity's attempt to take advantage of the Dane's poor start saw him slide hopelessly wide at the opening corner, an error which let Leinders into fourth.

Vinella's Vector was hardly to his liking, and Giorgio held up the pack, giving Gay the chance to sprint away. And Patrice was holding a massive advantage when he arrived at Surtees on lap three, only to find the track covered in dirt from tailender Marco Schumann's gyration the lap before. The hapless Mygale driver rotated out of the lead and into the gravel, promoting a surprised Vinella to the head of the field.

Meanwhile, Kolby slipped back further, to sixth, when his car jumped out of third gear exiting Clearways. McGarrity then scythed past Leinders for second at Paddock, Kevin showing all the aggression that the Belgian had lacked in his semi-final, when he simply tailed the Ulsterman for the majority of the race.

Vinella's erratically handling car proved little obstacle for McGarrity, and Giorgio also quickly fell prey to the works Swifts of Leinders and Miku Santavirta. At the same time, Kolby's ever-slimming chance was finally vanquished by Dutchman, Sepp Koster, whose Geva Racing Swift whacked the Dane for six over the Graham Hill Bend boundary.

Leinders homed in on the leader, but the wildcard here was Santavirta. The Finnish teenager was the only man able to hold a candle to Kolby's lightning pace all week, and Miku felt he had been unfairly docked a position when he was adjudged to have gained a place from Leinders under yellows in their semi-final battle.

And Leinders's inability to pass McGarrity – although the Belgian did ram the Van Diemen a couple of times – seemed to make Santavirta even more angry. Finally, Miku appeared to have got through at Paddock, but Bas pulled alongside on the run up to Druids. The pair had already banged wheels once – and they did so again – this time the works Swift duo spearing into the barriers, both seemingly happy with the fact that the other hadn't finished ahead.

This left McGarrity to coast to victory, Kevin admitting that he had lost time to the distant Vinella in the closing laps because he'd been laughing so much!

Vinella was an ecstatic second from Mario Haberfeld. The Brazilian snatched third from Mark Webber right on the line, the Australian having made a hugely impressive UK debut in a works Van Diemen. Giorgio's ecstasy was shortlived, however, for his Vector was deemed to be fitted with illegal camshafts, and thus Van Diemen scored a 1-2-3-4.

The Zetec-powered element of the Festival overshadowed the FF1600 version, which was dominated by Finnish talent, Topi Serjala, despite a loose undertray in the final.

Pos.	Driver	Car	Time
1	Kevin McGarrity (GB)	Van Diemen RF95	16m14.61s 88.91 mph/143.09 km/h
2	Mario Haberfeld (BR)	Van Diemen RF95	16m18.94s
3	Mark Webber (AUS)	Van Diemen RF95	16m18.96s
4	Robert Lechner (A)	Van Diemen RF94	16m19.21s
5	Luciano Crespi (RA)	Swift SC95Z	16m19.95s
6	Tim Verbergt (B)	Van Diemen RF95	16m20.11s
7	Kristian Kolby (DK)	Vector VF95	16m20.44s
8	Hans Willems (B)	Van Diemen RF94	16m21.19s
9	Cyril Prunet (F)	Van Diemen RF93	16m22.03s
10	Raphael del Sarte (F)	Van Diemen RF93	16m25.35s
DQ	Giorgio Vinella (I)	Vector VF95	16m16.31s

Fastest lap: Kolby 47.47s, 91.27 mph/146.89 km/h

The story of the second half of the season: PSR dominates the front row prior to either Jonny Kane (1) or Juan Pablo Montoya (4) scoring a win.

PSR, I LOVE YOU

FORMULA VAUXHALL REVIEW *by Marcus Simmons*

LAT Photographic

Are you an ambitious young driver? Do you want to make it in motor racing?

You do?

Well, why not follow the tried and trusted method of the 1990s? It's simple: first, you win a handful of karting championships; second, you succeed either in Formula Ford or Vauxhall Junior; third, you go to Paul Stewart Racing to win the Formula Vauxhall Championship. Then it's up to you . . .

For the third year running, the Milton Keynes outfit cleaned up. Following in the footsteps of Dario Franchitti and Owen McAuley, the champions of 1993 and '94, Jonny Kane overcame the tremendous early-season form of Rowan Racing's Martin O'Connell to dominate the second half of the year along with his team-mate, Juan Pablo Montoya. O'Connell, seemingly invincible at mid-season, simply fell under the path of the PSR streamroller.

Just one year after forecasters had predicted its demise in both Britain and Europe, 1995 was the season in which Formula Vauxhall truly came of age: David Coulthard became the first category graduate to win a Grand Prix; Gil de Ferran (the Scot's PSR FV team-mate back in 1990) did likewise in Indy cars; Rubens Barrichello, Mika Häkkinen and Heinz-Harald Frentzen reinforced their reputations as three of F1's hottest properties; Vincenzo Sospiri, Ricardo Rosset and Tarso Marques won in F3000; and Franchitti and Jan Magnussen became continental superstars in Class 1 touring cars.

This season five drivers, none of whom would be out of place in a leading F3 team next season, fought it out for the British Formula Vauxhall title. But even with talents like Kane, O'Connell, Montoya, Darren Manning and Peter Dumbreck, the racing was still, in the main, deathly dull.

Why?

Wings! Great though they may have been for aviation pioneers and Paul McCartney's post-Beatles activities, wings are the plague of modern motor racing. GM's motorsport gurus attempted to rectify this for 1995 by augmenting the front wings in a bid to negate the loss of front-end downforce which invariably occurs when one driver tries to follow in another's slipstream. But it made little difference in the UK!

Formula Vauxhall is often unfavourably compared, racing wise, with Formula Renault Sport in this country, but for some reason the GM category just doesn't seem to sit well with British circuits. Go to Zolder, Spa, Estoril or Imola to watch a round of the Formula Opel Euroseries, and you will often see racing that is just as good as that at the Formula Ford Festival – simply because the teams have to run a low-downforce configuration for the long, long straights which characterise continental circuits. Consequently, the drivers have to slide their cars around, make mistakes and abuse their tyres, all of which make for compelling racing.

On their own, Formula Vauxhall cars are spectacular beasts. The chassis was outdated even when the category was instigated in 1988, and its brilliant two-litre, 16-valve, 167 bhp Vauxhall Family 2 engine provides more than enough power for it to cope with. The sight of a flamboyant Kane taking pole position at Knockhill is one that will stick in the mind for a long time.

Apart from the front wing alterations, stiffer chassis sideplanks were introduced for 1995, as well as smaller diameter Bridgestone Potenza tyres that actually fitted their rims! For seven seasons Formula Vauxhalls had rolled their rubber badly on the rims, obligating a slow-in approach to corners, which detractors claimed made the category unsuitable as a nursery for F3. The improvements generally lowered lap times by half a second and made the cars a touch more taxing to drive for the novice. To the naked eye, however, it made no difference whatsoever.

They didn't, if you look at the season overall, cause a substantial upheaval of the Formula Vauxhall landscape either. Paul Stewart Racing, with all its resources and personnel, was once again able to provide the championship-winning car.

Team Manager Graham Taylor – demonstrating a perspicacity his footballing namesake would have died for – had fallen in love with the abilities of Kane when the Northern Irishman dominated the 1994 Formula Vauxhall Winter Series at Pembrey, on his category debut with the team.

'He's the driver I want,' declared Taylor, and it was no surprise when the signing was formally announced in the New Year. But brilliant though his display in the wet Welsh event had been, and magnificent as his Formula Ford record was, Kane still needed to adjust to the peculiarities of the Formula Vauxhall driving style.

A win in round one at Donington, in which he bullied his way past pole-position man Manning on the Craner Curves, disguised the fact that Kane still hadn't ironed out his sideways habits. And when O'Connell came on song for the next few races, Jonny's campaign started to suffer. May saw an unimpressive run to fifth at Thruxton, as well as a couple of foolish errors at Oulton Park. Was the 22-year-old from County Down all he was cracked up to be?

The answer was, emphatically, yes. Kane worked and worked and worked, PSR gave him the environment in which to do so and, by the time the circus arrived at Donington Park in late June, Jonny and team-mate Montoya were unbeatable.

Save for an aberration at Knockhill, where both Kane and Montoya crashed in qualifying, the team has not been beaten since early June.

Kane's uncanny ability to go hard on cold tyres from the start served

Kane scrutiny

LAT Photographic

With the black mark of last year's controversial National Formula Ford Championship against his name, Jonny Kane *(right)* answered any criticism of his ability with a superb victory in the 1995 Formula Vauxhall Championship.

The cloak and dagger events of 1994 – when he lost the title because of an engine irregularity that was beyond his control – may even have contributed to Kane's success with Paul Stewart Racing, for they forged a steely edge off the track to a man whose on-track prowess should never have been called into question.

'Everything that happened in Formula Ford made me realise that things don't always run smoothly,' recalls the 22-year-old from Comber, County Down. 'I'm probably in a better position to accept things in the future now.

'After all my problems, I wanted to go to a team that everybody knew was whiter than white . . .'

With four car racing seasons to his name since he graduated from the Ulster karting scene, winning a title championship in each – Irish Junior Formula Ford 1600, Ford of Ireland FF1600, Formula Ford Eurocup and Formula Vauxhall Winter Series – Kane ripped through Formula Vauxhall, in spite of the huge head start enjoyed by Martin O'Connell, courtesy of five straight wins.

'I always knew it was going to be really hard,' confirms Kane. 'Everybody had me down as favourite, but I didn't really know why I should be – I didn't have as much experience as a lot of the others. Even though I won the first race, I still didn't drive the car right. After that I had some bad qualifying results, and it's so important to qualify these things well.

'Martin had five wins, but he was always there to pick up the pieces, and there should always have been one person to beat him. Everybody else made mistakes, he didn't. We've been pretty quick all year – it was just a matter of stopping making those mistakes.'

In the end, Kane matched O'Connell's record of five victories. He also finished the year with a much smoother (albeit still aggressive) driving style.

'I always drove spectacularly in Formula Ford. If you saw my driving graphs from the start of the year to now you would probably think it was someone different!' he grins. 'You have to change the way you drive to suit the cars, and it's the same all the way up through the formulas.'

One reason for Kane's success is, paradoxically, his relative lack of funding compared to other drivers. It means that he only graduates to a higher category when a team in that class is willing to show faith in his ability. Being on the PSR treadmill, which could conceivably take him all the way through F3 and F3000 to the brink of F1, may help him considerably in this respect.

'I think it was very important for me to do well this year. I've never had a full budget, but I've had a really good sponsor this season in Arrow Abrasives [whom he has managed to get mentioned in a major yearly publication!] and, hopefully, they'll stay with me next season. The team's really pleased – they've now won the Formula Vauxhall Championship for a third year in a row, and that's what they set out to do.

'I've made a few mistakes, but I feel I've learned from them, and I should be in a good position to go into Formula Three now. I'd love to go with PSR – they've definitely got the best F3 team – but it all depends how much money I can get together and what sort of deal I can come up with.'

One part of that deal is in place already: as Jonny suggested when he dominated on his Formula Vauxhall debut in last year's Winter Series at Pembrey, and has emphasised numerous times since then, the biggest plus in his favour is talent.

him well in all five of his race wins, none of which was inherited. As well as that, he and Montoya dominated one race apiece when the Euroseries visited Donington in July.

Excellent driver that he is, Kane undoubtedly had to hand equipment that was second to none. Rivals scratched their heads in disbelief at the advantage which the dark blue and white cars enjoyed at Donington and on the short circuit at Oulton Park. There was no secret to it, however, they were just brilliantly engineered.

Montoya, too, played his part in the success. Three British race wins (plus one in the Euroseries) is a terrific record for the Colombian, who had never seen the majority of the circuits before this year.

He arrived as a hot tip from a successful karting background, but had also made his mark in Colombian Formula Renault and 'Touring Cars' (a curious anything-goes class with some monster machinery), as well as taking third in the Barber Saab Pro Series in North America.

A naturally smooth driver, Juan Pablo soon added an aggression to his style which made him a formidable race rival (you could almost hear Manning shout 'Ouch' at Silverstone in May) and, ultimately, a top qualifier. Pole position for the last two rounds preceded two wins, which included a breathtaking round-the-outside manoeuvre on team-mate Kane at Silverstone's tight Brooklands left-hander, on his way to third in the championship.

Match Kane's record of five wins during the season he may have done, but for Martin O'Connell 1995 was very much, as the football pundits

Right: **Five victories in a row gave Martin O'Connell the series lead. But he was unable to stave off the PSR challenge in the second half of the season.**

Below (left to right): **Wayne Douglas was sensational in his year-old car.**

A regular podium finisher, Darren Manning never achieved the win his efforts deserved.

Peter Dumbreck was the 'racing' disappointment of the year. The Scot should be a threat next season,though.

Photos: LAT Photographic

Paul Milligan made the switch from Caterhams to single-seaters, but was only moderately successful. The chassis was in its eighth season, having outlived all initial predictions.

Sutton Photographic

say, a game of two halves. So much so, in fact, that his five victories were scored in a memorable streak between rounds two and six!

The Walsall man, last year's Class B champion, stayed in Formula Vauxhall for a third season with his uncle Ray Rowan's team. But this was no cottage industry – this time the money was there for a serious, and professional, attack on the championship.

Those five successes were bookended by two wins in the wet at Brands Hatch, but in between there was fine driving in all weathers. O'Connell's greatest talent is his outstanding ability to rocket from the second row of the grid into the lead on cold tyres, and his wins at Thruxton and Silverstone owed much to a couple of lightning getaways.

Apart from that, there was a superb victory (from his first pole position) at Oulton Park, in which he blitzed his rivals in wet but drying conditions.

Then came the decay. Save for a pole position at Snetterton, Martin never recaptured that golden form, and was criticised once or twice for what rivals felt was unnecessary wheel-banging. As hard a charger as you'll come by, O'Connell was praised in a magnanimous gesture at the season's end by Rowan, who claimed it was the team which had lost the title rather than its driver.

Darren Manning's second Formula Vauxhall season with Mike O'Brien's Speedsport Racing Team drew a similar graph: a contender at the start of the year, the North Yorkshireman was struggling to keep up with the PSR twins by the end of it.

Pole position for round one promised great things, but somehow – and this remains one of the year's great mysteries – he never won a race. Darren stood on the podium nine times, but never at its highest point. Although he took a maximum score in the second Knockhill race, he still finished a close second behind Class B sensation, Wayne Douglas.

Speedsport drafted in Chris Weller from the crack German F3 outfit WTS Motorsport, on freelance engineering duties, but the vital spark never came. Always with the leaders, Manning stayed in contention for the title right until the penultimate round. The consistency

FORMULA VAUXHALL CHAMPIONSHIP – Class A

	Driver (Nat.)	Entrant	Car	1	2	3	4	5	6	7	8	9	10	11	12	13	14	Points
1	Jonny Kane (GB)	Paul Stewart Racing		15	0	(6)	1	7*	12	12	16*	16*	(1*)	16*	15*	12	13*	146
2	Martin O'Connell (GB)	Ray Rowan Racing		6	15	16*	15	15	16*	0	8	(5)	0	8	12	10	8	129
3	Juan Pablo Montoya (COL)	Paul Stewart Racing		8	0	10	(4)	12	0	16*	12	8	8	10	10	16*	15	125
4	Darren Manning (GB)	Speedsport Racing Team		13*	(8)	12	0	(5)	10	10	10	12	15	12	9*	8	10	121
5	Peter Dumbreck (GB)	Martin Donnelly Racing		10	13*	8	2*	10	0	0	6	10	0	0	0	6	3	68
6	Shinichi Takagi (J)	Team JLR		(3)	5	5	3	0	0	3	3	6	6	6	3	5	5	50
7	Jamie Campbell-Walter (GB)	PTM Motorsport		4	6	0	5	0	8	5		3	10	5	–	0	0	48
8	Paul Milligan (GB)	Martin Donnelly Racing		5	0	4	10	–	0	2	1	2	0	2	5	2	4	37
9	Hiroshi Sakai (J)	John Village Automotive		–	–	–	–	3	4	6	0	0	5	4	6	3	6	37
10	Marcel Romanio (BR)	PTM Motorsport		–	–	–	6	8	5	8	5	–	–	–	–	–	–	32

KEY

* *one point for fastest lap*   () *dropped scores*

Key to rounds: 1 Donington Park, 2 April; 2 Brands Hatch Indy, 17 April; 3 Thruxton, 8 May; 4 Silverstone National, 14 May; 5 Oulton Park, 29 May; 6 Brands Hatch Grand Prix, 11 June; 7 Donington Park, 24 June; 8 Donington Park, 25 June; 9 Knockhill, 29 July; 10 Knockhill, 30 July; 11 Brands Hatch Indy, 13 August; 12 Snetterton, 28 August; 13 Oulton Park Fosters, 10 September; 14 Silverstone National, 24 September.

was there, but the package just didn't deliver the goods.

If Manning thought he'd had a hard time, he just had to look at Peter Dumbreck, who was most definitely Formula Vauxhall's Mr Unlucky.

The Scot came to Martin Donnelly Racing as the reigning Vauxhall Junior champion, but had proved a disaster in the Formula Ford Festival and been totally blown off by Kane in the Vauxhall Winter Series.

Any doubts over his ability were dispelled, however, when he set the pace in pre-season testing, his ultra-smooth style reaping dividends on the stopwatch. But in competition – well, it didn't quite happen, did it?

Maybe Donnelly's set-up missed departed team manager, Jonathan Lewis. Chief engineer Gavin Jones, the Yorkshireman's replacement, may produce a first-rate car and be an extremely nice chap, but he's not the sort to go around hyping up his charge and bruising the others' egos.

Dumbreck was the form man in early-season qualifying, but his decidedly leisurely starts were never going to work in Formula Vauxhall, where it's so difficult to overtake. Accidents from mid-season onwards, as well as a trivial exclusion for having a rear wing attachment a gnat's whisker out of shape at Brands Hatch, pushed him further into the mire.

Peter plans to remain at this level for 1996, though, and will be a hard man to beat.

The other MDR car was occupied mostly by Lancastrian teenager Paul Milligan and, although the Caterham Vauxhall champion looked to be making progress early on, he rarely troubled the leaders. Kirsten Kolby drove a third car at the tail-end of the season on her return to the formula, but twice collided with Milligan!

Japanese drivers Shinichi Takagi (Team JLR) and Hiroshi Sakai (John Village Automotive) showed flashes of form during the season.

Takagi, who hadn't even sat in a Formula Vauxhall until a few days before the first race, quickly got into the top six but then suffered a rash of accidents. Composed once more, his last half-dozen races showed him to be capable of racing well.

Sakai, with experience of French F3, joined the series at Oulton Park in May and soon posted some useful performances. At present, he qualifies better than he races, but the promise is there.

The urbane Jamie Campbell-Walter, who ran virtually the whole year with Peter Thompson Motorsport, was probably the most improved driver of the season. Although funds were in short supply, the Vauxhall Junior graduate got on sensibly with the job – sometimes without having tested at all – and was closing on O'Connell and Manning in the final round at Silverstone when his steering arm broke.

Campbell-Walter, whose first motorsport competition came only two years ago, may lack the flair of some of those who have been in karts since they were eight, but he's a very competent driver and capable of a lot more than his form suggests.

The other PTM driver, for five races anyway, was Marcel Romanio. The tiny Brazilian was another without a great deal of money, but showed bravado on a major scale with his racing ability and often threatened the top contenders.

Bellringer Motorsport was the only other outfit to compete regularly in Class A, but Sean McNally struggled to adapt from Vauxhall Junior and wasn't seen in the last four races.

Formula Vauxhall has a fairly tricky winter ahead of it. Vauxhall Sport is committed to the future of the category, but there are those who are tempted by its still burgeoning rival, Formula Renault Sport. Most of the leading contenders from 1995 are graduating to F3, and there aren't too many youngsters ready to replace them yet from Vauxhall Junior.

While we wait for the present crop of 16- and 17-year-olds to sort themselves out for a move up the ladder, maybe we shouldn't expect too much from the series in 1996.

Wayne's World

When Vauxhall Sport introduced Class B to the formula, in May 1994, nobody could have expected that a contestant in this 'shoestring budget' division would win a race outright.

But that's exactly what Wayne Douglas *(below right)* did. Armed with the ex-Guy Smith chassis, the former Irish Formula Opel champion from County Antrim provided one of the sensations of the season with victory at Knockhill, holding off Darren Manning throughout an epic 15 laps.

Run by his former rallycrosser father, Richard, the 21-year-old had shown sparkling form in the preceding races, tailing Class A's 'Big Five' in the early going at Thruxton and humbling the rest of the Formula Vauxhall elite.

Class B cars ran to pre-1995 specification during the season, so the front wings were still carrying the single plane and the chassis sideplanks were not quite as stiff – yet Douglas knuckled down to fight against superior machinery. He won Class B in every race he finished, save at Oulton Park, where he goofed on tyre choice in tricky conditions and conceded victory to his friend, Alan Dallas.

Having wrapped up the title at Brands Hatch in August, Douglas sat out the rest of the season – except for a one-off Class A outing with PTM at Oulton – hoping to save the money to join a professional team in 1996. In many ways the star driver of last season, his fantastic car control and gutsy battling have to be rewarded soon.

Alan Dallas was the man most capable of matching Douglas. Another underrated Ulsterman, he ran a few races in the first half of the season with the Richard Peacock Mainland outfit, and was inspired at Oulton Park. But then he picked up a 90-day ban thanks to a third licence endorsement at Knockhill.

With the whole field having been similarly punished in an arbitrary fashion for behaviour under yellow flags at Silverstone, it could be argued that draconian officialdom has temporarily wrecked a promising racing career.

The other RPM driver, Chris Ward, ultimately placed second in the championship. A former FF1600 Champion of Oulton, Ward proved a better racer than he was a qualifier, and took two wins on the trot at the end of the season to edge out Amanda Whitaker for the runner-up spot.

The latter, a country and western singer from Durham, impressed at times, especially bearing in mind that she ran all season without the benefit of fuel injection (introduced to the formula's engines in 1993). The Amaron (Amanda and Ron – her father) Racing entry finished consistently, thanks to Whitaker's uncanny ability to get out of the accidents which afflicted most of her rivals.

Marcelo Battistuzzi was unlucky to be placed only fourth. The amiable Brazilian won the first round at Donington, before Douglas's arrival, and was always consistently placed from then on. He missed Knockhill because immigration officials wouldn't let him back in the country, and then crashed heavily at Oulton Park and broke his leg.

Michael Graham, who was run alongside Battistuzzi, had an accident-prone season, but was quick when he kept it on the island and scored a victory at Snetterton.

If it hadn't been for Douglas's win at Knockhill, then Alex Jack's performance (third overall with Jim Russell Racing) would have looked similarly sensational. The underfunded Scotsman didn't appear many times, and nor did Irish series contender Sam Thompson, who won in the wet at Brands Hatch.

Of the other regulars to score top three placings, Neale Blunden looked fairly handy, despite having experience of nothing more lofty than pre-1990 FF1600, but Mark Youde found the going a touch harder than he had in Formula Renault.

The majority of Class B Formula Vauxhall drivers come from a variety of club racing championships. Most of them enjoy being part of the TOCA package while competing on a low budget and, every now and then, they get a chance to measure their ability against a young star like Wayne Douglas.

There's no reason why it shouldn't continue to thrive.

LAT Photographic

FORMULA VAUXHALL CHAMPIONSHIP - Class B

	Driver (Nat.)	Entrant	1	2	3	4	5	6	7	8	9	10	11	12	13	14	Points
1	Wayne Douglas (GB)	Douglas Motorsport	–	16*	16*	16*	12	0	16*	16*	16*	16*	16*	–	–	–	140
2	Chris Ward (GB)	Richard Peacock Mainland	0	12	12	0	0	12	0	10	–	–	12	0	15	15	88
3	Amanda Whitaker (GB)	Amaron Racing	12	(4)	8	4	5	6	12	8	0	(3)	4	10	11*	6	86
4	Marcelo Battistuzzi (BR)	Team SER	15	10	10	12	10	4	0	0	–	–	6	9*	0	–	76
5	Michael Graham (GB)	Driver	6	8	2	10	0	3	10	0	12	0	0	15	0	10	76
6	Neale Blunden (GB)	Driver	10	0	5	0	4	0	2	6	8	6	8	0	12	0	61
7	Mark Youde (GB)	CBS Motorsport	–	–	1	8	8	8	8	0	2	1	3	12	4	5	60
8	Jan Ivan Powell (GB)	Speedsport Racing Team	8	0	6	0	0	2	4	4	4	8	5	8	–	–	49
9	Jon Tandy (GB)	CBS Motorsport	0	5	0	6	2	0	5	5	3	4	–	–	8	8	46
10	Kelly Rogers (GB)	Team Mota World	0	3	4	5	6	1	0	1	6	5	2	0	5	3	41

KEY

* *one point for fastest lap* () *Dropped score*

Key to rounds: 1 Donington Park, 2 April; 2 Brands Hatch Indy, 17 April; 3 Thruxton, 8 May; 4 Silverstone National, 14 May; 5 Oulton Park, 29 May; 6 Brands Hatch Grand Prix, 11 June; 7 Donington Park, 24 June; 8 Donington Park, 25 June; 9 Knockhill, 29 July; 10 Knockhill, 30 July; 11 Brands Hatch Indy, 13 August; 12 Snetterton, 28 August; 13 Oulton Park Fosters, 10 September; 14 Silverstone National, 24 September.

Ben Collins (27) was one of those just unable to prevent Marc Hynes from moving into the foreground.

HIS ROYAL HYNES

by Charles Bradley

LAT Photographic

Almost without fail the youngsters of Formula Vauxhall Junior provided the most exciting races of the TOCA package. Many had predicted that a mixture of teenage angst and competitive single-seater racing would lead to chaos but, in between sitting exams and mumbling shyly to inquisitive journalists about 'understeer', the majority of these F1 wannabes raced with great good sense, while a mixture of their on-track naivety and the forgiving and – crucially – low-downforce chassis gave rise to a legion of memorable dices.

And after this season of classic racing, Martin Donnelly's charge Marc Hynes came out on top. The 17-year-old fought off challenges from Darren Malkin, Ben Collins and Justin Wilson to take the crown, winning Donnelly's team its first-ever title in the process.

Hynes started the championship as joint-favourite with Malkin, the two having tied on points in the previous season's inaugural Junior Challenge Cup (for 16-year-olds, would you believe). Four victories and six pole positions were the statistics behind Hynes's title win, the MDR pilot vitally being the most consistent qualifier in the championship.

Yet the season was no easy ride for Marc. A serious electrical fault wiped out his championship lead at the Knockhill double-header in July, while a Brands Hatch 'jinx' saw him make his only major mistake of the year. On that occasion, the Tetbury-based student threw away valuable points in the final race at the Kent track by going off while in the lead, with only three laps to go. Otherwise his driving was exemplary, with only one clash with any of his numerous title rivals. That came at Donington, where Malkin clawed back a huge deficit only to collide with Marc at the Melbourne Hairpin, ending Darren's race as Hynes went on to win.

For Malkin, the outcome of the season was slightly disappointing. The Warwickshire John Village Automotive racer – son of Mitsubishi rallying guru Colin – had already scored an FVJ win at Silverstone in 1994 with Mike O'Brien's Speedsport outfit, and so was expected to feature highly in this year's championship.

He did. But he expected more.

He scored an impressive victory in the opening round at Donington, chasing down poleman Hynes and passing him easily. This early-season form was punctured, however, by an electrical failure at Brands Hatch and demotion to the back of the grid at Silverstone for overtaking under yellow flags – from which he could only climb up to eighth. From that point, he was always playing catch-up to Hynes, but began his chase with a flourish, winning convincingly at Oulton Park in round five.

This was a momentum he couldn't quite sustain. From Knockhill onwards, Darren seemed to struggle for a reason even he wasn't quite sure of; in testing, he would fly, but in qualifying he just couldn't put it together. An inherited win at Brands notwithstanding (when Hynes went off), he didn't feature on the podium for five of the last eight rounds – a surprising and costly statistic.

In fact, Darren was fortunate to hold onto second in the championship. As the red flags fluttered to herald a premature end to the season at Silverstone, due to a rainstorm, he spun down the order, which would have allowed Wilson and Collins to leapfrog above him in the table.

Wilson was the wild card in the championship, the lanky 16-year-old following Team JLR precedent by breaking bones during the year! Former champions Ralph Firman Junior and Peter Dumbreck had broken an ankle and wrist respectively, while Wilson broke both in a pre-season racing school shunt at Brands . . .

That meant the quietly determined Rotherham-based charger missed the opening round of the championship, and raced in the next few races while still walking with the aid of crutches. Despite this, he finished a quite remarkable third at Thruxton. Like Malkin, however, he had already won an FVJ race, taking a victory in the Winter Series at Pembrey the previous year.

One of the quietest drivers in the paddock (although it was easy to forget that he's only 16, due to his six foot four inch height), Wilson has huge self-belief and should succeed in Formula Vauxhall next year – if he can fit in the car! He gelled well with the down-to-earth northern environment of the Robert Lee-run team, and proved that he's no pushover when he endured a run-in with team-mate Richard Tarling at Silverstone.

Justin equalled Hynes's number of victories (four), winning three of the last four rounds in fine style. Mechanical failures at Donington and Brands in June, plus a collision with Charles Butler-Henderson at Brands Hatch in August, accounted for his non-scores, while controversy over the nose cones on the Team JLR cars did a little to unstable the team after its dominant performance at Oulton Park. But it is worth considering that if Wilson had finished first or second in the race he missed at the start of the season, he would have been the champion . . .

Before the season got underway, one-time Formula First racer Ben Collins was regarded as an outside bet for title honours, but the likeable 20-year-old came closer to winning the championship than most had anticipated, and he was unlucky to finish only fourth in the points table.

Ben proved that his racecraft was without equal in this year's series – a fact no doubt aided by a season in the equally frantic FFirsts, in which he was more than a little accident-prone.

In contrast, this season he was a model of consistency which, ironically, proved to be his downfall in the final reckoning, when the increasingly blond-streaked Exeter law student had to drop two scores. He actually completed every lap of the FVJ year – the only driver to do so, and a remarkable statistic in a championship where three-abreast dicing is the norm – and he appeared on the podium eight times in 15 races.

A good racer. Consistent. So what went wrong? The root cause behind his lack of title success can be summed up in one word: qualifying. Regularly he would have to claw his way through the top ten after a poor qualifying performance. Unable to put a finger on the reason for this failure, he learned the hard way that it was costing him dear when he duly converted his one pole of the season into a win. His other victory also came from a front-row position, and he is determined to raise his one lap game next season.

Fortunately, his ability to pass on the first lap helped; it was rare not to see the blue-and-white Paston Racing car scythe past two or three others in the opening corners of each race. His defensive driving was also without equal and, sometimes, right on the limit of being judged downright dangerous. Rival team boss John Village was moved to point out at Donington Park that Collins's defence of a position from his driver Malkin would have stopped New Zealand rugby winger Jonah Lomu!

Worthy of mention is Paston Racing which, in its first season of FVJ, excelled upon its graduation from Formula First. Rod and Phil Blow (the latter a former Donnelly employee) established the team in a highly impressive and professional manner and should be in demand for '96.

The fact that Chris Buchan finished fifth in the points table, despite missing four rounds, emphasises how he was right in the title hunt until he hit trouble. The Scot had collected three licence endorsements by Knockhill (two in two days at the Scottish circuit) and picked up a three-month ban as a result.

So it was a season of 'what might have been' for Buchan. He should have guessed that it wasn't going to be his year when, in the second round at Brands Hatch, he would have won but for a broken fuel pump while leading with 200 yards to go. He bounced back to win at Silverstone in May, and then took a superbly judged win at a greasy Brands GP meeting in June; as the circuit dried, he had made sure not to wear out his wet tyres in the early stages and surprised leader Malkin with a swooping passing manoeuvre.

A switch from Bob Krstovic's team to Bellringer Motorsport coincided with this upturn in form, and Buchan was in touch with the title contenders going into the Knockhill round. But two yellow flag offences during the weekend saw him banned from competition for the rest of the season. Having beaten both Hynes and Malkin to the Junior Challenge Cup in 1994, and proved his pace by running at the sharp end of the field this year, it was a bitter conclusion. Totally disenchanted with the situation, Chris contemplated quitting the sport.

Richard Tarling sprung to prominence with a stunning performance in the season's opener at Donington Park, the 16-year-old Team JLR pilot driving assuredly to third place on his car racing debut. The Pangbourne College student also impressed in his Formula Ford 1600 outings in the early part of the season, but inexperience was mainly to blame for his unpredictable year, Richard having no real karting experience to his name.

Despite flashes of blinding pace, he only made it onto the podium once more, finishing second in a Team JLR 1-2 at the Oulton Park Fosters circuit, having led an FVJ race for the first time. He set his only pole of the season at the Silverstone finale, and should be a major contender in next year's championship with a more measured approach.

Don Hardman's charge Ben Spouse showed his wet-weather abilities in the Winter Series at Pembrey last year, and whenever it was raining you could depend upon him to set the pace. In between, however, he was prone to making the most ridiculous mistakes. His first pole position – at Oulton Park – was nullified when he started when the red lights came on. You might think that was down to nerves, but he didn't even realise he'd jumped the start until after the race, even though he couldn't have seen a car in his mirrors for the first two laps! Perhaps he never looked . . .

Fine performances at Brands Hatch and Snetterton in August were interspersed with numerous excursions. The mistakes could be put down to a lack of kart experience, but if the 22-year-old computer programmer can muster a more considered approach next season, he could be one to watch. Seventh in the championship was obtained during his saner moments.

Eighth in the championship fell to Neil Moulton – brother of Formula Vauxhall racer Simon. He gradually

Quick off the Marc

One of the first beneficiaries of the RACMSA's decision to allow 16-year-olds to race cars as from 1994, Marc Hynes capitalised on his learning year in last season's Formula Vauxhall Junior series to win this year's championship.

The 17-year-old's first step towards the title came when he signed with former Lotus F1 racer Martin Donnelly's team: 'Martin was quite keen to run me and put in an attractive offer and I think he runs the best team,' enthuses Marc. 'From the start of the year I think I was the quickest driver out there, and I knew I could win the championship.'

He proved this by setting pole and leading the first race of the season. On the other hand, this race proved that the year wasn't going to be easy, as John Village's charge, Darren Malkin, overhauled him and took first blood. His confidence took a knock, and an-all season low was achieved in the following round at Brands Hatch. 'I drove like an absolute plank!' the always-honest Hynes admits.

'I had to step back and look at myself, because if I drove like that every time, then I'd very quickly end up not driving racing cars. It was basically a lack of aggression. I had the speed, but when it came to the racing . . . I don't know what the hell I was playing at really. Maybe it was a one-off bad day, but I looked at myself and thought "Christ, I've got to turn this around." '

To his credit, it became the platform from which he launched his championship campaign. A terrific scrap with Ben Collins at Thruxton put paid to any doubts about his aggression, and this win was followed by another victory, at Silverstone. Very soon, Hynes had won four races out of six, with three poles to boot.

But unlike many of his F1-hopeful contemporaries, out of the car the highly amiable Marc sometimes appears to have his head in the clouds – nobody else in the FVJ paddock lists painting as a hobby! In fact, he is a well-rounded and intelligent individual, while in the car he has shown he's got what it takes to graduate from the junior formulae with honours.

The Knockhill double-header proved to be the next hurdle for the Nestle/Lyons Maid-backed ace, where a stubborn electrical fault refused to go away, costing him finishes in both races and allowing Collins into the championship lead.

After changing everything on the engine, it was back to Hynes's bogey circuit, Brands Hatch. 'I put it on pole, was leading the race and then just fell off,' he remembers, a mistake which dropped him to fourth and promoted championship rival Malkin to the winner's circle.

He then lost out at Snetterton by using a 'duff' set of tyres in the wet conditions, and the race was won by late-season dark horse, Justin Wilson. Two further wins by Wilson put him right in the title reckoning. But Hynes opines that he really set himself up for the title at Oulton Park, where both Malkin and Collins struggled in qualifying. A steady run to third meant that Marc arrived at the Silverstone double-header in September requiring two steady performances to clinch the title. 'I had a pitboard system which told me where Malkin and Collins were, so it was no problem really,' he says.

Having proved his mettle in such a rough-and-tumble category, he will graduate to 'wings and slicks' in 1996 in the form of either Formula Vauxhall or Renault Sport.

Hynes cites his racing philosophy as: 'Qualify as high as you can, because it makes it so much easier in the races. It's so important to break the tow in Juniors, so you've got to go for it on cold tyres and try and make a break.'

It is an outlook which will certainly serve him well in the more senior formulae, where overtaking is so restricted by the nature of the cars.

LAT Photographic

Marc Hynes emerged as champion ahead of Darren Malkin *(bottom)*, whose title challenge faded as the season progressed.

LAT Photographic

gained speed with Paston Racing as the year went on, and learned much about racecraft and FVJ tactics as a result. Unfortunately, he also learned that it is possible to have enormous accidents in a Vauxhall Junior. Two of the biggest shunts of the year befell the 20-year-old: a qualifying accident at Brands had him somersault three times and break his foot, while a double flip at Silverstone in September saw him fracture vertebrae in his neck and back . . . Back for more in '96, Moulton should be a front-runner, his best result this year having been a third at Knockhill in July.

Leighton Walker took ninth in the championship. The super-confident 16-year-old from Stoke-on-Trent won the loan of a chassis via the Vauxhall Kart Challenge and completed the early-season races with SP Motorsports. A superb performance at Thruxton, where he diced with Malkin, reaped an early podium finish.

The rest of the season was not quite as rewarding, Leighton switching to Marque Cars Racing mid-season and also teaming up with ex-JLR man Bob Krstovic. A bout of chickenpox forced him to miss the Donington double-header, otherwise he showed good pace but was prone to the odd shunt.

Martin Donnelly's second pilot was Damien Faulkner. The Irishman had a strangely up-and-down season and rounded out the top ten. Thoroughly expected to be a front-runner on the basis of his Irish FF1600 and Formula Ford Festival (where he took pole for the Kent class final) performances, he benefited from Buchan's misfortune to snatch a win at Brands early in the year. But, after that, the high point of his season was a fourth place at Donington in June.

The 20-year-old's season was interrupted by a serious bout of appendicitis, although he raced even when advised not to drive a road car by his doctor. Maybe his illness had a Coulthard-like effect on his driving, for Damien never regained his early form.

Also worthy of mention is Rowan Racing's Shingo Tachi, the son of the TOM'S boss, who was on the pace more often than not. The 17-year-old suffered through missing a couple of races due to exams, though. Scottish racer Craig Murray also featured well in his Dave Forster (a former Mini special saloon preparation ace) entry, the confident 17-year-old

Right: **Malkin leads the pack at Thruxton.**

Below: **Chris Buchan (9) headed the field in the races too, only for his season to end in acrimonious circumstances.**

Photos: LAT Photographic

Shingo Tachi *(below)* flies high at Knockhill.

Bottom: A full grid and a forgiving chassis provided some of the most exciting racing of the TOCA package.

LAT Photographic

Justin Wilson was the form man at the end of the season. He was another major threat to Hynes.

scoring a fine second place at Knockhill in the opening race. He was then used as a launch pad by Tachi in the second race; a misfire caused him to slow directly in front of the Japanese, forcing Shingo to endure a wild ride over the top of him!

Charles Butler-Henderson also impressed by putting his JVA car on the front row at Brands in his first season of cars, but the 16-year-old didn't really feature at the sharp end again, having clashed with Wilson in that race. Jeremy Gumbley made an amazing transition from tail-ender to front-runner at Brands, benefiting from a mistake by Hynes to finish a fine second. Again, after that race, he was never to feature prominently.

Andrew Kirkaldy contested the last couple of rounds for Lewis Motorsport with great success, the promising young Scot leading at Snetterton on his debut and finishing an excellent second. A major prospect for the future, should Andrew stay with Lewis next year he is sure to start as a title favourite.

Team-mate Alberto Jacobsen made the brave step of attempting to restart his career after a disappointing run in the Formula Opel Euroseries with Draco Racing, by teaming up with Lewis. Two fine drives in the Silverstone double-header at the end of the year emphasised that his karting form in Brazil was no fluke.

Lewis himself returned to Juniors after his Formula Renault Sport deal with Derek Cook went sour. Having proved his managerial abilities in just about every junior category in Britain, Jonathan was determined to make a splash at the end of the year and did so with chargers Kirkaldy and Jacobsen. He is likely to be a key player in the 1996 season.

One of those to disappoint this year was Alex Deighton, the reigning Formula First Champion enduring a nightmare half-season with Jim Russell Racing. Alex seemed to get involved in every accident available, including a big shunt at Brands in April and a huge roll at Oulton when he tangled with Buchan. Swedish kart sensation Milton Ryttarbris was another not to fulfil his promise, the blond 21-year-old only scoring at Thruxton before returning home.

The Junior Challenge Cup for 16-year-olds was predictably won by Wilson. This was the final year of the sub-class, the just-out-of-karts brigade having proved themselves in possession of the pace to challenge for overall honours. Tarling was classified second, the complex points system also taking into account their overall points score, as well as in relation to fellow 'juniors'. Walker was third from Tachi and Murray.

Doubts over the competitiveness of the field in the 1994 season were confirmed, as lap records tumbled at almost every circuit during '95. Driving standards were also higher than ever, with only the accident-prone Moulton and Deighton having large shunts, while Buchan was the only driver to fall foul of the stewards.

A low-cost Class B will be introduced in 1996 for the older, lower specification chassis, as the 16/17-year-old class is made redundant.

FORMULA VAUXHALL JUNIOR CHAMPIONSHIP

	Driver (Nat.)	Entrant	1	2	3	4	5	6	7	8	9	10	11	12	13	14	15	Points
1	Marc Hynes (GB)	Martin Donnelly Racing	13p	0	16p	15	8	4	16p	16p	0	0	9p	4	10	12	13p	136
2	Darren Malkin (GB)	John Village Automotive	15	0	12	3	15	13p	12	0	(2)	6	15	8	4	10	10	123
3	Justin Wilson (GB)	Team JLR	–	10	3	10	10	0	0	3	16p	12	0	15	16p	15	8	118
4	Ben Collins (GB)	Paston Racing	(3)	12	5	6	12	10	10	10	10	16p	6	(2)	0	6	15	118
5	Chris Buchan (GB)	Krstovic Motorsport/Bellringer Motorsport	8	9p	1	13p	0	15	8	12	1	–	–	–	–	–	–	67
6	Richard Tarling (GB)	Team JLR	10	0	2	0	0	8	0	4	6	8	5	0	12	6p	0	61
7	Ben Spouse (GB)	Marque Cars Racing	0	0	0	8	5p	0	6	0	0	5	10	10p	1	0	0	46
8	Neil Moulton (GB)	Paston Racing	0	4	8	4	0	–	5	2	0	10	1	1	8	0	1	43
9	Leighton Walker (GB)	SP Motorsport	4	5	10	0	5	2	–	–	0	3	0	5	0	4	5	43
10	Damien Faulkner (IRL)	Martin Donnelly Racing	0	15	0	2	2	–	0	8	0	4	4	0	2	2	3	42

KEY

p pole position

Key to rounds: 1 Donington Park, 2 April; 2 Brands Hatch Indy, 17 April; 3 Thruxton, 8 May; 4 Silverstone National, 14 May; 5 Oulton Park, 29 May; 6 Brands Hatch Grand Prix, 12 June; 7 Brands Hatch Grand Prix, 13 June; 8 Donington Park, 24 June; 9 Donington Park, 25 June; 10 Knockhill, 30 July; 11 Brands Hatch Indy, 13 August; 12 Snetterton, 28 August; 13 Oulton Park Fosters, 10 September; 14 Silverstone National, 23 September; 15 Silverstone National, 24 September.

FORMULA VAUXHALL JUNIOR CHALLENGE CUP

	Driver (Nat.)	Entrant	1	2	3	4	5	6	7	8	9	10	11	12	13	14	15	Points
1	Justin Wilson (GB)	Team JLR	–	25	15	25	25	0	6	15	31	27	0	30	31	30	23	293
2	Richard Tarling (GB)	Team JLR	25	6	12	0	6	23	0	19	14	20	17	6	24	18	(5)	190
3	Leighton Walker (GB)	SP Motorsport	14	15	25	0	125	12	–	–	0	13	8	17	0	14	15	148
4	Shingo Tachi (J)	Rowan Racing	10	18	–	–	–	–	19	0	18	0	10	13	16	11	18	133
5	Craig Murray (GB)	Dave Forster Racing	18	10	8	0	18	6	9	8	24	0	0	0	13	0	0	114
6	Charles Butler-Henderson (GB)	CBH/John Village Automotive	6	5	6	17	9	0	15	0	10	8	0	0	6	5	7	94
7	Jeremy Gumbley (GB)	SP Motorsport	5	4	0	8	5	17	0	0	5	0	27	8	0	0	4	83
8	A.Premadasa (SL)	Jim Russell Racing	0	3	0	10	0	8	12	11	–	–	–	–	–	–	–	44
9	Juan Jose Font (YV)	Rex Hart Racing	0	0	0	0	0	0	0	0	0	0	6	5	0	6	10	27

KEY

Key to rounds: 1 Donington Park, 2 April; 2 Brands Hatch Indy, 17 April; 3 Thruxton, 8 May; 4 Silverstone National, 14 May; 5 Oulton Park, 29 May; 6 Brands Hatch Grand Prix, 12 June; 7 Brands Hatch Grand Prix, 13 June; 8 Donington Park, 24 June; 9 Donington Park, 25 June; 10 Knockhill, 30 July; 11 Brands Hatch Indy, 13 August; 12 Snetterton, 28 August; 13 Oulton Park Fosters, 10 September; 14 Silverstone National, 23 September; 15 Silverstone National, 24 September.

Lots of rubber is laid down as a few thousand horsepower rockets off the grid at Oulton Park.

KENT IN TUSCANY

by Paul Lawrence

LAT Photographic

Unstoppable in the early races, John Kent romped to his first TVR Tuscan title. It was a year in which the TVR veteran did everything right. Never out of the top four in a demanding 24-race campaign, he took the title in one of the best seasons of Tuscan racing yet. The arrival of the AJP engine gave the cars even more power and crowds were consistently wowed up and down the country.

Martin Short, Ian Flux and Colin Blower were the main pretenders in a year when the only downside was a spate of engine failures. In the second half of the season, engine changes were a constant sight in the paddock but, with 15 new cars on order for '96, the success of Britain's most powerful one-make category is set to continue.

Any remaining doubts about the pace of the AJP engine were emphatically dispelled when the season kicked off at Silverstone in March. Superior in terms of power and torque, the AJP-motivated cars simply left the Rover V8 cars gasping for breath in their wake. As the pack streamed out of Luffield 2 onto the pit straight, the Rover cars were easily visible – they were the ones going backwards.

Kent's performance that weekend showed all the hallmarks of someone who had tested extensively in the run-up to the season, for he was simply in a class of his own. This was far from the case, however. Only on Thursday was the decision taken to drop an AJP lump into his car. John duly tested the following day – his first time in a race car since the final round of 1994.

Though Steve Cole and Blower gave valiant chase, John was peerless and started his campaign in the best way possible. Short drove on the limit to get his Rover car up to fifth in the first race, but it was clear that an AJP was an essential for a title bid. 'I'll have an AJP for Oulton Park,' promised the former Rover racer.

Kent ensured it was a very Good Friday in Cheshire by making it four wins in a row, but at least the chasing pack was closer than it had been at Silverstone three weeks earlier. Cole and Short ran him close in the races, with Short stunned by the performance of his brand new AJP unit.

The Kent steamroller showed no signs of faltering as the teams moved to Donington in late April. He just drove away for win number five, as an inspired Nick Cresswell headed the rest. Flux, still without an AJP, pushed his Rover to the limit and beyond to grab fourth.

Finally, at Castle Combe on May Day, Kent was toppled. A tardy start from pole left him fourth and, when the race was red-flagged two laps early, Blower had stemmed the tide.

Castle Combe was also significant as the first race with AJP power for Flux, but it would take a couple more races before Ian was able to capitalise on his new-found bhp.

Failing to win at Castle Combe was not on Kent's script; he was back on top with a vengeance at Brands Hatch as Blower tried every which way to demote the Bauer Millett car. A second podium finish of the year for Gavin Cooper and a first podium for Steve Guglielmi heralded the arrival of two of the new breed of Tuscan pretenders.

Short had been bang on the pace from the start of his TVR racing at the tail end of the previous year, and could not have picked a better place than Spa-Francorchamps to score his first win. He's an ace around the daunting Belgian circuit and used all his experience of the Ardennes track to beat Flux there in June.

Certainly, Flux had been stricken by a late-race gearbox problem, but Martin reckoned that he had caught the leader before his gearbox had started to jump out of fifth gear. Whatever, they had been the class of the field and Kent accepted that third was the best he could expect from the weekend.

But you can't keep a man like John down for long; when the series returned to Castle Combe at the start of July, another two victories started people talking about him settling the championship. With 11 of the 24 races run, he had won nine times and it would take a disastrous second half to the year for him to be overhauled.

Significantly, he would not win again until the very last race of the season, although he should have won at Donington at the end of July: leading into the Esses for the final time, with Flux hunting him down, Kent spun and handed Ian his first victory of the year. But the series leader recovered to salvage second just before Short arrived.

The heat of the summer was just what Blower had been waiting for. His car was perfect for the 30-degree heat of Oulton Park in August, his car working its tyres with far more sympathy than any of the others. The reward for his efforts was two dominant victories as Kent, Flux and Short trailed him home in both races.

Colin carried that dominant form forward a week to Brands Hatch, where 31 cars for a 30-car grid meant a qualification race (won by Flux) for everyone except Blower, who had been quickest in qualifying.

In the championship race Blower duly netted win number four as Flux, Kent and Short battled for second. When Flux departed with a failed front hub, John bagged yet another large dose of points to make the title look ever more certain.

Right: **Steve Cole (3) and Colin Blower (5) lead the packs at Donington and Oulton.**

Ian Flux *(bottom)* was the form man in the second half of the season and won twice at Silverstone.

At Snetterton in early September, the Tuscan pack enjoyed perhaps its best-ever race. The results show a brace of wins for Flux, but the second race was an event of the very highest order. As many as seven cars contested the lead with quarter neither asked nor given in what was a battle of racecraft and not barging.

Kent bagged a second and third from his weekend in Norfolk, while Guglielmi drove his race of the season and was unlucky to drop to third when his gearlever detached itself at the start of the final lap.

His points scoring was such that Kent headed to Silverstone for rounds 18 and 19 in early October needing only a modest finish to settle the title. In the 18 races held thus far he had accumulated nine wins, five seconds, two thirds and two fourths. No one else could hold a candle to such consistent front-running speed and reliability.

The Silverstone weekend was remarkable for two things. In dire qualifying conditions, Colin Blower escaped with minor injuries from an horrific accident when his car went through the barriers at Brooklands. Only the strength of the car saved him from appalling injuries.

On a far brighter note, two races of the highest quality were played out in front of a bumper crowd as Flux and Short battled furiously for the lead. Ultimately, the former won both as Short 'bowed to the superior experience of the older man!' A rather frustrated Kent trailed Guglielmi home to take fourth in both races, but his patience and self-control were richly rewarded as he put the title beyond reach.

With such considerations now out of the way he could go racing again, and he relished the prospect of two late-season double-headers at Donington. But Flux remained in stunning form at the first to extend his winning run to six victories, one longer than Kent had enjoyed at the start of the season.

This left Ian with a long shot at snatching second in the series from Short, and he had no reason to aim at anything less than victories. Kent was his closest rival that weekend, as Short struggled to balance his chassis. But fourth and third were enough to keep him on track for second in the championship.

Back at Donington in early November, Flux and Kent shared the victories in another pair of classic races. But Flux lost the chance of making it eight in a row when he 'lost control of the vehicle' at the Old Hairpin in the second race.

Kent, after a moment with Short in the first encounter, went into the second race on a mission and accomplished it by ending the season the way it had started – spraying the champagne. Third and second was enough to confirm Short as the runner-up, his progress aided by Blower's enforced absence from the last six races.

Kent started racing TVRs back in 1980. He has contested the Tuscan Challenge since it was created in 1989. Until this year, however, the title had eluded him, though he had finished runner-up twice.

Supremely experienced, his blend of consistent speed and necessary aggression was a recipe for title success. 'We had an advantage,' he acknowledges of the opening weeks of the season, modestly overlooking the fact that it was largely a self-made advantage.

Ten wins, seven seconds, two thirds and five fourths from 24 races is a remarkable record that pays ample tribute to the efforts of the works mechanics who tended his car. Spending the second half of the season looking for solid finishes rather than racing for victory was not his way, but by July he could only really have lost the title through errors or mechanical trauma. Neither happened and he finished the season a thoroughly deserving champion.

If you had told Short at the start of the season that he would end the year as runner-up, he would have been rather surprised. However, such is the ability of the former front-wheel drive ace, he quickly joined the 'establishment' of leading Tuscan racers in his first full year in the class.

Running a six-year-old chassis with his own Rollcentre Racing team, Short learned quickly about the tricks of Tuscan racing and adapted his driving well to suit rear-wheel drive and excess amounts of power. Enjoying his racing enormously, he revelled in the challenge and, but for the troublesome handling of the ageing chassis, he would surely have won more than once.

'It's nice to race a car that, no matter what kind of race you've had, you've enjoyed it because they're such a thrill to drive' says Short. 'That was a *real* thrill,' he admits of his Spa victory, but elsewhere

John Colley Photography

LAT Photographic

John Colley Photography

Martin Short *(opposite)* was impressive in his first full season with V8 power, and scored his inaugural Tuscan win at Spa.

'Hello John, got a new motor?'

'I think it's been the best year ever in Tuscans.' As the newly-crowned TVR Tuscan champion, John Kent could be slightly biased, but it certainly has been a marvellous season for the 450 bhp machines.

What does it take to win the title?

'Firstly, you need a lot of luck. We've had superb reliability and the car has finished every race. And every round counts in this championship . . .' says the softly spoken rest home owner from Preston.

Even when he finished out of the top two, the car had winning speed and there was usually a good reason for 'only' finishing third or fourth.

'It was a new car in 1993; we did the development work last year so, by the end of the 1994 season, I was flying. It was difficult until about the middle of last season and then we got the speed in it,' he explains.

The switch to an AJP engine from the traditional Rover V8 unit could have upset the balance of the car, but the chassis took it with barely a murmur. The result was a car that was right as soon as the season started.

'I was going to run a Rover; I thought it would be the smart thing to do for the first couple of races while we saw how the AJPs went. They were loading the cars up on the Thursday prior to going testing at Silverstone on Friday. At about 2 p.m. that day, the decision was made that we were going to run an AJP! There was a lot of swearing in the workshops when I went up.'

Rather than a winter of testing, John had parked the car in the paddock at Donington after the last race of 1994 and only got back into it on the Friday before the opening race of 1995!

Though the engine undoubtedly offered more power, the balance of the chassis was not quite as good, but that was of little comfort to the field left floundering in his wake at the start of the year. 'It *was* better than everybody else's, but I think we had it better with the Rover engine. The rest were a little bit further away from a balance than we were.

'Usually, the races you win are the easiest races you have. We got a head start on everybody and managed to get five wins on the trot to start the season. Then, provided you've got the reliability, you'd have to be an idiot to lose it.'

While others struggled with engine problems, Kent had a faultless year with his AJP. The motor came out of the car only once for a routine mid-season inspection.

Initially, race wins were the target before what John describes as something of a 'mental crisis' in the middle of the year. 'You're thinking you must, at all costs, finish and score points. You must keep it tidy and not take risks, and that mode lasted until the championship was secure.

'The driving throughout the year from everybody has been terrific. There's been no dirty stuff at all, it's been very clean. I think it's been a very well-behaved year.'

A title defence is on the cards but Kent does harbour one desire to race elsewhere . . .

'This would be a good time to have a change, and the only thing I'd change to would be GTs . . .'

frustrating understeer hampered his race pace.

The 1991 title-winning chassis was pulling along some 60 kg more than many of its counterparts but, by the Donington final, on-going suspension development had the car bang on the pace. A new chassis was ordered by his sponsors, Station Hill Garage, even before mid-season and so Martin will emerge for 1996 ready to pitch for the title.

Of course, Flux will have other ideas. The fact that he ran the first five races with a Rover engine in his Team Central entry cost 'Fluxie' a shot at the title. By the time his AJP was installed and running properly, Kent was out of reach and Short had a healthy points advantage.

'Our season really started at Spa,' says Flux, who recorded just three top six finishes in the first eight races. Aside from a dire misfire that ruined his chances at Castle Combe, he was the dominant force in the second half of the season and his nine wins were only one less than the champion. Like Short, his chassis is of 1989 vintage, but Flux drove it brilliantly in his first full Tuscan season.

'We borrowed the car from Nigel Tustain and I'm pleased to say that we handed it back today in the same unmarked condition' said Ian after the Donington finale. 'We lost the title in the first half of the season, but John was better organised and took advantage of everyone else messing about,' continued Ian, who was only twice outside the top three after July.

A front hub failure stopped him at Brands in August, and then there was that rare driver error in the Donington Park final when trying to work a way around a determined Cole. Pulling 174 mph at Spa was one of the highlights of the year for a driver who just loves to race. If someone gives him the chance, he'll be back next year.

Though he was understandably absent from the closing stages of the season, Blower had a typically strong year in one of the four cars run by his team from its Hinckley base.

Champion in 1992 and runner-up in '91, '93 and '94, he started out confident, only for his year to be peppered with early-season engine failures and then, of course, ended dramatically at Silverstone. With a set-up that suited the warmer weather, Colin lost early ground on Kent. 'The car was excellent, but the engine problems meant I had no chance of fighting John for the title,' says Blower.

Victory at Castle Combe in May preceded three wins in 10 days at the end of August and, before the Silverstone accident, he was tussling with Short and Flux for the runner-up slot. Many a lesser man would have hung up his helmet after such a terrifying accident, but Colin is determined to be back, and a new chassis is being readied for 1996.

These 'big four' – Kent, Short, Flux and Blower – were the class of the field and no-one else won a race, but in a season when grids reached record levels, there were plenty of other contenders chasing those podium finishes.

Cole is another TVR 'vet', having won the title back in 1991, in the chassis that Martin Short raced this season. A brace of seconds in the Silverstone opener was a good start, and more top six results kept him second in the title race throughout Spring.

However, it all went wrong at Spa when he wrote the car off in a substantial accident. He knocked himself out for some 10 minutes . . . 'We built a new car from a load of bits,' he says, 'but lost ground getting it sorted properly.' Late in the season he was back on the pace and concluded with a fighting third at Donington. Fifth at season's end was due reward for his persistence.

You had to feel for Cresswell. In a season when engine problems struck a number of people, his was far and away the worst experience; his engine tally for the year was into double figures. When he had an engine running properly, he featured strongly and coloured his patience-busting year with a fine second at Donington in April.

Aside from Short, one of the most impressive newcomers was former BMW champion, Guglielmi. He managed to persuade his employers, H.R. Owen, that he should pilot its car and more than repaid its support with a fine learning season.

'It's a dream come true. I'm hooked,' grinned Steve, who topped his year with a brace of thirds at Brands, having got his AJP motor in time for the first meeting in Kent. Though his season ended early as funds were stretched, Guglielmi is a potential race winner if he can realise his ambition to return in '96.

Another driver to shine in the tight confines of the Brands Indy circuit was Rod Gretton. Back racing after a lengthy lay-off, he also had his share of engine problems, but was fourth at both Brands meetings. His year ended on a down, however, when – unsighted – he ploughed into the stationary car of Gavin Cooper at Donington Park and inflicted considerable damage to his mount.

It was a difficult season for Bob Sands. Another of the series stalwarts who have supported the championship since its inception in 1989, he ran a works-tended car

John Colley Photography

with backing from Naughty Nobbies Novelty Condoms!

Unfortunately, his '89 vintage chassis endured a few knocks, including a major off in qualifying at Castle Combe in July when an oil line fractured going into Quarry. And only late in the season did the team discover that the chassis was bent!

'I spent all year driving round the problem,' admitted Bob, who chalked up a pair of fourth and a pair of fifth place finishes in a disappointing year. 'I'll be back on the pace for 1996,' he promises, with a new chassis on order.

Cooper grew in stature in only his second season of racing cars. The former motorbike trialler piloted the WLA entry from his family's garage and finished third three times as he climbed steadily up the grid. A few DNFs due to shunts and engine problems cost him points, but considering his limited experience, it was a worthy campaign. He should become a regular contender next season.

Another youngster to join the fray and make a useful impression was former single-seater racer, Jason Yeomans, who joined Colin Blower Motorsport after a year out of the sport. A testing shunt at Brands in May interrupted his progress; but when team boss Blower was docked ten seconds for a false start at Castle Combe in July, Jason picked up second to Kent. That was his best finish in a strong learning year.

Also from the Blower stable was Martin Stewart, who capped his year with a sixth place at Oulton, while at the end of the season, novice Mark Preston, finished a bold sixth at Donington Park.

Chairman of TVR, Peter Wheeler, continued to race against his 'customers' to very good effect. A fifth place on home ground at Oulton Park in Easter was a rather happier result than when the series returned in August. Then, a hefty first-lap shunt at Cascades wrecked his car. 'I've never seen so many cars spinning and out of control,' he declared.

Finally, from the many one-off or 'guest' appearances, three drivers stood out: Mark Hales, the 1994 champion, ran a works car a couple of times and flew in the Donington final to battle with Kent, Flux and Short; Robin Brundle drove the same car to fifth at Snetterton, while Pro-Sport racer, Chris Lord, finished fourth in a superb trial run in the second Henley Heritage car at Donington Park in October.

TVR TUSCAN CHALLENGE

	Driver (Nat.)	*Entrant*	*1*	*2*	*3*	*4*	*5*	*6*	*7*	*8*	*9*	*10*	*11*	*12*	*13*	*14*	*15*	*16*	*17*	*18*	*19*	*20*	*21*	*22*	*23*	*Points*
1	John Kent (GB)	Driver	21*	42*	21*	42*	63*	39	20	40	45	20	40	54*	18*	34	51	15	34	13	26	17	34	13	42*	744
2	Martin Short (GB)	Rollcentre Racing	12	16	13	34	36	45	10	12	63*	15	36*	45	13	26	45	4	22	17	36*	13	30	15	34	592
3	Ian Flux (GB)	Team Central	10	20	0	16	39	33	1	24	51	10	2	60	15	30	0	20	40	21*	40	21*	42*	21*	0	516
4	Colin Blower (GB)	Blower Motorsport	15	0	15	26	45	63*	18*	36*	39	13*	30	33	20	42*	63*	17	0	–	–	–	–	–	–	475
5	Steve Cole (GB)	Driver	17	34	17	30	33	51	11	2	0	0	14	39	12	24	0	13	20	12	24	0	22	12	30	417
6	Nick Cresswell (GB)	Driver	6	14	10	0	51	36	0	20	36	13	26	27	0	2	36	8	16	8	0	9	12	7	0	337
7	Gavin Cooper (GB)	WLA Specialist Cars	13	30	12	–	0	30	15	0	27	11	22	36	0	8	0	9	18	1	20	15	0	0	16	283
8	Jason Yeomans (GB)	Blower Motorsport	4	18	0	–	24	15	–	–	–	17	24	0	8	0	33	12	28*	11	22	0	20	9	24	269
9	Rod Gretton (GB)	Driver	8	10	9	14	30	0	8	26	33	4	16	18	4	16	39	7	2	0	10	5	10	0	–	269
10	Steve Guglielmi (GB)	H.R. Owen	7	24	2	0	21	–	12	30	0	–	–	30	11	22	12	11*	30	15	30	–	–	–	–	257

KEY

** Fastest lap* *Points divided at double-header meetings, with two-thirds allocated to second race*

Key to rounds: 1 Silverstone National, 26 March; 2 Silverstone National, 26 March; 3 Oulton Park, 14 April; 4 Oulton Park, 14 April; 5 Donington Park (Short), 23 April; 6 Castle Combe, 8 May; 7 Brands Hatch Indy, 21 May; 8 Brands Hatch Indy, 21 May; 9 Spa-Francorchamps, 11 June; 10 Castle Combe, 2 July; 11 Castle Combe, 2 July; 12 Donington Park Grand Prix, 30 July; 13 Oulton Park, 19 August; 14 Oulton Park, 19 August; 15 Brands Hatch Indy, 28 August; 16 Snetterton, 10 September; 17 Snetterton, 10 September; 18 Silverstone National, 8 October; 19 Silverstone National, 8 October; 20 Donington Park (Short), 22 October; 21 Donington Park (Short), 22 October; 22 Donington Park (Short), 5 November; 23 Donington Park (Short), 5 November.

BINTCLIFFE'S EDGE

by Charles Bradley

Right: **A calm drive at Silverstone netted John Bintcliffe *(below)* his second one-make title in as many seasons.**

LAT Photographic

In a season highlighted by some dubious driving standards and tactics, John Bintcliffe stole a march on his rivals in just about every respect. But it was still far from easy for the talented Yorkshireman, who has now achieved back-to-back Elf Renault Clio UK Cup and Ford Credit Fiesta Championship titles. Rob Hall made him fight every inch of the way, and his second title in as many years was only secured at the season's finale.

Bintcliffe's was a year of changing fortunes. The BIM Motorsport team struggled to give him the machinery he needed to do the job in the early rounds and, after a terrible qualifying session at Donington Park in April, it decided to go away and do some private testing. The plan worked to perfection and, by May, John was back in the hunt, although the car's set-up was still far from perfect, the blue Fiesta running on a knife-edge at Thruxton and Silverstone. At least points-scoring finishes were attained, and the first win eventually came at Oulton Park.

That success was followed by one of the craziest finishes in national motorsport history at a very wet Brands Hatch. Bintcliffe had held a race-long lead over Norwegian Clas Esbjug, but a slight mistake at the last corner allowed the youngster to draw alongside on the drag to the finish line. The cars collided in the process and the Briton slammed against the armco before spinning lazily across the line in second place.

Equally unimpressive was the unruly driving that prevailed at Donington Park in June, a result being declared after two starts and only three laps!

Bintcliffe's season really came alive at Knockhill, the Harrogate man dominating proceedings in spite of a praiseworthy attack from young Graham Jennings in both races. Another narrow win over Jennings, at Brands Hatch, moved Bintcliffe into the championship lead for the first time, and it looked to be plain sailing from here on for the 28-year-old.

A risky tyre choice for the first race of the Snetterton double-header seemed to have put that in jeopardy, however. On a soaking wet but drying circuit, Bintcliffe chose slicks and spent the first few laps slithering around, a balancing act that almost concluded with a huge shunt at Coram, his car spinning off and rearing precariously up onto two wheels before he could regain the track. Yet he fought back in brilliant style and, with by far the best Fiesta drive of the season, overcame everyone to take a famous win. He also won the second race, albeit in less exciting circumstances.

But with the championship almost won, disaster struck. The off at Snetterton had damaged the back axle, and when the offending item was replaced, a preparation error allowed non-standard shims to be fitted to the stub-axles. So after setting pole on Oulton Park's Fosters circuit, he was promptly thrown to the back of the grid and forfeited six points by way of a penalty for this technical transgression.

To compound his misery, another poor tyre choice was made and, having carved his way into the top ten in soaking conditions on slicks(!), he spun out of the points. Fortunately for him, title rival Rob Hall had his victory rescinded when he was excluded for dangerous driving. This all ensured that the title would go down to the wire . . .

Bintcliffe took pole for the all-important finale, but a poor start saw him slip behind Hall. However, second place was sufficient (fourth place would have been enough) and, despite a few half-hearted attempts to take the lead, he settled for the runner-up spot and the championship.

As a reward for his endeavour, he will receive a serious run in a works BTCC Ford Mondeo.

A sterling tale of talent triumphing over adversity, it would be a travesty if Bintcliffe doesn't find his way into a Super Touring drive for 1996. What more does he have to do?

You have to feel sorry for Rob Hall. If Bintcliffe hadn't arrived on the scene, the Lincolnshire man would have walked away with the championship. The ex-Formula Vauxhall Lotus racer – once a teammate of Kelvin Burt – was a frontrunner in the '94 season, and missed out on this year's title by just two points. This slim deficit is attributable to a couple of exclusions from points-scoring positions for dangerous driving – both at Druids, yet at different circuits! At Brands Hatch, in April, he was unlucky to be thrown out for an incident with Gary Burridge, while his seemingly ruthless attack on Gareth Downing at Oulton Park in September – the Silkolene-backed machine slamming into the latter and punting him off very comprehensively – can perhaps be explained by the wet conditions.

Run by dealers Tim Norton, the 28-year-old won three rounds – at Silverstone (twice) and Donington Park – and was always at the front of the field; but those disqualifications cost him dear.

Despite his Oulton Park excursion, Downing came through strongly during the year to take third spot in the championship standings, the 24-year-old also taking the Junior class title as well. A maiden Fiesta victory was gifted to him by the antics of Bintcliffe and Esbjug at Brands Hatch in June, but this was a low-budget effort from a family-run team, so his eventual place in the championship was an excellent achievement.

He was actually given the car as a 21st birthday present, and raced it initially in Production Saloon events. But he wasn't precious about it, showing his mettle by pressing on when it was in a very battered state at Oulton after being wiped out by Hall when dicing for the lead. This determined effort maintained his impressive 100 per cent finishing record in the top three of the Junior Championship.

The early-season revelation was Burridge, the former motocrosser beginning the season brilliantly with back-to-back victories at Donington Park. Unfortunately, these were the only times that he would stand on the top step of the podium. The closest he came to repeating the feat was at Thruxton in May, but a collision with leader Colin Stancombe saw him drop down the order.

Short on finances, Burridge pressed on, but gradually slipped as the year progressed. After his initial success, misgivings over his car's legality proved completely unfounded, making this an excellent second season in one-make racing for a man who was often seen changing his own tyres during qualifying. Gearbox problems proved to be the real bane of his season, however.

Mike Gorton was a steady points scorer, but he was unable to register a win in 1995 with the impressively presented MGA Motorsports outfit. However, his several sterling drives were rewarded by a share of the *Motoring News*-backed Ace of the Race award, for which he too receives a run in a works Mondeo.

One-make or break

In 1994 John Bintcliffe won the Renault Clio UK Cup. He had hoped that this success would be a passport to the British Touring Car Championship. It wasn't. Instead, he found himself caught in a familiar trap: unable to convince a works team to take a flier on a proven one-make winner, and without the ready cash necessary to tackle the Total Cup for privateers, the BTCC was out of reach.

Thus the Ford Credit Fiesta series became his only option for 1995. This was hardly the realisation of his dream, but the winds of harsh reality blow cold for the impecunious racing wannabe. He knew that it was vital to remain within the TOCA package, for to keep winning in front of the BTCC spin-doctors was his slim, but only, hope.

He was actually approached to drive for the Mobil at Halfords-backed BIM team before he'd clinched the Clio crown in '94, and substituted for Robert Speak at Brands Hatch. It went well. Qualifying on the front row, he finished third in the race: 'For whatever reason, everything seemed to work that weekend. The team were suitably impressed, as the car had been struggling until then. At the time Richard [Kaye, who graduated to the Total Cup from Fiestas this season] was swamping everyone, and for me to qualify so close to him shook everyone up a bit! Obviously, the team thought, "Bloody hell, if we can get the money, it would be good to run him next year," ' comments the 28-year-old Yorkshireman.

It did. It was.

The Clio/Fiesta double feat had been achieved before – by Matt Johnson – although not in successive years, and is something which cannot be repeated as Clios will not play a part in next year's TOCA package.

'I didn't really want to do Fiestas to be honest,' admits Bintcliffe. 'I wanted to do the touring cars this year, so the team thought that they'd go along with what I wanted to do. It got to the point where we'd been to see some privateer cars and we were about to sign a deal . . . but it just wasn't the right thing to do.'

The decision was made to do Fiestas. 'It was always going to be difficult this year, as we had to catch up on the teams that had years of experience on us.'

The beginning of this season was a living nightmare for Bintcliffe. The car was late and featured untested fundamentals such as a Yortech rollcage and Proflex suspension which all had to be dialled in to make the package work. Although they would ultimately prove to be championship-winning materials, initially the car was comparable to an Asda shopping trolley . . .

'The car was finished the night before and we drove to Snetterton to test – it kept breaking down. Then we literally drove to Donington for the first race,' he remembers. 'It wouldn't start at one point during qualifying and they had to push me off the circuit! At that point I was ready to go home. It wasn't like I was throwing my toys out of my pram or anything, it was just that there wasn't any point in racing.'

Time in the car was what was required, and the team gambled on skipping the next round at Brands Hatch – where the car/driver combination had gone so well previously – to do some much-needed testing.

Bintcliffe was back for Thruxton: 'Of all the places to return; we'd got the car right by testing on short, twisty circuits, but we went there with the same hard settings and I could hardly keep it on the track in qualifying,' he grimaces. 'In the race, we did a guess job and softened it all off, and that seemed to work.' Work it did, John storming from a lowly grid position to finish fifth, almost mirroring a similar drive with a hastily finished Clio in the '94 season-opener at the same circuit.

From that point progress was made, despite sacrificing much of the testing budget in pre-season preparation. 'We were left just doing the official TOCA one-hour tests, while everyone else was out every week,' he says. 'I still feel that, if we'd had the time, I could make the car quicker still.'

In this respect, Bintcliffe is quick to sing the praises of his engineer, Rob Speak. 'I can give him the information and feedback he needs, and he can understand exactly what I'm saying. That's how I think we won it really. Without him – or without someone he could rely on to give him a good opinion of what the car is doing – then I think it wouldn't have worked at all.'

The driving side of the equation was certainly impressive. Bintcliffe's fierce pace is that of a front-wheel drive natural. His initial forays with the tricky Honda CRX saw him on the front row of this competitive series within three races, and he made a seamless transition into Clios a year later. 'The other good thing, other than winning the championship, is that I've proved to people that I can set a car up,' he reasons. 'Also that I can do it in a short space of time and for all sorts of circuits. If you look at my times in TOCA tests, and in qualifying, I can do the times within a handful of laps.'

Zero points from the opening two rounds is no way to win a one-make championship, but five consecutive wins were the reason that Bintcliffe was able to turn his season around. 'Since we really got the car sorted – at Knockhill – we've set pole for every race to the end of the season,' boasts John.

The Harrogate ace would routinely set these on his third lap and sit out the rest of qualifying, saving his tyres for the race. Hang on, isn't that what they do in the BTCC? 'Yeah! I almost did it on purpose in a way, to show people I was capable of doing it,' he agrees.

But was anybody watching? He can but hope. For all this work will be rendered irrelevant if he doesn't get the BTCC opportunity he so craves. Part of his Fiesta prize is a test in an Andy Rouse-built Ford Mondeo, although a similar prize run in a Renault Laguna in 1994 did nothing to benefit his career, other than to give him a frustrating feel of what he's missing.

'I'd like to think I could go straight into a touring car drive without worrying about all the money and everything. But I think that's just pie in the sky these days,' he shrugs.

But with a mixture of money, abundant talent and a bit of luck – Vauxhall sensation James Thompson being the prime example – that goal can be attained.

Bintcliffe just lacks money and luck . . .

Jason Minshaw *(above)* leads the pack into Redgate. But it was Gary Burridge *(right)* who scored a back-to-back surprise at Donington in April to take an early lead in the championship.

LAT Photographic

LAT Photographic

Right: **Veteran Colin Stancombe endured an up-and-down year.**

Samantha Hill, Damon's sister, made her racing debut at the Silverstone Grand Prix meeting *(below right)*.

Below: **Bouncing the kerbs at Thruxton.**

Bottom: **Rob Hall was Bintcliffe's nearest challenger. This battle with Gareth Downing at Oulton Park concluded violently and Hall was excluded. This cost him the championship.**

LAT Photographic

Simon Hildrew

LAT Photographic

LAT Photographic

Graham Jennings *(right)* scored two second places at Knockhill, but he lacked the consistency to match Bintcliffe *(centre)* and Hall, who join him on the podium on this occasion.

The former XR Challenge runner started the year well with a pole position at Donington Park, but he was unable to repeat this despite being a top five regular.

Sixth in the championship went to class stalwart Colin Stancombe who scored two wins, but was unable to put together a serious title challenge. Always a good bet around Brands Hatch, he towed around his protégé Esbjug to win on the Indy circuit in April.

His second victory came in the following round at Thruxton, having tangled with early challenger Burridge at the chicane. A racer who always enjoys his sport, the 'ash blond' wasn't able to repeat his early championship form and fell out of the title race.

Graham Jennings was another to show promising early-season form which only flattered to deceive. He held the championship lead after Thruxton but, like Stancombe, had dropped out of the title equation by mid-season.

A close-season recovery saw him chase Bintcliffe to second places at Knockhill and Brands Hatch, but he just couldn't find the consistency to move up the points table.

Others who occasionally impressed included Esbjug, the Norwegian gaining a reputation for being fast but wild. Always quick at Brands, he finished second there in April, and should have done likewise at the Grand Prix circuit meeting in June; instead, a rash attempt at taking the lead right on the finish line saw him smash spectacularly into the pit wall. Another moment worthy of note was his roll at Snetterton's ridiculously tight Russell chicane, from which the Scandinavian – rally-style – calmly selected first gear and continued!

Another to gain an Ace of the Race Mondeo test drive, he could be a saloon star of the future if he can temper his aggression.

Scot Robert Ross was run by 1994 champion Matt Johnson to some decent results, although consistency wasn't his strong point. Peter Sowerby also made a good impression with some top five results and strong drives in his ex-Rob Hall car. Meanwhile, Mark Russell notched up some praiseworthy results at the end of the year, finishing in the top five at the Silverstone finale.

Now that the Clios have departed from the TOCA fray for 1996, the Fiestas should prosper as the only one-make saloon series to support the BTCC. That is, if its organisers and competitors can address the wild driving streak that pervades it at the moment.

LAT Photographic

FORD CREDIT FIESTA CHAMPIONSHIP

	Driver (Nat.)	Entrant	1	2	3	4	5	6	7	8	9	10	11	12	13	14	15	16	Points
1	John Bintcliffe (GB)	BIM Motorsport	0	–	–	6	8	9	12	10	10	12	12	12	12	12	0*	10	119
2	Rob Hall (GB)	Tim Norton Motor Services	8	7	0	10	12	10	8	0*	12	9	9	6	10	10	0	12	117
3	Gareth Downing (GB)	Driver	4	(2)	9	5	7	8	(3)	12	7	8	4	9	7	9	0	9	98
4	Gary Burridge (GB)	Driver	12	12	0	7	10	12	7	3	9	6	8	4	0	0	0	5	95
5	Graham Jennings (GB)	Pro Plus Sound Ltd	10	10	4	8	5	0	0	0*	5	10	10	10	0	6	0	2	74
6	Mike Gorton (GB)	MGA Motorsport	3	8	0	4	0	4	10	5	0*	7	7	0	5	2	12	8	69
7	Colin Stancombe (GB)	Stancombe Vehicle Engineering	7	0	12	12	0	0	9	9	0*	0	2	5	9	8	0	0	67
8	Jason Minshaw (GB)	Driver	9	9	6	0	6	6	0	7	0	3	5	0	4	4	0	0	59
9	Robert Ross (GB)	Johnsons Motorsport Ltd	2	0	0	0	0	0	5	6	0	5	0	2	6	7	10	6	49
10	Roy Tunney (GB)	Croydon Race and Rally Centre	6	6	8	0	9	7	–	0	0	0	–	3	0	0	–	0	39

KEY

** 6 points deducted in accordance with sporting regulation 4.1.1.c.* *() dropped scores*

Key to rounds: 1 Donington Park, 1 April; 2 Donington Park, 2 April; 3 Brands Hatch Indy, 17 April; 4 Thruxton, 8 May; 5 Silverstone National, 13 May; 6 Silverstone National, 14 May; 7 Oulton Park, 29 May; 8 Brands Hatch GP, 11 June; 9 Donington Park, 25 June; 10 Knockhill, 29 July; 11 Knockhill, 30 July; 12 Brands Hatch Indy, 13 August; 13 Snetterton, 27 August; 14 Snetterton, 28 August; 15 Oulton Park, 10 September; 16 Silverstone National, 24 September.

Lee Brookes prevailed in this 'small family' car class.

LEE'S SHAW THANG

by Charles Bradley

John Colley Photography

In the final year of the Clio's participation in the TOCA package, Lee Brookes finally wrapped up the title, having come close to the feat last season. His competition came in the shape of David Shaw, another of 1994's beaten championship contenders, and things got a little out of hand as the tension increased . . .

The season started perfectly for Brookes, the 27-year-old from Willenhall winning the first two races in his Mates condoms-backed machine. In fact, besides Brookes and Shaw, only Guy Povey managed a win in 1995, and then only when the battling title duo took themselves out!

Shaw fought back, winning the next two rounds, but Brookes countered with an impressive run of four victories. To make matters worse for Shaw, he was excluded from a second place at Donington Park in June, when the rear axle of his Harlow Motorsport-prepared car was deemed to be illegal. The team appealed against the decision, an action which clouded the championship points situation until an RACMSA tribunal at the season's end.

Shaw also invoked his 'claimer' option at Donington, whereby any competitor could buy a rival's engine. Unperturbed by all of this, Brookes succeeded in winning the next round at Knockhill, thus proving that his engine wasn't the reason for his superior performance.

Sunday's race at the tight and undulating Scottish circuit saw yet more controversy, as the title hopefuls collided at the infamous Duffus Dip – much as they had done in the corresponding race the year before. This time Brookes's car was tipped into a roll, the Renault appearing to pick up speed as it slithered on its roof down the steep hill. As Shaw was forced to pit, a surprised Povey inherited the win.

Brookes protested Shaw's driving, but this was thrown out after the stewards had viewed video evidence of the shunt, stating that both parties were equally to blame.

At the following Brands Hatch meeting, Brookes – perhaps not surprisingly – was content to sit behind leader Shaw for the duration. He was happy to let David win as long as he could pick up the points for second. But Shaw was to further his championship push with another victory at Snetterton, as Brookes struggled to a lowly sixth with a down-on-power engine.

In the penultimate round at Oulton Park, Brookes and Shaw collided yet again. The pair rounded Lodge side by side, and exited the corner with Brookes bouncing into the barriers while Shaw went on to win. Again the stewards were consulted, Shaw admitting that he'd outbraked himself initially, but taking no blame for the actual contact which resulted in Brookes's violent exit.

This still left Lee with the seemingly simple task of finishing fifth in the Silverstone finale to make sure of the title and ensure that Shaw's ongoing appeal became irrelevant in championship terms.

And the title race effectively ended at the first corner, Shaw making a poor start and then being forced into the Copse gravel. In stark contrast, Brookes found a gap and was able to make a break. A fine recovery drive from David saw him eventually net second, albeit aided by some diabolical driving by those in front, but Brookes cruised to his seventh win and the title.

For his troubles – and successes – he benefited from a Silverstone test drive in a Williams-built Renault Laguna BTCC car, when he impressed with his calm, professional approach and speed.

As in '94, the Riverside Packaging-backed Shaw had to settle for second place in the title race. Although the 35-year-old former Formula Ford racer had his Donington Park disqualification hanging over him like the Sword of Damocles for the latter half of the season, he pushed Brookes all the way.

Best of the rest was Dave Cox, the Clio veteran scoring a number of top five places. Always amongst the front-runners, he – like the rest of the field – couldn't hold a candle to Brookes or Shaw.

Cox just fended off Harlow Motorsport's Charlie Postins for third by eight points. The latter, a team-mate of Duncan Vercoe in his Formula First days, was in his first season of saloons, and it saw him on the pace from the middle of the year onwards. A late-season burst of top placings helped him rise to fourth in the final points positions, although a collision with Cox in the last race at Silverstone put the latter out and dropped Charlie to eighth in the race.

Jim Edwards Junior made a very welcome return to the mainstream series, having competed in the Renault 5GT Turbo category for a number of seasons. The SMC Racing driver just managed to hold off Glenn Board to place fifth in the championship. These two were eliminated in the same accident at the final round, a shunt which neither actually instigated.

Sixth-placed Board's distinctive Pinnacle-backed, Harlow-run car was often in the wars, but when Glenn kept it on the island he was a regular top six finisher. A hard racer, his best outing was at Brands Hatch in August, where he fought out a monster scrap with ex-Formula

RENAULT
elf
MICHELIN
SHADRAKE GROUP
RENAULT
RIVERSIDE
HARLOW
MOTORSPORT
Renault Fina
elf
CHAMPION
MICHELIN
Car S

The story of the season: David Shaw (2) dices with Brookes. On occasion, this battle became a tad over-zealous.

John Colley Photography

Guy Povey was the only other race-winner, inheriting his Knockhill success when Brookes and Shaw collided.

Fordster Mark Cole and Cox, which he won to place third behind Shaw and Brookes.

Povey may have been the only person other than Brookes or Shaw to win a race, but he was disappointed to finish an unrepresentative seventh in the championship. The former Production Saloon ace accepted his Knockhill win with open arms, but had been bang on the pace at the start of the year at Donington. He sold his car before the end of the season, but still stayed ahead of Julian Pilling in the points table.

Julian was another to stray from the straight and narrow on a couple of occasions, his repertoire including a spectacular roll at Thruxton. He had shown what he was really made of in the previous round at Brands Hatch, when he led for the first few laps and only fell prey to champion Brookes in the terribly tricky conditions.

The *Coupe des Dames* element of the championship produced a really good scrap between Sasha Pearl and Paula Stephens – a battle that became distinctly unladylike at Knockhill, where the pair spent much of the weekend driving into each other!

Pearl came out on top, although she was lucky to escape without a ban from the bruising Scottish encounter, as she'd obtained a number of previous licence endorsements. The Tarmac-backed Scot impressed last year in Renault's celebrity car at the Scottish circuit, and her decision to switch from single-seaters reaped dividends.

Stephens, partner of F3000 team boss and driver management supremo David Sears, was in her first full season of racing, having only contested a couple of Formula First races. She made the transition to Clios very impressively and the 25-year-old's Brookes Motorsport machine was often in the top ten overall. Both women featured well in the overall scheme of things, winding up ninth and tenth in the championship.

Of the rest, Adrian Cottrell's first season of Clio racing was a disappointment. The ex-Formula Renault man suffered a huge engine blow-up at Knockhill, and only really came good in the last round of the championship at Silverstone, where he finished an impressive third.

The Clios are to be replaced on the TOCA package by the all-new Renault Spider sports car next year, the French saloons finding sanctuary in the world of club racing for 1996.

They have been good value over the years.

Bubbling Brookes

After a season-long struggle with David Shaw, Lee Brookes won the Elf Renault Clio UK Cup crown – in a car prepared by his own team, Brookes Motorsport.

There is a plethora of outfits which specialise in one-make racing, a form of the sport that looks easy from the outside but can prove a minefield for the uninitiated. The on-track antics are tough enough, so why double your workload?

'It was a lot of hard work!' understates Lee of his title bid. 'At the beginning of the year we did a lot of testing, we tried loads of different settings. We learned what would give us a consistent race pace and what would give us a quick qualifying pace,' he adds.

This was Lee's third season with the Clio, and this year he meant business. To win he knew that a driver has to understand the car from top to bottom. Both he and the team had the experience. He'd come close in 1994. It was time to make it count.

He began his career in karts before jumping straight into a saloon, a strange move one might think. 'It was, but I just didn't have the money at the time. I was already 19 when I was in karts and these days you need to be in F3 when you're 19! Karting is one of the best learning grounds you can get, though,' he asserts.

Last year, Brookes was always among the fastest in Clios, but reliability was the problem: 'We felt we were quick enough at the end of last year – obviously with getting three straight wins. It was just a case of tidying up the edges and making sure we had the reliability.'

And Brookes worked well with his family-run team: 'I gave them the feedback they needed to know and they'd adjust it and say, "Try this, then that." We learned between us, and seemed to get it all sussed out!'

He did not click with Shaw, however, his rivalry with whom was the main talking-point of the Clio season. 'To be honest, at the start of the season we were a little bit quicker than him. Then he got quicker about halfway through – but we were still beating him. Then, at the end, it started to get a bit rough,' says Lee. 'By the middle of the season, we needed two non-finishes for us not to win it . . . and we had two non-finishes!' he grimaces.

As for their tangles, Lee feels a lot of them were unnecessary. 'He was losing the championship and was paying a lot more money than I was . . . He bought my engine at Donington, so we had to build a new one for Knockhill – which we did and won the race . . .'

Brookes was eliminated from the second race at Knockhill after a clash with his rival.

A re-shell was required after that episode. 'I stuck it on pole at Brands, so that was another sickener for them! I just sat behind him in the race to collect the points. Then this thing at Oulton happened.' They collided again. If he was to prevent Brookes from taking the championship, Shaw had to win the race while his rival failed to finish. Lee was leading. David was second. They touched. David won. Lee retired. Controversy and recrimination followed.

The deck was stacked against Shaw at Silverstone, as he was also appealing against an exclusion for back axle irregularities. 'Even so, there was a chance he could still win it at the last round,' stresses Brookes.

It all came right, though; Shaw's trip into the gravel at the first corner saw him drop down the field, allowing Brookes to notch up his seventh victory of the year. 'In the end, I decided to either sit in second and watch how it all goes, or just go for it. When Jim Edwards made a mistake at the first corner, I thought, "This is your chance, you've got to go for it," so I just went and the gap kept increasing . . .'

His success has been double-edged, the workshop manager hugely encouraged by the way things are going on the business side, reporting much interest for next season, when the team plans to move into the Ford Fiesta series.

For '96, Brookes himself wants to step up to the BTCC: 'I'm hopeful, because I've had words about a few tests. I just want to get in there and show them that it's worth giving me a try. That's the way I'd like to go. I'm sure I can do a good job.' He has since tested a TOM'S GB Toyota Carina at Snetterton in impressive fashion. With David Sears now managing him – 'he knows the people who you need to know' – he could be set for great things.

Photos: John Colley Photography

ELF RENAULT CLIO UK CUP

	Driver (Nat.)	Entrant	1	2	3	4	5	6	7	8	9	10	11	12	13	Points
1	Lee Brookes (GB)	Brookes Motorsport	32*	30	25	27*	32*	30	30	32*	0	25	16	0	30	309
2	David Shaw (GB)	Harlow Motorsport	0	22*	32*	30	25	27*	E	2	2*	32*	32*	32*	27*	263
3	Dave Cox (GB)	M-Sport	0	10	20	20	22	20	22	22	25	20	20	20	0	220
4	Charlie Postins (GB)	Harlow Motorsport	16	14	0	22	20	0	18	25	20	18	25	22	12	212
5	Jim Edwards (GB)	SMC Racing of Woking	22	16	22	0	14	18	20	14	18	12	22	18	0	196
6	Glenn Board (GB)	Harlow Motorsport	0	18	18	0	16	22	16	20	22	22	14	25	0	193
7	Guy Povey (GB)	GT Services	25	8	16	16	12	10	27*	0	30	16	18	–	–	178
8	Julian Pilling (GB)	Harlow Motorsport	20	25	0	E	18	12	14	12	0	14	6	16	18	155
9	Sasha Pearl (GB)	Driver	14	4	E	8	0	8	4	10	14	6	10	6	16	100
10	Paula Stephens (GB)	Brookes Motorsport	4	1	0	12	0	6	8	4	10	10	3	8	14	90

KEY

** Fastest lap (2 points)   E Excluded*

Key to rounds: 1 Donington Park, 2 April; 2 Brands Hatch Indy, 17 April; 3 Thruxton, 8 May; 4 Silverstone National, 14 May; 5 Oulton Park, 29 May; 6 Brands Hatch Grand Prix, 11 June; 7 Donington Park, 25 June; 8 Knockhill, 29 July; 9 Knockhill, 30 July; 10 Brands Hatch Indy, 13 August; 11 Snetterton, 28 August; 12 Oulton Park Fosters, 10 September; 13 Silverstone National, 24 September.

THE MOST COMPREHENSIVE CIRCUIT GUIDE EVER PUBLISHED

The updated 1996 Autosport Guide...

...now even more essential!

IF YOU'RE A COMPETITOR, A MARSHAL OR A SERIOUS ENTHUSIAST THEN THIS ANNUAL A5 LOOSE-LEAF MONO GUIDE WILL BE INVALUABLE TO YOU!

Now with
- Five more UK circuits
- Five European circuits
- UK hillclimb venues

ONLY £24.99 plus £5.00 for rugged binder

OVER 500 PAGES

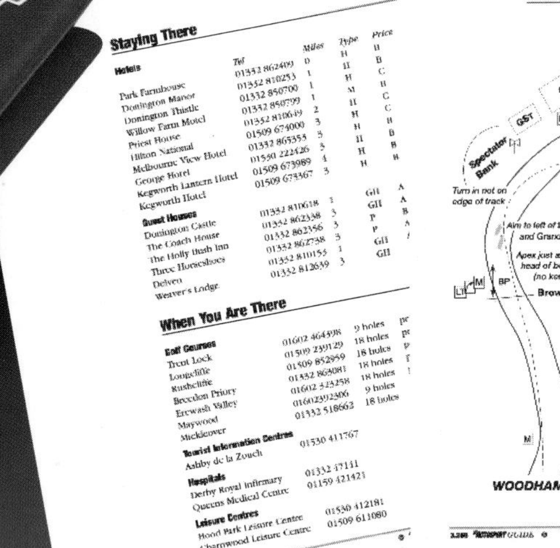

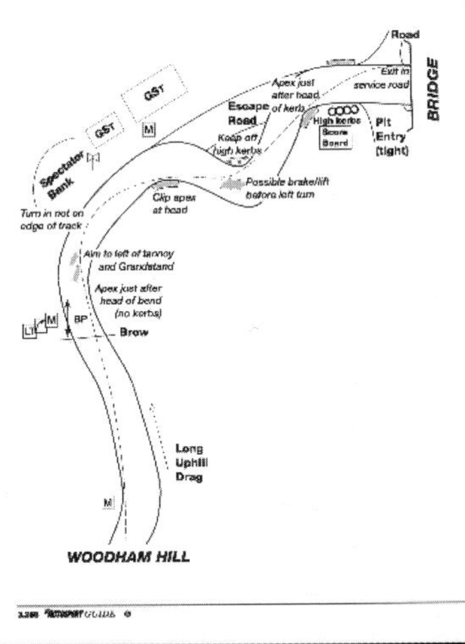

COMPLETE CIRCUIT LISTING:

Brands Hatch *(GP and Indy circuits)*, Cadwell Park *(Long, Woodlands and Short circuits)*, Castle Combe, Croft, Donington Park *(GP & Short circuits)*, Goodwood, Ingliston, Jurby IOM, Kirkistown, Knockhill, Lydden, Mallory Park, Mondello Park, Oulton Park *(International, Island and Fosters circuits)*, Pembrey, Silverstone *(GP, National & Stowe circuits)*, Snetterton, Thruxton, Le Mans Bugatti circuit, Nurburgring GP circuit, Spa, Zandvoort, Zolder

BENEFITS...

- Corner by Corner Circuit Diagrams *including Racing Line*
- Detailed Written Circuit Notes
- Improve your Circuit Familiarity
- How to Get There, Where to Stay
- Comprehensive Events Calendars
- A-Z Autosport Directory

WHAT THE PUNTERS SAY....

'Absolutely excellent...' Mark Beynon

'Very impressed by the quality throughout...' Chris Mellor

' A great concept...' Stephen Mummery

' A great guide... made my novice outing (in a Morgan at Thruxton) much more succesful' Simon Orebi Gann

WHAT THE JOURNALISTS SAY....

'An essential for the novice circuit driver and useful to the most experienced' John Barker, *Performance Car*

'...a boon to the beginner and seasoned competitor alike: you're never too old to learn.' Art Markus, *Cars and Car Conversions*

Phone our 24-hour order line on

01993 891000

DENT PUBLICATIONS LTD,
Newbarn Court, Ditchley Park,
Chipping Norton, Oxfordshire OX7 4EX
or fax our Order Line on 01993-891100

Access and Visa accepted

John Colley Photography

Mary Harvey

RACING ROUND-UP

Mary Harvey

by Paul Lawrence

John Colley Photography

Both Caterhams and Minis provided spectacular action over the year. Here are the champions *(anti-clockwise from left)*: Simon Harris (Caterham K), Michael Jackson (Mini Seven), David Walton (Caterham Vauxhall) and Chris Lewis (Mini Miglia), here on the outside of series rival, Bill Sollis, at Brands.

But of them all, the small-engined Caterhams were perhaps the most spectacular. *Autosport* journalist, Tom Clarkson *(left)*, leads a typical group at Oulton Park.

John Colley Photography

CATERHAM VAUXHALL CHALLENGE

WALTON'S MOUNTAIN

Going into the final round of the Caterham Vauxhall Challenge, David Walton had it all to do. His arch-rival, Keith Farrance, had a 13-point advantage and, having finished third, second and third in the previous three years of the championship, Walton needed something special to claim the title he had been chasing since the start of 1992.

No one could have predicted such a thrilling climax. Both Walton and Farrance qualified poorly but were soon storming up the order, until Keith had his gearbox jam in fourth, that is. Pushing just too hard, he slithered off into the McLeans gravel trap and could only stand and watch as Walton netted the title by finishing fourth in a blanket finish.

Seven wins in the 19-race championship could have retained the title for Farrance. But the ex-Formula First champ was left to rue Silverstone and Castle Combe retirements, as well as the Donington Park finale.

But Walton also had his share of misfortune. His elation at winning the first round at Silverstone was shortlived when he was excluded for a technical infringement relating to the carburettor. Then in round two, at Oulton Park, an out-of-control celebrity car took him out of a safe lead. Later in the season a sudden change of team could also have hampered his bid, but he endured to take the title he so badly wanted.

At the start of the season Shaun Balfe gained most from Walton's bad luck. Even at the final race, he retained an outside chance of taking the title. Shaun was always in contention, despite never quite repeating that winning form.

As is typical of the championship, the racing was frenetic as long gaggles of cars contested the lead. Among the many leading protagonists were K Series graduate Clive Richards, Bart Hayden, Guy Parry and Verney Wood.

CATERHAM K SERIES CHALLENGE

SIMPLY SIMON

If any class of racing was able to beat the Caterham Vauxhalls for breathtaking action, it was their less powerful brethren. The championship for Rover K Series-engined cars stunned crowds up and down the country with the sort of racing not seen since the epic years of Formula Ford.

With 30-plus grids and a host of potential winners, the achievement of Simon Harris in clinching the title before the end of August is all the more remarkable. For his third season of Caterham racing, he ran with Chas Berger's team in a new car and began the year with what would prove to be his worst result of the season – a fifth place at Silverstone.

Where Harris scored over his rivals was his ability to stay out of trouble and secure the best result available on the day. Seven wins later, the championship was his.

But it could have been very different if young Dan Eaves had hit the top of his form earlier in the year. As soon as the season started, the Cheltenham teenager was right on the pace. But he got involved in a few incidents mid-season that cost him any chance of the title. Later in the year, however, he was superb and six wins from the last eight races marked him out as a very promising talent – a talent that possesses the uncanny ability to win by fractions of seconds, a vital asset in this series!

Aside from a guesting John Barker, who won both Good Friday races at Oulton Park, no one else won more than once. Tim Fuller, Mark Humphrey and Peter Venn all triumphed, but it was the consistent front-running drives of Warren Gilbert and Mike Neumann that counted for more in the points race. The latter impressed greatly having started the year very much a novice. Sadly, his season ended with a scary accident at Donington from which he was lucky to escape unharmed.

UNIPART DCM MINI MIGLIA CHALLENGE

LEWIS TAKES SOLLIS

The fact that Chris Lewis won the Unipart DCM Mini Miglia Challenge for the second time in a row – and the fourth time in all – would not come as a surprise to anyone who witnessed his early-season hat-trick of victories. By the end of April it seemed a formality that the Yorkshireman would run away with the title, just as he had the year before.

But Bill Sollis had other ideas. Throughout the preceding winter and into the first part of the new season, the London fireman had been working hard to discover the edge of power that he knew Lewis had over him. By mid-season Bill had found the best air-intake arrangement for his engine and was to make Chris work immensely hard for the rest of the year.

At the Silverstone final, with Sollis winning the race, Lewis needed third place to take the title. Stewart Drake was second and . . . Lewis only snatched that vital place by less than half a second from Ian Curley!

Even then it took a tie-break to declare Lewis the champion, thanks to his seven race wins to the six of Sollis! Impressively, both drivers were only out of the top four once in 16 races: Lewis struggled on the wrong tyres at Spa; Sollis risked ten laps at Mallory Park without an oil cooler and paid a heavy penalty.

Drake, third in the series, had by far his best season despite a very modest budget. It was topped by wins at Spa and Snetterton.

Curley, the reigning Mini Seven champion, endured a tough start to his year as he learnt the tricks of Miglia racing. He won at Mallory Park, though, on his way to fourth.

Nobody else won races, as Ian Gunn and Peter Baldwin were the best of the rest.

UNIPART DCM MINI SEVEN CHALLENGE

THE JACKSON SEVEN

When did anyone last win the first six Mini Seven races of a season? Not recently, for sure. But that is precisely what Michael Jackson did this year and, as far as the championship was concerned, the rest never saw him again.

Champion in 1992, Jackson emerged from the winter break on a charge. With his car's chassis sorted to perfection, he blitzed the opening races, and it was not until Spa in June that he faltered, outbraking himself into the Bus Stop chicane for the final time and allowing young Matt Hayman to nip through for a famous first win. To complete his joy, Jackson took home the road-going Mini-Cooper that goes to the overall Mini champion.

The runner-up slot was decided on a tie-break, Shaun King just pipping Dave Banwell. King – in his best season so far – won the final round to add to a Castle Combe double. Banwell had another front-running season, but was frustrated to miss out once more on a victory.

Dave Braggins was almost relieved not to be runner-up – for three years in a row he had finished second. Having shaken off the 'bridesmaid' tag by finishing fourth, he will mount a fresh bid in 1996.

Tim Sims climbed up to fifth with a strong second half to his season, while Hayman never repeated his Spa win, but was usually in the action on his way to sixth.

Remaining race winners, Steve Bell (Thruxton) and Rob Selby (Mallory), were next in the standings.

Left: **Mark Jones won the Rover GTi title at his fifth attempt, while Simon Crompton *(right)* won the ICS Historic Saloon Car Championship in only his first full season of motor racing. His BMW held off a host of American monsters and Lotus Cortinas in the process.**

LAT Photographic

Colin Taylor Productions

Gary Haggity

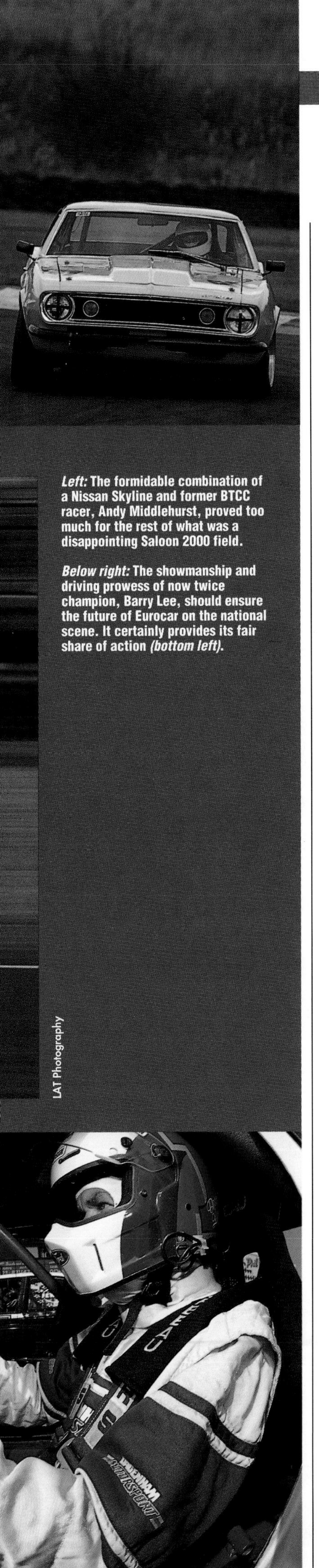

Left: **The formidable combination of a Nissan Skyline and former BTCC racer, Andy Middlehurst, proved too much for the rest of what was a disappointing Saloon 2000 field.**

Below right: **The showmanship and driving prowess of now twice champion, Barry Lee, should ensure the future of Eurocar on the national scene. It certainly provides its fair share of action *(bottom left)*.**

DUNLOP ROVER GTi CHAMPIONSHIP

NO JONES ABOUT IT

Championship victories don't come much tighter than this one. For half the season nobody seemed to want to win more than one race in the Dunlop Rover GTi Championship and, in the closing stages, Vince Martin still headed the title race even though a win had eluded him. Finally, at Silverstone in October, Mark Jones ended the race level on points with Martin and, thanks to two victories against the still-winless Martin, the title was his.

The Southampton garage owner has remained faithful to the GTi throughout its five seasons as a race car but, until April of this year, had yet to win a race. Then, on a dire day at Silverstone, he was without peer in the rain. He repeated his success when the series produced a pair of fantastic races at Donington Park in the heat of July. That victory brought to an end a remarkable run: aside from the fact that Gary Till won both parts of a double-header at Brands Hatch in May, the opening six meetings produced a corresponding number of winners.

Young Rupert Deeth stunned the 'establishment' by winning on his championship debut at Snetterton in April. Never again did he repeat that form, but he had pace aplenty and could have won the final round at Silverstone had he not speared off into the Copse gravel at the start of the second lap.

After wins for Jones and Till, Carl Blakely was victorious at Mallory. A real hard-charger, he was to win again at Donington. Elsewhere, patchy results kept him out of the title race but, with a proper budget and a little more consistency, he could be a champion.

The same can be said for Alfonso Emanuele. 'Alfie' was a master of the fast tracks and won at Thruxton and Castle Combe during a season when he was invariably in the thick of the action.

At Cadwell Park, John Griffiths, in only his second season of racing, was victorious. A month later he contained a snarling pack for ten laps of the Oulton Park Fosters circuit to add a second win. He made it three in the Snetterton rain – a promising year that belied his modest experience and netted him fourth in the championship, just ahead of Emanuele.

While others were doing the winning, Martin was busy chalking up the points in the top six. Vince pulled off the best drive of his season at Donington in July; punted into the Redgate gravel at the start of the first race, he started from the back of the grid for race two, yet tigered through to salvage points for sixth.

Going into the final race, Jones had sneaked ahead of Martin by four points. Yet both were under threat from a late-season attack from Spencer Baker.

The Leeds racer had been threatening to win races since the start of the year and was always a contender. But it was a win at Snetterton, then two more at Pembrey in September, that set him up for a charge. And once he had watched Deeth fly into the gravel at Silverstone, he was dominant to take his fourth win. A loose filler cap at Brands and a driver error when leading on cold tyres at Oulton had cost him his title chance, however.

SALOON 2000 CHAMPIONSHIP

MIDDLEHURST, MIDDLE-DISTANCE

Over the winter, the Group N Championship was remodelled into a two-class affair and branded Saloon 2000 in deference to plans to create a two-litre-only single-class championship. To simplify the racing in 1995, cars were split at two litres, but the result was not what the promoters wanted. Grids were generally small, and the series reached an all-time low at Oulton Park when just six cars started the race.

The combination of Andy Middlehurst and a Nissan Skyline was to prove the class of the field. The former BTCC racer and his team did the job properly – victorious in 11 of the 18 races, they won the title commandingly.

His rivals were the Escort Cosworth pack of Michael Woodcock, Graham Coomes and – for part of the season – Robin Rex. Woodcock won five times, including a brace at Mallory Park, where the long, long Gerards rooted the Nissan's tyres, to take the runner-up slot.

Coomes and Lionel Abbott (Saab 900) took a win apiece, while Geoff Kimber-Smith pedalled his Sapphire Cosworth further up the field than it really should have been.

The two-litre class was often full of drama as the Astras of David Pitcher and Peter Morss were locked in a combat that was sometimes rather too robust. However, a popular class winner was Bill Stilwell in his Honda Civic. Two double-headers at Brands proved the highs and lows of Bill's season: in May, he beat a bumper entry in both races to set up his title bid; in August, he nearly ended it by crashing heavily!

Warren Briggs would have been a contender had he not dropped out mid-season.

ICS HISTORIC RACING SALOON CAR CHAMPIONSHIP

CROMPTON BATTERY

To win a championship in your first full season of racing is some achievement. But that is precisely what Simon Crompton did in the ICS Historic Racing Saloon Car Championship. As before, the series supported the BTCC and thrilled the attendant bumper crowds with some great racing.

During the winter, Crompton acquired the BMW 1600 that Tony Hill had developed so well in 1994. Though badged a 1600, the car actually benefits from a very potent 2.1-litre engine, and was more than a match for the Lotus Cortinas that packed the class.

Simon took to the car immediately and, though beaten in the first two races by the Cortinas of defending champion Sean Brown (Donington) and Nevil Smith (Brands), was soon on a winning streak. Only a second win by '93 champion Smith, in the rain at Brands, and a self-imposed penalty at Snetterton, kept Crompton from winning more than ten times. When the BMW spun out of the overall lead at a damp Snetterton, impressive novice, Rick Tanton (Ford Lotus Cortina), took the class victory.

Most of the race wins, of course, went to the American muscle-cars in Class A. By winning half the races, Roly Nix proved himself to be the top dog in his 6.2-litre Chevrolet Camaro. Series creator, Pete Hall, was the closest challenger to Nix in yet another Camaro.

When it rained at Oulton Park in May, Nick Swift won the hearts of the crowd by taking overall victory in his Mini-Cooper S. A giant-killer in any conditions, he claimed the Class C title before putting the car up for sale. For the time being, he will concentrate on making other people's Minis go faster!

EUROCAR SALOON CAR CHAMPIONSHIP

GENERAL LEE

It was sometimes hard to believe that the Eurocar movement was only in its second season: huge grids of identical V6 Ford Mondeo-based spaceframe racing saloon cars thrilled the crowds everywhere they went.

The fields comprised a heady mix of drivers from varying backgrounds, with numerous oval racers signing up alongside a number of drivers with circuit racing experience. But it was the most versatile of them all, the legendary Barry Lee, who claimed yet another title after a superb campaign.

The man of most concern to the defending champion was Mike Jordan, who moved from traditional saloon car racing and made the transition brilliantly. Though finally outpointed by Lee, Mike was always pitching for the lead.

Former hot-rodders, Kevin Clarke, Graham Miller and Phil White, battled for the lesser placings with ex-Formula One Stock Car champion, Pete Falding.

For 1996, an additional championship for V8 monsters will only serve to heighten the action.

Mick Walker

Left: **Pete Chambers's Carrera 2 (5) won the Pirelli Porsche Cup's 'big' class.**

Below: **Rob Schirle (14) was a surprised Vento champ. Dave Green (8) was eighth.**

PIRELLI PORSCHE CUP
AND PIRELLI CLASSIC PORSCHE CHAMPIONSHIP

BUSSELL HUSTLES

Following a season-long battle with defending champion, Caroline Lucas, the overall Pirelli Porsche Cup was scooped by John Bussell after a mighty campaign in his Pickup Motorsport-tended Class 3 924S. It was the second year that the overall crown had been won by a contender from the class for the least powerful cars.

In his sixth year of Porsche racing, Devonian circuit instructor Bussell faced a constant challenge from the 944 of Lucas, who could have won the title again but for a major shunt at Brands in May when she collected a spinning car.

Adrian Grieves travelled from the opposite end of the country to Bussell to finish third in the class with his 944.

At the top of the field, the Class 1 cars did all the winning, and it was the Eurotech-prepared 928GTS of David and Godfrey Jones that was the most successful car. Had either of the twins contested a full season, one would probably have been overall champion, but by alternating in the car, they finished the season second (David) and fifth (Godfrey) in class. Lots of pre-season work had the all-new car bang on the pace right from the opening race, and even the mid-season addition of a 70-kilogram weight penalty failed to stop it winning. Only at Oulton Park did the car falter when Godfrey was elbowed out onto the unforgiving run-off area.

The biggest challenge to the 928 came from Porsche stalwart, Peter Chambers, who developed his new Carrera 2 into a race-winner. Victories at Donington and Snetterton, plus consistency elsewhere, put the car on target for the class title, despite problems with its ABS.

Graeme Langford had to push his older 911 Super Sport to its limit to stay on terms with the newer cars, and a hefty shunt at Snetterton did not help his year. However, he was invariably in the points and grabbed third in class from Robert Babikan when the latter's 911 ended its year in a Silverstone gravel trap.

Des Winks was a contender through the first half of the season in his 968, but only did selected races in a car that was always for sale.

From the summer onwards, two 'new' drivers arrived in the 'big' class and both made a major impact. Phil Hindley stepped up from Class 2 into the top division with a 944 Turbo, and was on the pace from his very first outing. When Godfrey Jones was excluded for passing under yellows in the Silverstone final, he took maximum points. After Stephen Radcliffe was forced to step down from racing his Carrera 2 for business reasons, Mark Hales readily accepted the drive, and won twice in the searing August heat at Oulton Park, but only after mighty battles with Chambers. He remained a pacesetter in the remaining races.

Class 2 was a straight battle between Paul Edwards and Tom Segrue. Though the 944S2s, notably those of Segrue, Diane Osborne and Peter Owen, had the legs of the older 911SC, Edwards battled hard. And when Segrue suffered a gearbox failure in the penultimate race, the rear-engined car was able to clinch the class title.

The older cars had a series to themselves – the Pirelli Classic Porsche Championship – which was a resounding success, with big grids and close racing. John Williams had a marvellous year in his Eurotech 911E to win overall from Class 2, while Chris Heeley (Carrera RS) and David Barnard (911T) took the other class titles.

John Colley Photography

John Colley Photography

LUCAS VOLKSWAGEN VENTO VR6 CHALLENGE

SURELY SCHIRLE

The Vento VR6 Challenge started year two of its life without the Polo G40 Cup for numerical support. It had also come out from under the wing of VAG to be taken over by Magnus Laird and his Hyperion Motorsport concern. Grids remained modest, with a peak of 15 cars, but those drivers who tried the Vento enjoyed the experience, and the field was usually strong on quality if not quantity. The signs are that the series will benefit from further steady growth in 1996.

Three races had already been run before Rob Schirle decided to join in. The versatile former Rover Turbo racer was busy establishing his own Cirtek Motorsport team, but seized the chance of contesting the mid-May Zandvoort double-header in a Tim Sugden-entered car vacated by the financially-troubled Simon Hill. Little did he know that he would go on to win the championship!

Two weeks later Rob was victorious in both races at Knockhill. Suddenly he was on course for the title, although it was not until September that it was finally sealed after further wins at Cadwell Park and Snetterton. His mission accomplished, he stepped down from the series to concentrate on running his team and sorting out some GT drives.

With seven victories, defending champion, Mark Lemmer, won the most races, but some dire luck when the big scores were at stake cost him any chance of beating Schirle. He will now continue to run 'customer' Ventos, while switching his own attention to TVR Tuscans – a racing culture shock if ever there was one.

Consistency was the key to Colin Wells's year, as the former BMW champion beat Lemmer to the runner-up slot in his Mardi Gras Motorsport-tended car. The Shrewsbury driver adapted well to front-wheel drive, winning at Brands Hatch in August and always being in contention.

More was expected of Frank Greenway in 1995. The former Group N front-runner never found the pace that had marked his earlier career. However, he came close to stealing third overall from Lemmer, and only when Mark squeezed home ahead of him at the Thruxton final was the matter resolved.

Mark Grady stepped up from Polos and won twice to edge Chris Boon down to sixth in the standings, while saloon car legend, Dave Brodie, capped what was a surprisingly modest season with a victory at Thruxton.

Numerous drivers tackled one or two races, including a gaggle of Rover Turbo racers: Jeremy Cotterill, Laurence Plummer and Brian Heerey all scored podium finishes.

CATERHAM VAUXHALL CHALLENGE

1	David Walton	159
2	Keith Farrance	156
3	Shaun Balfe	144
4	Clive Richards	131
5	Bart Hayden	118
6	Guy Parry	109
7	Verney Wood	94
8	Simon Jackson	78
9	Paul Kite	76
10	Howard Walker	72

CATERHAM K SERIES CHALLENGE

1	Simon Harris	214
2	Daniel Eaves	172
3	Warren Gilbert	154
4	Mike Neumann	136
5	Tim Fuller	133
6	Mark Humphrey	124
7	Rod Robson	97
8	Peter Venn	70
9	Neil Delargy	55
10	Bruce Robinson	51

UNIPART DCM MINI MIGLIA CHALLENGE

1	Chris Lewis	122
2	Bill Sollis	122
3	Stewart Drake	105
4	Ian Curley	98
5	Ian Gunn	65
6	Peter Baldwin	60
7	Myk Cable	47
8	Mick Best	39
9	Ian Scott	37
10	Jonathan Lloyd	32

UNIPART DCM MINI SEVEN CHALLENGE

1	Michael Jackson	123
2	Shaun King	90
3	Dave Banwell	90
4	Dave Braggins	87
5	Tim Sims	81
6	Matt Hayman	79
7	Steve Bell	63
8	Rob Selby	57
9	Phil Manser	43
10	Genny Cooke	41

DUNLOP ROVER GTi CHAMPIONSHIP

1	Mark Jones	180
2	Vince Martin	180
3	Spencer Baker	176
4	Alfonso Emanuele	148
5	John Griffiths	146
6	Nigel Reuben	110
7	Carl Blakely	92
8	Rupert Deeth	92
9	Gary Till	82
10	Russell Clark	40

SALOON 2000 CHAMPIONSHIP

Over two-litre class

1	Andy Middlehurst	Nissan Skyline	127
2	Michael Woodcock	Ford Escort Cosworth	81
3	Graham Coomes	Ford Escort Cosworth	65
4	Lionel Abbott	Saab 900	53
5	Robin Rex	Ford Escort Cosworth	51
6	Geoff Kimber-Smith	Ford Sapphire Cosworth	45

Under two-litre class

1	Bill Stilwell	Honda Civic V-Tec	102
2	David Pitcher	Vauxhall Astra GSi	99
3	Peter Morss	Vauxhall Astra GSi	65
4	Warren Briggs	Honda Civic V-Tec	39
5	Michael Cullen	Honda Civic V-Tec	27
6	Roger Moen	Honda Civic V-Tec	25

ICS HISTORIC RACING SALOON CAR CHAMPIONSHIP

Class A

1	Roly Nix	Chevrolet Camaro	59
2	Peter Hall	Chevrolet Camaro	47
3	Dennis Clark	Chevrolet Camaro	44

Class B

No starters

Class C

1	Simon Crompton	BMW 1600	69
2	Sean Brown	Ford Lotus Cortina	39
3	Nevil Smith	Ford Lotus Cortina	33

Class D

1	Nick Swift	Mini-Cooper S	65
2	Graham Churchill	Mini-Cooper S	47
3	Gordon Streeter	Ford Anglia	42
	Bob Bullen	Ford Anglia	42

Class E

1	David Bridger	Austin A40	21
2	Ken Grundy	Mini-Cooper	19
3	Ron Parker	Hillman Imp	13

EUROCAR SALOON CAR CHAMPIONSHIP

1	Barry Lee	4950
2	Mike Jordan	4450
3	Kevin Clarke	3975
4	Peter Falding	3775
5	Graham Miller	3365
6	Phil White	3200
7	Lester Stacey	3140
8	Tony Gale	3055
9	Mark Willis	2795
10	Jeff Simpson	2765

PIRELLI PORSCHE CUP

Class 1

1	Peter Chambers	Carrera 2	235
2	David Jones	928GTS	204
3	Graeme Langford	911 Super Sport	150
4	Robert Babikan	911 Carrera	144

Class 2

1	Paul Edwards	911SC	293
2	Tom Segrue	944S2	262.5
3	Diane Osborne	944S2	228
4	Peter Owen	944S2	227

Class 3

1	John Bussell	924S	314
2	Caroline Lucas	944	308
3	Adrian Grieves	944	159
4	Jason Saunders	924S	145

PIRELLI CLASSIC PORSCHE CHAMPIONSHIP

Class 1

1	Chris Heeley	911 Carrera	258
2	Darren Litten	911	167
3	Martin Harvey	911 Carrera	144
4	Nick Cremin	911RS	141

Class 2

1	John Williams	911E	318
2	Mike Clapham	911SC	215
3	Rob Williams	911E	200
4	Anthony Oliver	911SC	155

Class 3

1	David Barnard	911T	259
2	Bob Mason	911T	184
3	Gerald Alticosalian	911T	153
4	David Benett	911T	137

LUCAS VOLKSWAGEN VENTO VR6 CHALLENGE

1	Rob Schirle	223
2	Colin Wells	201
3	Mark Lemmer	165
4	Frank Greenway	158
5	Mark Grady	139
6	Chris Boon	137
7	Andy Kraemer	119
8	David Green	115
9	Dave Brodie	108
10	Steve Deeks	83

Steve Jones

BEWILDERING VARIETY

by Marcus Simmons

Without a shadow of doubt, Great Britain is the world's leading producer of racing cars, in terms of both quantity and quality. So it's little surprise that this country's national racing scene should contain so many championships for single-seater machinery. Once a car has become 'last year's model', there is always a new home for it . . .

And Formula Renault 1700, the latest addition to the roster of sub-TOCA package series, illustrated the point perfectly.

With Formula Renault Sport taking over for 1995, the now obsolete 1700 cc-engined, road-gearboxed Formula Renaults of old found a new role as one of Britain's premier club-level series, and its grids stayed mainly around the 20 to 25 mark. That has to be encouraging.

Not only that, but Formula 2000 enjoyed a revitalisation which resulted in fields being boosted and a talented young champion emerging in the form of Stuart Saggers. ARP Formula Three, for cars built before 1993, also enjoyed entries in the high teens.

As usual, Formula Ford 1600 had the numbers, but its halcyon days are past and it has become increasingly marginalised, particularly in England: large grids of enthusiastic amateurs battled out the numerous regional series, but the national BRC affair was poor. Scotland and Northern Ireland can now lay justifiable claim to possessing superior championships.

BRITISH ENGINE INSURANCE
FORMULA RENAULT 1700

HENDERSON'S BIG FEAT

Formula Renault 1700, then, was the success of the season. Renault UK gave the initiative plenty of support as it left the security of the TOCA package, while the BARC sourced a sponsor brand new to motor racing.

Round one at Snetterton saw a superb field number well into the twenties, but by the end of the season financial constraints had taken their toll and several competitors had fallen by the wayside.

There had been controversy, too. David Henderson, who by rights should have been exhibiting his ability in Renault Sport, was compelled to remain in FR1700 with Haywood Racing's lead Swift SC94R. His main rival was to be Neil Riddiford, the inaugural Formula Renault UK champion – back in 1989 – driving Tarry Racing's Van Diemen RF93.

With Henderson seemingly set for the title, there was drama at Castle Combe in late August, when the Durham youngster was excluded from third position for a driving offence. Then, at Snetterton, a clear victory for Riddiford was handed to Henderson when the Tingewick veteran's reverse gear was found to be non-operational in scrutineering.

It all left a bad taste in the mouth. A disgusted Riddiford missed the penultimate round to debut the new Renault Sport Ray at Silverstone, and Henderson doesn't know to this day at which round he actually clinched the title! But there should be no tarnishing of his crown, for an exemplary record of seven wins from the 12 races leaves little doubt as to who deserved the championship.

Riddiford, as ever, battled well to take two wins, but – provisionally – looks to have lost the runner-up spot to late-season sensation, Simon Graves. With just half-seasons in FF1600 and Class B Renault under his belt in single-seaters, the former VW Polo man arguably proved the pace of the field at the end of the year with his Streatfield Motorsport Swift. Haywood boss, Jim Warren, is very interested in his services for the 1996 series . . .

One driver leaving Haywood is Adam Wilcox. The teenage gearbox karting graduate took fourth in the standings with his Swift, but his natural speed was let down by an inability to qualify well. He plans to move to Class B Formula Vauxhall for '96 and could be a title contender.

Ex-Formula Firster, Ian Astley, in another Swift, never quite breached the top three, but was consistent in taking fifth in the championship ahead of the Cramer brothers. The redheaded Gloucestershire siblings shared an ex-Manor Motorsport Van Diemen RF94, Marc and Eric notching up two podium finishes each.

Uruguay's Daniel Fresnedo tied on points with Norwegian, Jarle Gaasland, another rapid Haywood pilot who is attempting to raise the finance for a full season in '96.

As it did when it ran under Renault UK's auspices, the FR1700 series also had a Class B, for pre-1992 machinery. Run by fellow Devonian Gavin Wills's West-Tec concern, Adrian Crawford won the first four races with his Swift FR91 and never looked back. The former rally driver is hoping to join Henderson in Renault Sport next season.

Second and third were cousins, Jason and Jeremy Timms, once again campaigning their ex-Martello Orions. Jason scored four wins and Jeremy one, accounting for every non-Crawford victory.

Andy Thornton arguably should have had a win, too, but the Liverpudlian spent too much time dicing with the Class A boys and often paid the penalty.

ALLIANCE & LEICESTER
PERSONAL FINANCE
FORMULA 2000 CHAMPIONSHIP

JOCKY STUART

Under the leadership of Ray Bacon, Formula 2000 International did a superb job of promoting what was formerly known as Formula Forward, bringing it back into the spotlight as a potential avenue for the penniless, but aspiring racer.

A generous sponsorship package allowed drivers of the Van Diemen-built, Ford-engined slicks and wings chassis to compete for realistic

***Opposite:* FR1700 titlist, David Henderson.**

***Below:* Stuart Saggers (41) and Tim Spouge (64) won the F2000 and FFirst titles at the last gasp.**

prizes, including a Formula Three test drive for the champion.

That proved to be the diminutive Stuart Saggers. The 22-year-old from Cambridgeshire had been out of racing since taking runner-up spot in the 1992 Formula First standings. But with the help of loyal friend and mechanic, Brian Clark, the shoe-string-budgeted Saggers scored three wins in a consistent campaign which saw Graham Fennymore, his major rival, cruelly edged out at the final round.

A Junior FF1600 contemporary of David Coulthard, Fennymore had made a successful return to racing in 1994 with victory in the Pre '90 FF1600 Championship. The Oxfordshire man linked up with Team Verdan, one of the most successful Formula First teams ever, for his season of F2000, and was unlucky to lose the title at the last hurdle due to a puncture.

The initial pacesetter was Mike Kirkham, the Formula Renault convert driving for F2000 stalwarts, ME Motorsport. But as Saggers and Fennymore found their feet, so Kirkham's results suffered. He still comfortably outpointed his team-mate, Elliot Lewis, who was the highest placed of the drivers already with experience of this class. That, and the failure of 1994 champion, Mike Doble, to finish higher than equal sixth in the championship, showed just how much more competitive the formula had become in '95.

Standards rose higher still when Alex Jack, a vastly under-used talent, was drafted into the Alliance & Leicester-backed car at mid-season. Run by Sceptre Racing, the gifted Scot won race after race and shot up to fifth in the rankings, comfortably ahead of Sceptre mainstay, Mike Bey.

FORMULA FIRST CHAMPIONSHIP

JUST IN TIM

As Formula 2000 gained in popularity, so the other Brands Hatch Leisure-originated single-seater class – Formula First – waned. Grids for the Van Diemen-built starter formula plunged to around a dozen by the season's end, despite being on the right side of 20 when the year kicked into action at Mallory Park.

A new bodykit for the virtually standard Ford CVH-engined car certainly improved its looks. The racing was good, too. But with around 150 chassis in existence, and 42 of the new bodykits sold, the lack of numbers is a mystery.

Like the 2000s, the Firsts settled their championship at the very last round. Texaco-backed Lincolnshire youngster, Tim Spouge, took advantage of James Beales's accident at Donington Park to seal the title at the 11th hour.

Run by Mark Burdett – himself a rapid FFirst pilot – Spouge won the opening round, but added just two more wins in a consistent season. Perhaps his experience from the 1994 Winter Series counted in the end: former karter Beales took four wins in a plucky privateer effort, but his early-season form as a raw novice hadn't hinted at what lay in store. The Norwich teenager picked up some late-season tweaks from ex-FFirst outfit, Paston Racing, which ran him in the Vauxhall Junior Winter Series at the end of the year. Spouge has loftier ambitions, and is looking towards Renault Sport.

Category mainstay, Joe Chedid, took his first win on his way to third in the championship, ahead of two-times victor, Steve Dutton.

It was a poor season for double champions, Team Verdan: neither James Hills (fifth in the points) nor Owen Mildenhall (seventh) won any races. Team boss, Mike Dance, drafted in the penniless Daniel Stilp, but after two victories he started crashing and was dropped from the Wetherby outfit's squad.

Other winners in a very open year were early points-leader, Andy Berg, who ran out of funds, and the occasionally rapid Martin Wallbank.

ARP FORMULA THREE CHAMPIONSHIP

TATE HARRIES ROLF

This is a championship for F3 cars built before 1993, split into two classes: pre-1987, with mechanical fuel injection; post-1987, with electronic fuel injection. The two classes are equalised by the imposition of a smaller diameter air restrictor on the newer cars, limiting straightline speed.

The season saw a showdown at its

Steve Jones

Steve Jones

Steve Jones

Left: **Simon Tate (15) battles with his chief ARP F3 rival, Jason Rolf.**

Bottom: **Topi Serjala celebrates his FF1600 Festival victory.**

Donington Park finale, between Simon Tate and Jason Rolf. The latter only needed a top six finish, even if the former won, but his hopes turned to dust when he spun out of second place. Tate duly collected his fifth win (to Rolf's one) of the season and unexpectedly, but deservedly, took the championship silverware.

Tate made life harder by missing a mid-season round to go on his honeymoon! He returned early, and won at Castle Combe on the last day of their holiday, while his new bride looked on!

Rolf, a former Mini racer with one season of ARP F3 under his belt, actually graduated to Class B of the British F3 Championship at the start of the season, but costs were beyond his reach and he soon returned, successfully, to the less financially taxing ARP series.

Third in the championship may have been a disappointment for reigning titlist, Dave Karaskas, but it wasn't all bad news for the Ralt RT31 driver, who won his first-ever single-seater race! Winless during his victorious, but consistent, 1994 campaign, he had at least laid a ghost to rest.

Other race winners were Gareth Burnett and Ian Walker, while former Monoposto champion, Jim Blockley, won the post-'87 class in his ex-Andre Ribeiro Reynard 923.

A category for pre-ground effect Toyota-engined F3 cars was run too, with Chris Fearon proving dominant in his Chevron B43.

FORMULA FORD CHAMPIONSHIPS

STILL CRAZY . . .

Yet again there was a multitude of Formula Ford 1600 championships. But Britain's flagship series, the BRC, was arguably the weakest of them all.

Scott Ramsay took the title with his Van Diemen RF92, but the Glaswegian did so without winning a single race. More often than not, he was beaten by local drivers venturing out for a one-off. Had Kevin Mills travelled further away from Castle Combe more often, he could have added this title to his Combe crown, but five wins with his Swift SC92F still left him a point behind Ramsay in the reckoning.

Like Ramsay, Barry Pomfret was a regular in the series who failed to win, but the Bletchley biology teacher's Van Diemen ended up third in the rankings.

A mid-season run of wins marked Scotsman, Andrew Kirkaldy, as a man to watch, while Vauxhall Junior runner, Richard Tarling, undertook some races with a Marque Cars-run Van Diemen. The 16-year-old won at Snetterton in April, but he also got involved in too many incidents for his own good.

Scandinavians, Topi Serjala and Fredrik Sørlie, won races on the rare appearances of their Apollo Motorsport Swifts, and these two were to dominate the Formula Ford 1600 Festival at Brands Hatch. In the end, Finn Serjala pipped Norwegian Sørlie to the post, with another Finn – Risto Virtanen – bringing his Andy Welch Racing Swift home in third.

As if that wasn't enough, Mikko Lempinen – from Finland, if you hadn't already guessed – won his heat with a third Apollo Swift, before crashing out of the final with fellow heat-winner, Mark Marchant, the 1994 Champion of Brands returning for a singleton foray with the works Jamun.

Scotland enjoyed a considerably more competitive FF1600 series, but the – hopefully – temporary closure of Ingliston for racing meant that this became a one-circuit series, i.e. Knockhill.

Putting his reputation for occasional wildness behind him, Ricki Steedman clinched the title with a round to go in his Van Diemen RF91. Having added a calm, authoritative style while under pressure to his undoubted speed, Steedman was also the man to beat whenever he ventured south to Oulton Park. He now wants to race full-time in England, and has tested a Zetec-engined Van Diemen for Mick Gardner, whose teamn took Kevin Wallace to the 1995 First Division title

Opening round winner, Stuart Thorburn, also RF91 mounted, took second in the championship, but came under threat towards the end of the year by returnee, Stewart Roden. Armed initially with the unloved Van Diemen RF94, Roden was off the pace, but he gradually honed it into a decent weapon which was formidable whenever the weather turned wet, a frequent occurrence at Knockhill! He took pole position in soaking conditions by 2.7s at the 'anti-clockwise' meeting in October.

But perhaps the biggest name to emerge from Scotland this year was that of Kirkaldy. Only narrowly defeated by Thorburn in his first-ever car race, it seems incredible that his Van Diemen RF92 didn't win once in the Scottish series, especially bearing in mind the string of victories accrued when he ventured south for some mid-summer English outings.

The Kirkistown-based Northern Ireland Championship was also pretty competitive – five men had a chance of the title entering its final round!

Eventually, it was Chris Paul who won through, for the second year running. The Ulsterman's River Rock Van Diemen RF92 prevented a clean sweep for the teenage sensation, Tim Mullen, who had already secured the Ford of Ireland and Star of Tomorrow championships down south in the Republic.

As well as this success, Paul was to prove the top non-Scandinavian in the Festival at Brands, with a steady run to fourth that was a monument to his ability to stay out of trouble over the weekend.

Leading the Northern Ireland series prior to the final round, incredibly, was sexagenarian Tommy Reid, but the Reynard 91FF driver just didn't have the pace when it mattered. Also in with a chance were George McAlpin and Simon Woodside, but they will have to wait another year.

Arguably the best of England's single-circuit championships was the HEAT-backed series at Castle Combe. Both Gavin Wills and Bob Higgins were bidding to take their fifth title, but both were upstaged by Kevin Mills, a comparative novice.

This promising Swift SC92F driver won fewer races than the similar car of Wills, but still pipped the Plymouth man by a point, thanks mainly to the West-Tec supremo tripping over a backmarker and retiring from the penultimate round with mangled suspension.

Higgins, a legend at this track, won the first round, then crashed, then announced his retirement, then announced his comeback and finished the year in his Van Diemen RF94! He, Alan Cooper and Dave Williams were the best of the rest.

The Champion of Oulton series went to Mike Bennett, his first such title. His Swift SC93F won the first round, then twice more to wrap things up with a race still to go. Major opposition came from the likes of Colin Boal, Colin Nield and Bryan Mullarkey. Boal took two wins in his Mondiale over a successful April meeting, but was unable to triumph again. Swift driver, Brian Scowcroft, was another race winner.

Apart from that, rampaging Scots – Ramsay, Kirkaldy and Steedman – tended to put the locals in the shade when they appeared.

Oulton's successful Class B, for pre-1987 machinery, saw Malcolm Barfoot's Crossle 25F triumph over the Swift of Mike Newton.

The Star of Mallory series enjoyed backing from the circuit's racing school, Everyman, once again. Justin Sherwood jumped into an early lead with two wins in his Swift SC92F, but Alan Brunton – a top six regular in Scotland – decided that he rather liked Mallory Park and stayed on to win the championship in his Van Diemen RF91.

Former champions, Steve Shirley and Stuart Kestenbaum, were also race winners, as was underfinanced karting graduate, Tommy Field.

With the number of race meetings at Brands Hatch significantly cut for 1995, the once great Champion of Brands series metamorphosed into the Kent County FF1600 Championship, with Brands and Lydden sharing the races. An early-season burst of form from John Hayden saw

LAT Photographic

This blue Van Diemen RF90 won the Kent County FF1600 Championship in the hands of David Hardisty *(right)*. It also finished third in the points thanks to the early-season victories of John Hayden.

his Trevor Stiles-run Van Diemen win the first five rounds, but Hayden then retired from the sport and sold the RF90 to habitual third place-finisher, Dave Hardisty.

As Hardisty got used to the car, so Peter Alexander moved into the lead thanks to a consistent run of results in his Swift FB91. But then Alexander's season fell apart, the decline scarcely arrested by a switch to the works Jamun. By now at home in the ex-Hayden machine, Hardisty romped to three wins to take the title from Alexander by 17 points.

Despite not racing since May, Hayden still placed third in the standings from Ray driver Darren Rayfield. Mention should also be made of Donny Barrett, whose late-Seventies vintage Royale RP29 is now surely the oldest car to win a contemporary Formula Ford race, at Lydden in July!

Britain's three national series for older FF1600s each enjoyed strong support. The newest of them – the BRSCC's Pre '90 Championship – was also extremely wide open . . .

Lacking the finance to venture into mainstream junior single-seater racing, kart star, Darren Rayfield, was forced to compete in local events and the Pre '90 series, in which his Ray 89F took the title with four race victories.

Second and third were Nicholas Jeory and Ken Parkinson, but these two took just one win between them, the latter prevailing at Oulton Park. Simon Davey, thrice a victor in his Reynard, was right behind them and tied for fourth with Swift driver, Mark Jackson.

The BRSCC also organised the Pre '85 Championship, which went down to the wire. This provided another triumph for Ray Formula Cars, with Simon Homewood's 1984 example getting the verdict from Welshman Bruce Evans's Reynard.

Chris Whittingham, the outgoing champion, took his share of wins with a Lola, but the sensation of the season was Kevin Hall. The 16-year-old was dominating the series finale by a country mile when his Reynard was suddenly slowed by bent valves.

Jointly promoted by the BRSCC and BARC, the Classic FF1600 Championship finally went the way of Dave Lowe. The Guernseyman has been campaigning his well-driven Lotus 61 for donkey's years, initially in the Pre '74 series: seven wins in Class A saw him comfortably home on this occasion.

Ray driver, Alan Crocker, was next up, but it was a shame that the ultra-quick Bob Berridge and Paul Sleeman didn't appear more often.

Class B, for the '74 to '80 models, was taken by Steve Pearce's PRS RH02. Pearce won the first two races only, but scored consistently thereafter to take the title. Behind him, Stephen Hare's Van Diemen pipped Royale driver, Peter Chippindale, at the final round for the runner-up spot.

Steve Jones

THE REST

THE BIG BOSS

With plenty of championships for smaller cars, the Boss Formula initiative allowed F1, F2, F3000 and F5000 machinery to enter the fray in a well-promoted, short series of races. The brainchild of 'big banger' enthusiast, Roger Cowman, Boss enjoyed strong support from its inception and should become an integral part of the racing calendar.

German Klaus Panchyrz won the first two races with his Reynard 92D. Bearded Scot, Ron Cumming, was victorious at Donington in his March 88D, while the similarly facially-haired Tony Worswick triumphed at Silverstone with a Reynard 93D. The finale was dominated by Interserie regular, Johan Rajamaki, whose Footwork-Judd set a new outright lap record around Donington Park's short circuit.

The 1600 cc F3 cars of the 1971-73 era were catered for in the BARC's Oregon Timberframe Homes-backed championship. This was dominated by the Chevron B20 of Nick Crossley, one of the founders of Delta Racing Cars back in the 1970s.

A consistent season gave Nigel Bigwood's Ensign LNF3 second in the rankings, ahead of Bob Sellix, Peter Harrington and Mike Barnby. Harrington, a northern FF1600 star of the Seventies, might have challenged Crossley for the title had he started his Brabham BT40-mounted campaign sooner.

The BARC was also responsible for that curio, the Universal Racing Services Pre '83 Formula Ford 2000 Championship. Increasingly a one-make series for Van Diemen RF82s, some of the cars have actually been built to the classic design – in which Ayrton Senna originally starred – during the past few years.

Traditionally dominated by the same drivers, the series saw a new winner in 1995, Nick Pearce. He won the first round, but didn't really come on strong until he took three victories to secure the title with one race still to go.

Tony Hancock was the only man to stay remotely in touch, he and Pearce scoring twice as many points as anyone else. Consistent driving allowed Nick Owen to place third, ahead of Paul Bayley and David Hutchinson. In Class B, for older machinery, Simon Loynes's Lola T580 took the honours from the Reynard of Colin Wright.

No major changes are in the pipeline for Britain's single-seater championships in 1996. And, with most of them strongly supported, there seems little reason to alter anything anyway. Yet British motorsport has to be on its guard against too many championships: if and when Formula Vauxhall, for example, drops onto the national club racing scene, maybe it would be time to pension off Pre '83 FF2000 to the Monoposto Racing Club or 750 MC.

But too much variety is better than too little. As this country's racing industry continues to churn out cars by the hundred, there is little prospect of this state of affairs changing.

BRITISH ENGINE INSURANCE FORMULA RENAULT 1700

Class A

1	David Henderson	Swift SC94R	151
2	Simon Graves	Swift SC94R	108
3	Neil Riddiford	Van Diemen RF93	98
4	Adam Wilcox	Swift SC94R	83
5	Ian Astley	Swift SC94R	58
6	Marc Cramer	Van Diemen RF94	42
7	Eric Cramer	Van Diemen RF94	36
8=	Daniel Fresnedo (URG)	Van Diemen RF93/4	34
8=	Jarle Gaasland (N)	Swift SC94R	34
10	Matt Bettley	Van Diemen RF93	26

Class B

1	Adrian Crawford	Swift FR91	128
2	Jason Timms	Orion FR91	125
3	Jeremy Timms	Orion FR91	103

ALLIANCE & LEICESTER PERSONAL FINANCE FORMULA 2000 CHAMPIONSHIP

1	Stuart Saggers	139
2	Graham Fennymore	137
3	Mike Kirkham	119
4	Elliot Lewis	89
5	Alex Jack	78
6=	Mike Bey	55
6=	Mike Doble	55
8	David Thirsk	38
9	Neil Cox	28
10	Alan Bonner	24

FORMULA FIRST CHAMPIONSHIP

1	Tim Spouge	128
2	James Beales	127
3	Joe Chedid	107
4	Steve Dutton	99
5	James Hills	81
6	Andy Berg	75
7	Owen Mildenhall	68
8	Martin Wallbank	63
9	Daniel Stilp	54
10	Mark Piercy	49

ARP FORMULA THREE CHAMPIONSHIP

1	Simon Tate	Reynard 863-VW	121
2	Jason Rolf	Reynard 863-VW	115
3	Dave Karaskas	Ralt RT31-VW	96
4	John Wilcock	Reynard 893-Toyota	74
5	Jim Blockley	Reynard 923-VW	69
6	Chris Fearon	Chevron B43-Toyota	65
7	Kevin Sherwood	Ralt RT32/33-Toyota	58
8	Keith Baldwin	Reynard 873-Alfa Romeo	54
9	Douglas Fairbairn	Ralt RT30-VW	46
10	Tom Bellamy	Reynard 863-VW	38

THE BOY WHO WOULD BE KING

by Marcus Pye

Photos: Marcus Pye

Andy Priaulx, at just 22, is now the 'king' of the RAC British Hillclimb Championship at his first attempt in a 575 bhp 'Formula One' car. This was a remarkable achievement in itself, but the manner in which the brilliant Guernsey man defeated the sport's 'establishment' was nothing short of phenomenal.

Ten victories from the 14 rounds he contested (the other two were abandoned – Craigantlet after Mark Colton's terrible accident and the September Wiscombe meeting because of rain) earned Priaulx the maximum possible score of 100 points, a feat last achieved by the maestro Roy Lane, *en route* to the first of his three championships, exactly 20 years ago.

The speed with which Andy got to grips with the former-Ken Ayers four-litre Pilbeam MP58-Cosworth DFL – a learning process aided by intuitive engineer David Gould, constructor of the eponymous car which carried Chris Cramer to the 1985 title – took his rivals by surprise. They knew he was good. The question was, how good?

They did not have long to wait for the answer – Andy smashed the hill record to win the third round at Prescott. But what they were utterly unprepared for was the dominance that followed this breakthrough. He plundered six more outright records in the Bank of Bermuda-sponsored car before the summer was out, capping his campaign with the first sub-38-second ascent of Doune. This awesome drive, a heady melange of skill and immense bravado, had onlookers quaking in their boots.

Lane, who turned 60 in May, and had annexed seven of his 66 RAC Hillclimb round wins before Andy was born, believes that he is truly exceptional: 'He's made a few of us look like has-beens this year, but it's tremendous news for the sport. He's changed the face of British hillclimbing. It needed new blood.'

The evergreen Lane won the opening round at Loton Park in his Steel King Safety Footwear Pilbeam, and led the way until the Isle of Man encounter in May. Priaulx then took over at the top, a position the 'crown prince' was not to relinquish no matter how hard the opposition tried.

David Grace, 46, bidding for a hat-trick of RAC titles, proved to be Priaulx's closest rival over the course of the season, but a single win at his former bogey hill, Wiscombe in April, suggested that he was not as focused as before. His mercurial challenge was effectively thwarted when he crashed crossing the finish line in Guernsey – for the third time in four years! The factory-rebuilt Hart DFR-powered Pilbeam chassis was sharper for Shelsley Walsh's 90th anniversary meeting three weeks later, but it was too late.

Lane, who won his first RAC round in 1969, and has not been out of the top three in the championship since 1986, had 700 bhp under his right foot (from a Judd EV F1 engine enlarged to four litres), but progress was hampered by its lack of low-down punch.

Roy's points tally was equalled by Priaulx's extrovert father, Graham, whose weather-assisted second career win at Shelsley Walsh in June was inspirational. A sportscar ace on the hills a decade ago, the architect of Andy's success was, without doubt, the most improved driver of the year.

Despite its extraordinary highs, the season was overshadowed by the death of Mark Colton in Northern Ireland. Last year's runner-up, the only front-runner to make the trip to Craigantlet, was killed instantly during practice when his Pilbeam MP72 reared up (apparently when a front wing failed) and struck the only telegraph pole adjacent to the course. One of the sport's hardest triers, Mark had rapidly sorted the brand new car (a V8 derivative of the all-conquering MP62) in the early part of the season – often qualifying top for the run-off – and was eagerly making up ground in the title race. He smashed his own course record at Lerghy Frissel on the Isle of Man but, sadly, it was to be his final victory.

British Sprint champion Patrick Wood, who scored his first RAC Hillclimb win at Barbon last year, struggled with his Target Advertising MP58 (which boasts a deriva-

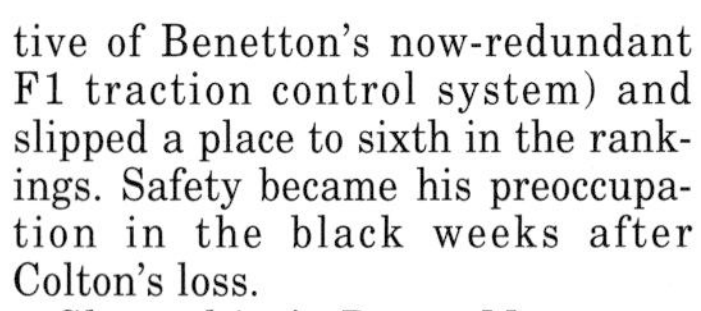

tive of Benetton's now-redundant F1 traction control system) and slipped a place to sixth in the rankings. Safety became his preoccupation in the black weeks after Colton's loss.

Shropshire's Roger Moran retained his RACMSA Leaders title, and finished seventh in the British series, having moved up from the 1600 cc class to the two-litre division with a wailing 300 bhp version of Swindon Racing Engines' four-pot Vauxhall engine, which also powered former hillclimber John Cleland's Cavalier to the BTCC title.

Moran's speed was prodigious, but it only served to inspire his young classmates, Justin Fletcher (in a similar, but slightly less potent Vauxhall-engined car) and Tom Brown. Both raised their game to beat Roger on occasion and, typically, he was the first to congratulate them. Brown – son of Shelsley record-holder Richard – pipped Moran by one-hundredth in the sensational run-off at Doune's finale in September, proving David Gould's F3 Ralt RT37-based car to be a match for the Pilbeam after a year's development with Hart power.

Moran and former Scottish champion, George Ritchie, who finished eighth in the RAC table with Lane's original MP58 (with Judd EV power these past two years) are to share a new MP72 in a serious title assault next season.

Simon Durling broke a leg when he shunted heavily in Lane's subsequent MP58 at Doune in June, but was back in harness by the end of the season, and will share the rebuilt DFL-engined machine with two-litre graduate, Tim Barrington, in what should be a stunning battle of the V8s.

But speed hillclimbing is not only about big single-seaters. The popular Midland Hillclimb Championship – run over three rounds each at Prescott, Shelsley and Loton Park – was captured for the third time in five years by former Caterham ace Rob Stevens, on this occasion in one of Yorkshireman Steve Owen's OMS sports racers, powered by a 1300 cc Suzuki motorcycle engine.

Andy Priaulx *(left)* sweeps to a 'home' win at Val des Terres. He was simply untouchable this season.

Justin Fletcher *(bottom)* hurtles through the farmyard at Harewood.

Young, but no pretender

The first Guernsey resident to win the RAC British Hillclimb Championship in its 49-year history, and the first Channel Islander since Jersey's Arthur Owen claimed the crown with a Cooper-Climax in 1962, Andy Priaulx is by far and away the most exciting young find of a generation in this exacting sport.

From one of the island's oldest motoring families – grandfather Ernold was a tearaway in his youth, and father Graham's (above pictured alongside his son) sportscar exploits fired his interest – Priaulx arrived on the hills at a tender age, at the wheel of the family's Mallock-Vauxhall Clubmans car. With his competitive instincts already honed in both karting and motocross (at which he was Channel Island champion), he was a revelation from his national debut in 1992. Eighth place, a tenth adrift of his dad, on home soil at Val des Terres in St Peter Port was a portent of things to come.

Armed with a 340 bhp Pilbeam-Hart MP57 for 1993, the motor technician learned the rest of the hills and, despite the power deficit, was soon scaring the cream of the V8 drivers. After a couple of near-misses, he secured a long overdue and immensely popular maiden victory at Wiscombe last September. The 'establishment' welcomed a new member, knowing that the writing was on the wall if he could finance the jump to V8 power . . .

Renewed backing from the Bank of Bermuda, assistance from Team Guyson's Tim Thomson (brother of James, the 1981 champion at 21, and a double RAC round winner himself), plus the tireless efforts of his entire family and mechanic, Ian Skyba, made it possible. The rest is now inscribed in history, the title their reward.

Having tested a Formula Vauxhall at the end of last season, the Elf Winfield school graduate is keen to try his hand at circuit racing, although he must first raise a budget. 'I want to race cars, but could not turn my back on hillclimbing completely,' he says. 'It's part of me, something I've been brought up with and can share with my family. Besides, you can't match the exhilaration of taming a brutal car on a narrow course. I love it too much.'

Mark Colton

17 March 1961–5 August 1995

The freak accident which claimed the life of Mark Colton at Craigantlet devastated a sporting community unused to tragedy, despite the relative lack of primary protection at its scenic venues. His was the first fatality among the top-line speed hillclimbers for more than 30 years, and was also the first in the Belfast hill's 82-year history.

Colton, 34, was a self-made man, whose genius in the world of computer software allowed him to indulge his passion for fast cars. In leisure, as in business, he was intensely competitive. A complex character, yet one with the driest sense of humour, he was also committed to a local children's charity, for which he twice cycled the length of the country.

The protégé of triple British champion Roy Lane, he joined the big guns in 1991, and scored the first of his 12 RAC round victories at Doune – the king of hills – the following year.

Apparently fearless – his 144 mph through the finish at Shelsley Walsh has not been approached – he missed out on the 1994 title by 0.31s! This merely doubled his determination, and few doubted that he would have been champion one day.

Photos: Marcus Pye

Above: **Mark Colton's death shook the sport to its very core. He will be much missed.**

Left: **Roy Lane was overshadowed by Priaulx but, even at 60, is still a threat for victories.**

It's not just about V8 grunt: Roger Moran *(below)* won the Leaders Championship, while Rob Stevens *(below left)* was the MIdlands Champion in his 'bike-engined flyer.

RAC BRITISH HILLCLIMB CHAMPIONSHIP

1	Andy Priaulx	4.0 Pilbeam MP58-Cosworth DFL	100
2	David Grace	3.5 Pilbeam MP58-Hart DFR	88
3	Roy Lane	4.0 Pilbeam MP58-Judd EV	76
4	Graham Priaulx	4.0 Pilbeam MP58-Cosworth DFL	76
5	Mark Colton	3.5 Pilbeam MP72-Judd CV	72
6	Patrick Wood	3.5 Pilbeam MP58-Cosworth DFZ/R	44
7	Roger Moran	2.0 Pilbeam MP62-Vauxhall	42
8	George Ritchie	3.5 Pilbeam MP58-Judd EV	29
9	Simon Durling	4.0 Pilbeam MP58-Cosworth DFL	29
10	Peter Harper	2.5 Vision Viper-Hart	26